Drilling Ahead

Drilling Ahead

The Quest for Oil in the Deep South
1945–2005

Alan Cockrell

Published for the Mississippi Geological Society
by University Press of Mississippi / Jackson

Also by Alan Cockrell: Tail of the Storm, University of Alabama Press, 1995

The University Press of Mississippi is a member of the
Association of American University Presses.

Photographs courtesy of Alan Cockrell unless otherwise noted
Manufactured in the United States of America

First edition 2005

Library of Congress Cataloging-in-Publication Data

Cockrell, Alan, 1949-
    Drilling ahead : the quest for oil in the deep South, 1945-2005 / Alan Cockrell.— 1st ed.
    p. cm.
    Includes bibliographical references and index.
    ISBN 1-57806-811-8 (cloth: alk. paper) | ISBN 978-1-4968-4969-4 (trade paperback)
1. Petroleum industry and trade—Mississippi. 2. Petroleum industry and trade—Alabama.
3. Petroleum industry and trade—Florida. I. Title.
    HD9567.M7C63 2005
    338. 2'7282'0976—dc22   2005007867

British Library Cataloging-in-Publication Data available

§ The paper used in this publication meets the minimum
requirements of American National Standard for Information Sciences—
Permanence of Paper for Printed Library Materials, ANSI 239.48-1984.

Book design: David Alcorn, Alcorn Publication Design

Dedicated to the memory of James W. "Buddy" Twiner

Contents

Figures

Acknowledgments

In his book *Oil in the Deep South: A History of Oil Exploration in Alabama, Mississippi, and Florida, 1889-1945* (University Press of Mississippi, 1993) Dudley Hughes wrote inspiring stories about oil people and their accomplishments that changed the way of life in the Deep South and, in some ways, the entire country. I read his book and waited with anticipation for the continuation of the story to modern times. So did thousands of others. But when people asked him to write the sequel he balked. The book took time he needed for his family, his work, and his hopeless addiction to the fly rod and the shotgun. Then a friend urged me to pick up where Dudley left off and bring the story up to date. When Dudley committed his full support and encouragement I decided to write. The result is this—a companion book to Dudley Hughes' work.

I spent twelve years in the business of hunting petroleum. During that time I examined mountains of logs, drew miles of contours, screened hundreds of deals, and even managed a small exploration department. Then I became an independent, as some unemployed geologists call themselves. That's when I learned firsthand the loneliness of standing on a busy Houston street corner cold-calling. I loathed thumbing through the Yellow Pages in a phone booth, hoping to find yet another oil executive who would spare a few minutes to hear me tell him where a bonanza of oil was and how he and I could get it—with his money, of course. I did find a couple of puddles of oil and several puffs of gas, but mostly my contribution to the oil business was insignificant.

I wrote this for a general audience, not just for oil people. The oil heritage of the Deep South belongs to all its citizens, and I want them to enjoy in full measure the fascinating world of petroleum exploration. Consequently, I have salted many explanations of oil field concepts and terms along the way and repeated most of them in a glossary. The lay reader should note that the word *well* as used in the oil business does not necessarily refer to a producing well but is used interchangeably with *hole*. Thus to say that a certain company drilled a well at such and such a location does not imply a successful producing well; it could have been a dry hole. Remembering that oil people often refer to all holes as wells will help avoid confusion.

Because I don't want to overwhelm the reader with numbers, I have tried to keep the statistical monster in its cage, appeased with rounded or approximated numbers. You wouldn't hear two oil people sipping coffee saying that a field produced 4,879,345 barrels of oil, they would say "almost five million." To make this book more readable I have chosen to use coffee counter statistics as well. The reader seeking more detailed factual data can find it all in the public records of the various state regulatory agencies.

Speaking of agencies, the on-line databases of the Alabama and Mississippi Oil and Gas Boards and of the Florida Geological Survey—free to the net-surfing public—are an unsurpassed public service which I have used extensively and with great appreciation. Those agencies also have some dedicated and conscientious people working with them who helped me.

One of my best sources of chronologically organized information was the combined work of Dr. David Sansing of the University of Mississippi and Jackson geologist Gerald Kinsley, both of whom were commissioned to compile data for the book Dudley Hughes intended to write but didn't. Their work was made available to me, and I used it so extensively that to cite every use would have burdened the reader. This acknowledgment will have to do, but I sincerely thank them both.

A last word about sources: To avoid a text laced with annoying superscripts and a bibliography stacked with ibids I departed from the formality of flagging every isolated quote with a note number. I used hundreds of quotes but normally only the first quote in a chapter by a particular person bears a source number. I apologize to readers who may want to check out the source of a quote and must search backward to find it.

I've presented the story as accurately as I could, though no doubt there are inaccuracies. Much of the material is presented in interviews with people who were a part of or close to the stories. Memories grow dim with age, and perception is always subjective.

There are many players in this vast story of a region and a people whose dreams, risks, hard work, and dedication have affected the economic life of the entire country, but there is room for only a few in these pages. Furthermore, big is not always better when history is being recounted. Frequently the small oil and gas discoveries had a more profound significance than large ones. I found the accounts of independents struggling to find production generally more compelling than the methodical operations of corporate exploration teams. Yet I included at least a mention of most significant discoveries and told interesting stories about many of them. I've even a recorded a few fascinating failures. I worked from interviews with over a hundred people, about half of them done by Dudley Hughes. Additionally, I made many appeals for information through letters and notices in petroleum publications. I fully understand that I have left out some noteworthy stories, simply because I never connected with the people who made them happen.

Certainly the people in these pages are not perfect. They had their faults and vices—some more than others. Readers interested in dirty laundry and tell-all will have to dig it up themselves. Here I emphasize the positive traits that led oil people to make a meritorious and lasting impact on the quality of modern life.

I want to offer my sincere gratitude to those who helped make this book a reality: The Allar Company, Larry Baria, Fleming Browning, Dave Cate, Robert Chaney, Callon Petroleum Corporation, Jim Furrh, Gardner Green, Bob Gaston, Ralph Hines, Dan Hughes, Dudley Hughes, J. Bradley Jeffreys, John McGowan, Tom McMillan Jr, Charles Morrison, Marvin Oxley, John T. Palmer, Julius Ridgway, Louis Ridgway Jr., Jim Stewart, Tom Sylte, Harry Spooner, Howard Stover, Vaughey & Vaughey Corporation, Vaughan Watkins, and Stewart Welch.

Others who have influenced me immeasurably over the years deserve recognition. Here are a few:

Mike Epsman, who reviewed the manuscript objectively and made many valuable suggestions. Friends don't get better than Mike.

Dr. Gary Hooks, who ignited a fire in me for geology while I was his student at the University of Alabama.

Lars Johnson, who hired me in my first job in the industry. I hope I didn't disappoint him.

Alex Sartwell, retired librarian and historian of the Alabama Geological Survey, who helped me find some gems.

Bob and Susan Schneeflock, who shared their home with me on numerous visits to Jackson. Thanks especially to Bob for taking great chunks of time from his work to make contacts and arrange meetings. He occasionally zipped me to interviews in a bullet shaped machine that is more rocket than plane, and I felt safe—I taught him to fly. It was Bob who urged me to write this book.

The late *Buddy Twiner,* my mentor at Grace Petroleum, under whom my learning of oil and gas exploration and development began in earnest.

The late *Gene White,* petroleum engineer, who took me under his wings while I worked at the Alabama Oil and Gas Board and who taught me much about petroleum field operations.

Charlie Williams, general manager of Vaughey & Vaughey, Inc, and former president of the Southeast Region of the Mid-continent Oil and Gas Association. Charlie's wise advice and counsel on the accuracy of the manuscript was vital.

Other fine geologists who have been my longtime friends encouraged me whether they realized it or not, among them Alvin Byrd, Tom Joiner, Phil LaMoreaux, Jay Masingill, Gene Pollock, Richard Raymond, Dave Stevens, Ron Tisdale, and Rusty Ward.

I've been in good company.

Prelude

The Salt of the Earth

The frozen, crusty mud crackled with a depressing crunch as he carefully stepped along Perry Creek's marshy banks, his breath billowing clouds of gray vapor. His clear, focused eyes systematically scanned the clay outcrops for the evidence. He knew it was there—somewhere. He took off a glove and pulled out the map he had created over a year ago when he worked these hills as a state geologist employed under a federal grant. And now he was back—compelled to come back and verify that which he had seen in the map's contours.

For weeks Fred had sat in his office, meticulously creating vast flowing contours on his maps after gathering his field data. The trace of his pencil had crept over the paper connecting points of equal elevation. His bright eyes had grown broader as his contours began to turn back on themselves like a snake in pursuit of its tail. Steadily his pencil worked its way through the clusters of data points until it met its point of origin, forming a great closure, the center of which was an obscure backwoods place near the Tinsley railroad switch.

An uninitiated eye staring over his shoulder would have seen only a crude and curious bullseye image taking form, but Fred saw much deeper. In his intuitive geologist's mind he saw a broad but subtle swell in the earth's crust, like a blister that had burst leaving only a crusty rim as evidence that it had been there. He knew that the slow but certain pace of erosion had burst the blister. And he had realized that he must go back and gather more data points to verify his hunch.

He folded his map and slogged along further until he spotted his objective. A subtle smile steadily grew across his trim, young face. He withdrew his rock pick and stabbed at the outcrop, sending chunks crumbling to his feet. He checked the topographic map again and looked around.

Yes, the location was correct and the elevation verified. There was a dome of some sort here, he reasoned, certain of it now. Something deep within the earth's crust—something enormous—had pushed the surface layers upward. The young Frederick Mellen[1] had only a scant idea of what that force might have been, but he knew enough about the fledgling science of petroleum geology to know he was on to something big. In Texas and other regions west of the Mississippi River such domal *structures* were the lair of oil. Yet strangely, Fred wasn't the first person to recognize the potential of this blight on the earth's surface.

Twenty years earlier, in 1916, Tom Slick, a successful Texas oil man, had gazed out his coach window as his train left the flats of the Delta regions and chugged through a rising valley. Somehow he envisioned a giant oil field underlying that hummocky countryside. Maybe he had information about surface oil seeps in the area, although there is no known evidence that seeps occurred. The legend lives on that Slick simply felt it. Upon reaching Jackson, he immediately hired an agent to buy land in the Tinsley area.[2]

But Fred knew nothing of Slick's bizarre premonition, and even if he did he shrugged it off. Fred was a scientist. He would always seek evidence to support his hunches. And now he had it. Yet Fred Mellen was also a gentleman of character. Those who had the privilege of knowing him in the years to come would marvel at his unassuming honesty and unwavering integrity. Fred had found the Tinsley Dome doing taxpayer-funded work and in his mind the citizens owned the information. He didn't rush out to buy oil leases. He rushed to his typewriter.

On April 12, 1939, the press release by the Mississippi Geological Survey reported that a large structural "high" as much as nine and one half miles in diameter had been mapped in Yazoo County.[3] Among those whose passions were ignited by the news was the former Mississippi State Geologist Henry Toler.[4] So sure was Toler of Mellen's find that he declared to his wife, "If the Tinsley structure does not produce, then we will leave Mississippi!" His pledge was understandable in view of the multitude of dry holes that had been drilled in Mississippi over the preceding years while oil hunters in Louisiana and Texas continued to bring in astonishing discoveries. The dearth of production had even prompted one of Toler's contemporaries to proclaim boldly that he would "drink all the oil found east of the Mississippi River."

As Fred resumed his government mapping projects in other counties, a gigantic spire of wood and steel, festooned with blocks and tackle, lines, ladders, and pipework, rose above the hardwood forests at Tinsley. Soon after, in September 1939, the Union Producing Company's No. 1 Woodruff pierced a prolific oil sand at a depth of 4,500 feet, unveiling one of mother earth's largest hidden treasures in the Gulf Coast region. Immediately oil companies and lease speculators alike descended in chaotic hoards on the sleepy hills of Tinsley, Mississippi.

By the end of 1940 over 133 wells would be flowing or pumping the slimy, sweet-smelling, dark brown stuff of which dreams are made and upon which empires are built: crude. It was the chosen fuel of the twentieth century, the potion that would set the standard of modern living, and the substance that would power the engines of the coming war. Thirty of those wells would produce from Tom Slick's estate.

Eventually, Tinsley would produce over 200 million barrels of oil—a "double giant" in modern oil lexicon. After decades of disappointment, hundreds of dry holes, and only a few natural gas finds, the hunt for oil in the Deep South was on—in earnest.

And Henry Toler stayed.

Petroleum Geology 101: A Five Minute Primer

Mellen, Toler, and their contemporaries were only beginning to understand the processes that produce oil, particularly in the Gulf Coast. With Tinsley, their learning curve started a dramatic climb. They knew that like many regions of a constantly changing world, the land area we know today as the Gulf Coast of the United States dropped below sea level numerous times. Each episode of submergence lasted millions of years and resulted in the deposition of thousands of feet of sediment that was transported and dropped by oceanic currents. During periods of emergence, streams, rivers, and winds shaped the landscape with erosion and deposition.

Under this steady process, layer after layer of sand, mud, and carbonate material began to weigh so heavily that the earth's crust sagged into a huge basin under the growing overburden. And the basin fed itself, inviting more sediment at the top as it sagged ever deeper at the bottom—a process that continues today.

As the layers settled they became compacted, consolidated, and in some cases chemically altered. These sediments would be transformed into hard rocks by the time they were visited by the drill bit: the sands to sandstone; the muds to shale; and the reefs and organic matter to limestone. But one of the thickest and most important layers would remain relatively soft—even fluidlike, by geologic standards; it would become known as the Louann Salt. Figure 1 is a simplified geologic "column" that identifies the relative vertical position and age of the major producing sedimentary rock layers in the southern portions of Mississippi, Alabama, and the Florida panhandle.

In the early stages of the basin's development, 180 million years ago, the climate was very arid, causing a great deal of evaporation from highly saline waters resulting in the precipitation of thick layers of salt. Since these deposits were among the first in the development of the basin, they lie near the bottom. The bottom of the basin—referred to as the "basement"—is the granite bedrock of the continental crust. The powerful effect that the Louann Salt exerts on the sediments that overlie it has given rise to the basin's name: the Mississippi Interior Salt Basin, or commonly the Salt Basin.

As the overburden built, the salt began to move laterally away from the areas of highest pressure into adjacent areas of less overburden pressure. Where it found those areas of lower pressure it billowed upward, pushing the sedimentary layers above it up into bulges. Some of the bulges eventually pierced the overlying younger sediments and climbed thousands of feet through them. A few even reached the surface. These "piercement" features

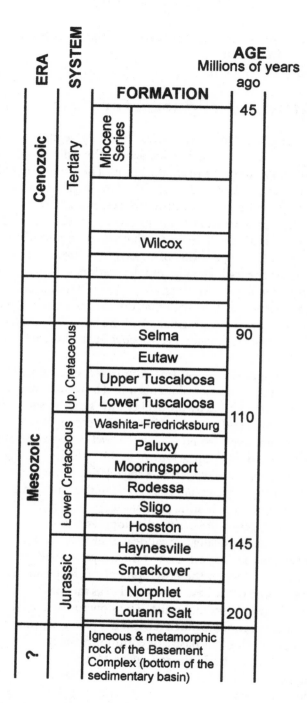

Figure 1. Simplified geologic column of Mississippi Interior Salt Basin, showing the relative vertical position and age of the major drilling targets commonly referred to in the text. (Depth depends on location.)

became known as salt domes. The various movements of the Louann Salt immeasurably influenced the ability of the overlying sediments to trap petroleum.

The salt layer is at its thickest underneath Perry, Forrest, and Lamar counties in south Mississippi, where it is buried 30,000 feet below the surface. Farther south it thins out and becomes absent under Mississippi's coastal counties. It also thins northward until completely "pinching-out" at depths of about 9,000 feet along a northwest/southeast trending line through central Mississippi into south-central Alabama. The Salt Basin and other major geologic features of Alabama, Mississippi, and the Florida panhandle are depicted in Figure 2.

But the Louann Salt is neither the source nor the repository of petroleum accumulation in the basin; it is only a source of brute force that is needed to shape the rock layers above it into large petroleum traps. The *trap* is one of four primary components required to form an oil and/or gas field. The others are source rocks, reservoir rocks, and a seal.

Contrary to popular belief, the source of oil is not dinosaur carcasses but the bodies of countless microscopic organisms that live in the sea. They die and settle on the bottom in great oozes, and become buried and compacted. The heat and pressure of a steadily building overburden initiates chemical changes in the organic matter and result in the formation of hydrocarbons. Both oil and natural gas are hydrocarbons. The rock that houses this process is called the source rock, and is usually shale or limestone. The hydrocarbons may eventually be "squeezed" out of the source rock by the pressure of the overburden. When this happens, the hydrocarbons take refuge in the pore spaces of an adjacent reservoir rock.

A *reservoir* rock needs two qualities to accept oil or gas from the source rock: good *porosity* and good *permeability*. Porosity is the ability of the rock to hold fluids between its tiny grains. Permeability—or *perm*, in geology-speak— is the ability of the fluid to move from pore space to pore space; i.e permeability is the connectivity of the pore spaces. (Only a few oil reservoirs in the world consist of actual large subsurface caverns, as is the popular belief.) When geologists refer to an oil or gas accumulation as a "*pool*" they actually mean the petroleum that is contained in the reservoir rock. Petroleum will push through the reservior rock, at rates of perhaps only millimeters per year, under the influence of pressure, until it reaches a roadblock—he *trap*.

Figure 3 illustrates three common traps. In the classic *anticline*, oil will move upward and accumulate at the highest point. Deep-seated anticlinal structures in sedimentary basins, even though huge in the subsurface, are rarely expressed on the surface where erosion has eaten away at them. The earliest oil fields were found where anticlines could be seen on the surface, such as Tinsley. After the obvious surface swells were drilled up, the hunt for oil got harder.

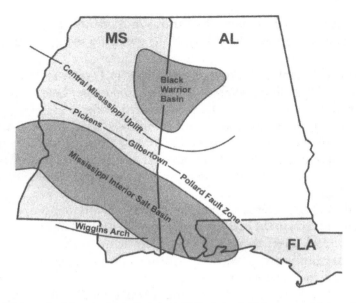

Figure 2. Major subsurface geologic features of Mississippi, Alabama, and the panhandle of Florida

Often a *fault* forms a trap. A fault is a crack in the rock layers along which one side shifts relative to the other side. The displacement may be tens of feet or thousands. When a faulted reservoir rock is thrown against a non-permeable rock, petroleum can become trapped at the fault. As with the anticline, faults in the Gulf Coast basins are rarely expressed on the surface.

In the *stratigraphic* trap, petroleum stops its upward migration when it reaches nonporous or impermeable sections of a tilted reservior rock. This permeability transformation is most common where porous sandstones grade into *tight* (low porosity/permeability) shales. This kind of trap is also referred to as a *pinch out*. The stratigraphic trap is the hardest of all oil fields to find.

Whether the trap is an anticline, fault, or stratigraphic trap, a nonporous *seal* must be present above to stop the oil's upward migration. Shale is the most common seal rock in most basins.

In the Salt Basin, the salt itself is the predominant mechanism that causes traps to form in other rock layers above it. What Fred Mellen had discovered at Tinsley was the surface expression of a huge mound of salt, the top of which would eventually be found 11,000 feet below the surface. Numerous layers of reservior rocks stacked upon each other lie draped over the salt mound, and each one would constitute a separate oil pool independent of the others. The upward pressure of the salt also caused faults to develop in the overlying sediments, meaning dozens of separate pools would eventually be discovered even in the same layers.

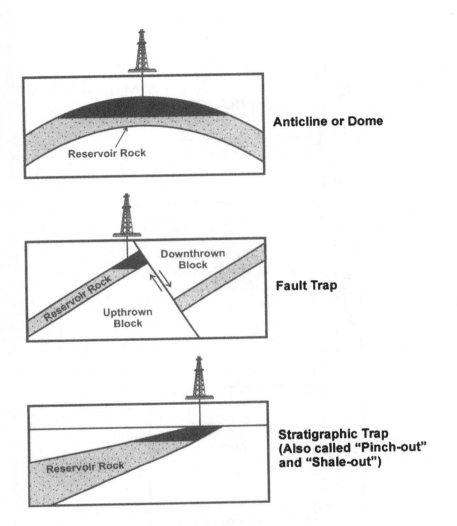

Figure 3. Three common types of oil traps

But the Mississippi Interior Salt Basin is not the lone petroleum producing basin in the Deep South. An even older basin lies north of it—the Black Warrior Basin (Fig. 2). The rocks of this basin date back 400 million years. The two basins are separated by a high ridge in the basement rock, which runs through central Alabama and Mississippi. Like the Salt Basin, the Black Warrior Basin also consists of mainly marine (oceanic) deposits, but the rocks are generally much harder on the drill bit, and less porous. Figure 4 is a simplified geologic column depicting the common producing rock layers of the Black Warrior Basin.

The Black Warrior Basin's rocks lack a dynamic force, such as the salt underneath them to produce large structural features. Consequently its traps

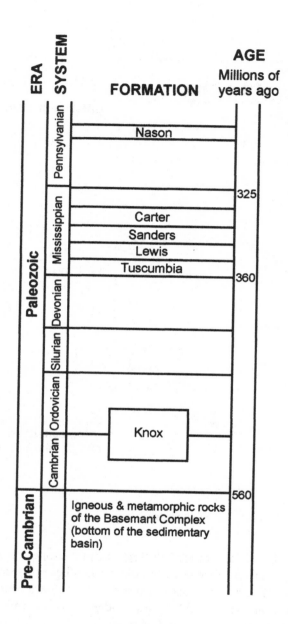

Figure 4. Simplified geologic column of the Black Warrior Basin, showing the relative vertical position and age of the major drilling targets commonly referred to in the text.

are relatively small and often subtle. Small faults and numerous stratigraphic traps are the basin's production trademarks. Due to the extreme age of the basin's sediments, the petroleum maturation process has left little crude oil. Most production is methane gas. In 1902 the Black Warrior Basin earned the honor of offering up the first commercial production in the southern states east of the Mississippi River. The citizens of Huntsville, Alabama, enjoyed gas streetlights for a short period before the shallow wells depleted.[5] The Black Warrior Basin is also a prominent region for coal and coal bed methane production.

But the Black Warrior Basin drew little attention from oilmen who stampeded into south Mississippi after the excitement at Tinsley. Armed with a growing repertoire of oil hunting skills and tools they attacked the Salt Basin with legions of drilling rigs. And it was in the nick of time.

The Hunt Intensifies

A dark cloud moved over the enormous excitement generated by the Tinsley discovery. Germany invaded Poland and began its march on the Galician and Romanian oilfields. War broke out across Europe and quickly spread into North Africa and the Pacific.

The U.S. Government immediately set out both to conserve oil and to encourage exploration. In a cooperative effort between government and industry, the Office of Petroleum Coordinator (OPC) was established and staffed with experienced oil industry specialists. Some observers squealed about conflicts of interest and pointed accusatory fingers at oilmen appointed to government jobs related to the oil business; but OPC mandated conservation, and exploration flourished under its control.

This suited the oil people of Mississippi—those few who were not called into the fray. Their state was the newest of the major oil producers and in their minds the potential was unlimited. Drilling reached record levels. From 1943 to 1945 large oil finds were logged at Brookhaven, Eucutta, Cranfield, Heidleberg, Mallalieu, and Baxterville. Important gas discoveries turned up at Gwinville, Soso, and Hub. By the war's end the fields discovered to that point in time would ultimately prove out reserves of over one billion barrels of oil and 3.5 trillion cubic feet of gas.[6]

Alabama drew scant attention from oil explorers during WW II, but the state's first oil production came in at Gilbertown, in Choctaw County, in 1944. By the war's end only twenty-five wells were producing oil in Alabama, but the future looked bright to oil explorers who relished the opportunity to press their exploration efforts in the Heart of Dixie.

Florida was the farthest Gulf Coast state from the oil provinces and suffered from even less attention during the war, yet a discovery was made at Sunniland by Humble Oil Company in 1943 near the northern edge of the

Everglades. Otherwise, efforts there during the war years were largely disappointing.

Despite enormous demand, the resolve of the OPC and the oil industry paid off. Fueled by oil and resolve, Allied forces defeated Germany and Japan, cutting both off from their petroleum supplies. The United States was producing over 50% of the world's oil supply when the war broke out, and 67% when it was finally quelled.[7] The U.S. was the only country that had discovered the petroleum resources to restore the world to normalcy.

Within twenty-four hours after Japan's surrender gasoline rationing ended in the United States. The Office of Petroleum Coordinator was dismantled and the individual states regained control of their own oil and gas industry.

Millions of war veterans hung up their uniforms and put skills learned in the war to work. Others turned to attacking college textbooks. Many had saved their military pay, and the glistening shine of new automobiles caught their eyes. Cars came into a tremendous demand. America's old love affair with the motor car flourished again.

Sixteen million new cars hit America's roads in the first five years after the war. Gasoline sales shot up 42% and the overall sale of petroleum products soared 67% by 1952. Under such demand the price of crude oil doubled in three years.

Companies and investors had thrown tons of money down dry holes across the South, but the lucky ones had also reaped enormous profits from new strikes in Mississippi. Just as important, much had been learned. Innovation in oil field technology had bounded ahead to keep up with demand of the swelling economy. In pursuit of those demands more oil companies cast expectant eyes on Alabama, Florida, and Mississippi. For the visionaries at their maps, like Fred Mellen, the hunting grounds of the Deep South lay broad and beckoning.

PART I
Late 40s to Mid 50s

Chapter 1

Tours of Duty

B ob Womack thought his timing was lousy. He had followed his calling, inspired by his older brother Brane, a geologist who had stalked oil along the Gulf coast since the 1930s. Working part time for Phillips Petroleum and Kerr-Lynn Oil Company, his apprenticeship began even before he graduated from the University of Oklahoma, one of the finest soft-rock geology schools in the country. With all the exciting things happening in the oil industry, especially the fervor down in Mississippi in which Brane was actively involved, Womack's appetite for oil hunting burgeoned.[1]

But that was the summer of 1941 and mankind was preoccupied with more sinister conquests. The draft board sent Womack an invitation he couldn't refuse. With the ink still wet on his new degree, he walked off the OU campus and into the Navy recruiting office. Four and a half years later, Womack hung up his uniform and cast a longing eye upon the oil fields. And he found his timing wasn't so bad after all.

Many new oil fields had been found and exciting new *plays* had developed. Petroleum professionals call the heightened period of exploration activity in a particular subsurface rock layer a *play*. He saw that the drain of personnel to the war effort had left the oil industry critically short of trained professionals. And while many of his contemporaries were only starting college training, he knew he was locked, loaded, and poised to go oil hunting.

He accepted an offer from Gulf Refining Company, which was delighted to find a degreed geologist fresh from the war. His assignment came swiftly: Mississippi. He rushed to the oil boomtown of Laurel, where Gulf had set up district headquarters in an old schoolhouse. There he met his new boss, Tom "Sparky" McGlothlin,[2] who was responsible for Gulf's ambitious southeast Mississippi drilling program. Sparky had held the fort down during the war years, performing a job normally requiring several men, and he was ecstatic to have reinforcements.

Womack found a room only a block from the schoolhouse in the Pinehurst Hotel, which was becoming a landmark in Mississippi's oil culture. Immediately he sent for his wife, Vee. She arrived at five o'clock one evening, just in time to see him off to work. He didn't see her again for three weeks.

Like every petroleum professional, Womack soon discovered that the learning process doesn't stop with college graduation but begins in earnest on the first job with an oil company. For the geologist, that usually meant paying his dues by examining core cuttings at the drillsite and becoming thoroughly familiar with drilling, testing, and production operations. Making maps and looking for new places to drill would come later. Womack's work was cut out.

McGlothlin threw him into the thriving beehive of Gulf's drilling operations, where he joined other budding geologists to become a *well-sitter*. In that capacity they examined the cuttings of the drill bit, brought to the surface by the *drilling mud* that constantly circulates through the drill pipe and back to the surface. The bit's diameter, wider than the pipe's, makes circulation possible. Holes in the bit eject the mud under pressure and force it back to the surface through space between the pipe and the borehole wall. The circulation of the mud cleans the hole out as drilling progresses and helps the driller control any natural high-pressure fluids or gases he encounters. Figure 5 is a diagram of the procedure, which is basically unchanged since the 1930s.

The cuttings are filtered from the returning mud and examined under a microscope or a hand lens, and the observations are logged on a strip of paper annotated with depth marks. The folded paper strips are called *mud logs* and are correlated with those of nearby wells to determine how the current well is *running*. The technique is still in use today. If the well is running excessively *low* to nearby wells, that is normally bad news. It means the well is drilling in rock layers that are either downfaulted or tilted downward (*down dip*) of known production. In such a case water might be expected at the target depth, rather than oil. Conversely, a well running *high* to its neighbors is a good sign. Thus Womack and his co-workers provided valuable information to the company in monitoring the progress of their drilling activity. But Womack found out quickly that the term "well sitter" is a gross misnomer. He did anything but sit.

When a well *spuds* (begins drilling), operations continue unabated until target depth is reached. Weather and holidays are ignored. Geologists long ago concluded that drilling crews probably conspire to reach target depth on Christmas Eve. The crews then get to spend the holiday at home while homesick geologists evaluate the well.

Crews of *roughnecks* rotate eight or twelve hour shifts called *tours* (pronounced *towers*) but a single geologist is usually responsible for the well. He or she visits frequently to collect the cutting samples and analyze them. (Female petroleum professionals did not appear in substantial numbers until the late 1970s and today there are still relatively few.) Often a company employs a *mudlogger* to make the mudlogs, not usually a degreed geologist but a trained observer of rock cuttings. The geologist responsible for the well then uses the mudlogs in conjunction with other data to evaluate the well. His presence is required during critical operations such as wireline and diamond coring, electric logging, and testing.

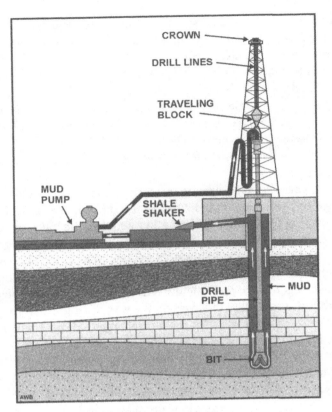

Figure 5. Diagram of drilling operators.

Womack and the other new geologists needed to develop a working knowledge of all analytical operations quickly. Gulf was running up to fifty drilling rigs in such widely spaced fields as Heidelberg, Eucutta, Baxterville, Gwinville, and Soso, all discovered during the war years.[3] Also numerous exploratory, or *wildcat*, wells were drilling at the same time as the field wells.

The rooky geologists rapidly picked up the lingo of the oil field. They learned that "drilling ahead" and "turning to the right" were phrases drillers boastfully used to indicate that their big rigs were "making hole," or proceeding downward without problems. Managers in the home office dreaded reports that their rigs were stuck, fishing, or tripping. A *stuck* drill string, a *fishing job* for lost pipe, or a *trip* back out to change a bit were all costly delays. The four geologists responsible for Gulf's fifty rigs, turning frantically to the right, learned the language and the methods, and they lived the lives of hummingbirds: zipping from rig to rig, rarely seeing home, rarely resting.

Like most oil companies, Gulf sub-contracted its drilling operations. Womack came to know the drilling contractors and their personnel well. He remembered H.L. Hunt, owner of Penrod Drilling Company, and one of the world's richest and most powerful industrialists. "You never knew when old man Hunt was going to drive up on the rig," he recalled, "and he would drive out there at two in the morning!"

In September 1947 after two sleep-starved years of rushing from rig to rig, Womack had enough. He submitted his resignation, but McGlothlin talked him into staying on another two weeks. The last ten days were hell. "I had a wildcat well somewhere between Gwinville and Baxterville, and I was coring two wells in Gwinville and three wells in Baxterville. It was eighty-five miles from one end to the other, and for ten days the only sleep I got was in the car, and that was not unusual."

Congress gave Womack and his co-workers some relief when it rectified the shortage of professional personnel in the oil industry, as well as many others, by passing the GI Bill. Among other benefits, the bill provided veterans up to four years of college. The booming oil industry was generating excitement and new wealth. Thousands of jobs were available, begging for qualified applicants, prompting many vets to earn degrees in geology, petroleum engineering, or other petroleum-related fields. Colleges bulged to capacity. With four years snatched away by the war, during which they learned the real meaning of responsibility, most discharged veterans returned to civilian life with an unusual level of maturity and determination.

Opportunity in blue-collar jobs blossomed as well. Many veterans returning from the service to their native South found jobs offering high pay in an industry which sprang up and flourished while they were away.

Toward the end of the forties, new graduates began to swell the staffs of oil companies. Geologists and engineers were being hired at exorbitant salaries, some up to $300 per month—a big salary in 1946. Exploration blazed ahead in a frenzy throughout the producing states, driven by high oil prices that eventually reached $3.00 per barrel—triple the wartime ceiling price.

In 1946 almost 200 companies were at work in Mississippi, busily developing their strikes. Most of the oil and gas activity in the state at war's end was development work, drilling additional wells in existing fields. During 1946 and 1947, some 600 new wells were completed in fields discovered during World War II. Daily production reached 130,000 *BOPD* (barrels of oil per day) from almost 1,300 wells. Annual oil production increased from over 24 million barrels in 1946 to almost 40 million in 1951.

The romance of the oil business has always been wildcatting. Oil exploration fires imaginations and electrifies spirits. A wildcat may be drilled only a mile or two away from an established field, or a even in the middle of one, seeking new production from a different depth; or a wildcat may step out hundreds of miles from known oil provinces to hunt in an entirely unexplored basin. The latter, called frontier exploration, is usually left to the big corporations with deep pockets. The former is an open season for anyone who believes in his dream strongly enough to win financial backing.

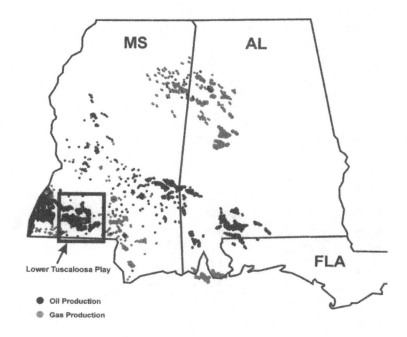

Figure 6. Map of Lower Tuscaloosa Play.

By 1945 most of the oil and gas in Mississippi and Alabama had been found in the younger and shallower formations of the Salt Basin, including the Gas Rock, the Eutaw, and the Lower Tuscaloosa (figure 6). Those were still the main targets of wildcat wells in the late 1940s. A hot new trend started to develop in the Natchez area, however, extending from its origins in Louisiana, that would eventually spark more wildcat drilling than all the other trends combined. Its target was the prolific but largely unpredictable sands of the Eocene age. It became known as the Wilcox Play (figure 7).

Those Funny Little Sands

Oil production in Louisiana spread slowly eastward and across the river into Mississippi, where operators lusted after the oil-saturated sands of the Lower Tuscaloosa. The first big strike after Tinsley came in 1943 at Cranfield in Adams County.[4] Cranfield swelled into an enormous field and eventually yielded tens of millions of barrels. Geologists sitting the wells in Cranfield noticed strong oil shows in some shallow sands they passed through on the way down to the Lower Tuscaloosa, the Wilcox Sands, which had yielded good production in Louisiana. Some completion attempts were made in the Wilcox in Cranfield but were mostly failures. The sands were brittle. They crumbled

7

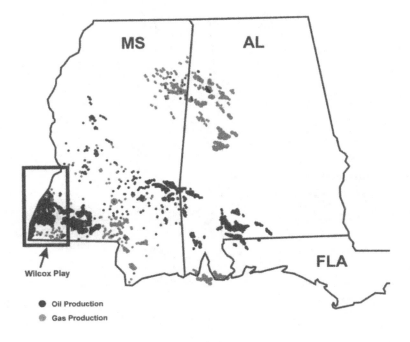

Figure 7. Map of Wilcox Play.

and caved, causing cement seals to fail. Most operators shrugged the Wilcox off and concentrated on the Lower Tuscaloosa. They had no idea what a bonanza they were ignoring until Bud Norman came along.

Norman, a Texan, signed on with Gulf after collecting his geology degree from TCU in 1929. Gulf sent him to the wild frontier state of Mississippi where he joined Sparky McGlothlin and others mapping surface features along the Pickens/Pollard/Gilbertown fault zone. Later he worked in Texas until being assigned back to Mississippi after the Tinsley strike. He left Gulf in 1942 and threw in with Buzz Morgan, an independent who had just found production in the Pickens field.[5] Later he joined independents Emmett and Bill Vaughey.

The Vaughey brothers, Bill and Emmett, were successful lease brokers involved in almost every major oil discovery since Tinsley, but they had grown tired of leasing tracts for other people to find oil on. "When a major oil company wants you to take a block," Emmett said, "they call you into their office, show you the outline of the structure, and you have that very valuable information, you have to keep this very confidential and we always did. However when you are trying to find oil for yourself, this sometimes comes into conflict, so we decided to abandon a very good brokerage business.... This was a very hard decision for us to make, because we liked the brokerage business. It fed us a lot of information, paid well, and it's exciting."[6]

"The Vaughey brothers were the highlight of the oil business in Mississippi," remembered James Furrh, who came on the scene in 1954. "Bill was a very handsome fellow, tall and robust. He was the smooth talker of the two, and the salesman type—very warm and friendly. Emmett was shorter and very slender—a heavy smoker. He was the one who came up with the ideas and Bill sold them."[7] The brothers invested in a Lower Tuscaloosa wildcat six miles southwest of Cranfield operated by Roeser & Pendleton and Sohio. Bud Norman evaluated it for them.

The well reached *TD* (total depth) in early 1946, encountering shows in the Lower Tuscaloosa. Production casing was set, but the Lower Tusc sands at 10,500 feet proved to be noncommercial. After six months of testing, the group halted operations after producing only 4,500 barrels. The well was a teaser. They prepared to plug the hole. But Bud Norman had an idea.

Norman approached Wilbur Knight of Union Producing Company. Raised in Laramie, Wil Knight was a product of the University of Wyoming's geology department. Union Producing Company hired him as a geological scout immediately after graduation and sent him to Jackson where he became heavily involved in the Tinsley development. His Army ROTC reserve commission was activated in 1942, snatching him away to the war. Union snatched him back after his discharge in 1945. He worked his way up to district geologist, where he was actively involved in almost every major play in the Southeast in the forties and fifties.

Norman pointed out some interesting zones uphole. "What do you think about these funny little sands here in the Wilcox?" he asked Knight. "Why don't we try them?"[8]

But trying them wasn't as simple as it sounded and the two knew it. The Wilcox sands occurred at approximately 6,000 feet in the well. The base of the casing, however, was almost a mile deeper at 10,500 feet, where the Lower Tuscaloosa completion had been attempted. That presented a serious problem.

When *production casing* (usually 5 or 7 inch diameter pipe) is set in a hole, it must be cemented in place. A calculated volume of cement is pumped down the casing. When it reaches bottom, it comes back up through the open space (the *annulus*) between the casing and the borehole wall. The amount of cement used for the upward journey is calculated to be sufficient to cover all potential producing zones so that they will be sealed off. The cement pumped down the pipe is followed by a plug, then a column of water. When the plug reaches bottom, the cement is allowed to set. Then, a gunlike device lowered on a wire line shoots perforations into the formation. The shots are powerful enough to penetrate both pipe and concrete and drive deep into the reservoir rock. Another smaller-diameter pipe called tubing is placed in the casing. If the rock is sufficiently porous and permeable, whatever fluids are present (gas, oil, or water) flow into the tubing and to the surface.

On the well Norman and Knight were working, it would have been highly impractical to circulate cement from a TD of 10,500 feet back up to the Wilcox sands at 6,000 feet, even though the engineers had tried. They doubted the sufficient cement seal behind pipe at the 6,000-foot level in the brittle and crumbling Wilcox sands was sufficient. In fact, most engineers thought that circulating cement across the Wilcox not only failed to seal it but damaged it as well. They feared the cement, flowing under pressure from surface pumps, would drive into the exceptionally porous Wilcox sands and permanently damage their ability to yield oil. They thought a perforation attempt would only draw salt water from some higher or lower water zone through imperfections in the cement seal, like the earlier Wilcox attempts in Cranfield. The problem had long plagued and discouraged exploration and development of the Wilcox and for good reason.

Salt water is particularly bad on the environment. It kills vegetation and pollutes freshwater sources when dumped onto the ground. As state oil and gas conservation laws now require, production-associated saltwater can be safely disposed only by pumping it down a borehole into a naturally occurring saltwater bearing zone far below the freshwater aquifers.

No—trying the funny little sands would not be easy, but Norman had an idea. Based on his Texas experience, he would *perforate* above and below the Wilcox sands and squeeze more cement behind the pipe to ensure a better concrete seal. Maybe the *squeeze job* would prevent cement failures like they had at Cranfield.

Soon he had Knight and others convinced. They decided to attempt a Wilcox completion using Norman's suggestions. Norman recalled the procedure as if he were still at it. "So now I'm squeezing below or re-cementing—was the way I looked at it—below pipe and kept the pressures as low as I possibly could in keeping with the belief that you [shouldn't] pump into the sand, and with about 2,600-2,700 *psi* maximum pressure, the squeeze job appeared to be all right."

They drilled out the cement and perforated. The well kicked off, flowing 100% oil, establishing the No. 1 Baker-Maier as the discovery well for the LaGrange field. "We had erased the belief that you ruined the Wilcox Sand [by squeezing cement into it]," Norman added. Production engineers had given up on the Wilcox cementing problem, but the person who solved it—resulting in a stampede in Wilcox exploration—was a geologist.

Consequently, oil people across the region were happily surprised in August 1946 when the No. 1 Baker-Maier flowed 300 BOPD, water-free. The Wilcox suddenly captured peoples' passions.

The next significant assault on the Wilcox came under the bit of Big Chief Drilling Company of Oklahoma, a newcomer to the Mississippi scene, but there was still an enormous problem to overcome if people were to get serious about drilling in the southwestern counties of Mississippi. And it had nothing to do with geology.

The first complication began before a company leased the first acre. The counties along the river in southwest Mississippi were a landman's nightmare. They had been divided by old Spanish land grants into sections having no pattern or standard size. Instead of the standard one-mile squares—as in most parts of the country, including most of Mississippi—section boundaries in the southwest corner of the state ran along creeks, roads, ridges, rivers, or whatever suited the surveyors' fancies in the early days. Land maps looked like jigsaw puzzles. The irregularity made it extremely awkward to form square, systematic 40-acre *drilling units*, long the accepted size of oil well spacing units. The problem was a real head-scratcher until J.P. Evans Sr. figured it out.

Evans, a Shreveport *landman*, involved in Mississippi since the 1920s, had an eye for spotting opportunity in the midst of mayhem, as he had demonstrated years earlier. He was familiar with the Tinsley area, having leased property there in the 1920s for Amerada. After Union's strike in 1939, he cruised the back roads of the Tinsley area, yelling out to landowners as he passed, asking them if they had leased their land. One inquiry had netted him 145 acres that eventually were the home of six oil wells.[9]

Evans eyed the jagged, patchy land patterns along the Mississippi side of the river and crafted a clever scheme to open the area for easy leasing and drilling and make him a ton of money in the process. Knowing the oil companies were interested in the area, he leased a core area of 8,500 acres in Adams County and subdivided it into 40 acre square lots with each with a number. The lot boundaries were independent of official section boundaries. Landowners agreed to accept them as drilling units, sharing the royalty in each, in proportion to the number of acres each owned in the 40-acre lots. Next, Evans offered 215 of the lots for sale to the industry. His block became known as the "J. P. Evans Subdivision." Many companies, including the Vaughey brothers, bought the lots.

One of the most respected men in oil circles nationwide in 1946 was Bill Payne, another Oklahoman and the founder of Helmerich & Payne, Inc. With the increased fervor in the southeastern states, Payne decided to move one of his drilling companies, Big Chief Drilling, Inc., to Mississippi. He made Harold L. Rowley the partner in charge and sent him to Laurel. The bookkeeper for Big Chief, operating out of Shreveport, was George Jett. Jett had an oil fire in his belly and regarded his clerical job as a launching point. He was destined to make oil patch history in the years ahead, for both his illustrious achievements and his career-ending destination—prison.

Payne was anxious to participate in wildcat prospects as a paying partner in addition to providing contract drilling. Over the years he established a good relationship with a group of investors in New York, who provided the money to take interest in other people's deals. His need for local representation to make the necessary connections led to an association with the Vaughey brothers. Rowley ran the drilling company while Vaughey & Vaughey located *drilling deals.*

The Vaugheys were enjoying good cash flows from their early successes and needed somewhere to re-invest. Accordingly, they cut a deal with Payne, which reserved for them the right to buy a quarter interest in each deal.

The Vaugheys put Big Chief into the J.P. Evans Subdivision, and soon the R. L. Parker No. 1 was spudded on Lot 137. The geologist was Benton Vernon Sr., and Bud Norman performed the engineering work. The well hit. That success sold the Big Chief people on the Wilcox and in concert with Vaughey & Vaughey, they went on to drill 16 producers in the LaGrange field. Union Producing, still not convinced that the Wilcox production would hold up, farmed out its lots to Vaughey & Vaughey, as did others. By the end of 1949, 114 oil wells had been completed in the field. In time, LaGrange was to become the largest Wilcox field in Mississippi, producing 45 million barrels.

Subsequent development work by the Big Chief group showed that some 30 sands in the upper 2,000 feet of the Wilcox are potential production targets. The depth of the potential producing sands ranged from 4,000 feet in northern Adams County to 9,000 feet in southern Wilkinson County. Most production was found around 5,000 to 6,000 feet. Hundreds of oil fields were found from the sands in Jefferson, Adams, Franklin, and Wilkinson Counties.

J.P. Evans died in 1954 in a plane crash, returning from a duck hunt with several other oilmen from Louisiana. He never saw the Wilcox play that he started at LaGrange reach its boom stage. The advances he made possible spawned the exploration that eventually resulted in hundreds of Wilcox fields. Bud Norman's contribution earned him the title "Father of the Wilcox."

The beckoning Wilcox play attracted more companies and continued to intrigue oil hunters. The funny little sands often exhibited strange, almost unpredictable geological characteristics. Mack Cox, who studied the sands, also discovered that some strange people lived above them.

Messages from the Stars

After the successes at LaGrange, Phillips Petroleum took notice and set out to find themselves some Wilcox prospects. They transferred Cox to Jackson from Shreveport to build up their Mississippi subsurface maps. Cox was a second generation oilman who earned his geology degree from the University of Texas and his practical experience from the University of Hard Knocks. "Phillips," he said, "was a firm believer that a man being groomed for leadership should be accustomed to the end of a shovel."[10] As a new geologist, he laid pipe and set tank batteries as a *roustabout* before he was ever allowed to lay eyes on a rock or pick up a contouring pencil.

Cox tackled the Wilcox geology and convinced Phillips to send brokers into Adams County. Soon after beginning leasing operations, the brokers reported an encounter with a rather strange, mystical family—the Artmans. Cox tells of the bizarre meeting that led to a very sweet oil field. "The Artmans, who owned the land, were spiritualists. They required that the formal signing of the lease should occur in the eerie atmosphere of the Natchez Trace, all covered with moss, along the banks of the Mississippi, at midnight, under a full moon."

Phillips went along with the strange idea, and in December 1946 they completed the No. 1 Artman flowing over 100 BOPD a mile down, opening the Pine Ridge field and possibly the first exploratory well to be targeted exclusively for the Wilcox.

But the Artman family's strange ways dogged the drillers every step of the way. "On subsequent locations after the discovery," Cox said, "old man Artman was always right on [with] his predictions of whether we would get a producer or a dry hole. I finally told Bartlesville [Bartlesville, Oklahoma, company headquarters] that his information was better than mine and must be coming from the stars, and they didn't need me, but should retain Artman." They didn't.

The Pine Ridge field was Phillips' first production in Mississippi since their success in the old Pickens field, discovered before WW II. Eventually Pine Ridge would swell Phillips' coffers with the financial harvest of over four million barrels of oil.

As Phillips moved out from the field and began shooting *seismic* in search of deeper Lower Tuscaloosa structure, the old wizard followed them. "The party chief, Doug Hoyer, called me in Jackson to say he had been all over the world but he had never come up against a guy like Artman. Seems most every time he started drilling a shot hole Artman wanted to move it to prevent drilling into pots of gold and precious jewels."

Mr. Artman soon proved correct again—the shot-hole locations were moved slightly, at his urging, and not a single pot of gold or jewels was disturbed. The family name became indelibly etched in oil history, as the sand dubbed the 'Artman' developed into a favorite drilling objective of the Wilcox players.

There were no Wilcox discoveries in 1947, but Harry Elliot found one field, South LaGrange, in 1948. South LaGrange, located in the J.P. Evans subdivision, became a six million–barrel field.

After two slack years, Wilcox activity picked up in 1949 with the discovery of three fields. Sohio and Jones & Kemp found the Armstrong field; Hodge, Gilster & Kemp discovered the Oldenberg field; and Danziger turned up the Possum Corner field. Of the three, only Oldenberg produced over a million barrels from the Wilcox. Those were the beginning of swarms of small Wilcox fields found over the years.

Dozens of meticulous geologists in small, back-alley offices in Natchez and Jackson would pore over well logs in the densely drilled Wilcox trend, trying to track down the elusive Eocene-aged sands with maps scaled at 1 inch=500 feet, while using structural contours of only five or ten feet contour interval. Precise attention to minute detail became the recognized mark of a Wilcox geologist.

As the trend matured, these specialists typically generated small four to five well prospects, many of which exhibited no more than 50 feet of structural closure. (To visualize that, imagine a hill only 50 feet high.) The equally numerous stratigraphic prospects they worked up were commonly lenticular sands draped across a plunging structural nose. Those risky little deals drew an abundant cadre of small investors because of the relatively cheap drilling costs and the proximity to Wilcox production, sometimes only a stone's throw away.

But the chief reason the Wilcox afforded so much romance to investors was the role of serendipity. In essence, a Wilcox prospect was only an excuse to drill; the funny little sands themselves offered up their own surprises to those bold enough to sink a hole and have a look. Some of those daring speculators came from vastly different walks of life.

Everybody in Natchez wanted in on the action. In the midst of the Wilcox hubbub, the quiet, stately river town became a regional oil center. Equipment yards, strewn with huge piles of pipe, hordes of pumps and valve assemblies, rows of heater-treaters, and clusters of holding tanks sprang up.

The Natchez Eola Hotel housed oilmen who left their rooms and swaggered down the street to Emmett's Bar (no relation to Emmett Vaughey) to swap lies and trade rumors. At lunch they discussed business over hamburgers at D.A. Biglane's diner. Emmett Vaughey, a central figure in the Natchez oil culture wrote, "He [Biglane] listened intently to what everybody said and, as a consequence, came out pretty well."[11]

Jim Furrh, who came into the Wilcox later, knew Biglane very well. "He was short and robust, quite heavy. He was not a tutored fellow. He didn't go beyond high school. But he was sharp as a tack. He got all his oil information from the oil people that came in. He started drilling his own deals."[12]

John Callon, another player who came onto the Wilcox later, also knew Biglane well. "He opened a restaurant here in Natchez called Topps Grill on Main Street. It was very, very successful. Biglane didn't have a clue about the oil business but he was an opportunist extraordinaire." (So was Callon.) "He [Biglane] stood in the front door of the restaurant and he got to know every person who came in regularly. They would tell him what they were doing. Pretty soon, they would be drinking coffee and he was able to pick up things. He didn't know a damn thing about the oil business, but he had that ability to see an opportunity and to get information."[13] Biglane began turning the profit from the Topps Grill into leases and royalty, based on the clues and leads he gleaned from the oil crowd. He eventually drilled wells and spread his operation into the Lower Tuscaloosa play. "He just had an innate ability to work hard and get to know people," Callon said. Callon himself was destined to become one of Mississippi's most successful self-starters in the oil business.

Drilling steadily increased into the 50s, resulting in 42 Wilcox fields by the end of 1952, but the steadily increasing stream of oil flowing from Mississippi's rocks into the country's refineries were no match for the black tidal wave approaching from the far East—a wave that heightened the competition for market share.

Chapter 2

"As pretty as anything you've seen"

In 1950 the Abqaiq Field in Saudi Arabia became the world's largest producer at 450,000 barrels per day, exceeding the super giant East Texas field. Other super giants in the Middle East followed. Cheap foreign oil imported into the U.S. market began as a trickle and soon became a torrent.

The resulting downward pressure on domestic oil prices frustrated Mississippi wildcatters, but they continued to sink holes where the contours closed on their maps. In their scramble for leases and drilling dollars, they wove intricate deals that tended to grow and fragment as various partners promoted their interests and hedged their risks. A little deal in Wayne County, Mississippi, in 1947 was typical.

Independently of each other, a couple of young but street-wise oil hunters decided to play the same hunch. One of them was a popular, outgoing fellow who regarded his idea so highly that he declared he had an oil field—before he drilled it. The other, who played his cards closer, displayed an immense determination and a cocky, swaggering style that often rubbed people the wrong way. The two opposites met head-on at the spud point.

Merrill Harris was another Sooner drawn to Mississippi. He came out of an Oklahoma town even Will Rogers had never heard of and took a geology degree from OU. He also brandished a hot saxophone in a ragtime band, which kept bread on his table until Union Sulfur picked him up for its expanding oil and gas operation. They sent him to Jackson during the Tinsley fervor. After a few years he turned independent, partnered with Butch Payne, and opened a consulting office in Jackson. Union Sulfur retained him as a consultant.

Harris had been scoping out an area near Waynesboro, Mississippi, where Humble Oil and Refining Company (which later became Exxon) was busily probing a *graben* structure they had found with gravity and seismic work. *Graben* is a German word geologists adopted to describe a common geologic feature. The dynamics of salt movement often caused two approximately parallel *faults* to form in the rock layers draped over the salt. The area between the two faults dropped, leaving the flank areas of the structure *upthrown* and the central block *downthrown*. Wildcatters commonly found oil in one or both upthrown blocks of a graben, and sometimes even in the downthrown block. Figure 8 is a diagram of a typical graben and Harris' concept.

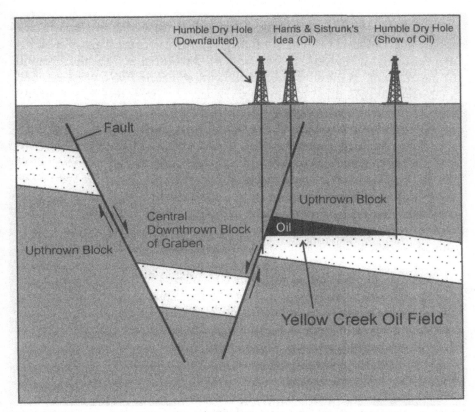

Figure 8. Diagram of the Yellow Creek Graben illustrating how Harris, Sistrunk, and others keyed off of previous dry holes to find the pool.

Humble put five holes down at various points on the structure. All turned up dry. Then, Harris learned, Humble elected not to renew a major lease on the prospect belonging to the Masonite Corporation. Apparently they had given up, but Harris was not satisfied that Humble had drilled in the right place. His assessment was simple.

"The last well Humble drilled was downthrown, just barely into the graben. And then, out here on the other side, there was a well [with] about two feet of oil show. . . . And, of course, Geology 101 says that if you can get that, come up to the fault [and] you've got an oil field!"[1]

Harris oversimplified the concept. It was not something generally taught in classrooms. It took lots of log study and subsurface mapping to put his concept into practice, but it didn't necessarily take a geology degree to comprehend it, as Harris was about to find out.

He leased the Masonite acreage and then went to New Orleans to get a farmout on the rest of Humble's block. A *farmout* is a deal in which a lease-holder contributes his acreage in a given area to another operator who agrees to bear all the expense of drilling. If the well is successful, the leaseholder usually backs in for a portion of his original interest, commonly 30 to 40%, after the operator recovers his costs from production sales. Thus the farmout arrangement offers the advantage of allowing someone who owns leases but is reluctant to drill them to convey those leases to someone who wants to drill but doesn't have them. Both parties benefit if the well hits.

Calling Humble to request the farmout, Harris learned that a shrewd poker player named Walter Sistrunk Sr. had upstaged him. Sistrunk was a self-made man who had bolted for the oil patch after an abortive attempt at college. He paid his dues roughnecking, but when the rest of the crew went home after their tours, he stayed and picked the brains of the geologists, engineers, and landmen. Eventually he built enough knowledge to try his hand at wildcatting and began a career that rode the roller coaster of fortune and famish. Sistrunk thought that was the most thrilling ride in the oil park.

Sistrunk got to Humble first, and they offered him two 80-acre tracts plus $10,000 *dry hole money* to drill a 5,000-foot Eutaw test. Dry hole money is an incentive leaseholders sometimes use to entice someone else to drill. It is paid only if the hole is dry. If the well hits, the leaseholder benefits from his share of production or simply from the additional information he gains.

Hearing of this, Harris rubbed his chin, wondering how to approach the plucky Sistrunk, then met him. "I saw Walter," Harris recalled, "and I said, 'Well, there's no use us sitting here fighting each other. I've got part of it— you've got part of it. We're going to have to work together.' He [Sistrunk] said, 'Well, that suits me.'" Maverick though he was, Sistrunk was also a realist. He knew when it was time to be a team player.

"So I called Lyle," Harris said, "and told him I had an oil field for him." Lyle Cashion, a drilling contractor, had just moved in an enormous rig from South America and was looking for a place to drill. In 1928 Cashion was the first petroleum engineer to graduate from Rice University. He spent most of his career with Gulf before forming his own company. Harris could hardly believe his eyes when he saw the rig. "I went down to see that rig come in, and it came in on flatcars. Looked like the Barnum Bailey Circus. He had flat cars stretched for two miles."

Harris offered to let Cashion drill the hole if he would take a piece of the deal. Cashion presented the proposal to his Texas financial backers. He was rebuffed. They told him it was too risky and too small.

Cashion told Harris he couldn't do it, but Harris was a persistent guy. "I'll give you one more chance to take this deal; if you don't take it you're going to kick yourself for the rest of your life because this is an oil field!"

Harris' certainty that he had an oil field was more than presumptuous, especially in light of Humble's five dusters. His was a brazen—even arrogant—self-confidence that was and still is the compelling obsession of oil explorers. Though the same could be said of lunatics, fools, and gamblers, the oilman is a visionary. Or at least he regards himself so.

"Let me talk to them again," Cashion said. He was persistent too. He pressed his appeal again and his backers finally loosened their purse strings.

Meanwhile, Walt Sistrunk crossed paths with J. Willis Hughes, yet another Oklahoman, at the Walthall Hotel in Jackson. Hughes was sent to Mississippi in 1943 with Atlantic Refining Company and later became an independent. The two sounded each other out, and Sistrunk offered to sell Hughes part of his interest in the deal. Hughes shied away from going after Humble's risky culls. He turned Sistrunk down. After a while Sistrunk pitched his proposal to Hughes again and was shown the door a second time. The tenacious Sistrunk then made a third run at Hughes with a proposal to trade half his interest in the deal, which they named the Yellow Creek Prospect, for half of Hughes's interest in a salt dome prospect Hughes was preparing to drill. Like that of Harris and Cashion, Sistrunk's dogged persistence also paid off. Hughes finally relented and threw in with the group. At last the deal came together.

Cashion spudded with his circus rig, drilled ahead, and reached the Eutaw in December 1947. They took a wire line *core* and pulled it out. They all examined it. They smelled it. They tasted it. All of them, that is, except Willis Hughes. He couldn't bear to watch and stayed in his car. But Harris and his seasoned partners knew the sweet taste of crude. "It [the core] was as pretty as anything you've seen in your life," he said.

Harris went where Hughes sat in the car with his wife and children. "After I got through smelling and tasting and aahing about it, I went to Willis and I said, 'Don't you want to come see what you've got?' He said, 'I don't know whether I want to or not.'" Hughes finally got the nerve and went to have a look. He promptly rejoined his family and drove to Florida for a lavish vacation.

Tasting a core was a ritual Harris observed time and again throughout his career. His daughter, Judy Harris Green, remembered that he urged her to taste the oil when she was young. "He told me it was good luck to taste the core."

Officially completed on December 21, 1947, the Sistrunk and Hughes No. 1 GM&O Land Co. was the discovery well of the Yellow Creek Field. It flowed nearly 200 barrels of 19.5 degree gravity oil per day from a depth of 5,000 feet. The following year, Walt Sistrunk and most of the same partners drilled a well two miles to the east and discovered the east segment of the Yellow Creek structure. That well was completed as the East Yellow Creek Field. By 1956 a total of 123 producing wells had been drilled in the Yellow Creek complex of fields, and they ultimately produced 35 million barrels of oil.

Each of the artisans who helped pioneer the early Eutaw play in south Mississippi went on to make a significant impact on the Deep South's oil history. Merrill Harris helped open the Lower Cretaceous a few years later.

J. Willis Hughes put together scores of Wilcox deals. Lyle Cashion became a legendary driller in Mississippi. And Walt Sistrunk eventually became a key player in exploring the Black Warrior Basin of northwest Alabama. All four had vastly different personalities, backgrounds, and methods, but they all had a couple of vocabulary deficiencies in common. They didn't recognize the words *no* and *quit*. There were many others like them.

Yet crafty, persistent men like Merrill Harris, Walt Sistrunk, and Willis Hughes weren't the only ones with the kind of street savvy to go after a good hunch. Some company men were also excellent opportunists.

A Profitable Country Ride

A couple of years after the Yellow Creek find, word leaked out that a Jones County, Mississippi, wildcat operated by Red Wing Drilling Company tested gas on a block of leases they had farmed out from Humble. Union Producing Company's geologist, Wil Knight, needed to get out of the office for a while. He asked Union landman Robert Hearin to ride along with him.

Born in Demopolis, Alabama, and raised in Montgomery, Hearin graduated from the University of Alabama with a liberal arts degree, but he took a number of geology courses, which interested him in the oil business. Hence he often called himself as a "half-ass geologist." He found a job checking land records during the Tinsley fervor and eventually signed with Union Producing as a landman and *scout*.[2]

Knight and Hearin's joyride turned out to be a very profitable excursion for Union. They drove to the Red Wing rig and pulled over to look. They remembered a set of Tobin maps in the car's trunk. Tobin was a service company that made and sold mineral leasehold maps, not always accurate but excellent tools for giving an interested landman or geologist a general idea of who owned leases in a particular area. The two unfolded the map and jabbed their fingers at the area of the wildcat location. Soon something odd got their attention.

Within 330 feet of the well location lay a 680-acre tract that had expired only two days earlier. It was not unusual for companies to drill on tracts that were almost at their lease expiration date, but the Red Wing well was not on the 680-acre tract. It was on the one next to it. The two men raised their eyebrows and eyed one another. Surely, they thought, Red Wing must have renewed the lease on the offset tract. But maybe they didn't. After all, the Tobin map was not entirely up to date.

Up the road a piece sat a farmhouse on the 680-acre tract. Knight recalled stopping at the house. "I'll be dammed if Bob didn't go up there and talk to the guy. He asked, 'Haven't you signed a lease?' The man said, 'Been on a lease for ten years.'" Ten years sounded like a long time to Hearin. He asked to see a copy of the lease. Sure enough the lease had expired, only two days before, and nobody had renewed it. Knight was aghast. "Nobody had done a thing!" Hearin offered the man $50 an acre, and he signed immediately.[3]

Hearin and Knight rushed to Laurel to call their boss for authorization to spend the money while the farmer thought over the offer, but when they got back, they found another cherry picker at the man's door.

"We got back there and found that Fred Hodge had gotten to this guy and offered him $60 an acre," Knight said. "Bob and Fred got into a big hassle. Finally we wound up with a compromise. We gave Hodge a little piece of the pie, and we bought the lease."

Knight and Hearin's quick thinking netted Union two fine Eutaw wells in what was to become the Sharon Field.

Deeper Probes

The search for oil and gas in the deeper formations between 1945 and 1950 was sparse, only a few wildcats in search of Lower Cretaceous and Jurassic-aged targets. At the close of 1952 only one commercial success rewarded those deep efforts—the Chaparral field, which produced from the Lower Cretaceous in Wayne County.

Early successes in Mississippi spawned the growth of a number of independent companies, chiefly Roeser and Pendleton. Charlie Roeser, an Ohio boy from an oil lineage that dated to the industry's beginnings in Pennsylvania, came to a stranger's aid in a Wichita Falls, Texas, bar fight in 1922. Tolbert Pendleton was in trouble. He hailed from West Virginia and had been an All-American quarterback at Princeton and a WW I fighter pilot. Not surprisingly, those three aspects of his background qualified Pendleton as an expert bar brawler. The two of them emerged from the fray bloodied and tattered and retired to Roeser's room at the Crazy Horse Hotel where they proceeded to knock off a bottle of rye whiskey. Their resultant drunken brainstorming hatched a partnership that would last out their lives and burgeon into one of the biggest independent firms in the South.

Although active in Mississippi's Upper Cretaceous plays since the Tinsley discovery (mainly Brookhaven Field, where they drilled the confirmation well), Roeser and Pendleton decided to try their hand at the emerging Mississippi Wilcox play. They bought into the J. P. Evans Subdivision, where they became joint operators on the LaGrange Field discovery well. That success encouraged them to branch out into other plays in Mississippi.

They then took a farmout from Sun Oil Company on 2,400 acres in the expanding Brookhaven Field in Lincoln County. There they agreed to drill 24 wells to earn one half Sun's interest. They made a similar deal with Superior Oil Company in Baxterville Field on 10,000 acres. These and other successful deals proved to be extremely profitable for Roeser and Pendleton and established them as the largest independent oil company in Mississippi during the late 1940s. In 1949 Roeser died and Marshall R. Young took the company private, eventually changing the name to Marshall R. Young Oil Company. The company went on to add production in the West Lincoln, Ansley, Waveland, and Jay fields to their earlier successes at Brookhaven, LaGrange, and Baxterville.

Roeser and Pendleton, along with other wildcatters, enjoyed the spotlight in the mid forties. While they continued to ride a happy wave of successes, the owners in Cranfield Field were becoming alarmed. Located in Adams and Franklin counties, Cranfield was Mississippi's second largest oil field. The bottom hole pressures were falling quicker than anyone had predicted. Disaster was at hand.

The Experiment at Cranfield

The California Company discovered the field in 1943. By 1945 more than 33 wells were completed at 10,500 feet in the Lower Tuscaloosa "Massive Sand." Cranfield was a huge salt structure with a large *gas cap* underlain by a thick rim of oil.[4] The natural pressure in the gas cap kept the downdip oil flowing to the surface, but the gas was flared at the wellhead, there being little or no market for natural gas at that time. Thus the reservoir pressure started to deplete, and the owners faced the specter of placing their wells on pumps and leaving millions of barrels of oil unrecovered.

The solution was a new technology called *pressure maintenance*. The engineers reasoned that if they could inject the gas back into the gas cap itself they could maintain reservoir pressure and recover more oil. It had been done in Texas, but the idea faced a serious problem: the diverse mineral and lease ownership.

Under the plan certain wells still producing oil would have to be converted to gas injection wells. Other wells would benefit from the conversion by making more oil. Obviously, the owners under the injection wells were not willing to give up their income so their neighbors could make even more money. The only solution to the ownership problem was *unitization*.

With unitization the entire field could be declared a single production unit, as if it were one lone well. It wouldn't matter where or under what well an individual owner had his lease or minerals; he would share in the profits of the unit's production based on the ratio of his total acres to the total size of the unit. It was not a completely fair solution but it was the best anyone could offer. The unitization agreement, a cooperative effort between the state regulatory agency, the various field operators, and the mineral owners, included a daily allowable for the entire field rather than for individual wells.

Unitization made higher rates of fieldwide production possible by drilling more or fewer wells, as the case may be, within the unit with no spacing restrictions. Then the field could be water-flooded to increase ultimate oil recovery, and the better wells could produce more oil. All of those measures resulted in more income for the owners. Unitizing a field made it one giant producing property in which all owners shared proportionately.

The major problem, however, was that unitization would be entirely voluntary. At that time no state laws allowed *forced unitization* provided at least 75% of the owners consent, as is the case today. So in November 1947 the operators at Cranfield set out to educate the owners and win them over to the idea. It was a miracle of sorts that numerous oil operators and nearly 500 royalty owners agreed to the formation of the Cranfield unit.

The group built a $4.2 million plant to remove the marketable components—oil, condensate, and LPG (liquid petroleum gas)—from the gas before it was re-injected. The California Company, Gulf, and H.L. Hunt's Placid operated the plant jointly. The Cranfield unitization, Mississippi's first such effort, became a tremendous success, resulting in the recovery of almost 50 million barrels of oil and several hundred billion cubic feet of gas from 90 wells.

Cranfield had dodged a deadly bullet, but that bullet highlighted an increasing need to refocus Mississippi's oil and gas conservation efforts. Some perceptive people started to realize that the oil business in the state was becoming its own worst enemy. Reserves were being drained almost indiscriminately and wasted at an alarming rate. Something had to be done.

War in the Capitol

In 1930 as he vetoed the first conservation statute passed by the Mississippi legislature, Governor Theodore G. Bilbo declared, "What Mississippi needs is to give every man . . . the right to drill and sink wells upon every hill and in every valley of the state."[5] The governor's intent to preserve individual rights was noble but proved disastrous for the rights of many oil and gas property owners. Beginning in 1932, an Oil and Gas Board, consisting of the governor, lieutenant governor and state geologist regulated the state's oil industry, but their regulations lacked scope and enforcement powers.

World War II prompted the federal government to insist that all oil producing states promote conservation of oil resources. Washington allocated scarce pipe and material and denied them to states that did not comply. Of particular concern was the drilling of unnecessary wells.

Some states required 10-acre spacing and some none at all. Mississippi's Oil and Gas Board generally favored 40-acre oil spacing, but the regulations had no teeth and political favoritism allowed too many exceptions. Operators commonly spaced wells as they pleased. Another concern was high production rates, which could result in premature loss of reservoir pressure. Tinsley Field had suffered a great loss of pressure in that portion of the field developed on 10-acre spacing.

In 1944, Everette DeGolyer, a geologist famous for his pioneering work in Mexico's "Golden Lane" and President Roosevelt's wartime director of conservation, made a speech to the Mississippi legislature. He issued an inflammatory ultimatum from the federal government, demanding that the state pass a conservation law that included 40-acre oil spacing and requirements for efficient production rates.[6] A similar demand was made of all oil producing states in conjunction with the war effort. Alabama hurriedly passed legislation establishing conservation laws creating a strong Oil and Gas Board, even though there was little production at the time. Mississippi found itself surrounded by states with modern conservation laws.

DeGolyer's ultimatum from Washington did not sit well with some of Mississippi's politicians who were still sympathetic to the old Confederate Cause. They characterized the Washington group as "officeboys." A conservation bill was introduced but failed. Similarly, the 1946 legislature passed no bill. Meanwhile, the waste continued, and even the politicians began to notice it.

When the 1948 session began, the legislature turned about and gave priority to passing a conservation bill. Many of the reservoirs in Mississippi's oil fields had shown an alarming drop in pressure. Over-drilling and over-production left a staggering amount of oil in the ground, oil that could have been produced with controlled reservoir pressure and properly spaced wells.

Salvos of strong words thundered from both sides of the spacing issue during hearings. The landowners and small independent operators generally favored 10-acre oil spacing, while the major companies favored 40-acre oil spacing. The Vaughey brothers knew something had to be done and took the initiative. Emmett recalled his efforts to bring about the needed reform. "All the major companies, of course, wanted oil and gas regulations like the other states, but peculiarly enough, Bill and I were the only independents [who wanted them]. [The opposition] did not realize how wasteful it would be to the reservoir to produce [in the old] manner. The major companies asked us to take the lead in presenting it to the legislature because, as you know, the legislature sometimes opposes anything favored by big corporations and we, as independents, could [do a better job of presenting it]. The Mid-Continent Oil and Gas Association had recently been formed, and Doug Kenna had been hired as the director. Working with Doug and the majors, we argued our case before the legislature."[7]

It wasn't easy. In the minds of many Mississippi landowners and royalty holders, conservation was another way of saying "pro-ration"—a detestable word implying government regulation. They believed that any law for conserving oil and gas would impede rather than promote development. Emmett described the deep emotions his opponents held. "He [Ike LaRue] got up to testify . . . at the hearing at the King Edward Hotel . . . and said, 'Sure . . . they [the Vaughey brothers] are being paid off by the majors.' I waited till I got in the petroleum club before I called him a son of a bitch."

The legislators were torn between the strong arguments presented by both sides. The non–oil community sat back amazed and watched as the oil players turned upon themselves, but the Vaughey-led group won its case. Emmett elaborated further about the battle. "Bill did a lot more than I did at the time, but both of us drank a hell of a lot of whiskey with legislators down at the King Edward Hotel to get the thing passed, and we were rebuked by all our fellow independents. I can't think of an independent operator at that time that wasn't against us, because they wanted to take their oil out as fast as they could and get their money back."

House Bill Number 80 finally passed both houses of the legislature, and Governor Fielding Wright signed it into law in 1948. The bill was "to protect the public and private interest from the evils of waste [and] to permit each and every oil and gas pool in Mississippi to be produced up to its maximum efficient production."

Oil spacing was set at 40 acres and natural gas at 320-acre units. (Gas migrates through reservoirs farther and faster than oil.) Section 10 of the statute also provided for forced pooling (unitization): "for the prevention of waste or to avoid the drilling of unnecessary [wells] . . . require such persons to integrate their interest and to develop their lands in a drilling unit." Thus future unitization efforts would not depend solely on voluntary participation.

The 1948 law also established a new five-member Oil and Gas Board to regulate Mississippi's petroleum industry and supersede the old Board, created in 1932. The governor made three appointments to the Board, one from each of the state's three Supreme Court districts. The lieutenant governor made one appointment, as did the attorney general. To shield the Board from political interference, members served staggered, four-year terms.

The law also authorized hiring a Supervisor and a full-time professional staff to advise the appointed Board and provide administrative services. It stipulated that the Supervisor be a petroleum engineer or a geologist with five years experience in the oil business and without connections to any petroleum company or individual operator in Mississippi.

The conservation law also required that a record be filed with the Oil and Gas Board on all wells drilled in Mississippi within thirty days after completion. Additionally, it required monthly reports on each producing well. Those records were open to the public. Also, the monthly meetings of the Oil and Gas Board would be open to the public.

The results pleased the Vaughey brothers and the larger companies. Emmett heaped praise upon the state for this dramatic legislative move: "By the grace of God we did convince the legislature that we were right. . . . As it turned out we were the last state, at that time, to write the regulations for an Oil and Gas Board. We looked at the ones [similar governmental bodies] in Oklahoma, California, Texas, Louisiana, and Arkansas, all the [major] producing states, even Alabama. As a consequence we came up with practically the best of everything and have one of the best regulations and laws on oil and gas production in the country."

The vast amounts of oil and gas Emmett and Bill Vaughey discovered, or caused to be discovered, may actually be the least of their contributions to the oil industry. Their extraordinary courage and vision in developing good conservation laws was one of the Mississippi's petroleum industry's greatest historical advances.

That done, Mississippi oil people could get on with business. And, for those dealing in natural gas particularly, a major business opportunity was developing.

Shivering Yankees

Since the 1800s, the major cities along the East Coast, including New York, used coal-manufactured gas for cooking and fuel oil or coal for heating. Both these fuels were expensive and dirty. Most people in the metropoli along the Eastern Seaboard didn't realize that cheap, clean, abundant fuel awaited them below the Mason-Dixon Line. To make matters worse, the Southerners sitting on the bounty weren't sure what they should do with it. A vast amount of excess gas was behind pipe—some actually *shut-in* in Oklahoma, Kansas, Texas, Louisiana, and Mississippi. Markets for the gas in the southern states, where the population was relatively low and the winters mild, were limited. The energy needs of Southerners were minuscule compared to the potential that sat in the natural gas reservoirs they had found.

In 1946 a handful of people realized that a massive market lay in wait in the North, but there were no private pipelines to supply that enormous concentration of industry and population. The expense would have been staggering. N.C. McGowan, founder of United Gas Corporation, Shreveport, was one of those visionaries.

Early in his career, McGowan represented Chicago's Palmer financial interests and with their powerful backing combined a number of small companies to create United Gas in 1930. During the Depression, United took over many gas interests from companies in financial trouble, including Southern Natural's pipeline in south Mississippi. Thus, McGowan built and headed a major gas company by 1946, and he had a novel idea to keep the Yankees warm.

At the beginning of WW II, crude oil was transported by ship from the Gulf Coast to the northeastern refineries. But German submarines sent many of them to the bottom. The government figured there had to be a better way. There was.

Soon a pipeline that became known as the "Big Inch" was built to carry crude oil from Texas to the East Coast. Following the Big Inch's completion, the "Little Inch" was laid along the same right-of-way to carry refined products. They were the first long distance pipelines connecting the petroleum-rich states of the Gulf Coast with the northeast. But at war's end, the U.S. government–owned pipelines had no further purpose.[8]

McGowen figured on converting the Big Inch and Little Inch pipelines from their original purpose of carrying oil to carrying natural gas to the northeastern markets. He organized an effort to encourage the government to bow out of the pipeline business and transfer ownership of its lines to the private sector—especially his own sector.

Tennessee Gas Transmission Company, supported by a group of gas interests including McGowan's, negotiated a lease from the War Assets Administration (WAA) to convert the lines to natural gas. On December 5, 1946, Tennessee Gas engineers turned gas into the Little Inch, and four days later into the Big Inch, to test the conversion feasibility. After a short period of testing, the lease with the WAA expired and operations ceased.

The group liked the test results. They formed a new company, the Texas Eastern Transmission Company. On November 14, 1947, Texas Eastern bought both the Big Inch and the Little Inch from the government. United Gas benefited greatly from the new acquisition. It could deliver natural gas to the Texas Eastern pipelines through its own network of gathering systems. One of those was to be a 30-inch gathering line from Mississippi's newly discovered gas fields and fields in Louisiana, to deliver gas to Texas Eastern at a tie-in at Kosciusko, Mississippi.

The vast new market boosted the demand for natural gas and sparked renewed exploration. The future looked bright for natural gas and, as markets continued to expand, Transcontinental Gas Pipe Line Corporation was chartered October 4, 1948, with Federal Power Commission approval to build a 1,840 mile 30-inch pipeline from South Texas to New York. The 235 million dollar project was completed from Hidalgo County, Texas, to New York City on August 22, 1949. The local gas distribution companies in New York converted from manufactured gas to straight natural gas, delivered on a regular basis to New York City after December 28, 1950. The Transcontinental line went through Mississippi and opened another market for the state's new gas discoveries.

Although the rig count declined slightly as the 1940s drew to a close, optimism soared in the ranks of oilmen hunting in the Deep South and elsewhere. Many millionaires were created, and tens of thousands of families saw their standard of living rise to unexpected heights. The future looked bright and inviting. They were excited and busy with more schemes to harvest the earth's bounty. In their enthusiasm they never dreamed that the industry could do anything but rocket upward continuously.

Chapter 3

"Hell, this is real!"

No doubt they snickered and guffawed at the mention of Howard Nason's name over their coffee at the King Edward Hotel, the morning gathering place of the Jackson oil crowd. Who, they crowed, could believe a crazy old north Mississippi mule farmer anyway? Was he smarter than the oil companies? They shook their heads and chuckled, but their mockery of Nason would soon cease.

Years before the fun started, Carter Oil Company was one of the few companies that found the Black Warrior Basin in northern Mississippi tempting. The basin was largely ignored after its only significant find—the Amory Field—depleted and was abandoned in 1938.[1] With a cumulative production of only a billion cubic feet of gas (*Bcf*), total sales never returned enough revenue to pay for the Amory wells. Over the following years only a handful of wells were drilled in the basin, all promoted by small independents and all dusters, although many had decent *shows* of oil and gas.

Carter did some extensive seismic work across the area in the early 1940s and turned up some interesting geology. The data showed that the old Paleozoic-aged strata dipped gently to the southwest toward the axis of the basin until a set of huge regional faults stair-stepped them thousands of feet down. But up-dip of that fault system, where the target beds were shallower, numerous small *counter-basin* faults sliced through the strata. To envision the counter-basin fault, imagine walking down a flight of stairs and encountering an upward step along the way. Those faults, in which the basinward side was thrown up in relation to the up-dip side, were often good traps in other basins. The Carter people also saw subtle anticlines developed here and there, usually along the faults.

The company assembled several lease blocks in Monroe, Clay, and Chickasaw Counties, Mississippi. In July 1941, Carter spudded the No. 1 Sanders well in Monroe County near West Point. Carter halted drilling at the planned total depth and called Schlumberger in to run electric logs.

The Schlumberger Company (pronounced Schlumberjay) was an early pioneer of electric well evaluation. Typically the company backed its highly specialized trucks up to the drilling rig after the drill pipe had been pulled out and lowered a series of devices to the bottom of the well on a wire line. In the early days those tools measured only the resistance of the fluids in the rock to an electric current. Geologists were interested in that information.

A rock with low *resistivity* usually meant a reservoir was salt water saturated. Relatively high resistivity could signal the presence of gas or oil. As years went by, Schlumberger and its competitors developed wireline tools to measure other important rock properties such as porosity, relative permeability, angular inclination (dip), and radioactivity. The *logs* were printed in the logging truck on long folded paper with depth marks down the center. Geologists huddled in the truck, waiting for these logs to print out so they could lay them alongside their mud logs, pick out important rock layers, and determine their capacity to produce petroleum.

With the logs in hand, Carter's geologist saw two thick sands between 5,300 and 5,500 feet in the Sanders well, both exhibiting very high resistivity. He shrugged them off as granite wash, a type of sandstone composed of reworked granite fragments, commonly found on or near the bottom of a basin. (Those particular sands were actually thousands of feet above the basin's granite floor.) It's not clear why he and his company were prejudiced against granite wash; it produced some prolific oil fields in other parts of the country. In any event, the two sands ultimately proved not to be granite wash but rather a more common quartzose sandstone originating from an ancient depositional environment such as a barrier island or certain parts of a delta—ideal reservoir sands.

Carter abandoned the Sanders well in November 1941 and folded its tent to go and explore elsewhere. Later, Carter's geologist would be given an extended remote assignment to South America—as punishment, some observers thought, for misinterpreting the potential gas reservoirs.[2]

Soon after the Carter Oil Company left, local residents strolled out to the drillsite to bemoan and lament the boom that might have been. As they approached the drillsite they heard a hissing sound. They located the source and held a match to it. It burned.

Oil scouts learned of the little flare, and the Dixie Scout report of February 18, 1943, mentioned it, but the oil community paid little attention. Property owners on whose land a dry hole has been drilled often believe their well could have been a producer if it had not been plugged and abandoned. T.J. Sanders was no exception. With the abandoned well on his farm leaking gas, he had more reason than most to suspect the well could be productive. After seven years an increased demand for natural gas finally convinced Sanders and several other locals to join in reassembling the old expired Carter lease block. Two of those partners were Malcolm McCaskill, an old time driller, and Howard Nason, a mule farmer. The year was 1950.

The partners leased several thousand acres from their friends and neighbors and offered the block to Carter Oil Company again, insisting that the old well was leaking gas. The manager of Carter's Jackson office rebuffed them, telling them that he was not interested. He insisted there was nothing there and that Carter had plugged the well properly.

Disappointed but not deterred, the grass-roots group shopped the deal around to other companies and generated some interest, but the curious invariably called the Carter people to ask their opinion. Carter told them not to waste their money.

Soon the men realized that no oil company would take their judgment over Carter's. Carter's condemnation blackballed them and made it impossible to sell the deal to the established oil community. They wondered what to do.

At length, a landman buying right-of-way for a new gas pipeline from north Mississippi to Virginia told Charles McCamic, a practicing attorney in West Virginia, about the deal. McCamic got interested and contacted the group, agreeing to put up the $19,000 needed to clean out and test the old well.

They hired a crew and moved a small workover rig in, beginning operations in October 1951 with McCaskill overseeing the work. For 18 days they cleaned and reamed. On November 6, Nason and his associates dove for cover as the zone to become known as the Sanders Sand introduced itself to northeast Mississippi.

Geologist Fred Mellen—an early believer in the potential of the Black Warrior Basin—stayed close to the operation. "They drilled the first plug at the bottom of the surface casing at about 1,000 feet. Then the well kicked on them. It scared them but they went on down."[3]

Kick is driller's slang for the sudden ejection of drilling fluid from the hole when a gas bubble surfaces. It may jolt the rig and scare the crew and in extreme cases may warn of an impending blowout. Nason and his crew should have heeded the warning. Mellen said, "They drilled a plug at 2,950 feet and all hell broke loose. It just blew out wild."

The well flowed furiously and out of control for days. Oil scouts quickly learned of the blowout and reported it to their companies. Wil Knight remembers the call he got from his scout, Claude Smith. "He called and said, 'They've got a blowout!' I said, 'Oh, my God,' and he told me that the highway patrol had come in and blocked the roads. I mean it was just a panic situation."[4]

Knight called his landman, Bob Hearin, and proposed another leisurely drive into the oil patch like the one that netted two nice wells in the Sharon Field for Union Producing Company. Upon reaching the site they got out of the car and heard the well before they saw it. The wild roaring shook the ground like a powerful rocket engine. Hearin thought to himself, "Hell, this is real!" After seeing the furious blow, they knew they had to move quickly.

"We contacted Howard Nason," Knight remembered, "and he was in a panic because he didn't have any money, and his two backers, the drilling manager and the attorney . . . weren't that rich. Bob [Hearin] was a good dealer. He made the deal. . . . He said, 'If you give us half of [all the leases] you own and let us keep all the revenue until we get our money back for killing this well, we'll take over, kill the well, and see what we've got here.'"

The thunderstruck Nason quickly agreed. It was a sweetheart of a deal for Union. Knight and Hearin then called Walt Spears, the vice-president in charge of exploration, to get approval for the deal. According to Knight, Spears said, "Oh my God, you guys are crazy!" But he approved it.

Union hurriedly moved in a large rig and killed the flow with heavy mud 40 days after it blew out. During the next 54 days they fished out the drill pipe, which had fallen into the hole. After cleaning out to a depth of over 5,000 feet, they set production casing. They open-hole tested the well at a calculated rate of 3,500 MCF per day. Thus the No. 1 Sanders became the discovery well of the Muldon Field. Completion date was official on March 3, 1952.

Union developed the field, completing eight gas wells and four dry holes by early 1954, using the newly developed *frac* treatment on some wells. In that procedure, ultra-fine loose sand grains in a solution of acidic water are pumped down the pipe and out into the natural fractures of the rock under immense pressure from hydraulic pumps on the surface. That, in effect, props open the natural avenues of gas flow through the rock. Sand-fraccing ultimately proved to be one of the important innovations that made the Black Warrior Basin's tight sands commercial producers.

Union's success kicked off a frantic lease play and a robust round of new exploration in the Black Warrior Basin. Newcomers to the Black Warrior soon found that the principal drawback to drilling the hard Paleozoic rocks was the high cost of wells. Drilling a 6,000-foot well took from 75 to 90 days, compared to 10 to 15 days in the Wilcox trend of southeast Mississippi. This made the wells very costly and required large reserves or high-priced gas to be profitable.

Muldon Field was definitely profitable. Eventually it produced 65 billion cubic feet of gas before being converted into a gas storage reservoir in the 1970s. The reserves were estimated at 90 Bcf, far overshadowing the 1 Bcf the Amory Field produced. Muldon proved that the Black Warrior Basin held great potential for significant gas reserves.

But Union's rival, Shell Oil Company, had been eyeing the basin long before Knight and Hearin made their profitable drive to north Mississippi. Union's success at Muldon convinced Shell to make a serious play. They moved seismic crews into Monroe County and liked what the reflections showed them. By the end of 1952, Shell was drilling the No. 1 Mrs. Lee Harrington well, which eventually tested good gas flows in the Sanders and was completed as the Aberdeen Field discovery well in early 1953. By the mid-1990s the field had produced over 16 Bcf.

Howard Nason stayed active in the oil business. Born in 1901, he was involved in a variety of business ventures besides raising mules and farming. Some may not have been entirely legitimate. He claimed he once swam the Mississippi River to get away from "revenuers."

After the Muldon Field paid out and began to produce serious profit, Nason became involved in buying and trading minerals and leases. He also drilled a few wells, always on the Mississippi side of the Black Warrior Basin. Apparently Nason ran through his first fortune, only to replenish it several times over during the gas boom of the 1970s. Over the years he kept chasing another Muldon, though it was never to be—at least for him.

Even in his advanced years he continued to visit to the offices of Jackson geologists who worked the Black Warrior basin. Mostly he peddled stray leases or wild ideas during those visits. The young geologists, respectfully aware of his pioneer status, politely watched as his aged, bony fingers traced imagined trends across smudged maps devoid of contours. They dared not snicker as they listened to tongue-tied prattle that sounded as if it were coming through a mouth full of cotton. The years dulled his tongue but not his mind. When Howard Nason died in 1995 at age 94, he was a legend in the gas fields of north Mississippi.

Slow Drilling

The early fifties saw activity in the Black Warrior Basin, mostly on the Mississippi side. After Aberdeen Field was found, Chester Oil Company opened a small field at Trebloc in Chickasaw County that made three million cubic feet per day plus a little oil. The Vaughey brothers got into the act and found Coleville Field, also in Chickasaw. Neither fields approached the significance of Muldon.

Crow Well Company found a minor field in Itawamba County in 1953. Producing from several wells completed in a very shallow Mississippian Sand, the Beans Ferry Field was short-lived. But for 35 years it was the northernmost gas production in Mississippi.

Carter Oil Company licked its wounds in 1953 and got back into the Warrior, drilling the deepest well to date, the No. 1 Mattie McFadden eight miles southwest of the Muldon Field in Clay County. In that short distance the Mississippian target sands dropped some 3,000 feet due to enormous faulting. Still, they completed a small gas well, the Siloam Field. Later Shell Oil Company and others became active at Siloam and completed 16 producing wells from two Pennsylvanian-aged sands and two Mississippian sands, the deepest over 8,000 feet. The field eventually produced over 21 Bcf and 64,000 barrels of oil, though it did not generate much interest among other companies in the deeper part of the Black Warrior Basin until the late 1990s.

Glimmers of Hope in North Alabama

Oil and gas explorers in the fifties seemed uninterested in the Alabama half of the Black Warrior Basin. In the early 1900s small shallow gas reservoirs were found and produced near Huntsville, Fayette, and Jasper,[5] but they were short-lived and notable only in that they offered hope of future significant discoveries. Nonetheless a few small operators chased that hope.

In 1950 near Hamilton in Marion County, Harry Cullet blundered into a gas sand at 1,800 feet. He gauged a small gas flow from a relatively tight Mississippian-aged sandstone that he dubbed the "Bethel Sand," known later as the "Lewis Sand." Dr. Walter B. Jones, the Alabama State Geologist then, described Cullet's strike in the September 1954 issue of *The Petroleum Engineer*: "It is reported that plans have been completed for a pipeline to supply gas to Hamilton and other nearby towns." The pragmatic Jones, a civil servant with a profound vision for the mineral resources of his state, recognized that a discovery is not a success until it comes to the market. "When that has been accomplished," he continued, "the Hamilton Field will become a reality." Dr. Jones wrote further that "the oil-frac might be used to step up the capacity [of Cullet's well] considerably. So far, that method has not been used anywhere in the state."[6] Jones hoped, and knew intuitively, that the hydraulic fracturing methods introduced in Mississippi's Muldon Field would be the key to success for north Alabama's natural gas potential. He was profoundly correct. Cullet drilled two more producers and finally got a pipeline in 1955, but the field produced a paltry 168 million cubic feet until its abandonment in 1964.

The basin's first Ordovician-aged production was established 1953. In the New Hope Field in Monroe County, Mississippi, Magnolia Petroleum Company's No. A-1 Snow flowed 190 BOPD through perforations at 4,700 feet. Production did not hold up, but the recovery of free oil in the Black Warrior Basin raised eyebrows. Twenty years passed, however, before anyone one found a significant, lasting oil field in the basin.

Thanks to the Muldon and Aberdeen Fields, all but a skeptical few began to regard the Black Warrior Basin as a viable exploration target. It never rivaled the Salt Basin, and after the euphoria of 1951-53, it lay dormant until the late 70s. But Bob Hearin was prophetic—the Warrior Basin was indeed real.

Oil Parade

The thrill of the new Wilcox and Lower Tuscaloosa discoveries, and the new developments in north Mississippi created a fervor in Jackson. Mississippi was now a petroleum province on three fronts. Oil people could hardly contain their excitement. Times were good. That called for a grand celebration, and what better way to celebrate than a parade? In 1951 they had one, the state's first oil parade ever. It was also the last one.[7]

Irline Coen, a young girl from Hazelhurst, hired on as a secretary at Vaughey & Vaughey in 1942 and quickly became chief of the company's land records, as well as president of the Jackson Desk and Derrick Club. The Association of

Desk and Derrick clubs was organized in 1949 in New Orleans to promote the education and professional development of people employed in or affiliated with the petroleum, energy, and allied industries.

The 1951 oil parade was the largest parade Jackson had ever seen with the exception of Governor Hugh White's inaugural parade. It started with geological and land floats, followed by drilling, production, pipeline, and refinery floats, and ending with the distribution floats. The Desk and Derrick Club also had a float with Irline sitting in the front seat. Irline Han stayed active with Vaughey & Vaughey for 45 years and remains a consultant for the firm. But her boss, Emmett Vaughey, was too busy for the parade. His country needed him and he had answered the call.

A Buck a Year

The decade of the fifties started out looking not so fabulous to Emmett Vaughey. World peace must have been too boring, he guessed. Folks started shooting and bombing each other again. An oilman could hardly imagine that war could be more exciting than hunting petroleum.

On June 25, 1950, the Korean War started, and five days later Congress extended the draft and passed the Military Assistance Program for South Korea. National Guard units from several states were called to active duty, including the 31st Division from Mississippi, and many men left the oil field for the battlefield. A national rearmament program was soon underway.

As the shadow of war clouded the country Uncle Sam became jittery about fuel supplies. The U.S. was still producing over 50% of the world's oil, but a shortage of petroleum materials began to develop, including pipe and other equipment necessary for drilling and production.

America began looking for an energy czar, like it had in WW II. The search scanned all the big oil producing states before settling on Jackson, Mississippi. Emmett Vaughey got the call. He turned his thriving independent business over to his brother Bill and headed for Washington.

Vaughey's new job was Director of the Petroleum Administration for Defense (PAD). He immediately selected a few top oil people from both major companies and independents to staff the agency. All gave up their positions within the industry for the duration of the war and volunteered their expertise to the government for the princely sum of a dollar a year. This was the last time the government officially called on the petroleum industry for leadership and expertise to see it through an energy emergency, preferring instead to rely on industry outsiders. The fear of conflict of interest trumped the need for workable energy solutions.

Emmett's group set to work allocating the limited stores of pipe and equipment to carefully selected projects that would produce petroleum more efficiently. Emmett later recalled that no one in the volunteer group ever tried to influence decisions that favored their own companies or interests. He told Charlie Williams, Vaughey & Vaughey Corporation's general manager today, that the PAD allocated all steel goods "down to the last screw" to oil operations in the USA at a time when over 56,000 wells were drilled every year. He said that when a request came in, they made a decision and answered that day. Later Emmett told Williams that he doubted that a government agency could ever act with the speed and decisiveness that members of the private sector used to accomplish a critical function in their field of expertise.

The PAD was dissolved on April 30, 1954. Thanks to Vaughey and his staff, no shortage of petroleum developed at home or on the Korean battlefront. Emmett Vaughey returned to the Deep South to find the oil patch flourishing. During his absence, five southwest Mississippi Wilcox fields were discovered in 1950, several of them significant. Humble's Sibley Field produced over six million barrels. Another was Kingston Field, found by Plains Production Company, a subsidiary of Sinclair, which also yielded over six million barrels.

One of the best Wilcox fields ever discovered, Church Hill Field in Jefferson County, Mississippi, was found in 1950 by Robert Oil Company and further developed by a gentleman on his way to establishing one of the Deep South's most revered oil legacies—Lyle Cashion Sr.

"We've got a serious problem."

Lyle Cashion's small drilling company, which got its big break at West Yellow Creek in 1947 with Merrill Harris, Walt Sistrunk, and J. Willis Hughes, was becoming a leading operator in the Wilcox play. Like several other successful companies, Cashion both took an interest in deals and drilled contractually. The company had drilled a dry hole on a thousand-acre lease that the young geologist Verne Culbertson was evaluating. The landowners were asking Cashion to release their acreage.

Cashion told Culbertson, "If we've got a prayer of a chance, we don't want to lose that lease. Tell me what we should do with it." Culbertson remembered his thought, "Oh no! To be hit with this. First crack out of the bag!"[8]

Verne Culbertson had just arrived in Jackson. He grew up in Iowa, far from oil country, and entered the Navy during WW II without much thought about the future. His commanding officer asked the lanky young man what he was going to do after the war. Culbertson shrugged and said, "I probably won't live to finish the war."

The senior officer said, "Yes you will, and you'd better think about it."

Culbertson developed a curiosity about landforms and geology he saw from aboard ship in the Pacific. He found some geology books in the ship's library and became fascinated with them. They helped him make up his mind about what he was going to do when he got back home.

"Of course," Culbertson recalled, "I wasn't thinking about petroleum because Iowa State is in 'hard rock' country, but a very lucky thing happened. In my junior year the head of the department retired, and Dr. Roy Chalmers came up from Louisiana State University to Iowa State to become the new head of the department. It turned my life around when he exposed us to petroleum geology."

After graduation, Shell Oil Company hired him and put him to work in Houston, but in the late forties Verne left Shell to work for an independent. That didn't work out too well. "He [the independent] was a con artist," Culbertson said. "He couldn't tell the truth. I told him one day after eight or ten months, 'I can't stay. You're going to destroy my credibility, and then I'm finished in this business. You can lie to these investors all you want to, but you're not going to drag me into it.' So, I quit."

Culbertson's concern for ethics resulted in a lonely job search, but then the best thing in his career literally bumped into him on the street. "I was searching for a job in Houston, and I bumped into Mr. Lyle Cashion Sr. He came out the door of a music store. We literally ran in to each other! I had been on one well, a Shell well that his company had drilled, and he remembered me. He found out I was over there looking for a job, and before the evening [was over] I had a job with Cashion back here [in Mississippi]. And I stayed with them about five years before I decided to go on my own. That five years with a drilling company is what really helped me in this business. And I learned so damned much."

One of the first things Culbertson learned was that his new boss had confidence in him and was willing to take a risk on his recommendation. Cashion's latest dry hole had been on a 1,100-acre lease in Jefferson County, but Culbertson had seen a 20-foot difference in the oil/water contacts of two wells on either side of the lease. At first that made him think the two small fields were not connected. The big lease was apparently in the risky ground between them. Culbertson worked for several weeks on the area, going over all the details he could gather, and developed a different idea. He thought he had found a rare tilted oil/water contact, and if that was correct then the area between the two wells should be productive. He looked across the map at Cashion and said, "Lyle, I'll lay my head on the chopping block betting that this thing will produce!"

Cashion told him that the company's finances were not in good shape. They had just suffered losses with three costly fishing jobs. He told the rookie geologist they couldn't afford a dry hole. Then he said, "Let's do it!"

The first well found oil, as did five more. Culberton's risky hunch was right on target. The entire area was a single reservoir. The lease netted Lyle Cashion almost 600 barrels a day. Culbertson regarded the success as one of the most incredible things that happened in his career. Financially, it turned Cashion Drilling Company around. The Church Hill Field eventually approached eight million barrels of oil and established Lyle Cashion as one of the leading independent operators of the Wilcox. The following year, 1951, drilling in the Wilcox trend accelerated, but small independents conducted much of the wildcat activity in the trend.

In 1952 activity in the Wilcox trend increased steadily with 16 new oil discoveries. Of them, six exceeded a million barrels. The largest was the Sunnyside Field in Jefferson County, part of a deal turned to Union Producing Company by J. Willis Hughes. The discovery well resulted from a location Union's Wil Knight picked. Sunnyside eventually produced over four million barrels, mostly from the Artman Sand.

Oil fever abounded in southwest Mississippi. Almost anyone could put together a Wilcox deal, but only those who applied sound geological techniques had a reasonable chance of success. Yet one emerging Wilcox player would get his start in an amazingly creative way.

Chapter 4

"You had to protect against success"

The year 1952 saw the emergence of one of Mississippi's most successful homegrown oil companies, led by another of the many enterprising and opportunistic men of the day. But this upstart didn't hail from Texas or Oklahoma, as did many who came to hunt oil in Mississippi. He was a local boy, and the thing he did best was simply communicate with people. That was enough.

John Callon's first jobs as a Natchez lad were bumbling attempts at retail sales. The Benoit Clothing Store, a Natchez landmark business, hired him to sell clothes and keep books. That was a decent start for a better job when Sears Roebuck opened in town. Then WW II broke out and he enlisted in the Navy and went to sea. There he found his first opportunity to develop a quality he had long known he possessed—good people skills.

Callon found himself well adapted for administrative duties, but as he recalls, his greatest satisfaction came from working with the people. "I was a chief yeoman in the Navy. It was really a delightful job. As chief yeoman I acted as private secretary to the commanding officer, kept all of the personnel records, and all of the books."[1]

As the skipper's confidant and advisor, he began to hone his communication skills and developed a talent for recognizing and attending to people's needs, though he didn't yet realize that his talent for human relations was the key to his future.

After the Navy he returned to Natchez and again looked to sales for a living. Again he flopped. It left him wondering where he missed the boat. "I had an uncle here in Natchez selling life insurance and he suggested that I take the test for insurance. I took the test but did not do very well. I was told to stay away from selling, that I was not the type for selling, and should get another vocation."

Undaunted, he tried again. "I saw an ad in the paper about a job with Heinz in New Orleans. I went down there and took another psycho test with all those foolish questions and answers—sort of like the one taken for insurance. They told me they were sorry, but I didn't have any selling ability."

Returning to town after the war, he noticed "all these things sticking up behind the trees" that he couldn't identify, having never seen a derrick or an oil well in his life. Natchez had become an oil boomtown during his absence. He wanted to learn more. Soon he befriended a couple of geologists named Gulmon and Jones with whom he shared his interest in becoming involved in the oil business—to what extent he didn't have a clue, but he felt compelled to stake his claim in the exciting new industry. He remembered when his break came. "A man named L. M. Lockhart from Los Angeles came to town. He had a 'black box' man with him and wanted to run a black box survey all around the country, particularly in Franklin County. They became very excited about what they saw. He wanted to start buying leases but there was no lease man [available] in Natchez."

Through the years of petroleum history many people have invented devices they claimed could sense oil below the surface. Some of them had impressive credentials, while others were obvious kooks. Many of the devices were simply sniffers that detected gas molecules seeping up to the surface, a legitimate concept, assuming the machine wasn't sniffing oil that leaked out of someone's pickup. Otherwise the problem was that any gas that escaped to the surface would probably not come straight up. Other devices were mere science fiction. None ever proved decisively that they worked, but they did raise money. Oil professionals simply called them "black boxes."

"Gulmon called me," Callon said, "and said they needed somebody to start buying leases. I told them I didn't know anything about leases. He then ripped off a [standard mineral rights lease form] and told me to take it home and read it and that after reading it I would know as much as anybody else about leasing. So I became a landman on the spot.

"Mr. Lockhart told me he wanted those leases and didn't want me to come back and say that I couldn't get them, just buy them. I figured you might have to pay as much as $10 for them. He said go to $50 if you have to. So I did and I used the old deal of $1 per acre and 10% of what you pay for the lease as my commission. That is a horrible way to send a landman out. It is a definite conflict of interest, because the more [he pays], the more you make."

Callon learned the landman's trade quickly and soon saw an opportunity for a bold move. He had a lifelong friend, Gene Parker, heir to 10,000 acres in southwest Adams County. "I asked him [Parker] one day about leasing the land. Then I went to Lockhart and told him I was going to try and get the whole 10,000-acre block. My deal was two bits an acre commission. I thought the world had come to an end. That was the biggest commission you could think of on 10,000 acres of land. I didn't have to do a thing, just ask them to lease. They said okay."

Following Callon's assignment with Lockhart he put his navy record keeping and administrative skills to good use. He fell to the tedious task of making leasehold maps in selected areas of the Wilcox Play. As his pool of information grew he developed an ingenious idea to get wells drilled at little cost to him. For a young man still relatively new to the business the move was staggeringly bold.

"I started going to the courthouses with my pad and pencil and recording leases by hand. I would do this during the day and write down every lease, then take the list home at night and transfer to my maps. If it was Gulf Oil Company leases, I would color them orange; if it was Texaco, I colored the leases Texaco's color; Magnolia Petroleum, I colored them their color; Stanolind Oil & Gas, etc. Each company and their leases were color-coded."

Armed with that information, Callon looked for points where the corners of lease blocks of three or four companies came together. He then approached each of the companies and proposed a 40-acre unit that included some portion of each company's leases. He asked each company to contribute $1 per foot of drilling depth as dry hole money.

Callon's plan offered a cheap way for the companies to gather important geological information about their leases and was also a moneymaker for him. "You take that money and drill a 6,500-foot Wilcox test and get $1 per foot from three people, you're talking about $20,000 or so in dry hole money. Then you would take that $20,000 to a drilling contractor and tell him you would give him $15,000 and half interest in the well if it produces. Most times he would agree.

But, you had no contract. Everything was done back then with no contracts—just verbal. Those were great days, because you dealt with people all the time with no written agreement [just a handshake]. It is a little more difficult to do anything like that today."

The first 42 holes were dry. Eventually the law of averages prevailed, and Callon's worst nightmare came true. His dry hole luck ran out. Years later he recounted it with a laugh. "Then all hell broke loose. The 43rd and 44th wells both hit oil on the same day. We had no dry hole money! We had to pay our completion costs. The drilling contractor was happy because he had half interest in an oil well. So to protect against that, I had to start to selling out of the half that I had left. That way I would have some money to pay completion costs. So you, in a sense, had to protect against success." John Callon's failures resulted in the discovery of the Jeanette and Locus Ridge fields in 1952, but now he was forced into more conventional oil operator roles.

Soon he joined his brother, Sim Callon, who was working a few deals west of the river, and formed Callon Oil & Gas Company, later to become Callon Petroleum Co. John, Sim, and Jessie worked together raising money and putting together a team of geologists and many associates. Eventually they drilled or participated in over 1,000 wells expanded into other areas of North America and the offshore Gulf of Mexico. Callon took the company public, listed it on the New York Stock Exchange, and opened offices in Houston, but Natchez remained company headquarters.

The local boy from Natchez, with a flare for working with people, a willingness to learn, and an eye for opportunity, became one of the Wilcox's major players and one of Mississippi's leading industrialists.

Maps Don't Make Money;
Leases Make Money

By 1953 the major companies were beginning to scale down their Wilcox activity in favor of deeper prizes elsewhere, paving the way for more good discoveries by adventurous independents. Lyle Cashion took a deal from geologist Bob Alligood based on a farmout of leases in Jefferson County, Mississippi, owned by Gulf, Union, Cities Service, and Sohio. The farmout complemented a lease Cashion and others had bought previously. The well discovered the Idlewilde Field. Cashion went on to drill 13 successive wells without a single dry hole. Verne Culbertson was astonished by the company's good fortune. "Looking back, I still say it's impossible. You couldn't do that! There's no way in the world! It was a miracle! It was so easy—like falling off a log."[2]

That success, coupled with Churchill Field, propelled Cashion's company ahead. He bought airplanes and built a new company building on the outskirts of Jackson, which caused Culbertson to worry. He told Cashion, "We need to be downtown where the action is and see people, where drilling deals will walk in the door." But Lyle elected to stay away from downtown. Culbertson was upset. "After we moved out there the whole atmosphere of the company turned around. Nobody came out to see us. Everybody would come into town with a deal. And if you weren't there, you'd be bypassed. [Thus] we didn't look at drilling deals. I got a little bit disillusioned. We were generating a few things of our own but after having been active drilling wells all the time I got frustrated and finally I talked to Lyle about it. I said, 'I don't think this is what's going to get the job done for you.'"

As the 1950s wore on, Lyle Cashion Jr. assumed a major role in managing the company. Like his dad, "Bubba" Cashion graduated Rice University in petroleum engineering. According to Culbertson, Bubba's mode was different from his dad's.

"He did not like those drilling rigs. The old man loved them. He loved everything about a drilling rig. Lyle Jr. didn't mind the engineering—he loved the engineering part of it. He just didn't like the problems of a drilling rig, which were tremendous. His idea was to get rid of the drilling rigs—which he did—and invest in deals." But two things went wrong.

"First of all he was buying in at retail, and the other thing was that nobody was coming to show him the deals. By the time he learned about a deal the good ones were already sold. So it didn't work well, and they sat out there [on Woodrow Wilson Boulevard] for a long time, literally with nothing to do."

Verne Culbertson enjoyed a good working relationship with both the Cashions, but he especially remembered the elder Cashion's wisdom. He was working on a prospect to show to Lyle Jr. when Lyle Sr. walked in and said, "What have you got there, Verne?"

"Well," Culbertson said, "I've got a little area that looks pretty good." Cashion Sr. asked how many leases he had on it.

"Mr. Cashion, we don't have any yet. I haven't even talked to Bubba."

Cashion said, "Son, let me tell you something, and don't you ever forget it. Standard of New Jersey doesn't pay off on a geological map. They pay off on an oil and gas lease."

Culbertson never forgot that lesson. "That's why he's an oil finder." Culbertson thought Lyle Cashion was an amazing man. "He had that intuitive sense of where to go to find oil." Lyle Cashion Sr., one of the Deep South's most respected oil finders, died in 1969.

While the opening years of the 50s saw a high level of exploration and development in Mississippi, Alabama remained quiet with the exception of a few widely scattered finds in the state's southwest corner and southern border counties. The first of those was in northern Baldwin County. There in early 1950, Humble Oil targeted a domal structure they initially detected by a gravity survey in one of the most remote areas of Alabama, a swampy lowland along the flood-prone Alabama River.

There Humble struck oil in the Massive and Pilot sands of the Lower Tuscaloosa in the 5,200–5,500 depth range, but their hopes of a great discovery sank when they swabbed a thick, viscous, tarry crude to the surface. The stuff was so thick it sank in water if it was allowed to cool to ambient temperature. Nevertheless, Humble developed the discovery, which they named the South Carlton Field.

Because it was so hard to get in and out of the locations, Humble erected barracks and chow halls for its crews, who stayed for days at a time. As development progressed, South Carlton became a logistical nightmare. The thick oil had to be stored in heated tanks to keep the viscosity low enough for pumping to the barges. The company had to haul in huge volumes of diesel fuel to heat the tanks. With the syrupy oil, the field also produced great quantities of water, which had to be disposed of properly, further escalating costs and reducing the field's commercial value.

South Carlton's convenient location next to the Alabama River may have been its salvation, as Humble could move the oil out by barge, normally relatively cheap—but not so for Humble. It was expensive, because the barges themselves had to be heated to keep the oil in a liquid state. Yet the field grew to include over 64 wells and produced over 14 million barrels. Humble eventually gave up on the messy field, but South Carlton was cleaned up and reworked by Belden and Blake Corporation in the 1970s.

A Game of Blue Chips

Undeterred by South Carlton's ponderously thick oil, Humble and others were encouraged to step up the hunt for Lower Tuscaloosa oil across south Alabama, igniting a lease play that quickly spread eastward. A geologist named Dale Myers had believed in that area's Lower Tuscaloosa potential years before South Carlton. Beginning in 1948 he sifted through the dry hole data, test core information, and gravity and magnetometer surveys. The data strongly suggested the presence of an east-west trending fault, down-thrown to the north. Myers convinced his company, Stanolind Oil and Gas Company, of Oklahoma City, to shoot a seismic reconnaissance program across the prospect. Satisfied there was a structural swell against the fault, Stanolind bought 1,500 acres on a prospect ten miles southwest of Brewton, Alabama. Myers picked a location near the old Wolf Log Bridge across the Little Escambia River, and in August 1951 Stanolind began operations on the No. 1 F.A. Stewart.

The sight of the tall steel derrick going up above the pines excited people. Newspapermen and townspeople alike flocked to it. The *Brewton Standard* kept a daily score card for its readers on Stanolind's well, explained oil field terms to them, and described the costs and processes of drilling and evaluation. The paper quoted one of the oilmen as saying, "You can see that this is a game where they play with nothing but blue chips." Then it pointed out the irony of the amazingly low after-tax cost of refined products. A quart of motor oil cost forty cents then, "of which a fair percentage is taxes," it said.[3]

The August 30, 1951, issue of the paper heralded the news Brewtonians had waited for: "Promising Show of Oil is Discovered." Myers knew he had penetrated his hoped-for fault ideally above the Eutaw, but his only good show occurred in the Lower Tuscaloosa. He halted drilling at almost 6,000 feet and sent for a coring crew. The core recovered 40 feet of porous sand in the Lower Tuscaloosa, the top ten feet of which appeared to be oil bearing. The soft-spoken, reserved Myers was forced to reveal the core's results, telling the newspaper reporter, "This is more encouraging and we have more hopes than we had yesterday. After we run tests for pressure and get other information, we will know if it is a producer." He then ordered a DST—a *drill stem test*.

In a DST, a *packer* attached to the bottom of the drill string is set against the walls of the open hole to seal off drilling fluids. A valve is then opened, allowing fluids or gas under natural pressure to reach the surface through the drill pipe. The procedure is expensive, hazardous, and often inconclusive, but positive results on a DST are among the most thrilling of all oil field events.

As the DST progressed, the citizens pressing against the fences around the location saw it and smelled it—oil! But along with the oil came much salt water. The paper reported that Myers' hopes fell, though he remained optimistic. "Well, this won't be the last well drilled around here. There will be others, whether we [Stanolind] drill them or not." Even as he made that statement others were moving into action. Humble, who contributed a small amount of dry hole money to Stanolind, prepared to drill nearby.

"Oil all over everywhere!"

Soon after Stanolind plugged their well, Humble sprang into action and began drilling core holes to define more accurately the location and orientation of the fault Myers found. They concluded that Stanolind's exploratory well, although ideally located for a Eutaw test, was too low at the Lower Tuscaloosa horizon. Humble's location was one mile east of Stanolind on A.W. Moye's farm. On January 3, 1952, they cored a Lower Tuscaloosa sand, now known as the Moye Sand, at a depth of 6,000 feet. They found good shows in the core and commenced a DST. Within 24 minutes oil reached the surface. It spewed 100 feet into the air and onto the drill floor as pipe was pulled from the hole, providing a marvelous show for the crowd of onlookers.

A.W. Moye was in Atmore on business when his wife called saying, "This thing is spewing oil all over everywhere!" He knew that the oil company drilling on his farm in the Friendship community, six miles southwest of Brewton, had found some good shows in their cores, but he couldn't put off his errands. He had to go to town. "I got in the truck and drove back at 40 miles an hour," he said. "I told my daddy-in-law that I sure didn't want to have a wreck. I sure wanted to live to see it."[4]

Despite the Alabama Highway Patrol's attempt to control the crowds, Moye found his fences knocked down and his cotton trampled by hundreds of gawkers and curiosity-seekers, many his neighbors. But he didn't care. The black slimy stuff that shot up over the derrick and wafted in the wind across his field ruined the cotton anyway. He grinned up at it.

Moye was a member of the county school board and began to envision a small severance tax on oil that would go directly to the schools. "I'll never forget that day," he said in the *Ledger*.

Humble's engineers ordered production casing and tested the well at 315 barrels per day. Even more exciting to Humble was the fact that the oil was a relatively light 33 degree gravity, not the syrupy stuff they found at South Carlton and feared would prevail across the region.

In the following week, local hotels were forced to turn away the oilmen pouring in. Excitement swelled. Speculation abounded. A *Tri-City Ledger* columnist had fun with the new language of oil spreading along the streets. "Well, just what is an oil play?" he wrote. "I never saw one when Miller High took on Neal. Or maybe that's what beat Alabama!"[5] But the people of

Escambia County didn't need a definition of oil play. They understood it intuitively as they watched lease bonuses leap 100% and saw eager speculators from the oily regions further west courting mineral rights and royalties.

The Alabama Oil and Gas Board named the exciting new strike Pollard Field. It eventually grew to 38 wells and added more pools in the Pilot and Massive sands. The field eventually produced over 13 million barrels—not a lot by Mississippi or Texas standards but important, because it was Alabama's first truly significant find. The Gilbertown Field,[6] found in Choctaw County during WW II, produced only half as much.

A.W. Moye typified the humble and beholden nature of Southern farmers who found themselves suddenly showered with oil. "It's a wonderful thing," he told the *Ledger*, his wife standing by nodding in agreement. "But the best thing is it'll mean a lot to the whole country and not just us. We can only hope we can act according to what's right, now that it has happened."

State Geologist Dr. Walter B. Jones had been touring south Alabama for years talking to the citizens and the oil companies, promoting the area's petroleum potential. The new discovery made him beam with satisfaction. H. Gene White, staff engineer at the Oil and Gas Board said, "I went all over the place with Dr. Jones to make speeches to Kiwanis clubs and the like, and he would say, 'Now, this Pollard is just the splinter. We need to look for the logs.' I thought, 'How tacky can you get?' But he was exactly right. Those people understood that."[7] Unfortunately, eighteen frustrating years passed before explorers along the southern tier of Alabama counties found the logs.

Interestingly, Pollard field lay along a fault originally thought to be the same one that formed the Pickens Field in Yazoo County, Mississippi, 200 miles to the northwest. Today geologists recognize the Pickens-Gilbertown-Pollard fault as a system rather than a continuously connected fault.

Dale Myers, one of the first people to discern the fault's southeastern extent, and others at Stanolind deserve a share of credit in the Pollard discovery. They pointed the way. But Myers wasn't finished. Forty years later, he and partner Lloyd Spivey Jr. scored another Lower Tuscaloosa strike, the Osaka Field, just north of Pollard.

West of Pollard not much was happening, but the year following the discovery at South Carlton, Crow Well Servicing Company and J.D. Reese extended Langsdale Field from Clarke County, Mississippi, into Choctaw County, Alabama. Long Bell Petroleum originally discovered Langsdale in 1945. The field produced from the Eutaw at depths of about 3,800 feet in a narrow band of structural closure along the Pickens-Gilbertown-Pollard fault system. Crow and Reese's Alabama extension netted only a quarter million barrels but is still in production today. The Mississippi part of the original field consisted of 49 wells, which produced 5 million barrels.

Exciting finds like Pollard were the result of intensive work by visionary oil professionals, but a unique well was getting underway in south Mississippi under the control of a shady character who appeared from nowhere, knew nothing, shunned the established oil industry, and was arguably the unluckiest man to ever spud a well. Yet he too made a profound mark on drilling history.

Chapter 5

"Impossible! Absolutely nuts!"

One of the most bizarre events in the history of oil exploration came in the late 40s and early 50s when an untrained underworld figure named George Vasen contributed more to the annals of geologic and petroleum engineering knowledge than all the major oil companies' research labs could put together. He went to prison for it.

Most observers believed Vasen moved to Mississippi in the mid 40s from Chicago. He acquired a large tung tree plantation two miles northeast of the town of Wiggins in Stone County. The rare trees produced oils for paint products. He called it the Tung Corporation of America.

Wil Knight of Union Producing Company, one of the few professional oil people who knew Vasen, thought the farm was just another of the get rich quick commodity schemes popular at the time. Knight said Vasen "was a very profane, hard-nosed, almost criminal type of person."[1]

The oil bug bit Vasen in 1946, or perhaps he saw oil as another avenue of financial exploitation. Whatever his motive, he decided to promote a well on his plantation. To generate capital he sold interest to his wealthy underworld friends all over the United States and Europe. Vasen's promotional methods astounded Knight. "He didn't promote anybody in Mississippi that I know. . . . He was selling interest for much more than costs, and he would sell them by layers. He'd sell you from 10,000 to 11,000, and once you got to 11,000 . . . you were out. If you wanted to get back in the deal, you bought 11,000 to 12,000!"

Seasoned oil investors would have laughed at the absurd scheme, but Vasen's associates took the bait. His property sat on the broad crest of south Mississippi's most prominent subsurface geologic feature, the Wiggins Uplift, also known as the Wiggins Arch and Wiggins Anticline. The huge structure underlies a large part of four counties—Stone, George, Jackson, and Harrison—extending 65 miles east to west and 25 miles north to south. On the north flank, the strata plunge off steeply into the Mississippi Interior Salt Basin, while the formations plunge more gradually to the south into the Gulf of Mexico. The structure drops off to the west into Pearl River and Hancock Counties. To the east it is less well defined. Erosion and late deposition have eliminated most of the obvious surface evidence of the huge anticline.

The timing of the Wiggins uplift was an ongoing debate among geologists: if the structure was relatively recent, the odds of finding production were poor, because oil would have moved through the rock layers before the structure was formed, without being trapped. If the structure was very old and was present when oil began its migration, however, there was a good chance that the oil was trapped. A scattering of shallow dry holes along the broad spine of the structure had been drilled to the Eutaw and Lower Tuscaloosa. By the end of WW II, however, the Wiggins was disappointing.

Whether or not Vasen knew his property was on the Wiggins Uplift will probably never be known, and even if Wiggins' geologic riddles had been explained to him he would not have been daunted. He was determined to go for it.

Vasen hired an old rig that consisted of a 136-foot derrick, three oil-fired boilers, two mud pumps, and an old draw-works. Given the great strides in drilling technology of the postwar years, the rig was a relic, but Vasen spudded with it on August 21, 1946. The hole would reach its astonishing total depth almost six years later.

The well drew scant attention from the professional oil community; they didn't take Vasen seriously. But, along with Wil Knight, one other geologist took notice—Mack Cox of Phillips Petroleum.

Cox had pondered the question of uplift timing in the Wiggins structure while working in Phillips' Jackson exploration office. He saw Vasen's well as a welcome source of information. He contacted Vasen and offered his assistance.

"He [Vasen] agreed to deliver me his samples [drill cuttings] for confidential evaluation and asked what he could expect. I told him a target was the Glen Rose at about 12,500 feet, which would be impossible for him to do, but he replied that he could reach it. Although popular opinion projected that the Glen Rose would be much deeper, he said he would go until he found it. Slowly, he drilled to the target which came in where I expected but with no evidence of commercial showing."[2]

Vasen abandoned the well in the Paluxy sand at a depth of 11,209 feet in November 1946. He found no shows, and oil circles took little interest; but he was not easily discouraged.

Another group of investors furnished money to drill the hole to 14,000 feet, buying the rights below 11,209, but he needed a newer, bigger rig. No contractor at that time would offer a set price to drill to such a great depth, so Vasen leased a rig from Martin Harris Drilling Company on a day rate basis (as opposed to the more common *turn-key* basis, where a drilling contractor sets a price for the entire job). That rig, too, was ill suited for the challenge that not even Vasen realized lay ahead.

With interest in his affairs growing, the overly suspicious Vasen built a high chain-link fence around the location to keep scouts and other nosy people out. He even stationed armed guards and dogs inside. His crews cleaned out the hole and resumed drilling in 1949.

After several months the hole reached 14,038 feet. Vasen ran electric logs, set a string of casing, and perforated in several intervals between 13,600 and 13,900, but the test yielded mostly salt water. Still, Vasen would not relent.

He seemed driven to continue the well, somehow convinced that he was about to discover a giant oil field. He ordered the rig to drill ahead while he raised more money. Again, he turned to Cox for advice. "He wanted to know the next target. I told him, 'Well, that might be the Smackover.' He wanted to know how deep. I said, 'Oh, about eighteen to twenty thousand feet.' He said, 'fine,' and drilled ahead."

The depth at which the impulsive neophyte was drilling would have challenged even a large exploration company with the latest know-how and hardware. The rig Vasen hired was already far deeper than its rated depth capability. The last recorded temperature was 317°F, at a depth between 12,500 and 13,000 feet. No downhole thermometer then in use could read any higher. After many weeks of very slow progress, he reached a depth of 14,670 feet, and some measure of good fortune smiled on him.

He hadn't found oil yet, but the oil companies and the oil field service companies suddenly began to pay attention. He didn't want their attention. He was still very private and was guarded about his well. They had something that intensely interested him however—gifts and money.

Oil Based Mud, Inc., a service company, had developed a controversial new drilling mud known as "Black Magic." Whereas common drilling muds used various clay minerals suspended in a water-based slurry, Black Magic suspended the clays in an oil-based mud by chemically treating bentonite—which naturally absorbs water and repels oil—to absorb oil and repel water. That property helped it hold clays and heavy mineral material in suspension, caused the mud to hold up under higher temperatures, and furnished better lubrication for the drill pipe. The company realized that the Vasen well was a dramatic testing ground to prove the merits of its new product to the industry. It offered to furnish oil-based mud as well as expensive diamond core bits to Vasen free of charge. He eagerly accepted.

In January 1950 the water-based mud was displaced with oil-based mud. Coring was resumed with incredible results. By September 16, 1950, 51 cores were cut in 83 days, reaching a depth of 18,370 feet.

At depths below 14,500 feet, Mr. Schutz—the rig's *tool pusher*—found that diamond coring was faster than drilling with normal rock bits. Diamond coring uses a donut shaped bit with a ring of diamond cutting teeth around it attached to the bottom end of a heavy pipe called a core barrel. As the bit rotates, it cuts down through the rock and forces a core of undisturbed rock up inside the barrel. When retrieved to the surface, the core is extracted and laid out for the bulging eyes of geologists to examine. Because it is slow and expensive, such coring is normally only done when a target zone is reached, but since it was free, Schutz used it for *making hole*. It was the fastest way to drill at the depths he was drilling with his small rig.

The irony was that Vasen didn't care about the important geological data his cores contained; he was satisfied with the downward progress that the expensive diamond coring made possible. Although Schutz was a brilliant tool pusher, he also cared little for science.

Vasen's indifference to geology amazed Wil Knight. "There wasn't anybody that he was involved with that was really scientifically oriented," Knight said. "But the guy with the Oil Based Mud Company was smart enough to have some boxes built, and every inch of these cores was put in boxes and saved and stacked. . . . They cored three to four thousand feet of Lower Cotton Valley, which nobody had ever seen before down in that area. I mean brand new! They were really out in brand new territory, geologically. I mean they were just opening up a whole bunch of information. But it was all just in the boxes, and nobody had looked at it. I forget how we found out about it."

Actually, Knight found out about the cores from a scout's detective work. Oil company's scouts were unable to obtain much useful information on the Vasen well. About all they could do was sit in the woods with binoculars when the core barrel came out for a bit change, and count the stands of pipe. Knowing the length of each stand gave them and their companies an idea of Vasen's depth.

Knight vividly remembered Vasen's paranoid security measures. "They had this old beady-eyed guard with a tobacco-stained beard . . . had a big ole horse pistol sitting on his lap there in that dusty old guard room guarding that gate, and he'd wave you through if you were the right guy. If not, you'd better get your butt out of there."

Bert Lismon, a crafty scout for Gulf, befriended the beady-eyed guard and managed to get in for a look around. Lismon's colleague, Ray Stevens, who spent 30 of 38 years in Mississippi scouting for Shell, recalls what happened. "Burt got through the guard and walked up on the derrick floor, and George Vasen was on the derrick floor and Burt didn't know it. And he asked Burt what he wanted. Burt told him he was with Gulf and was down here to see what was going on to get some information. Vasen said, 'Well, goodbye. You can go. Get on the road. Get out!' Burt acted like he didn't hear him, kept on talking to him, and he [Vasen] pulled out a .45 and stuck it into Burt's stomach and said, 'Now, I mean get out, and get out now!'"[3]

Lismon retreated hastily, but the scouts managed to discern that cores were being taken and that they were samples of rock never seen before in any well in Mississippi. They carried the news back to their companies, and soon geologists were watering at the mouth to study the cores. Wil Knight called his boss and got permission to spend some money to get at the cores, if he could. He put together a cooperative effort with five other companies: his own

Union Producing, Gulf, Superior, Atlantic, Sinclair, and one other. Each contributed $6,000 to a $30,000 pot.

Knight called Vasen and offered the money. Vasen wondered why they were so interested in the rocks, but he did not let that opportunity slip by. He accepted, but he wanted cash—he trusted no one. Knight was aghast. "[He wanted] $30,000 cash! I mean this was cash—not a check!"

Knight and four other geologists, one from each of the five participating companies, drove to Vasen's rural residence with the cash. Vasen took them to a barn where the geologists vigorously pored over the cores, each taking a one-inch sample out of each foot. Later the United States Geological Survey (USGS) also contributed money to the project and obtained all the cores.

As the scouts reported that the hole had passed the 20,000-foot mark, Knight and his contemporaries sat shaking their heads incredulously. "It was just unbelievable! It was like the bumblebee that can't fly. That rig just couldn't drill that deep. It was impossible! It was absolutely nuts!"

The hole cored slowly deeper through 1951 and into 1952. At 20,227 feet, a 50-foot core was recovered, reported to be the Jurassic-aged Smackover limestone with a live oil show of 45-degree gravity oil. The well kicked hard while coring at 20,300 feet but was brought under control after spewing 100 barrels of mud into the derrick. It blew out again at 20,352 feet, losing 200 barrels of mud. The rig crew was uneasy about the rotten egg smell of hydrogen sulfide (H_2S) gas in the mud and cores. H_2S in high concentrations is lethal. At 20,450 feet Vasen decided to run pipe and try to complete the well.

With H_2S likely to come with the hoped-for oil, Vasen was advised that he needed a special grade of nickel pipe to ward off corrosion, but the Korean War had put federal controls oil field pipe. Vasen appealed to Washington to help him find the pipe. Petroleum czar Emmett Vaughey needed no persuasion. A Mississippi independent, he knew the importance of Vasen's venture. After a lengthy delay and with Vaughey's help, Vasen finely obtained the string of nickel tubing and liner.

They ran the liner, with the bottom 358 feet nickel and the bottom 40 feet slotted. No perforating gun then could operate at the high temperature at the bottom of Vasen's hole without firing prematurely. The slotted liner was a less effective alternative to perforating.

The well kicked again and was quickly brought under control. It flowed *sour gas* (natural gas mixed with H_2S) for several hours on September 7, 1952, and then died, probably due to faulty cement seal in the liner, according to Knight.

Vasen's investors became impatient and came to Wiggins for an on-site inspection. One spent several days waiting for the well to come in. He returned to Chicago after Vasen told him that the tremendous well pressure had blown a "rubber gasket" and delayed the start of the well's flow.

Soon thereafter, Vasen's only flow became a flood of lawsuits, followed by an indictment, on May 28, 1953, by a federal grand jury in Chicago. They accused him of defrauding 300 investors of approximately two million dollars, each of whom lost from a few thousand dollars each up to $300,000.

According to testimony at the trial, Vasen began raising money to finance his venture in 1946. Witnesses testified that he told them he was "drilling through oceans of oil," that his well would flow as much as 10,000 to 20,000 barrels per day, and that it would eventually be worth fifty to seventy-five million dollars. He told some of them he was even thinking about building his own pipeline between Wiggins, Mississippi, and the Gulf Coast to get his vast reserves to market. Vasen promised his financial backers a return of ten times their investment. The most damaging testimony came from a petroleum engineer from Houston whom Vasen hired to test the well. He said that he made core tests from 14,650 and 15,797 feet and found no oil-bearing sand.

Vasen pled innocent to all the charges and presented witnesses who claimed he made every effort to bring in a legitimate commercial oil well. A Chicago accountant testified that Vasen spent more than $2.5 million dollars "in a Herculean effort to strike oil." An unconvinced jury found Vasen guilty and sentenced him to five years in prison, a $25,000 fine, and five years probation following his prison term. He died a short time after his conviction.

The Mississippi State Oil and Gas Board took Vasen's well over and plugged it, a sad ending to an incredible saga in the history of the oil business. Yet from a technological standpoint the venture was a resounding success and inspired many companies to turn their sights upon drilling targets far deeper than they had yet imagined. Wil Knight summed up the hole's scientific success. "It was quite a contribution to the [knowledge of the] geology of south Mississippi. It was a landmark contribution."

Statistically, Vasen's well shattered the 15,730-foot depth record for the southeastern states, previously reached by the Superior No. 1 Cassie Bradford in Forrest County, Mississippi, but he could not lay claim to the world's deepest well of the time. Superior Oil Company set that record in 1949 in Sublette County, Wyoming, at 20,512 feet and established the world record. At 20,450 feet Vasen's well was the second deepest. Considering the equipment used, Vasen's achievement was far more impressive. Whether he was a crook, a fool, a fanciful dreamer, a determined entrepreneur, or any combination thereof, George Vasen's grit and perseverance earned him a place in petroleum exploration history.

As the exploration of the Southeast picked up in the decade of the fifties, another colorful personality began to emerge who proved to be George Vasen's antithesis. He knew about oil field operations, focused on business opportunities, and applied the skills and talents he developed from an early age.

"I told my daddy I was going to go to the oil field"

Grady Pruet worked hard trying to farm a small piece of west Texas dirt and raise a few head of cattle on it. Never able to afford a hired hand, he depended heavily on his lanky, hyperactive son to help out. Although the boy was never very interested in cattle, he did what most farm boys do—what their daddy tells them.

Years working the ranch made the young Chesley Pruet hard as nails, but his blond hair and well-chiseled features set him apart and drew inviting glances from girls. Gradually he developed a mischievous grin, an amusing banter, and many friendly mannerisms—all traits he put to good use in the business world later.

In those years on the ranch he was not sure what his future held, but he knew what he didn't want it to hold. He never forgot the day his father took him to the bank to cash a check for his class ring. "Does Grady Pruet have $20 in his account?" the clerk yelled to the bookkeeper. Chesley held his breath until the answer yes came back. He resolved then never to live that close to poverty.

He took a degree in animal husbandry and returned to the ranch in 1934. He enjoyed traveling around trading horses and cattle, and although he didn't make much money, he learned how to deal with people. His friendly smile and forceful, slightly raspy yet pleasant voice helped him make friends wherever he went. In the years ahead he had no trouble befriending all manner of people, from roughnecks to major company CEOs.

After a few more years of hard work in the cattle business with little to show for it, he decided to shift gears. "I told my daddy I was going to go to the oil field," he said, "and work and save $25,000 and go into business with him. At that time $25,000 was a big stake." Soon he found a job with Zack Brooks Trucking Company and, although he didn't realize it at the time, a relationship was born that profoundly affected the petroleum development of the eastern Gulf Coast. He remembered the hardships of those early years.

"I was making 50 cents an hour swamping, but I put in long hours and got up to be a driver and got 60 cents an hour. Then I got a lot better job roughnecking, which paid seven dollars a day for eight hours work. No time and a half or anything, just $49 a week, no withholding or anything at that time. I roughnecked and saved my money and bought a car.

"I then decided I wanted to go back and study petroleum engineering. I went to Texas Tech at Lubbock. I had one year of engineering and got out of school in 1938. I went back to El Dorado, Arkansas. I had been working for Delta Drilling Company, roughnecking. But I went to work with Hunt Oil Company on the rigs in Cotton Valley, La. When school time came the next year I didn't want to go back."[4]

Pruet worked hard, as all roughnecks do, sometimes working double tours (16 hours). After one long night he noticed a problem and offered to fix it before the daylight crew came on duty. He would wish many times he had left it to them and gone home.

"I told the driller that the chain on the drawworks rattled real bad last night and I think it needs to be changed. He checked it and said it did. (It was a steam rig.) I had always thought that I was pretty good with a sledgehammer. Another boy was holding back the stops with a hammer on the chain where it wouldn't slide across the floor. He was standing right over it. I was standing straight up, driving the pin out, and a piece of that pin flaked off and went in the bottom of my eye and lodged in it. They rushed me to the hospital in Shreveport. They sucked it out of my eye with a magnet. Of course, I lost all the fluid in the eye. An old doctor in Dallas thought he could do some good with it. I waited four or five months to see if he could do anything with it. He would put hot compresses on it. Anyway, I finally gave up on it and he did too. So I had it removed."

Pruet tried to enlist in the service in WW II, but the missing eye kept him out. He learned to live with a glass eye and didn't let it keep him from hard physical work. He even became a pilot. Later, as he developed vital business relationships, he learned to coordinate his good eye so that people he talked to never suspected he had a glass eye. [5]

After the accident he quit roughnecking and took a job looking after a boiler on a gas distillate well, which paid better, but he found it boring and unchallenging. "The job had gotten so easy. The guy I had worked for in trucking, Zack Brooks, asked me if I wanted a job. I told him yes because if I stayed here I was going to become the sorriest dadgum guy in the world because I wasn't doing anything. I took a cut in salary."

Eventually Zack Brooks decided to expand his business beyond trucking into drilling and he invited Pruet to partner with him and E.L. Erickson. The three pooled $45,000 and bought a drilling rig. With Pruet as managing partner, the three pursued drilling opportunities wherever they found them. As the company grew Pruet began to realize the value of combining his keen business talent with his roughneck brawn and his driller's skills. He told Brooks, "I could hire a tool pusher in my place, and I could get out and make deals for us and make a hell of a lot more money than we would have to pay the tool pusher. Zack agreed to that."

The change soon paid off. Pruet kept his rigs busy working for oil operators and also managed to edge in for a royalty or a working interest.

His expanding knowledge of oilfield operations, his energy, and his willingness to gamble soon produced even bigger pay-offs as the drilling trail led the company southeastward.

The Wiggins Surrenders

Whether the shows in George Vasen's well emboldened others to test the Wiggins is arguable, but Ohio Oil Company decided to give it a shot in 1952. Their seismic work in Forrest County had delineated an anticlinal substructure within the larger framework of the Wiggins. The gamble paid off with doubly good fortune, although it did not solve the geologic timing question clearly.

The No. 1 Coleman-Powe tested over four million cubic feet of gas per day, plus 80 barrels of condensate per day from the Eutaw sand below 7,000 feet. Condensate is a hydrocarbon type that exists as gas in the geologic reservoir but condenses into a light colored oil as it rises to the surface. Deeper still, Ohio's engineers tested over three million cubic feet per day, plus 125 barrels of condensate, from the Lower Tuscaloosa sands below 8,000 feet. That became the discovery well for the huge Maxie Field, which eventually produced over 300 Bcf.

A number of other small widely scattered discoveries occurred across the Mississippi Salt Basin in the early fifties, mostly in the Wilcox. Although the few modest Lower Cretaceous successes encouraged more deep exploration, none of them caused much excitement. Explorers kept drilling, but they wondered if all the big fields had already been found. They didn't know that the oil business in Mississippi—and unsuspecting Alabama—was about to blow wide open.

Chapter 6

The Big Three

I n 1953 the first of the decade's "Big Three" came in like gangbusters. Union's Bob Hearin described it succinctly. "They just kind of hit—Bang! Bang! Bang!—all about a year apart."[1]

The first bang was near a small town northwest of Laurel in Jones County, Mississippi. The town's name means small, trifling, or barely passable, but the residents of Soso like it there and recognize only one of Webster's synonyms—small. Like their town, their little gas field, discovered during WW II was not noteworthy. Twenty-five or so wells were producing gas from the Eutaw sands at a depth of 6,500 feet. In 1953 the wells began to lose pressure rapidly, which signified reservoir depletion. Because of the low price of gas, due to abundant supplies, the depletion of the Soso Field didn't seem such a big a loss until the operators remembered some critical clauses in their lease agreements. The dwindling gas wells of Soso held a staggering 10,000 acres of leases in force—as long as they continued to produce commercially. If the wells were depleted and abandoned, the vast block of acreage would be lost. Something had to be done.

Even though the Lower Cretaceous beds in Mississippi had so far been disappointing, the operators—Union, Gulf, and Humble—jointly decided to try to save the leases by finding deeper production. If they found even a few small gas wells, like the ones they found in the Eutaw, that would salvage some of the giant lease block.

The deep test well began drilling in early summer of 1953 and penetrated the Lower Cretaceous two months later. The numerous rich oil sands the operators logged amazed them. They completed the well in August 1953 for almost 200 BOPD from the Sligo Sand.

Lower Cretaceous fever ignited and swept across Mississippi. A rookie geologist fresh out of the Army, Dudley Hughes of Union Producing witnessed the logging of the well. He wrote, "I didn't realized the importance it would play in my future." He was to spend many months mapping the geology of the Soso structure, and in doing so he and others would glean immeasurable knowledge of the nature of Lower Cretaceous *stratigraphy* and of the structural aspects of salt dynamics.

Hughes and other geologists working the field eventually determined that the Soso structure was a *turtle*, Mississippi's first such discovery. A turtle, also known as an *inter-domal high* or *residual high*, is a relatively low mound of sediment between large adjacent areas of salt. The mound's turtleback appearance on a subsurface map gives the structure its name.

The numerous pay sands on such a broad structure produced an astounding find: 40 to 50 million barrels. Soso is a classic example of drilling a shallow, unimpressive field deeper to discover a mother lode of oil at its core. Not surprisingly, it sent other operators scurrying to drill deeper wells on old structures that either were dry or yielded shallow production. Before long, there was more to celebrate.

Second Bang

Another Lower Cretaceous strike hit in the heart of Mississippi, 100 miles northwest of Soso. Larco Drilling Company took a farmout from Gulf Oil to drill the No. 1 Lettie McAlpin on a salt structure near the cotton town of Bolton in Hinds County. In July 1954 they logged good shows in the Paluxy Sand and ran a drill-stem test.

Word of the test spread swiftly through the oil community. Bolton was a short drive west of Jackson, and hundreds of cars soon lined the road to the rig as people poured out of Jackson to watch. Oil gurgled from the DST of the McAlpin well, then sprayed onto the rig floor. The crew scrambled to reverse out before the flow got out of control. They succeeded but not before oil sprayed onto the shiny new company car Larco attorney Hap Owens had parked too close to the rig. The car's paint job was ruined, but Owens and operator Ike Larue thought it was the most beautiful paint job an oilman could want. Larco completed the well July 29, 1954, from the Paluxy sand, yielding almost 300 BOPD at a depth close to 10,000 feet.

Wil Knight left Union to join Larco's staff after the discovery and worked on the geological interpretation of the new field. Bolton quickly developed into a multi-pay field, producing oil from one or more sands in every Lower Cretaceous formation from the Hosston to the Washita-Fredericksburg. The discovery extended the massive lease play Soso started. Offers of up to $1,500 per royalty acre were turned down. However, Hinds County proved disappointing in the search for more good Lower Cretaceous fields.

Nearly 150 miles to the southeast of the Bolton discovery, a man scouted the ground and looked at a map. He imagined a straight line through Bolton and Soso extending through the ground he stood on, but others had already drilled there and walked away disappointed. They quit too soon, he reasoned. When he invited them to invest in his idea to go deeper, they scoffed and showed him the door. But he had a vision that wouldn't be denied.

Third Bang: "*The heavens* were filled with oil."

In the late 1800s, officials of the Gulf, Mobile & Ohio Railroad heard that a place along their track about 30 miles northwest of Mobile was the site of springs which, according to an Indian legend, had mysterious healing powers. Desperate for passenger revenue, the railroad seized the opportunity to exploit the legend and acquired a large tract of land at the site on which it laid out a town. It advertised the healing springs throughout the North, and soon tourists began pouring in. The town eventually became an active railroad hub with two hotels and a bustling tourist economy.

The boom began to fizzle after the turn of the century as the Yankees rode trains straight through town to the gleaming new resort areas along the Gulf coast. By the mid-twenties, For Sale signs decorated half the town's houses. Many families moved on, while others were too poor to pay their property taxes. The town shrank and fell into an agrarian existence that depended on an overworked lumber and tung tree industry. Young people left in droves and older folks died, leaving their estates to be divided. Hope of a better life seemed to have fled altogether.

Then in 1901, word spread through the town about the big oil strike in Texas at Spindletop. People who were land rich and cash poor tried to raise a few dollars selling oil leases. They held an auction in front of the courthouse, but no oilmen showed up.[2]

As the town's vitality ebbed, the mystical healing powers legend faded with it, and the real origin of the town's name became known: a plant whose oil is said to drive away mosquitoes, the citronella plant. With the departure of the tourist trade, life in Citronelle, Alabama, became routine, even dismal for some families. Then came Everett Eaves.

When Eaves first came through buying oil leases, no one really took much notice. Several wells had been drilled nearby in the years since the unsuccessful lease auction, all dry. Few people had much hope, but some leased to Eaves.

Eaves had seen a vision beneath the town in the contours of his maps. He knew the town sat higher than the surrounding countryside—a topographic *high*, geologists called it. The high was hardly noticeable to the eye but railroad surveyors had long known about it. It indicated a possible dome-like structure in the subsurface. The earlier shallow dry holes supported the notion that a structure existed.

Eaves wondered if the recently found deeper Lower Cretaceous production at Soso in Mississippi might extend southeastward into Alabama. Geologists had a name for that method of thinking—trendology. It was an extremely long shot; Soso was 85 miles away. If so, he reasoned, oil should be present in structures such as the one under Citronelle. All he had to do was convince investors to drill deeper.

Eaves, a 1937 graduate of the University of Oklahoma, worked for 25 years as a district geologist with Magnolia Petroleum Company, predecessor of Mobil Oil. Early in his career, he befriended Chesley Pruet. The two had met when the Zach Brooks Drilling Company drilled a well for Mobil. Pruet remembered urging Eaves to consider going out on his own. "He was sitting a well and I was looking after the rig. Everett said he [wanted to] go into business for himself. I told him the longer he waited, the harder it would be, because he would start thinking what a good retirement plan he had with the company."[3]

The Alabama Oil and Gas Board's Gene White remembered Eaves as "a scholarly man, very distinguished. He had a black mustache and was tall and a very handsome man. He was kind of the dean of geologists in those days. Everybody had tremendous respect for him."[4]

Eaves took Pruet's advice and left the comfort and security of his big company. Soon thereafter he acted on his hunch and began leasing at Citronelle. He also secured the necessary farmouts from acreage already under lease, most of which belonged to Gulf. But Eaves was short of drilling funds. "I walked all around the county for about six months before we could get the money," he said.[5] Part of his problem was the excessive taxation that Alabama levied against drilling rigs brought into the state. Many investors shied away from Alabama's transportation taxes, preferring the more oil friendly states to the west.

The breakthrough came when Eaves ran the deal past the Zach Brooks Drilling Company. They offered to buy a piece of it if Eaves would give them the drilling contract. "The reason we took the deal," Chesley Pruet said, "was that Gulf gave us [through Eaves] $70,000 . . . and gave us half interest in the 6,500 acres they had leased there." That paved the way for a few other investors to fall in line, but Eaves' funds were still low.

Eaves looked for ways to cut costs. "It would cost us about $6,000 to build a board road back to our [preferred] location," he said. "So we offered Mr. Donovan $150 to let us drill on a lot he had cleared for a used car lot. Then he could have it back after we got through." Donovan never got it back.

Drilling started and Eaves continued to acquire leases. He finalized the lease under the drill site location the day operations began. Citronelleans sat on the hoods of their cars, watching as the days passed. Mayor I.D. Wyatt told the *Mobile Register*, "'Electricity' has been with us for about three days. Everyone has been thoroughly expecting something to happen."[6]

Eaves saw some shows near 11,000 feet. He stopped drilling and ordered a DST. The packer was set and the surface valve opened. They waited. Eaves and Pruet looked at each other and shook their heads; there was no surface pressure. The townspeople saw Eaves' disappointment and dropped their heads.

Pruet had the crew recover the DST tool. After the first few stands of pipe came out, the water cushion, put into the pipe for safety reasons, suddenly blew out. Then came oil. It shot skyward through the crown block and fell onto the now upturned faces of the people of Citronelle. Unknown to Eaves and Pruet, 800 feet of oil had entered the pipe. The DST was a success. Pruet found out why there was no surface pressure. "The Haliburton guy was a young boy and he forgot and left the valve open at the top of the drill stem."[7] Even so, as far as Citronelle was concerned, it was a blowout.

The electrifying "Blow-out!" rang down the streets, as people scurried to tell their neighbors. Excitement stampeded the town. A local physician, Dr. M.L. Moore, accidentally walked into a real-life drama, the *Mobile Register* reported. "I had just parked my car about 150 yards away from the well," he said, "and I was approaching it when they started bringing up the drill. There was no sound when it exploded . . . and the whole heavens were filled with oil. . . . Most of the people ran around. They were tickled." Dr. Moore said his car looked as if someone had poured about 15 gallons of oil on it.

The Zack Brooks Drilling Company went on to complete the No. 1 Donovan on October 13, 1955, flowing 445 BOPD of sweet 45 degree gravity oil from the Rodessa at almost 11,000 feet. The gross pay interval was 850 feet thick. Initial bottom hole pressure clocked in at almost 5,000 pounds per square inch.

State Geologist Dr. Walter B. Jones and engineer Gene White went down to observe the test. "Dr. Jones was really high on getting down there and getting pictures and observing what was going on," White recalled. "It was a beauty, boy! They lit that flare up—natural pressure. It was blowing and going. We knew we really had something big."[8]

The field's geology was both fascinating and challenging to understand. Richard Stechmann, the Citronelle Field's unit manager in 1995, described the geologic characteristics of the field at the 50th anniversary of the Alabama Oil and Gas Board. "As new wells were completed and more geologic data became available, the reservoir was identified as being composed of a series of stacked sand lenses draped across a broad, dome-shaped substructure. . . . The sand bodies themselves are irregular in size, shape, and thickness, and are generally noncontinuous. One can get an idea of the structure by visualizing hundreds of pancakes of various sizes being thrown out on top of a rounded table. . . . The characteristics of the reservoir sands suggest that the environment during the time of deposition [approximately 130 million years ago] was similar to the present day Mobile Bay. Some 330 separate oil bearing zones have been identified; however the bulk of the oil reserves are located in about 100 of the thicker, more permeable sand bodies."[9] The pancakelike rock layers two miles beneath the town were pregnant with oil.

Citronelle's fortune, it seemed, had come full circle, and, predictably, a title wave of lease brokers washed across the community throwing money at anyone they thought might own mineral property. The June 16, 1956, *Saturday Evening Post* reported on the feeding frenzy in a feature article entitled "The Day it Rained Money."[10]

Many of the townspeople were not streetwise to the dealings of oil brokers. One family, the *Post* said, leased too quickly and only for the amount of the debts they owed, then found they could have leased for three times as much. Another elderly lease owner committed suicide under the pressure of being courted by numerous brokers. According to the *Post*, a broker was overheard assuring his company on a phone that the old man had signed a lease prior to killing himself.

A man named John Henry, a small crop farmer on the edge of town, was not so easily intimidated. He held brokers in suspense for days while rocking in the yard and talking about bird dogs. One exasperated broker eventually jumped up and shouted, "I don't want to hear anymore about bird dogs. I came here to do business!" He threw a bundle of money in the dirt at John Henry's feet. The farmer calmly called for his daughter to pick up the money and give it back to the man and then he continued his discourse on training dogs. Eventually John Henry leased for $1,000 an acre and an unspecified royalty.

The *Post* story also revealed Citronelle's character when it reported numerous accounts of cash poor citizens who stuck to their word, even when more money was offered later. The most compelling such story was about Carlton Stallworth, a car dealer. Stallworth agreed to lease his family's 6,000 acres for $180,000, but after days of haggling he was too tired to review the contract for errors before signing it. He asked that it be brought to his office the next morning. When morning came, another oilman appeared with a lease for $300,000. Stallworth looked at the two documents, then stared out the window for a long time. Finally he scrawled his name on the $180,000 lease.

As the field developed and the size of the strike became apparent, leasing gave way to trading of another kind. Everett Eaves' discovery well was drilled on Mrs. Donovan's property on the north edge of town. The second big producer came in two miles south, on land owned by the Boy Scouts of America. That revelation—that the bulk of the field lay underneath Citronelle—presented both problems and opportunities for the herds of brokers, speculators, title busters, and swindlers that descended on the town.

With almost 2,500 small landowners above the giant field, anyone with some cash had a shot at getting a lease or buying mineral rights. So fanatical were the speculators that when Alabama's state geologist, Dr. Walter B. Jones, visited the town, one of them approached him, wanting to know if he had anything to lease.

Opportunity abounded for title busters to track down absentee owners and to challenge deeds that people who were accustomed to doing business with handshakes had never recorded. Complicating the situation, many records had been lost in a courthouse fire. The pickings were ripe for crafty opportunists who overwhelmed townspeople with their offers, schemes, and claims.

The *Post* story reported that "the sea of the tax-deed buyers and their more reprehensible cohorts, the title busters, has led to some tense situations." One man showed up at the Methodist Church with a tax deed on its cemetery, claiming that the taxes on the property were long overdue and he had paid them thus earned title to the property. That was a gutsy bluff, since church property is not taxable in Alabama. The church's deacons—among them Carlton Stallworth, the man who had shone his word was more important than $120,000—didn't fall for it. They invited the man for an edifying walk in the woods where he was persuaded to give up his claim.

Citronelle soon burgeoned into a discovery of a gargantuan magnitude. It became every oilman's dream—a *giant* oil field. A *giant* is an oil field of over 100 million barrels proven reserves or a gas field of over one trillion cubic feet of gas. Citronelle was the Deep South's biggest Lower Cretaceous field and produced over 160 million barrels of oil from almost 500 wells. Alabama, no longer a fringe producer, had finally joined the oil fraternity with a mighty bang, and Everett Eaves had joined the ranks of the few oilmen to become giant killers.

Predictably, John Henry and most of Citronelle's other 2,500 small landowners never got rich, but houses were repaired and painted, some new pickups appeared around town, and church tithes doubled. John Henry himself, according to the *Post*, was happy to afford some new bird dogs and a fine horse to ride alongside his pack.

The *Saturday Evening Post* was wrong in one respect. It never really rained money on the town named for the citronella plant, but hope descended in torrents.

Smaller Bangs

The Lower Cretaceous trend had been extended almost 100 miles southeast of Soso (Figure 9). The total length from Bolton to Citronelle was 200 miles. All along the trend, wildcatters sank wells probing the deeper sections of salt structures, many of which had too little uplift to trap Eutaw or Lower Tuscaloosa oil but had just the right structural closure in the deeper layers.

There would be more successes along the trend, but not another Citronelle. Strangely, very little Lower Cretaceous oil was found east of the giant that anchored the trend's southeastern end. It was as if Citronelle were a sentinel blocking the way; however, in the decades ahead, deeper but riskier treasures lay in wait southeastward.

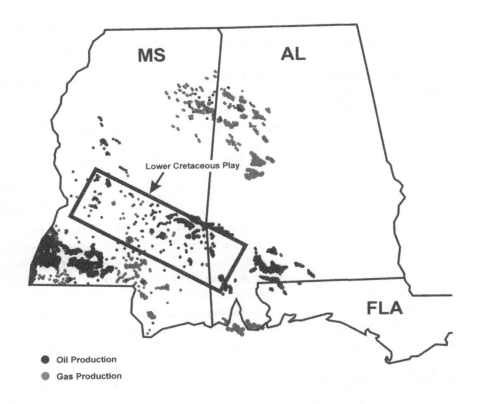

MS

AL

Lower Cretaceous Play

FLA

● Oil Production

◉ Gas Production

Figure 9. Map of Lower Cretaceous Play

In 1955 Marshall R. Young (formerly Rosser and Pendleton) discovered Ansley Field in Hancock County, opening the most southerly production in Mississippi to that time. The field has produced 15 Bcf from the Lower Cretaceous at about 10,000 feet.

Also in 1955, a new method of trouble shooting bad well completions resulted in a major economic breakthrough. Imperfect cement jobs when operators put production casing in the hole in anticipation of production tests had always dogged the industry. Often the cement did not circulate thoroughly through the annular space between the outside of the casing and the borehole wall, leaving channels of open space behind casing. Saltwater from higher or lower water sands found its way into the perforations through the channels, spoiling production tests. Then an oil field service company, Dowell, Inc., developed a radioactive tracer method of determining salt water source in channeled wells. The radioactive material was pumped into the hole under pressure so it followed any and all paths of communication and was then traced with a gamma ray log. Using the log, engineers could perforate channeled areas and squeeze more cement in to fill them. The method was similar to those Bud Norman pioneered in the early Mississippi Wilcox wells, though much more accurate. The new method helped control completion costs.

Innovative technology and a steady stream of small but lucrative discoveries helped boost Mississippi's oil production past the 500 million–barrel mark by the middle of the decade. Gas production approached two trillion cubic feet.

With the swelling industry, Jackson's oil cadre grew so large that their favorite lunchtime eatery, LaFleur's Restaurant, couldn't seat them all. They needed a place of their own, and with the establishment of their own place, they would bring Jackson into an exclusive fraternity of oil cities.

Deal Weaving at the Bar

With the threat growing from importers, oilmen began to depend on each other more than ever. The oil community grew tighter, although many old rivalries thrived. Ordinarily the early Jackson oil crowd banded together for food and drink at LaFleur's on South President Street at luncheon rendezvous where they not only bellyached about the industry's problems but also traded valuable information. Many deals were seeded in the LaFleur's private dining room. As the oil industry introduced new blood into the community, however, the old guard hatched the idea of organizing a petroleum club.

Petroleum clubs were popular in oil centers like Shreveport, Dallas, Houston, and Tulsa, and promoted the exchange of ideas, information, and capital investments. The LaFleur's crowd decided it was time for Jackson to join them.

They drew the by-laws and elected a board of governors with Ike LaRue as president. They found space for their new lair on the mezzanine of the Edward House, later the King Edward Hotel, which offered the space despite the objection of the ladies' beauty salon on the same floor. Renovations began, and the club opened in December 1946.

Struggling with financing, the young club installed slot machines to supplement its income. That, and the exclusion of women from the club, sent the beauty parlor packing to a new location, and the government eventually busted the slot machine operation. The club struggled to hang together into 1950 under the presidency of Rees Oliver who removed one of the two phones to save money.

Bob Hearin became president in 1951 and soon had the club in the black, but he irked some by replacing the poker table with a ping pong table. At the end of his term the membership presented him with a fur-lined chamber pot.

The Jackson Petroleum Club finally achieved financial stability and wide acceptance by the oil community under the leadership Bill Vaughey. Vaughey was applauded for converting the ping pong room into a cocktail lounge. Although Mississippi was a dry state, private clubs served alcohol to members. The bar became a strong factor in the club's success.

From 1952 on, the club entered a period of stable growth that continued for three decades and became a focal point for social activities of the oil business in Mississippi. The petroleum club was the Jackson oil community's ticket of acceptance into the elite club of oil producing cities.

By the middle of the decade, the club's growing membership relaxed at the bar and sipped their coffee and libations, telling tales, swapping lies, swabbing each other for well information, and drawing contours and faults on napkins. Many an oil field was born on the bar.

After the big strikes, and the shattered hopes, some in the club pondered the fortunes and perils in the years ahead. Plenty of both were in store.

PART II
Mid 50s to Mid 60s

Chapter 7

Cutting Teeth in the Oil Patch

As the fifties neared the mid-point new landmen and geologists poured into the Jackson regional offices of the major companies and began their education on the job. One was Bill Wooten, whose destiny was sealed on a handball court in Tulsa in 1955.

He had just gotten out of the Army and needed a job; his wife was expecting. A friend on the court introduced him to Bill Lackey, the head landman of Stanolind Petroleum, which eventually became Pan American Petroleum, which became Amoco. He asked Wooten if he would like to join the oil business.

"I don't know anything about it. I don't have a technical background at all—I'm just an English major," Wooten answered.

"That doesn't bother me. Hell, I majored in French!"[1]

Soon after he started working Stanolind transferred Wooten to New Orleans where he spent the bulk of his career. His boss was Joe Hildebrand, and his office was where most oil companies in Jackson did business—the Standard Life building. "We had no air conditioning," Wooten recalled. "The windows were always open, the wind blowing, and paperweights were on everything."

Along with many other company landmen, Wooten found himself under the wing of a legendary Jackson broker named Cuz Mayeaux. "He was about as wide as he was tall," Wooten remembered. "And he had a horrible coonass accent. He called everybody Cuz because he couldn't remember people's names. Cuz taught me the basics of how you talk to landowners and acquire leases. It was really interesting work."

Wooten's tutelage under Cuz laid the foundation for a long career that led to the formation of his own company, Orleans Exploration Company, and eventually to Exploration Manager at Pruet Oil Company. Jackson teemed with landmen like Wooten and Cuz, and geologists pored in.

By 1955 the Mississippi Geological Society had swollen to 149 members. Dudley Hughes was typical of those budding oil finders. He and his brother Dan came home from the Korean War as decorated artillery officers. Union Producing Company, their former employer, rehired them and assigned Dan to Texas. Dudley came to Mississippi where he worked under the tutelage of Wil Knight and Bob Hearin.

One of Hughes' most unusual experiences came early in his stint with Union Producing. The old Jackson gas field discovered in 1930 had long since depleted, and Union decided to convert it into a gas storage field.[2] Hughes' fellow geologist, Claud Smith, was assigned to the ambitious project, which involved plugging over 100 old wells, located randomly on the east side of the city of Jackson. "Houses had to be moved and bulldozers scraped the ground to find the old casings. Work-over rigs then re-entered the old holes and plugged them. One was found under an outhouse where the seven-inch casing had received many years of convenient use.

"Three wells blew out during the plugging processes and sent plumes of white saltwater and gas spewing into the air. From downtown Jackson these looked like huge feathers hundreds of feet tall swaying in the breeze. Red Adair was called to bring the wells under control. . . . The gas storage was finally completed and was very successful. With the very strong water drive, the gas can be injected or flowed back under almost constant pressure, at a differential of only 50 psi. Few people in Jackson know it exists."[3]

Later in Hughes' apprenticeship he noticed a more experienced geologist committing a serious blunder. Union had sent him to a well in Pistol Ridge Field in Pearl River County, Mississippi. I.P. Larue discovered Pistol Ridge in 1951 with production from an Upper Tuscaloosa Sand of questionable commercial value. American Liberty Company and LaRue started drilling another well, in which Union had a working interest, two miles northwest in September 1953. "Fresh out of the Army and inexperienced in well sitting," Hughes recalled, "I was sent to the well as Union's representative. While there, the American Liberty geologist in charge showed me how to plot drill time and correlate sands and shales. This was new to me.

"We were going to core the Massive Sand of the Lower Tuscaloosa where the previous well had hit a slight gas show in the top. The American Liberty geologist, with a bit of uncertainty, finally picked a coring point. The core had a slight gas odor but a DST tested water. However, it seemed to me that the drill time indicated the top of the sand was 50 feet higher than the core point. I called Wil Knight acknowledging my inexperience but saying it looked to me that we had drilled through 50 feet of sand before coring.

"Throwing all caution to the wind, Wil sent a fleet of brokers who worked all night and the next few days buying leases. When the well was logged there was 50 feet of gas sand in the Massive Tuscaloosa. The well was actually completed in the Eutaw and a well completed by Southern Natural three months later got credit for the discovery. By observing what the other participants failed to notice, Union got the jump on leasing and ended up with a larger interest in the field."

Hughes' days building experience went at a frantic pace. "Sitting on wells during the Soso deep oil development program," he said, "sometimes required watching four rigs at a time, [and overseeing] coring and testing. During one week alone, I caught 50 diamond cores and witnessed 15 DSTs. When a committee was picked to unitize Soso, I was selected as Union's geological representative and spent most of a year in Gulf's Laurel office working on the project." Hughes' service on the unitization committee gave his on-the-job training a tremendous boost. Unitization duty always broadened a young geologist's knowledge.

Other explorers were learning as well. *Salt tectonics*, the dynamic movement of subsurface salt formations, was a blossoming science, and in 1956 a significant breakthrough in the field occurred in Texas and spread enthusiasm eastward. Geologists knew for years that some salt domes exhibited a mushroom-like top in which the salt spread horizontally. Oil was sometimes found trapped under the *overhang* area of the salt dome. That knowledge kicked off another big lease play around the salt domes of the Mississippi Interior Salt Basin. No such field types were found until many years later, however, and then only a few.

The year 1956 was a milestone for Mississippi. The state's natural gas production peaked at 250 Bcf and began a steady decline for the next 20 years (Figure 10). Yet oil production rose steadily. The California Company discovered Raleigh Field in Smith County in January 1957, and completed in the Hosston, flowing over 300 BOPD. The field eventually produced over 26 million barrels from 37 Lower Cretaceous wells. When asked how thick the pay zones in the wells were, engineers commonly replied, "About a hundred yards!"

Later that same January, ten miles west of Raleigh in Simpson County, Central Oil brought in the Martinville Field, which eventually produced over 12 million barrels from 19 Lower Cretaceous pools and one Cotton Valley Sand. Excited speculators paid up to $2,000 an acre for royalty around Martinville.

In July 1957 Larco Drilling Company, led by Wil Knight's geological evaluation, discovered Diamond Field about six miles north of Waynesboro in Wayne County. To date, Diamond Field has produced over 15 million barrels from the Lower Cretaceous, Cotton Valley, and Smackover.

Over in Alabama where Citronelle was still the only Lower Cretaceous production, concern began to grow over the field's rapidly declining reservoir pressures. In 1957 an operators' committee was formed to determine if a secondary recovery process was feasible. The committee estimated the ultimate primary recovery to be 52 million barrels of oil or about 15% of the original 350 million barrels in place. It concluded that a water injection program could recover additional 55 million barrels.[4] The Citronelle operators embarked on the difficult task of developing a unitization agreement fair to all parties. It would take several years.

Crystal Ball

If Citronelle Field was the heartbeat of Alabama's oil industry in the late 50s, the *Mobile Register* was the stethoscope. The *Register* kept its readers abreast of developments in Alabama's oil industry, especially where it affected the southwestern counties. After the 1959 New Year celebration, the paper reported, "Despite a year that proved to be mediocre at best throughout the nation, 1958 was a banner year for Alabama." The paper made some bold predictions for the coming year: "Rubbing a crystal ball and a throbbing head, here is what we predict for 1959:

1. A new record in Citronelle with the addition of about 60 more producers.
2. Extension of the field by at least two miles.
3. Another record in state oil production.
4. Major steps in unitizing Citronelle.
5. Considerable political pressure for revision of state oil and gas laws.
6. A new oil field in Southwest Alabama. (Could be the holiday spirit, but time and the law of averages make this a ripe year for new production.)
7. A new commercial field in the Black Warrior Basin (We're getting brave, now.)"[5]

The *Register's* crystal ball turned in a mediocre performance. As for Citronelle's growth in 1959, it was on the mark—exactly 60 new wells added and the field expanded almost a mile on two sides. The state's oil production did not set a new record, but the *Register* blamed a refinery strike for it. Citronelle's unitization effort made good progress but, the hoped for revision of oil and gas laws failed in the legislature. Still more disappointing, the "law of averages" did not prevail with a new discovery in South Alabama. The *Register's* prediction for the Black Warrior Basin demonstrated its leadership in reporting on energy issues for the entire state, but its crystal ball lied again in that regard. No one found any significantly new gas reserves in North Alabama, although an operator reported testing shallow gas in the Nauvoo area of Walker County.

Still, the paper did some tall boasting in 1959: "Of Mississippi's 148 fields, only one (Baxterville) could boast a better record than the Mobile County field [Citronelle]. . . . Oil men gave a collective hee-haw when Dr. Walter B. Jones, State Oil and Gas Supervisor, predicted early in the life of the field that the giant would have 250 to 300 wells. 'That's absurd,' an oil executive told this reporter. 'I would say we get—conservatively speaking—100 producers.' Today, the field has 100 hundred producers and the limit is not in sight. 'I've studied oil fields all my life,' one independent petroleum engineer said. 'Usually, I can size a field up in three months. But after studying Citronelle for nearly four years, I still can't dope it out.'"

Later that year the *Register* reported big news about a sellout deal at Citronelle. Gulf Oil prepared division orders for almost 1,300 owners and over 3,500 separate interests. They had no desire for the inevitable and con-

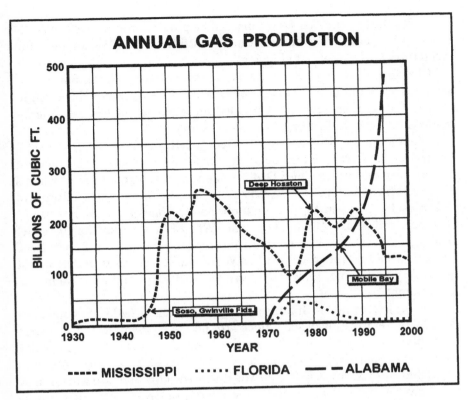

ANNUAL GAS PRODUCTION

Deep Hosston

Soso, Gwinville Flds.

Mobile Bay

----- MISSISSIPPI   ····· FLORIDA   — — ALABAMA

Figure 10. Annual gas production

tentious unitization effort with such fragmented ownership. They wanted out. Gulf halted its Citronelle development drilling program in 1957, just two years after Chesley Pruet and Everett Eaves discovered the field.

Black Bart and the No-Quit Man

Gulf didn't have to look far for an eager buyer. A group headed by Mobile attorney Bart Chamberlain and operator George Jett agreed to buy Gulf's working interest in the field. Chamberlain and Jett's company, the Citronelle-Mobile Gathering System, Ltd., was buying Citronelle's crude for $3.01 per barrel. The Mobile *Register* reported that Gulf sold out to Chamberlain's group for $6.75 million plus an overriding royalty interest.

Because of his love of messy litigation Chamberlain became known as "Black Bart," according to Tuscaloosa consultant and former Alabama State Geologist Tom Joiner. "He accumulated tremendous wealth," Joiner said, "and had a very strong personality. He actually ran the Citronelle unit. He's one of those people, though, that when you're talking about oil and gas in Alabama, you just can't leave out."[6]

When the Oil and Gas Board insisted he plug abandoned wells, Chamberlain told them, "We're in the business of drilling wells! We don't want to spend time worrying about plugging!"

Chamberlain was a behind-the-scenes oil power broker in South Alabama for years but eventually left the country under questionable circumstances. His partner George Jett also left an indelible but somewhat ignominious imprint on the Deep South's oil history.

Like the image his name evokes, George Jett was a restless, resourceful fast-mover. He started out in the oil field trucking business, then moved on to bookkeeping for Big Chief Drilling Company. According to Big Chief's Charles Hayes, "Jett was a very, very energetic person of small stature and wide hips. His penmanship was A-number one . . . one of the best typists I've ever seen, and he also [took] shorthand. When I first worked for Big Chief Drilling we didn't have a secretary in Shreveport. He typed up all the letters. The girls would get [bogged down] on W-2s or drilling reports, and he would say, 'Hell, give it to me.' He was that way. He worked his butt off from morning till night."[7]

In 1953 Jett teamed with Jimmy Kemp, a well established Dallas independent. With Kemp's money, Jett zipped around the oil towns of the southeast in his plane, taking one deal after another, sometimes several in a single day with different people. Often he had a well spudded before the paperwork was done. Bud Norman and Clyde Teel, who did most of his technical work, found themselves sitting so many wells they seldom saw each other. Jett's most significant mark may have been the takeover of Citronelle and his subsequent development work there. The March 18, 1963, *Oil and Gas Journal* called Jett "the man responsible for much of Citronelle's new optimism" and recognized him as the man with the "no-quit attitude." Jett's big problem is he didn't know how or when to quit.

"He was actually keeping two sets of books," Hayes said. "I mean, toward the end, he got to making a lot of money for the company and he [thought] 'Well, I'm not getting enough.' So he started keeping a set on the side."

Kemp accused Jett of raking off cash by not reporting all he had collected. The two parted company, and Jett formed George H. Jett Drilling Company in 1961, but Kemp eventually took him to court where Jett was convicted of fraud and spent a year in jail. Later, he worked for a company in Texas and rarely showed himself in Mississippi again. He died in 1996 at 81.

Jett discovered many fields and, although the conceptual credit for most of those discoveries goes to various geologists who generated the ideas, his involvement in buying an interest in those deals and drilling them was often the primary factor in making them happen. The oil and gas maps of the southeastern regions memorialize Jett. When anyone unfolds one of them, the name Jett invariably appears next to hundreds of well symbols from margin to margin.

A Vision for North Alabama

Most oil professionals gave no more than a hesitant nod to the Black Warrior Basin's petroleum potential, but a few promoters prowled the area, hoping to prove them wrong.

A small independent, Walter Pearson & Associates, decided to chase the Lewis Sand that had produced at Hamilton Field in Marion County. Near the settlement of Whitehouse they found gas in the Lewis, plus two other zones ultimately identified as the Bangor Limestone and the Hartselle Sand, all between 1,300 and 1,600 feet. The Whitehouse Field produced only 28 million cubic feet of gas from 1957 before its abandonment in 1973, but it stirred up enough interest that the Alabama Oil and Gas Board investigated the basin's general potential.

In February 1959, the Board's H. Gene White and Robert C. MacElvain published a paper on the Black Warrior Basin that was visionary in its prophecy. "Although all signs point to a large oil and gas producing potential in northwest Alabama, there are several very serious drawbacks. The most important one is that oil and gas do not seem to follow geologic structures. This is all important in locating oil and gas wells. . . . In northwest Alabama the rocks form beautiful traps, but they contain no oil or gas in commercial quantities, only oil and gas shows or residues. . . . Perhaps commercial pools of oil will be found to be related to, but considerably removed from, geologic faults and folds. If such a pattern of discovery is ever established, the walking beams of oil pumps will become a familiar sight across the landscape of the entire northwest portion of the state."[8]

White and MacElvain's predictions for the Black Warrior Basin proved accurate, although not quite as they envisioned. The "walking beams of pumping units" indeed became a familiar sight across the region, but they were not atop oil wells. A vastly new technology lay just beyond their vision, but they were correct in one respect: in a couple of decades the valve-studded assemblies of gas wellheads sprouted in abundance across the region.

Those Damned Geologists!

Cutting deals was a familiar activity of oil seekers, both big and small. Of them, none was craftier or more successful at it than Chesley Pruet.

The lost eye kept Pruet out of WW II but never handicapped him. He became an accomplished pilot, flying his own plane from job to job and meeting to meeting. Robert Mosbacher, one of Pruet's closest friends, remembered that Chesley once fell asleep with his plane on autopilot, en route to New Orleans. He woke up to see nothing but blue Gulf of Mexico in all directions. Fortunately he had enough fuel to make it back. Another time Pruet had Herbert Hunt on board when he got lost in a wild Nebraska snowstorm.

He found his way out by flying low down the Missouri River to Omaha. Mosbacher said, "He [Pruet] brought the two of them back from the brink."[9]

Pruet's proclivity for falling into sweet deals once happened almost literally. In 1957 he was en route to his office in El Dorado, Arkansas, from Mobile when his twin-engine Beech Travel Air developed engine trouble. He dropped into Jackson to get it fixed and went to the Petroleum Club for lunch. There he struck up a conversation with Ray Raines of Union Producing Company, who offered him a tantalizing proposal. Raines said that there were some very interesting Lower Tuscaloosa sands in Dexter, a gas field in Walthall County discovered in 1957 by Skelly Oil Company, that had not been tested. His company, Union Producing, wasn't interested. He offered Pruet a farmout of Union's interest to test the sands. Pruet immediately set out to lay off some of the risk.

"I [took it] up to get George Hunt's geologist to look at it," Pruet said, "and he said, 'We want a quarter interest.' I wasn't promoting it at all, but said okay. . . . I called Ted Weiner (Texas Crude, Inc.), and he said he would commit to one quarter. But he called back the next morning and said his geologists didn't like the deal. I told him people were running over me to get the deal. So I kept half and George Hunt had a quarter and some of his friends took the other. I drilled those wells and [soon] we were trucking oil out of there. They all made good wells." The field made eleven million barrels.

As the Dexter's production rate quickly reached 125,000 barrels per month, Ted Weiner, whose company had turned the deal down on its geological department's recommendation, called Pruet and asked how the field was performing. When Pruet told them how great it was, Weiner said, "Damn those goddamn geologists!"[10]

The Dexter experience and many others made the oil business fun for Chesley Pruet. Bob Mosbacher recalled that even in the worst of times Pruet was fond of saying, "The drilling business is pure pleasure and profit."

The same year the trouble on Pruet's plane plunged him into such good fortune, Alabama's oil fortunes were spinning collectively out of control. The state legislature was eyeing a situation developing rapidly in the south Alabama oil fields. It passed two bills vitally important to the oil and gas industry of that state in 1957. One levied a county documentary tax, or transfer fee, on leases but exempted them from ad valorem taxes. Many oilmen considered the other bill a life saver of their hopes to unitize the Citronelle Field in Mobile County. That bill authorized the Alabama Oil and Gas Board to require unit operation in any oil field if 75% of the royalty and lease interests signed a unitization agreement. Thus Citronelle was spared the lusty overproduction that victimized earlier giants elsewhere leaving pressures depleted and reserves forever unrecovered.

In the wake of the Board's action, the pace of development in the Lower Cretaceous reservoirs in Citronelle accelerated. By 1956 the field covered 3,000 productive acres.

More Celebrations

The Lower Tuscaloosa activity revived in Mississippi. In January 1958 Shell Oil discovered the Little Creek Field near Summit in Pike and Lincoln Counties. Little Creek proved out over 50 million barrels of oil and 26 billion cubic feet of gas from the Lower Tuscaloosa. The Little Creek Field discovery, which covers over ten square miles of productive acreage, set off another extended and concentrated Lower Tuscaloosa oil play. By June 1959, the 89 wells in Little Creek were producing more oil than any other field in the state.

On the heels of Little Creek and ten miles northeast of it came the discovery of the McComb Field in Pike County, orchestrated by J. Willis Hughes with Sun Oil. Operators drilled 25 successive producers at McComb until Lyle Cashion finally found dust. By the end of 1960, the field accounted for 20% of development activity in the southeastern states. Through 2004 McComb produced about 30 million barrels of Lower Tuscaloosa oil from 190 wells covering about 8,500 productive acres, more than 13 square miles. The Mississippi Oil and Gas Board's early emergency order setting allowables to 300 BOPD helped McComb preserve pressure. Both Little Creek and McComb are uncommonly large stratigraphic traps consisting of reservoir sands draped across a broad structural nose. Both Little Creek and McComb were unitized and converted to secondary recovery operations by water injection. Much later, both fields went through still another transformation—tertiary recovery involving carbon dioxide (CO_2) injection.

When McComb was discovered Charles Hayes had just left Big Chief Drilling Company to try his hand as an independent. On the way to New Orleans he noticed a rig sitting in a field alongside the highway and made a fortuitous decision to pull over. "I'm going down the highway and here's Reading and Bates' rig," he said. "The drill pipe was in the dirt and they're not tearing the rig down. [Hayes knew that if it were a dry hole the rig should have been being dismantled, but apparently it was awaiting delivery of a supply of production casing.] So, I just happened to go into the café and there's every broker, every person that I've ever seen in my lifetime, hustling leases at the Boyd Café. So, I went in and had my cup of coffee, went out and raised my trunk, looked and just happened to have a Pike County Tobin map. I looked at it and I heard a little conversation, and Dave Miller said, 'What are you looking at?' I says, 'None of your damned business!'"[11]

Miller, however, persuaded Hayes to meet with him and Dave Gammill, because he knew Hayes knew many of the mineral owners in the area. Working together, the three acquired several hundred acres of minerals, which were productive as the field expanded. Once again, a Tobin in the trunk, a keen eye for detail and opportunity, and the guts to gamble were highly profitable for an oil seeker.

Larco's Demise

In July 1958 Arkansas Fuel & Oil Company cut two major faults to discover the MaGee Field near the town of the same name on the Smith-Simpson County line. The discovery well, the No. 1 Lavon Womack, tested over 250 BOPD from the Sligo and was reported to have as many as nine pay sands in the Lower Cretaceous. The Magee Field covers only about 900 surface acres but has produced over eight million barrels.

That same month Larco scored again, discovering the Reedy Creek Field in Jones County. Early tests were disappointing and the field was considered marginal for years. But by 1991 the field redeemed itself, producing over 13 million barrels from 26 Upper and Lower Cretaceous reservoirs and 11 Cotton Valley wells.

Shortly after the 1959 Reedy Creek discovery Wil Knight left Larco. He saw the handwriting on the wall. "I left them because they were doing so well in the oil business that they couldn't stand to stay in the oil business. So they got this entrepreneurial spirit to get into the hotel business, and this business, and that business, and they wound up in the casino business in Las Vegas and went completely belly up."[12]

Knight went on to become an institution among Gulf Coast geologists. In his later years Wil used his depth of knowledge and his vast experience to establish a lucrative consulting business, appearing on behalf of his clients before various regulatory agencies as a geological expert witness. In that respect, some remember him as a hired gun, but a fairer view casts him as one of the Deep South's premier trailblazers in the search for oil. Wil Knight died in Jackson at 77 in 1998.

Eating Money

In September 1958, another of Merrill Harris' hunches came true, but not before he was forced to prove his talent at tap dancing between the big gunslingers' bullets.

He mapped a thinning of the Selma Chalk, using some sparse well control information near the town of Bryan in Jones County, Mississippi. He thought the thinning might indicate a deep-seated salt growth structure far below the chalk. He was busily putting a block of leases together based on his idea when Humble busted him. Other than Sun Oil, large companies almost never busted lease blocks being put together by independents, but "this was in the latter part of the year," Harris explained, "when if they had any extra money left over they always went out and spent it so they would get more money after the first. So they just sent a broker buying wild leases and damned if they didn't buy right through the middle of my block."[13]

First he made a tentative farmout deal with Gardner Green, president and principal owner of Central Oil Company, who owned leases in the area. Then he requested a farmout from Humble, only to be told they would take it under advisement. Harris was miffed when he learned that Humble subsequently approached Central behind his back and asked Green if he could get out of the deal with Harris and farmout to Humble on better terms.

Before Green changed his mind, Harris hit the trail to sell his deal and found an interested suitor in Shreveport: Lone Star. There he found that Central wanted to get in touch with him to cancel the deal. He hid out in a Shreveport hotel under a bogus name for a few days to avoid contact with Central while Lone Star looked the deal over.

When it looked as if Lone Star was on the hook, Harris called Gardner Green at Central. "I understand you're looking for me," he told Green. Green doubted Harris could sell the deal. Harris barked back, "Gardner, I've got it! I'll drill a well."

Geologist Marvin Oxley, working for Lone Star at the time, remembered that Harris compared his prospect to Soso, but Oxley thought the prospect was weak. "It was based on an isopach of the chalk, a gravity maximum, a Eutaw structure map, and one bogus—not bogus but it was misinterpreted—seismic line that supposedly showed a little bit of northeast dip."[14] That made Lone Star jittery about the deal. They wanted more information, namely better seismic data.

Harris told them he might be able to find another seismic line. He remembered that Gardner Green said Central had shot a line across the area. He went to back Green and told him he needed that information. Green explained that the quality of the line was poor, the result of a seismic company that had come to him saying they needed some "eating money." Green offered them a small job shooting the line across their leases, but he told Harris, "I don't know whether it's any good, or not." He let Harris examine the line. It offered very little useful information, but Harris worked it into his maps using his proven instinct with a contouring pencil.

"I approximated some dips," Harris said, "and fortunately the dips on the seismic line corresponded with what I had dreamed in. So I took it to Lone Star, and they thanked me. I found out later that the seismic company had gone bust about a month after Gardner made his deal with them and they never got out of town. Did all the shooting in their office!" Harris suspected the seismic company saved money by fabricating the data rather than by going out and shooting it.

The bogus seismic data didn't hurt the outcome. Lone Star and Central operated the initial well, the No. 1 Masonite, discovery well of the Byran Field, which proved out almost 2,000 acres with 61 wells and has produced over 30 million barrels from five Lower Cretaceous and three Cotton Valley reservoirs to date.

Marvin Oxley and Dan Herlihy wrote a benchmark paper, *The Bryan Field—A Sedimentary Anticline,* published in 1974 in the Transactions of the Gulf Coast Association of Geological Societies. The paper greatly advanced geologists' understanding of sedimentary anticlines, popularly known as turtle structures.

Bryan Field became the scene of some pioneering engineering work by Humble Oil. In 1959 Humble experimented with multiple completions in which they ran two and sometimes three strings of two-inch tubing in the same hole, with mixed results.

Steady String of Successes

In 1958 Gulf drilled yet deeper in Soso, a field that had progressively yielded so much hidden treasure. The No. 1 Z.B. Soso Field Unit bottomed at 19,040 feet in the Haynesville and was dually completed from the Cotton Valley and Hosston. That opened Mississippi's first Cotton Valley production and also scored as the deepest oil production in Mississippi to that date.

In January 1959, it was the City of Laurel's turn to celebrate. Merrill Harris, in his characteristic jocular portrayal of the obvious, described the seismic work around Laurel a few years earlier while he was with Union Sulfur. "They had a Petty crew that they didn't know what the devil to do with, I guess, and they said, 'Can you put the crew to work?'

"And I said, 'Yes, I'll find a place for them.' I didn't know a whole lot about Mississippi, but I knew there was a big fault section running from Laurel up north toward Hiedelberg. And we thought, well, I'll just put them in there and let them shoot those fault lines out.

"And they did about six months work, and came back and turned in a map and said, 'We didn't find anything of interest except there's an oil field under the town of Laurel, if you want that.'"[15]

Central Oil Company wanted it. With Chesley Pruet's Zach Brooks Drilling Company, they brought in the No. 1 Mississippi Investments, flowing 252 BOPD from the Paluxy below 11,000 feet. The new discovery, the Laurel Field, lay underneath the town. Like Citronelle, it was a colossal bucket of worms for the landmen. Only a few wells were drilled initially, and reserves looked small. The field did not see mature development until the 1980s and 90s. It eventually became a diverse and prolific field, producing from 29 separate pools ranging from the Eutaw to the Hosston formations. By 1998 it produced over 16 million barrels.

In September 1959 a group led by Jett Drilling Company discovered the Merit Field in Simpson County with a dual completion in the Mooringsport and Paluxy. Field development found 12 separate Lower Cretaceous reservoirs, a significant discovery in an area believed too far down dip for Hosston, Sligo, and Rodessa sand development.

That same month Pan American discovered gas in the Mooringsport at Grange Field in Jefferson Davis County approximately six miles southwest of Gwinville Gas Field. The well surprised everyone by drilling directly into salt from the Hosston. The common Jurassic target formations were absent. In the course of field development, other pools were found in the Rodessa, Paluxy, and Hosston.

Another significant dry hole that bottomed in the Lower Cretaceous was the result of Mississippi's only offshore activity between 1950 and 1954. C.A. Floto abandoned the No. 1 State of Mississippi near Horn Island at a total depth of 13,041 feet with no oil or gas shows reported. The deepest identifiable geologic horizon was the Paluxy at 12,651 feet.

The Giant Sleeps On

Only a few companies dared swallow hard and drill ahead through the Lower Cretaceous section to take a look at the intriguing Jurassic strata. Those rocks were truly unknown territory.

Big wells that flowed thousands of barrels per day from a Jurassic limestone known as the Smackover had been found in Arkansas, but the Jurassic interval was much shallower there. In coastal Mississippi it was deeper. Geologists often speculated that the Smackover might be present in Mississippi since it was found in Union's 12,000-foot dry hole on the Hatchetigbee anticline in Alabama in 1939.

In 1949, the California Company became the first to tackle the Smackover in Mississippi. They drilled in Washington County and found the Smackover at approximately 4,000 feet, but it didn't have the favorable porosity found in Arkansas. Following that, Carter, Murphy, Sun, and S.C. Oil Company drilled Smackover tests in Madison, Issaquena, and Washington Counties.

Rather than the anticipated limestone, Carter Oil surprised everyone by finding a thick sand in the upper Smackover in a deep test on the Pickens Field structure in Madison County. The sand showed gas and oil with a strong H_2S odor in an interval below 11,000 feet.

The same company established the first Smackover production of the 1950s in Mississippi. The No. 1 S.L. Brown in Madison County flowed 240 barrels of condensate per day, plus a huge volume of gas below 12,000 feet, but the production wasn't quite what they expected—the gas wouldn't burn. It was 73% carbon dioxide (CO_2). Nevertheless it was the discovery well for the Loring Field. For many years butane was injected into the waste gas to burn off the H_2S to recover the condensate. In time the well produced a little over a million barrels.

The curious encounter with CO_2 had been seen previously, when the old Tinsley Field was being developed. Union Producing Company's No. 1 Logan tested 2.5 million cubic feet of sour Smackover gas and 68 barrels of condensate per day from their No. 1 Logan. That gas was 93% CO_2 and 6.2% H_2S, which had very little sales value then and was dangerously poisonous. The well was never produced and was eventually plugged.

Interest in the Smackover zone was further stimulated in 1957 when the Phillips Petroleum Company ran a DST about five miles west of Quitman in Clarke County. The test produced a show of oil from oolitic Smackover limestone at 11,500 feet. The well was eventually abandoned below 12,000 feet in the Louann Salt, after penetrating 684 feet of Smackover limestone and dolomite.

In 1958, hope for Mississippi's Smackover revived again. In Scott County four miles northeast of Morton, the California Company drilled their No. 1 Forkville well to the Smackover and encountered nine feet of dolomitic porosity with oil shows at below 13,000 feet, but tests recovered only nine barrels of oil. More tests recovered live oil from the lower Smackover brown dense section, the first such showing east of the Mississippi.

Notwithstanding the encouraging shows, the Smackover eluded oil seekers in Mississippi throughout the 1950s. The failures were disappointing, but, to the profit of those who still hoped and planned for the deep unknown, the Smackover bided its time and awaited its heyday.

Chapter 8

"I don't get mad; I get even."

The rapid growth in the oil industry across the country stabilized by 1957. Oil prices held steady at about three dollars per barrel, and federal price controls held natural gas artificially low. Exploration continued but not at the rate of earlier years. Many oil people began to think that the industry had slowed down and even turned sour.

Geologist Mack Cox, who orchestrated Phillips Petroleum's Mississippi program, left the company to become a consultant and an independent in 1956. By the end of the decade he was burned out. "By 1957 the industry was stagnant, and it was hard for wildcatters to get major company support. The whole ball game changed. It seemed like it became a tax shelter gimmick with some very shady people. I was only 43 years old, but after 23 years, I felt burned out, although I was financially independent. I had moved to Dallas temporarily and then, full circle, came back to Mississippi in 1959 after Little Creek was discovered. To be perfectly honest, I wanted to raise my daughter in Jackson rather than Dallas."[1] Interestingly, Cox's comments on the relationship between the between majors and independents during that era have been echoed almost verbatim time and again.

Perhaps one of the reasons for the lack of cooperation between the little guys and the big guys was the diverse involvement in leasehold acquisition and management. As Mississippi grew into a mature oil producing province, independent operators and crafty individuals who considered themselves operators sprang up in abundance. Dozens of companies and hundreds of risk-takers scurried to take leases on suspected Upper and Lower Cretaceous prospects. Some proceeded on solid geological and geophysical evidence while others followed the pack, looking for culls.

Blockbusters flourished. Some were fairly large companies—Sun Oil, for one—that employed scouts to sniff out where the science-oriented companies were leasing. Most, however, were barbers, bartenders, insurance salesmen, and the like, even chiropractors, who canvassed their oil clientele for leads, then hurried out to lease a few acres in a block targeted for drilling. Where they gained a foothold they wrought havoc, bargaining for exorbitant royalties and onerous farmouts. The blockbusters became such a headache for the operating companies' land departments that they got notorious nicknames, like the "Brookhaven Bandits" and the "Mobile Mafia."

The blockbusting business continued unabated through the decades, prompting one angry Jackson independent, Bob Schneeflock, to counter-attack in 1982. The victim of a notorious blockbuster, he learned that the culprit himself was leasing a block. He quickly formed a paper corporation, busted the blockbuster's block, and sent him his new business card: *Vendetta Oil Company: You Busta My Block, I Busta Yours.* Another independent geologist, Les Aultman, remarked that he wanted to take a shower every time he rode an elevator with a certain loathed Jackson blockbuster.

Divvying up the Prizes

Problems even bigger than those the blockbusters posed troubled mineral ownership issues all across the Deep South. As the new wealth the oil finders created infused the countryside, petroleum leasing operations had to become managed precisely, or else operators stood to lose much of their hard won prize in the courts. Steadily, a new cadre of workers with an eye for detail and a mind for minutiae emerged and took on a vital role. Craig Castle Jr. was one of its pioneers.

The son of a Methodist minister from Madison, Mississippi, educated at Millsaps and Washington and Lee, Castle hung out a law shingle in Jackson. In the mid 1950s he recognized opportunity in the swelling oil industry and partnered with Heidelberg & Woodliff, one of two law firms dedicated solely to oil and gas concerns in Mississippi. The other was the Brunini firm.

He had his work cut out for him. When one of Castle's client oil companies made a discovery, it was his duty to *cure* the lease titles, a meticulous process of determining exactly who owned what. He also determined what portion of the production royalties and revenue each owner and participant would receive, and create that all-important document in the oil business called the *division order.*

"Most of the land problems in Mississippi," Castle said, "stem from the fact that we have large families and no succession—no probates back in those days. So oil people would find themselves sometimes with two families, and there would be an immediate squabble between one set of children and the other set of children, although the law did not make any discrimination."[2]

Other problems Castle and his contemporaries encountered were records lost in courthouse fires and *severed* minerals. Severed minerals resulted when a previous owner had conveyed all or some of his mineral rights to one buyer and his surface rights to another. Often surface owners with severed minerals weren't aware they would not share in a discovery. That almost always caused major headaches.

Other problems arose from tax sales and missing heirs. The underhandedness some mineral owners employed to cheat their own kin often amazed oil attorneys and landmen. "In the Depression more than a third of the land in Mississippi sold for taxes, so you had land that changed hands for sometimes $2.00 an acre—sometimes less than that. Actually there were people who simply couldn't afford to pay taxes. . . . But basically one of the problems was what we called 'missing heirs cases.' This was a case of somebody going off [to another part of the country to live] and other children who stayed, conveniently forgetting about him. And there were several devices by which you stole the land from your co-tenants, and one was to let it sell for taxes and buy it back."

It was difficult work but work that needed doing, and few wanted to do it. Castle's firm flourished with it. Among those he worked alongside were Harry Gwinnup, whom operator Charles Hayes called "the best, ever. The best of the best. . . A-number one!"[3] Others were Roger Jones, Henry Mack Kendle, and Martha Gerald. Gerald, one of the first women to venture into petroleum law, built a major law practice in Jackson. Castle firmly believed that the evolution of oil and gas law in Mississippi elevated the state's overall legal standards. "I do think that when the oil and gas industry came into Mississippi that it helped raise the standards of the lawyers who participated, and because of the presence of lawyers who were so meticulous, it raised the standards all over. Oil and gas lawyers brought a new meaning to real property law in Mississippi. If you were working for an oil and gas company, it was such a great privilege and so lucrative compared to the practice that was available on the street."

Castle closed out his career working independently. He switched hats and fell out of favor with many oil operators when he used his title experience to search the ownership records of producing properties with an opportunistic eye for finding mineral owners overlooked and unrepresented. Finding them, he offered to represent them in a case against the operator or to buy out their interest. The practice was perfectly legal, but operators bitterly dub such work *title busting*.

Mother of the Firm

Walker Watters was another attorney who devoted his career to what explorers considered the prosaic side of the oil business, but he loved it. Martha Gerald asked him to join her oil and gas law firm shortly after he graduated from Ole Miss. "I didn't know if I should," he said, "but I did, and I never regretted it."[4]

A lanky, unpretentious Mississippian with a pleasant personality, Watters' work as a petroleum attorney brought him into daily contact with almost every type of oil and gas person: geologists, engineers, landmen, accountants, corporate executives, and regulatory agency staff. As a result he saw the industry from a unique perspective and became one of the oil business' best apologists.

"The oil and gas business in Mississippi was an industry that provided opportunities that this state had never seen before. Mississippi was an agricultural state.... The opportunities here were limited prior to the oil and gas business. Either you worked in the agricultural industry in some capacity, or in a bank, or in a hardware store, or something like that. When the oil business came here and found a lot of discoveries, it created a lot of jobs and opportunities that the citizens of this state had never really had before.

"Any ambitious person could strike out and make it for himself and didn't have to leave the state to do it.... The person who was attracted to the oil business was sharp and was a risk taker. And usually these people had good personalities because they had to have good personalities to buy a lease or put a deal together, or sell a lease, or to work with people in the industry in any manner."

Dave Gammill was an example. "He [Gammill] could make it in any industry but the game in town at the time was the oil business. And he started his company and got wealthy. He had some reversals later on, but he epitomized to me the type of person who was well suited for the oil business and who prospered from it."

Another person Watters admired was Paul Radzewicz. "He was an unusual type. He came to Mississippi and got in the oil business and made some money. He started in Little Creek Field. Whenever he needed some money he would get in his car and drive to New York and sell a deal and drive back and get a well drilled. But there were all kinds of people in the business. Certainly the Paul Radzewicz type was one prototype. Dave Gammill and Rip Baker were another prototype. But they were all very capable and very interesting people."

Few were as interesting and as capable as the law partner who mentored Watters. Martha Gerald was one of the most respected oil and gas professionals in the oil business. "We were partners for 30 years," Watters said. "I spent more of my time with her than I did with my wife. She was one of the most remarkable women I've ever met."

Gerald walked bent over from a severe spinal deformity that resulted from a childhood bout with polio, but she never let her physical problem hinder her work or her relationships. Watters thought she was unique for many reasons.

Besides being "very, very bright," she was the pioneer female lawyer in Mississippi. She graduated from law school in 1943-44 when most men were away in the military. "Wells Law Firm at the time represented the Chevron Oil company. The war effort demanded a lot of drilling. They were doing the drilling but couldn't get their legal work. They hired Judge Ethredge, who is also a polio victim. And they hired Martha ... to do the title work for Chevron in Lincoln County. They got two of the finest legal minds in the state of Mississippi. Judge Ethrerdge later became the best judge ever on the Mississippi Supreme Court.

"But Martha had a good personality as well as a good mind. And she would stand toe-to-toe with anybody—would never back down when she shouldn't have. She is really one of the legends in the oil and gas industry in Mississippi. She probably had a better oil and gas practice than any one person in this state. As a human being, they just didn't come any better. She never married. The firm was her family. She was kind of like the mother of the firm. She nurtured everyone and was a very generous person. I can't say enough for Martha. I never heard anyone say anything bad about her."

Work like that done by Gerald, Watters, and their colleagues is vital, and oil and gas attorneys are frequently forgotten amid the glory and excitement of deal making and drilling. Yet without their careful behind-the-scene work, chaos would reign supreme throughout the petroleum business.

At the close of the decade, oil and gas law firms, banks, small independent operators, and government leaders pooled their resources to help quell a new panic. The majors didn't want anymore Mississippi crude; they could import it cheaper.

Breakfast with the Governor

The First National Bank of Jackson needed a new CEO. They wanted a savvy businessman with oil experience, and the man they wanted was Bob Hearin. Hearin was no stranger to banking. His father was a banker, but he didn't want to leave Union Producing Company where he was General Manager of Producing and Pipeline Operations in Mississippi, Alabama, and Florida. He was also being groomed to possibly run the company. After thinking it over a few months, he accepted the bank's offer. From then on he was technically out of the industry, yet still very much involved on the business side of oil. One morning in 1959 he received an unusual phone call. The governor wanted to talk with him.

"Ross Barnett asked me over for breakfast so I went over that morning and a fellow named Herman Presley, who was a public relations man for Humble Oil, was there and he had a message for us. Humble was no longer going to buy oil in Mississippi. This was a disastrous blow to us. I guess Mississippi crude was not economically competitive at that time.

"Several days later I got another call from Governor Barnett. He asked me over for breakfast again, and this time it was the executive vice president of Gulf Oil, and he announced that they, too, wanted to cease oil buying in Mississippi. Subsequent to that, Sun Oil Company announced that they wanted to stop buying oil in Mississippi."[5]

Hearin decided he wanted no more invitations to breakfast at the governor's mansion. The governor was concerned and for good reason. A recession in the state triggered by the collapse of oil sales was not what he wanted on his watch. Predictably, a panic began to swell through the Petroleum Club crowd. No one had any ideas how to deal with the blow.

Interestingly, Governor Barnett turned to neither his political advisors, nor the legislature, nor even to the Oil and Gas Board. He looked directly to the industry for help. Hearin's position with the bank made him the *de facto* leader of the Mississippi independent oil businesses. Hearin wasn't sure what to do, but he put out some feelers. He soon got a lead. "A friend of mine called and said, 'There's a guy in New Jersey who's building a refinery and who's looking for crude. They might be able to help here in Mississippi.' His name was Leon Hess.

"So, I picked up the phone and called Mr. Hess. He was pretty abrupt with me. The drift of his conversation was, 'Don't call me, I'll call you!'"

Hearin figured that was the end of that and began rubbing his chin, pondering other ideas, but two weeks later Leon Hess walked unannounced into Hearin's office at 7:00 A.M., saying he just wanted to chat a while. He was interested in crude. They spent the entire day together, and a productive day it was. Hess wound up buying the Gulf refinery at Purvis and the pipeline from Lumberton to Mobile. He then bought the gathering lines at Eucutta, Heidelberg, and Yellow Creek. Hearin said, "We laid a pipeline to McComb in 60 days and picked up that oil [that Sun had stopped buying]. So, I feel like he [Leon Hess] did a lot to bail this state out at the time we really needed bailing out."

Bob Hearin soon found himself sitting on the Board of Directors of Amerada Hess Corporation and a lifetime friend of Leon Hess, not a bad career for the self-professed "half-ass geologist" from South Alabama. Largely due to Hearin's efforts and Governor Barnett's trust in him, many Mississippi oil producers and royalty owners got a reprieve. Now the region's operators could fund their future plans from a reasonably steady and solid market for their existing oil. But market forces beyond even Bob Hearin and Leon Hess' influence were working against them.

A Flood of Oil

The 1960s opened to find the oil market glutted again. Oil poured in from Saudi Arabia, Kuwait, and Iraq. Rapid development of the Middle East fields began as soon as WW II ended. The oil companies that developed the vast reserves became known as the "Seven Sisters." They were Standard of New Jersey (later Exxon), Sony-Vacuum (later Mobil), Standard of California (later Chevron), Texaco, Gulf, Royal Dutch Shell, and British Petroleum. They put their expertise, influence, and financial muscle to work producing the huge reserves in the Middle East and flooded the United States with oil. Crude prices plummeted.

To protect against the surge, the big producing states, mainly Texas and Oklahoma, curtailed production by imposing strict *allowables* on producers. Allowables were quotas on wells, above which producers could not go. That prevented over-production, which could damage reservoirs, with the additional benefit of controlling supplies so oil prices did not fall artificially low; but as the flood of foreign oil increased, states were forced to prorate oil production to fewer than 30 days a month. In the super giant East Texas Field allowables got as low as 20 BOPD with only six days of production a month. The federal government finally reacted to protect the domestic industry and national security. Beginning in 1955 it limited imports to about 14% of domestic demand, a restriction which continued until 1973.

Still, drilling went on, mainly because of tax incentives. Oil producers along the Mississippi-Alabama-Florida coast were too busy to spend time worrying about international market forces. Some decided that to make money on low-priced oil, they needed to find a lot of it and to keep finding it. But at least one group of Southern independent producers adopted the opposite strategy to protect the value of the oil they still had in the ground.

During the oil surplus of the early 1960s, the operators of the Citronelle Field in Mobile County, Alabama, shut the field down rather than accept a threatened price cut of 20 cents a barrel. The shutdown involved a staggering 325 wells. The operators found another market for their crude oil and put the wells back on production in 1962.

No Complaints

While Lower Cretaceous activity stole the spotlight in the early sixties, the Wilcox players stayed busy backstage. In 1961 geologist James Furrh cut ties with his employer and began hunting for Wilcox oil on his own. Furrh was another deeply rooted Texan who found a home in Mississippi. After graduating from the University of Texas, he joined the Ohio Oil Company in 1954 and was sent to Jackson. Later he went independent. His first success was in the Lower Tuscaloosa. "The first well I drilled," he said, "was in the Knoxo Field in Walthall County, and it produced for about 20 years. It made two hundred something thousand barrels."[6] That wasn't a bad start for a new independent.

Furrh had a talent for making good money from small finds, proving that one-well fields need not be economic disasters. After some Wilcox work, Furrh returned to the Lower Tuscaloosa and drilled an extension to the West Lincoln Field in Franklin County between two dry holes, both of which had good shows. "I drilled it and we got 18 feet of Lower Tuscaloosa oil sand and that well is still producing about 50-60 BOPD. It's made over a million barrels since 1961." He and his group offset the well in every feasible direction and came up dry each time. "It had one of those lenticular sands that the Lower Tuscaloosa is so famous for—good permeability, good porosity, and good water drive. But it just didn't cover a lot of area. And to this day we're still puzzled as to why it made so much oil. But we're not complaining."

Furrh's main achievements, however, were in the Wilcox. "From time to time I've had great success in the Wilcox. Other times it's been dismal. But the good thing about the Wilcox back in the 70s and early 80s is it was still cheap to drill. And if you were lucky enough to find it, those wells usually made a pretty good amount of oil. Unfortunately they didn't cover a large area. But it was a very satisfying thing to drill and complete a well. Back in those days—the depth ranged from 4,500 to 7,200—you could drill them usually for about $80,000 and complete them for another $70,000. Many of them have made 400,000 barrels of oil. One of mine made 760,000 barrels. And there are only three wells in the field. It's the Magnolia Field in Adams County." Furrh discovered Magnolia in 1967.

Rarely did a young upstart independent like Furrh meet with quick success without a mentor. Jim Furrh had several, notably the Vaughey brothers, Emmett and Bill. "I think it's wonderful to have older men that will step in and back young people like I was at that time," Furrh reflected. "Army Dorchester[7] also took me under his wings and introduced me to people. He was from Texas. He had a lot of gravity information. As a result he was quite successful."

Furrh learned early to deal with a particular headache for Wilcox explorers, a trap Wilcox players could fall into very easily if they weren't careful. Many prospects had less than 50 feet of structural closure or, in the case of stratigraphic traps, only about 50 feet of height above water. Knowing the exact location and elevation of nearby controlling wells was critical. "Back in the 40s and 50s a lot of people just stepped-off the locations. [They didn't survey them properly.] I had many elevation busts that ruined prospects." Furrh learned never to rely on the accuracy of original surveys of the old holes.

Although Furrh loved doing the intensely detailed Wilcox geology, he discovered that the landwork was another headache. "There were so many people that owned ten acres and five acres, you had a hard time dealing with them. But it was pretty easy to deal with the larger ones. They usually wanted $25 an acre and one quarter royalty. Of course you did everything you could to get away from the quarter royalty. But the larger owners knew that was the going thing."

Despite the heavy royalty burden, the deals sold because they were cheap. "The wells were cheap to drill. If you were fortunate enough to make a well that would make 60-80 BOPD, you could get your money back in 6-8 months, even at three dollar oil. It was an easy way to get a good return on investment."

Furrh went on to drill about 350 wells in his career and made a number of Wilcox discoveries. In addition to Magnolia and Grafton, he discovered Clifford, Second Creek, Apple Grove, and Hutchins Creek, all in Adams County.

Due largely to the efforts of gutsy independents like Jim Furrh, the Wilcox continued to be the most prolific, although not the most profitable, pay zone in the Southeast. In 1964 alone, fourteen new Wilcox fields and thirteen new pools were added. The Clear Springs Field in Franklin County was one of the best and over seven million barrels from pay zones as thick as 30 feet.

The Lower Cretaceous also stayed busy in Mississippi in the early 60s with several significant strikes like Kokomo in Walthall County, which found over 50 billion cubic feet of gas. Another was Knoxo Field in Marion County, a monster whose reserves exceeded 150 billion cubic feet.

More hope for oil, still preferred over gas, arose when the Puckett Field was found in Rankin County. In a deal assembled by Jack Priar, the No. 1 R. H. Allen tested nearly 300 BOPD from Washita-Fredericksburg perforations at 8,600 feet. The field, which contained 35 small Lower Cretaceous reservoirs, eventually produced approximately six million barrels from 28 wells. Despite hope for a big new Lower Cretaceous play in Rankin County, it was not to be. Puckett was a teaser.

In 1961, internal quarrels in one of the most successful companies doing business in the Lower Cretaceous hunt led to a break up that created important new alliances.

Not One Say-So!

Chesley Pruet and Zach Brooks never got along with their partner, E.L. Erickson. Pruet and Erickson clashed many times over the way the business should be run, and Brooks always sided with Pruet. When the two of them worked to reinvest earnings and grow the company, they felt Erickson threw obstacles in their way. "We had a little trouble getting along with Erickson," Pruet said, "because he didn't know the business. Every time we would want to buy a rig or something, we would meet. Zack would tell him we weren't going to count his vote because he was always against it. He would get mad and go."[8]

Prior to his death Brooks arranged for his wife to sell his interest in the rigs to Pruet. Erickson tried to block the sale but failed. Pruet confronted Erickson and laid down the rules. "I told Eric, 'We have a lot of leases and whatnot together, and we are partners, but I am going to run this drilling company. You make the same salary I do, but you are not going to have one say so, because I am going to run it!' We had about $800,000 in the bank and the rigs. 'I told Eric that I wanted to buy his interest in the rigs or divide them up.' He said, 'All right.' We had seven rigs."

Erickson took the cash, and Pruet kept the rigs, though the partnership would continue with respect to their leasehold operations. Then came a severe test of the agreement.

Eric approached Pruet in 1961 and asked him to sign an AFE to drill on a 40-acre wildcat in Jones County, Mississippi, about nine miles east of Laurel. (An AFE, or Authorization for Expenditure, is an agreement to pay one's proportionate share of drilling/completion expenses based on his share of the leasehold ownership.) Pruet was taken aback that Eric wanted to drill a wildcat well on so small an acreage package. One of the wildcatter's basic rules is you don't drill exploratory wells to prove up someone else's acreage. You get as much acreage as you can around your intended test before risking the drilling costs. Pruet said, "Eric, you don't need to drill on just that little acreage we have in there." Now Erickson was forced to come clean. He admitted to making a deal with Union Producing Company for some acreage around the prospect. "I told him he would have to give me my part of that. (When I bought Eric out I told him that we would still partner in the leases we had.) He said, 'No. This is mine because I put it together.' I said, 'You can't do that. That's not oil field business. You're supposed to put that in with the other acreage.'"

They agreed to arbitrate the matter, and the arbitrator ruled in Pruet's favor. Pruet recounted what happened then. "Eric jumped up and said 'No!' He would not. He would give it back to Union first. Ray Raines, of Union, told me that if he (Eric) gave it back to Union, they would give it to me. But he didn't give it to me [my share]. He got it, and got a discovery on it." The discovery was the Pool Creek Field. Erickson's No. 1 Weems hit oil in Sligo and Rodessa, a nice find that produced over 11 million barrels from 33 wells in seven Lower Cretaceous and two Jurassic zones.

Pruet participated in leases he owned jointly with Erickson at Pool Creek, but they never partnered on another deal. Their relationship was sour, but Pruet harbored no ill feelings for Eric. "There is not a person living that I hold a grudge against," he insisted. Years later Pruet went to a hospital in Houston to visit the terminally ill Erickson to make peace with him. The two joked and Eric remarked that he heard Pruet was worth fifty million dollars. Pruet said, "I told him that with my daughters and everything, it might be worth that. But I think it's exaggerated. He hugged me. He was dead in three weeks' time."

As the Zack Brooks era came to an end, a new company that became one of the most successful of the early sixties started on the first day of that decade when a threesome gutted-up for a serious go at oil-finding but found the going tough and hectic.

The Million Dollar Map

Things were at a standstill at Union Producing Company, and Dudley Hughes was restless. Then a timely offer came. American Petrofina (commonly known as FINA), a Belgian company, bought out American Liberty Oil Company of Dallas and offered Hughes a district geologist position. He accepted and opened an office for them in Jackson. Carrol Jones, a landman from Shreveport, joined Hughes.

Hughes and Jones developed prospects and drilled wells for FINA but were confined to several thousand acres of lease inventory FINA jointly owned with Larco. They delivered only one discovery, Boykin Church Field in Smith County, Mississippi, in 1958. Another discovery—Valley Park—proved noncommercial.

Despite a lackluster run with FINA, Hughes and Jones later received an invitation for financial backing in an independent venture from the Vaughey brothers. Hughes, Jones, and Beadie Noel—a tool pusher on FINA's company rig—formed Triad Oil and Gas Company, with Emmett and Bill Vaughey as silent partners providing overhead expenses.

Triad's first order of business was to find a drilling rig for Noel to run, but after several months they had no success breaking into the drilling business. Meanwhile Hughes went to work mapping. Using available well logs, he built a structure map that spanned the Lower Cretaceous trend from Bolton to Citronelle, which soon became known within the company as the "million dollar map."

The map and research associated with it produced some unexpected, though welcome, results for Triad. When the 1960 convention of the Gulf Coast Association of Geological Societies (GCAGS) issued a call for papers, Hughes responded. He shared his ideas with his peers in a technical paper entitled *Faulting Associated with Deep-seated Salt Domes in the Mississippi Salt Basin*. The paper won the "Best Paper" award, and Hughes was invited to present it at the 1961 convention of the American Association of Petroleum Geologists (AAPG).

Suddenly, Hughes was in demand. The AAPG asked him to go on tour with his paper. He agreed and spent six weeks on tour, all expenses paid. "I was given one airline ticket with 35 stops. I made the talk almost every day for six weeks to geologic societies and universities throughout the central U.S. and Calgary, Canada. It opened doors to help sell deals."[9]

Finally, they sold a deal and drilled it, a 5,000 foot Eutaw wildcat. They found nothing. Still, they worked undaunted, farming-in acreage from major companies. Due to the Lower Cretaceous surge of the fifties, most of the trend was still under lease.

On the second try they found the Traxler Field in Smith County, Mississippi on a Chevron farmout in 1960. The well found good production from one Rodessa and three Paluxy sands. The partners' hopes soared but were short-lived. They drilled four dusters attempting to extend production. The new discovery turned out to be a dreaded one-well field.

The group shook off the disappointment and moved on to tackle another idea. Working strictly from subsurface well control, Hughes mapped a graben closure south of Taylorsville, Mississippi, with oil shows in dry holes on its flanks—an ideal drilling target. They checked the land situation and found that Pan American had a lease on the structure in three main tracts that was to expire in only two months. Triad would have to act fast.

Bill Wooten, then a landman in Pan Am's Jackson office, remembered the whirlwind that came through his door. "I was in the Jackson office and Carrol Jones came in and wanted to get a farmout on this block of acreage, much of which I had bought myself. And the leases were all about to expire. Carrol had the idea of creating a 40-acre unit by taking ten acres out of four different sections. Essentially, that would have held the guts of that block. The leases were expiring and we didn't intend to do anything about them."[10] Wooten quickly secured permission to grant the farm-out to Triad, retaining only an overriding royalty interest with no drilling obligation.

"It was very unusual for a major company to move like that," Hughes observed. But Triad had only two months to sell the deal and get it spudded. The partners lost no time. "I worked up some maps and a report and hit the road. The deal was priced at around $90,000. Drilling cost was around $70,000 for a 12,000-foot well." He quickly sold the deal to a number of companies and investor groups. He had retained a minimal one eighth interest for Triad, but upon returning to Jackson he discovered that Carrol Jones had traded half of Triad's interest to another party. That was a serious blow. Triad had a paltry sixteenth.

Compelled to hurry, Noel located a rig that could meet the deadline. Pan Am's land department worked into the night to give Triad a written assignment of their leases. Taxing their limited financial resources, Hughes chartered a plane and flew to Tulsa to pick up the assignment and went to the county courthouses to record the leases. Jones filed for a permit with the Mississippi Oil and Gas Board for a 40-acre drilling unit including a portion of each of the main tracts and filed pooling notices in the Jones and Covington County courthouses. The rig moved in and spudded at 10 P.M., beating the lease expiration by two hours.

The partners breathed a profound sigh of relief, then braced themselves for the anxiety of watching the bit's slow progress. As the hole inched downward the mudlogger recorded numerous shows in the sands of the Upper Tuscaloosa, Lower Tuscaloosa, Washita-Fredericksburg, and Paluxy, over 300 feet of mud log show. After they ran electric logs, they reduced the estimate to 150 feet of oil sand—still a phenomenal pay thickness. Smiling, the group ordered production pipe. The discovery well of the Summerland Field was completed flowing 250 BOPD with several lucrative sands still untested.

Even though Triad ended up with only a sixteenth interest, Jones was unwilling to borrow money to develop the offsets, still gun-shy from the failed offsets at Traxler. Instead he made a deal with the Vaughey brothers to finance Triad's development for half of its sixteenth. Hughes was not happy with the move and convinced the Vaugheys to limit their interest to only the first three offsets. After that, Triad would keep its full sixteenth in the rest of the acreage. That move saved the company.

Triad and its partners eventually drilled 20 wells and proved up 20 million barrels. Some of the wells had an amazing 300 feet of pay. The strike established Triad as a serious contender among independent companies. "We were the operator," Hughes said. "Beadie became production manager and hired field personnel. We added an accounting department and soon had the nucleus of an efficient oil company under way. Even with our small interest it put us in the oil business as a recognized company. . . . We hit the jackpot!"[11]

The euphoria dampened when the group sought a market for their bonanza. They learned a bitter lesson about the power of big oil companies. Only five miles east of the Summerland discovery sat the huge Soso Field in which Humble was buying oil at market price—$3.30 a barrel. The pipeline from Soso ran through the middle of Triad's new field, presenting apparently an easy and ready outlet for Summerland crude. Humble, however, refused to buy the Summerland oil and would not let Triad transport oil through their pipeline even for a fee. Humble, Gulf, and other major companies had a substantial interest in Soso, but no interest in Summerland. The big companies in Soso engaged in some exclusive back scratching, and Humble was allowed to take all the Soso crude. Triad was forced to sell to Miller Transporters at only $1.50 a barrel. Miller trucked it to a terminal where it sold to Humble at a greatly discounted price. The costly trucking and below-market selling continued until Amerada Hess began to buy Summerland crude a couple of years later at approximately $2.25 a barrel—still well below market price, but better for the independents.

Elsewhere, there were new strikes in 1961 with six new fields and twenty-two pool discoveries. In the Collins Field, just east of Collins in Covington County, Mississippi, Pan American Petroleum's No. 1 Windham tested almost 500 BOPD from Rodessa perforations at 14,000 feet—another "turtle" discovery that proved out five million barrels.

The industry was not the only sector with dynamic and energetic people like Pruet, Hughes, Hearin, and others during the early 60s. The government also had a few shakers and movers. In 1961 the watch changed at the helm of the Alabama Oil and Gas Board, in a move that profoundly affected the course of Alabama's burgeoning oil and gas industry. Walter B. "Doc" Jones, state geologist since 1927, had served the state effectively for 34 years. A native of Huntsville, he loved Alabama's woods, water, rocks, and people. According to Alex Sartwell, the Alabama Geological Survey/Oil and Gas Board historian, administration was not Doc Jones' strength, but he was a strong public relations man. He was a visionary and a dreamer, and his enthusiasm was contagious. He loved to travel and promote Alabama's resource potential.

As the state's oil and gas activity increased, so did the need for regulation and oversight. By the end of the 1950s, allegations of conflicts of interest, self-serving agendas, and personality conflicts clouded the climate at the Alabama Oil and Gas Board. Sartwell suggested that the politically appointed members tried to get too involved in the day-to-day management of the Oil and Gas Board and its technical staff. Doc Jones hired what Sartwell regarded as a highly competent professional staff—engineers Bill Tucker and Gene White, and geologists Boyd Bailey and Robert MacElvain—but the Board's bickering and interfering hamstrung their efforts to redefine the state's regulatory role. That took a toll on Doc Jones. "He [Jones] never could quite extricate himself from the Board's meddling," Sartwell said. "Walter B. got really burnt out."[12]

Clearly, the time was ripe for a change of command at the head of an important government agency. The oil and gas industry in Alabama was about to blow wide open, and the new state geologist wasn't quite ready for the magnitude of the challenges to come. But he was a quick study.

Chapter 9

You could fly across the oil fields
and see where the state line was!

Doc Jones knew exactly whom to recommend to the governor as his replacement. He saw no need for a search committee. Philip E. LaMoreaux was waiting in the wings.

Born in Ohio, LaMoreaux lived as a youngster in Arizona, where he developed a curiosity about rocks and landforms. Later, in college at Miami of Ohio, he studied journalism. There, he said, "I met Alton Wade, chief geologist of the Byrd Expedition. He was so interesting that I switched majors to geology."[1] Later he did graduate work in Wyoming and earned a Master's degree at the University of Alabama while he worked part time with the U.S. Geological Survey (USGS). While surface mapping in southern Alabama, he became familiar with oil and gas field operations and industry personnel. In time he became head of the USGS's Water Resources Division in Tuscaloosa.

There he became friends with Doc Jones and the Oil and Gas Board staff while working with them on joint federal-state research projects. LaMoreaux's journalistic talents immediately benefited the Alabama Geological Survey's publishing efforts. Historian Alex Sartwell remembered LaMoreaux's first days in Tuscaloosa: "Phil got along with everybody. He got along with Walter B., and you could see that all of a sudden there was new life in the survey publications. Phil and other people in the USGS were writing things [about] Alabama. Phil was not as much of an oil and gas man as Walter B., but they worked very closely together."[2]

When Doc Jones decided to step down, his replacement was a natural. In May 1961 Phil LaMoreaux took the reins as state geologist and oil and gas board supervisor. (The two positions involve separate but related duties and responsibilities. In Alabama they are vested in the same person.) Sartwell thought that LaMoreaux walked into an administrative mess. Tom Watson, a staff attorney at the time, also noted the profound change in management style. "Basically the Board did what Dr. Jones told them to do," he said. "Then LaMoreaux comes on board, having come from the U.S. Geological Survey Water Resources Branch, and being a federal type and having that background, things kind of tightened up a bit."[3]

The new boss focused on the core objectives of the two agencies he headed. He started by shedding some unrelated responsibilities that had encumbered Doc Jones' administration. He gave the Museum of Natural History to the University of Alabama. He gave the Moundville archaeological project and the Moundville state cattle ranch to another state agency. All the supplementary operations were sapping oil and gas funds. LaMoreaux's preliminary actions caught no one's attention in Montgomery and, as he geared up for his first budget presentation before the state legislature, the lawmakers were unaware of the broad swath he was about to cut through their midst.

LaMoreaux asked Bill Powell of the USGS to accompany him to Montgomery for his first pitch to the state legislature for funds. Armed with weeks of work done by their respective staffs, they arrived at the Senate Ways and Means conference room and sat up their exhibits. LaMoreaux became a ticking time bomb when only three senators showed up: Vaughn Hill, the committee chairman, E.O. Eddins of Demopolis, and Ryan DeGraffinried of Tuscaloosa. He corresponded with them so they already were familiar with the presentation he was about to give. He needed to get the word out to the rest of the committee, or else his work would likely not get proper funding. He checked his watch again as the appointed meeting time of 10 o'clock passed. "We were in this big conference room with a long table and chairs, and with only three senators," he recalled. His anger rose.

"I put up the first graph," LaMoreaux said, "and started to talk about it. Then I put up the second graph and began to get upset. Then I put up the third graph and got more upset." He finally turned to Senator Hill and said, "Senator, this is absolutely ridiculous! My staff has worked their hearts out getting this justification information for you and this group. There are only three of you here, and that's disgusting!" He turned to Powell and said, "Bill, let's pack it up. I don't even want to bother with this anymore."

Senator Eddins got up and put his hand on LaMoreaux's shoulder, calmed him down, and asked him and Powell to wait in the Senate lounge. "I was so mad, I could hardly talk," LaMoreaux said. Eddins came back later and said that the whole committee was present and asked them to come in and make the presentation. It was well received. "Over the next 19 years, whenever I went down there," he said, "there was never a time that there wasn't a full house. I don't think we ever came away from the legislature without getting what we asked." The meeting marked the beginning of an aggressive funding agenda that carried the Alabama Oil and Gas Board and Geological Survey through two decades and transformed it into one of the nation's best.

There was no formal job description for the state geologist, and hardly anyone considered "economic development" a part of the job; but the pragmatic LaMoreaux realized that conserving and developing natural resources created a direct economic benefit. Oil, minerals, and water made money for people. Every politician knew that. LaMoreaux knew what the politicians didn't realize—that Alabama's resource potential had to be marketed. And to be marketed, it had to be evaluated.

LaMoreaux described his program to use natural resources to invigorate the state's economic development: "We were able to get the funds to cover the state with topographic maps. And we began to get offers of cooperation from the counties on minerals, water, and so forth. Those counties were taking that to their chambers of commerce, and the chambers were helping them to get industry to come in [using the maps and publications]. So, people could see the value of water, minerals, and oil and gas maps."

Because LaMoreaux was with the federal government for 20 years he knew where to find federal money for different kinds of natural resource projects. He consistently convinced the legislature to allocate state matching funds, usually half or less, but after a while that began to affect Governor Wallace's programs. LaMoreaux said Wallace once called him and said, "You are going to have to slow down a bit. You are beginning to cut into my revenues!"

Although immensely successful with resource funding, LaMoreaux soon faced another challenge on a different front. The oil fields were a quagmire. The environment was damaged in some places. LaMoreaux recognized that a clean-up was needed, as well as a new and vigorous oversight program.

He knew his work was cut out when he took the job. "When I became Oil and Gas Supervisor in 1961 Alabama's oil fields were in pretty bad shape. We had, for example, salt water contamination and oil field waste strewn all over down in Choctaw County. Bad practices were rampant. This evolved over a long period of time from when oil was first discovered in the state up until the 1960s. The impetus was to discover as much oil as possible and get it out of the ground and not worry much about the environmental impact."

During LaMoreaux's administration, the Love Canal incident in New York sparked a nationwide environmental awareness. In Alabama the most immediate problem was salt water damage. The water some oil and gas wells produce is very salty and, if not properly disposed of, kills vegetation and aquatic life and contaminates freshwater aquifers. Only a few companies deliberately violated Alabama law by dumping saltwater onto the ground or into surface streams. Most practiced a form of disposal they believed to be legitimate, but according to LaMoreaux, was equally harmful.

The producing companies built massive evaporation pits and collected the salt water in them to evaporate, leaving solid deposits that were hauled out by truck. It sounded good, and the companies believed they were being responsible. LaMoreaux and his staff knew that was not the case. "Unfortunately," he said, "many of the oil fields in Alabama are in sandy, permeable [surface] formations and the saltwater was going right down through them into the fresh groundwater and we were contaminating groundwaters in many areas of the state." LaMoreaux challenged the companies. They claimed that the saltwater was evaporating and that the practice was safe. LaMoreaux knew he needed proof.

He turned to his former employer, the USGS Water Resources Division, and developed a monitoring program with their assistance. They drilled shallow monitoring wells around selected saltwater disposal pits and recorded the build-up of chlorides in the fresh water underneath.

LaMoreaux remembered taking the data to the Board. "They [the political appointees on the Oil and Gas Board] were concerned that they didn't have the authority to force the oil companies to clean up the fields. . . . But we [the technical staff] thought we had the authority to require it. If you read Alabama's laws, one of the precepts of the law is to protect natural resources. We considered water as a natural resource. And if a practice was causing groundwater to be polluted, then we had the authority to force a clean-up."

Presented with the data, the companies commenced a voluntary systematic clean-up of all their evaporation pits. Other, safer, means of disposal, like re-injection into deep saltwater bearing zones, became the accepted practice. (Selecting a deep disposal zone was not arbitrary and required technical testimony and Board approval). "It was amazing," LaMoreaux recalled. "Some companies cooperated more rapidly than others, but once we showed them what was happening we had this wholesale clean-up!"

LaMoreaux also hired more field inspectors, saw them properly trained, and required regular rounds and reports. Gradually the environment around the oil fields improved. "Seriously," LaMoreaux bragged, "you could fly from Alabama to Mississippi and tell where the state line was just due to the appearance of the oil fields." In Mississippi's defense, it had more oil fields to police than Alabama. It also had fewer leadership initiatives and less organizational funding.

Under LaMoreaux's leadership Alabama was one of the first states to initiate oil field clean-up programs. The Interstate Oil Compact Commission studied Alabama's research and soon other states followed suit. "It came at just the right time," LaMoreaux said, "because shortly after that we began to get big discoveries, and Alabama rose to about 15th or 16th in the country in the production of oil and gas."

In response to Alabama's growing significance in the world of petroleum production, a new building for the Board and the Geological Survey was dedicated in May 1962 on the University of Alabama campus. According to Alex Sartwell, one of the Board members had wanted to build it in his small hometown of Hamilton, far from the oil patch. LaMoreaux led an alliance of the other members and blocked that idea.

Locating the building on the University of Alabama campus was a prudent move. There the Board and Survey could take advantage of the faculty's knowledge and resources, and it was a prime location for research and development and for the cultivation of cooperative programs with the university, all of which symbolized LaMoreaux's commitment to excellence. "It was one of the finest survey/oil and gas buildings in the country," he boasted. They appropriately christened it Walter Bryan Jones Hall, after LaMoreaux's predecessor, the revered "Doc" Jones.

"We had one of the best three or four geological surveys in the nation then," LaMoreaux said. "We had really nice facilities and a top-notch professional staff. I was so proud of it I invited a bunch of senators to visit. We went down to the first floor and we smelled roasting peanuts. I thought, 'Lord, not now. What's going on?' At last they found the source of the fragrance. Edna Crowell, who for many years tirelessly washed and dried well cuttings for the Survey's sample library, was roasting peanuts for the lab crew in her drying oven. What might have been an embarrassment for LaMoreaux turned into a hit. The entourage enjoyed Edna's peanuts while surveying the new facility and its work.

LaMoreaux and his staff faced further challenges as Alabama rose to petroleum prominence, and, the record shows, they prevailed every time with a balanced approach to the needs of both the industry and the people. At the same time, though, the Mississippi Oil and Gas Board was not enjoying the best of times.

Hands in the Kitty

In 1961 the Mississippi legislature got interested in oil again, this time with vision. In a special session the body voted to float several important constitutional amendments. One paved the way for Standard Oil Company to build a $125 million refinery at Pascagoula in Jackson County, the largest refinery in the country then. Another authorized county supervisors and school boards to grant long-term leases on "sixteenth section" lands.

Early in Mississippi's history the minerals under the sixteenth section of each township had been given to the state by law. A township is composed of 36 numbered sections, each one mile square and containing 640 acres. The 1961 amendment transferred those mineral rights to the respective county school board where the sixteenth sections lay. With the new authority, the respective school boards could grant leases to oil companies and collect royalties for the county's school use. Another amendment extended *ad valorem* tax exemptions to new industry by ten years. Mississippi voters gave the amendments their wise and enthusiastic approval.

In 1962 the Mississippi governor appointed Fred Mellen state geologist and head of the Oil and Gas Board. Mellen was the man who sparked oil fever in the Southeast with the Tinsley Field discovery, yet never found much of it for himself. Somewhat similar to Alabama's Walter B. Jones—more visionary than administrator—he lacked Jones' public relations talents. Mellen's strength was his understanding of the science of petroleum geology and his

unfaltering integrity. Unfortunately the governor was haphazard about selecting and appointing some Board members. Mellen was a man of con-
science and could not work with unscrupulous Board members. "I had a
disagreement with my Board," he recalled, "and I resigned. Some of the members of my Board wanted me to get my hands in the 'kitty.'" He carried his
concerns to the state legislature. "They supported me. They had an audit of
the geological survey books and directed the attorney general and state audi-
tor to take steps to recover funds that were illegally managed by a couple of
members of our Board."[4] Fred Mellen resigned as state geologist in 1965 and
returned to what he loved best—consulting.

As Phil LaMoreaux began his tenure in Tuscaloosa in 1961, a breakthrough
occurred in the Citronelle Field unitization talks. Secondary recovery operations finally began after a long and arduous struggle. Engineer Richard
Stechmann explained the operation in a speech at the Alabama Oil and Gas
Board's 50th anniversary. "In May of 1961 the operators and royalty owners
agreed to the unitization of 139 tracts. The unit was basically located in the
center of the field in the town of Citronelle. . . . Waterflood operations began
in 1961, using the Donovan discovery well. Three additional wells were soon
converted to water injectors at various locations throughout the unit. . . .
Average daily production prior to waterflooding was approximately 6,000
barrels. Production after five months was about 11,000 barrels, almost
doubled."[5]

The mitigation skills of the technical staff at the Alabama Oil and Gas
Board catalyzed the many different interests at Citronelle into a cooperative
effort. The huge Citronelle Field was getting its second wind.

Exploration Spreads Steadily

During the sixties interesting work was under way in *rank* areas of Mississippi. (Rank is the term used for an area far from known producing regions.)
After extensive seismic work in northwest Mississippi, Amerada Hess drilled
a 9,500-foot wildcat in western Yalobusha County. They abandoned the hole
abruptly at 3,890 feet after drilling 510 feet of igneous section. Igneous rocks
are composed of the cooled and crystallized magma that forms the basement
of a stratigraphic basin. Below that point, oil and gas cannot exist, except in
rare situations in which it is squeezed into a fractured basement from overlying sedimentary source rocks.

Amerada-Hess also drilled a stratigraphic test below 3,000 feet in nearby
Panola County and reportedly encountered igneous rocks again. The
significance of those dry holes was the absence of classic producing sections
found further south, revealing a thinning of basinal sediments. That was bad
news for hopeful mineral owners in northern Mississippi.

Except for a few shallow cable tool drilled holes, Tunica County in north-west Mississippi saw its first rotary rig in 1962 when Amerada Petroleum, cueing on a seismic *high*, drilled below 6,000 feet. They bottomed in the Cambro-Ordovician-age Knox and plugged.

Placid Oil Company drilled a strange well in 1962 on the western side of the Jackson Dome in Hinds County. They lost mud circulation in the Gas Rock at about 2,800 feet, indicating that the well had pierced a highly porous layer that sucked up the drilling mud. A crafty local real estate developer suggested that the well would make an excellent sewage disposal well. The crew referred him to the Mississippi Oil and Gas Board who determined the matter was out of their jurisdiction. They in turn referred him to the State Board of Health, where his idea languished.

That same year in Smith County, Mississippi, Triad (Hughes, Jones, and Noel) developed another idea that didn't languish. They noticed that the California Company had drilled a dry hole some six miles west of Triad's Summerland discovery of the prior year. It appeared that the hole was upthrown on the same regional graben that formed the Summerland Field and that a structural closure existed in the downthrown block. The concept was a look-alike to Summerland. Triad wasted no time soliciting a farmout from California.

California agreed, but with a stipulation. They didn't believe in the downthrown potential and required that Triad drill its well upthrown near the dry hole California drilled. Triad balked at the idea but finally reached a deal by agreeing to drill first at their preferred location in the graben. That test would incur an option to drill outside the graben. California reluctantly agreed. In December 1962, Triad found oil in the graben, completing a 300 BOPD well from several of the same sands as Summerland but predomi-nately from the Paluxy. After drilling a dry hole upthrown at California's pre-ferred location, Triad developed a five million–barrel discovery that became the Mize Field.

Triad continued its hunt in Smith County the following year when Dudley Hughes mapped another turtle structure. The company acquired some leases and farmouts and drilled a 12,000-foot Rodessa-Sligo test. The well hit oil, and Triad drilled several offsets in what became the South Center Ridge Field. They quickly realized, however, that the reserves in the wells were too small to be reasonably profitable on 40-acre spacing. To reduce the number of wells by one half yet still recover the same volume of oil, Triad petitioned the Missis-sippi Oil and Gas Board for a special 80-acre exception to the statewide 40-acre oil well rule. Other independents and landowners threw up a furious opposi-tion, but the Board granted the exception. South Center Ridge eventually produced only 2.5 million barrels before being abandoned, but the wider spac-ing requiring fewer wells being made it profitable.

Triad's string of successes continued in 1963 with the discovery of Blackburn Field in Jones County, Mississippi. A graben structure was again the target. In an almost identical replay of the Mize Field deal, Triad farmed in a block of acreage from Sun, who had drilled an upthrown dry hole. Triad's 13,000-foot graben test found oil in the Washita-Fredericksburg and Paluxy with minor production in the Mooringsport and Rodessa. Blackburn has produced 2.5 million barrels from six wells.

Later in 1963 Jimmy Morgan and Alexander Field Chisholm approached Triad's Dudley Hughes seeking advice. They helped him and his brother Dan drill wells in the Hughes brothers' New Mexico venture a few years earlier. Returning the favor, Hughes looked at their deal. Morgan and Chisholm wanted Hughes to evaluate an acreage block and pick a location.

Jimmy Morgan was no newcomer to the oil patch. He worked as a roustabout in the 1930s and was the only man on record to descend a borehole. He was working on a rig in Marianna, Florida, in 1932 when the hole suddenly lost circulation. Morgan was lowered down the conductor pipe to a depth of about 20 feet where he found the hole had penetrated an open cave. "As far as I know I was the only stupid fellow who ever went down a hole," he said.[6] Later Morgan became a landman, scout, and independent producer.

Using only gravity and limited shallow well control, Hughes picked a location six miles southeast of Pool Creek Field in Wayne County, Mississippi, which Eric Erickson, Chesley Pruet's former partner, found. Yet again the target was a graben, and Hughes stuck with his strategy of targeting the downthrown block. The well struck oil in the Lower Cretaceous and the Lower Tuscaloosa. It became the Wausau Field, and the Chismore Company eventually completed 12 wells, which produced over six million barrels. More wells were added in the eighties and nineties. Hughes had no financial interest in the field but received a prized doubled-barrel shotgun for his help.[7]

Sun Oil paid dearly for valuable scientific knowledge in 1963 with a dry hole in northern Clarke County, Mississippi, where they drilled for the Smackover at a projected depth of 11,500 feet. After penetrating the Jurassic Cotton Valley, they encountered Paleozoic Pennsylvanian-age rocks at a depth of only 9,891 feet. The well provided additional evidence of the buried Ouachita Over-Thrust Belt in the subsurface of central Mississippi, believed to separate the Interior Salt Basin and the Black Warrior Basin. Additionally, Sun's well helped define the northern or updip limit of Smackover deposition. Many geologists were thankful Sun had recovered such valuable information about a largely unknown subsurface region. Others were thankful about the oil business in general.

In October 1963 the *Laurel Leader-Call* proclaimed Laurel, Mississippi, the "Oil Capital of the Deep South" and asked its readers a timely question: "Do you know the value of the oil producing industry in Mississippi?" The next nine pages answered the question. The story concluded with a resolute editorial counsel to the area's citizens. "We believe it is the duty of every good citizen to be familiar with the various industries which support our city's economy. . . . Please read about it, think about it, discuss it with your friends."[8]

One keenly observant citizen didn't need a newspaper to convince him of the opportunities the flourishing oil business offered. He didn't know much about it, but he knew he wanted to get his foot in the door. There were hundreds like him, but he had a mental attribute that helped him succeed in a business where perseverance is critical to success.

Total Recall

Jim Stewart was a determined man. His tall robust features caused heads to turn where ever he went. When he spoke—which was often—his passions came out with clarity and emphasis. Nobody had to wonder where Stewart stood on an issue.

He earned a degree in business administration from Southern Mississippi and started out in real estate, which he found patently dull. He knew nothing about the oil business but became interested through some oil people to whom he sold real estate. "I met Don Hugus, Jeff Tucker, Marvin Oxley, and Bob Bertolet—that's who I ran with. When one of them would go to a well to perforate, or something, they'd invite me along. After about two years, they said, 'Jim, you ought to go and buy some royalty.'"[9]

Stewart taught himself to run records at the courthouse and pestered his friends about geology. "I'd ask Marvin, 'Tell me about these sands that are shaling-out at McComb.' And Marvin would explain it. Then I would run into Dee Layman, or Hilton Ladner, or somebody, and say, 'Tell me what shaling-out of sands means,' or 'What's a fault?' So, I kept asking many questions. I can go to a party and not remember anybody's names five minutes later. But if it's something I'm interested in, like a well log, or a show in a well, or a name of a company man—things I'm interested in, like the oil business—I've got total recall of everything."

He told his father he was quitting his job to get into the oil business. He decided to start with his own family's holdings and headed to the courthouse. Passing the chancery clerk's office he stopped by and introduced himself and told the tax assessor that he was now in the oil business and if he (the assessor) heard of anyone who wanted to lease, to let him know.

Stewart had scarcely arrived in the records room when a phone call came for him. It was the tax assessor. The man told Stewart, "I've got a lady on the phone, Miss Maude Hare. She says they are moving a big rig in right across the road from her. She wants to lease her land. She's got 40 acres." Stewart could not believe his luck. He sped out to Maude's house and found the biggest drilling rig he had ever seen only a few hundred feet from her doorstep. Furthermore, Maude had called her friend Cora Bilbo, another elderly single lady who lived on the other side of the rig, and found that her 40 acres also were not leased.

Stewart checked the records and saw that both tracts were leased, but the rentals had not been paid, effectively nullifying the leases. (Rentals are small annual payments to a mineral owner to hold the lease until it is drilled.) He cut a deal with the women and borrowed some money from his skeptical father to pay them. Leases in hand, he headed for the office of the well's operator, Arkansas Fuel Company in Jackson. Presenting himself to the secretary he said, "I want to offer you two leases offsetting your well in Pearl River County."

She went back into the manager's office, and Stewart heard him say, "Tell that fool there are no leases available down there. We've got it all leased!"

She came out and told Stewart the manager was not interested. Stewart said loudly, "You tell that man in the back that he didn't pay his rentals!"

Suddenly the boss came out saying, "Hi. I'm Jack Phillips. How are you? Come back here, son."

Mr. Phillips' attitude changed miraculously, and he cut a generous deal. The well came up dry, but that didn't matter to Stewart. He made a profit, and he was now legitimately in the oil business. His learning curve took a sweeping turn upward as he bought and sold leases and kept an opportunistic eye on the happenings around the oil patch.

Yet he knew he couldn't just wait for fortuitous phone calls; he needed a method. He bought a 1 inch=1,000 feet Pistol Ridge field map—no geology, just well locations. He read the monthly production reports carefully and marked his map with symbols. "If [a well] made half million a day, I'd put a red x; less than half million, a minus red x; a million a day, two red x's; a million and a half, three x's, and so on. Then I'd watch the production and I would notice if a unit wasn't producing . . . in a particular zone."

The meticulous mapping soon revealed an opportunity. Stewart saw that Gulf Oil had completed a Eutaw well with no offsets to it that was making two and one half million cubic feet per day. He said to himself, "They [probably] won't give me a farmout on that [the Eutaw]. How in the world can I get it?" He had nothing to lose but his time. He asked Gulf for a farmout to drill the deeper Massive Sand test. He figured Gulf might grant the farmout because both he and they knew that the Massive was probably dry on that unit, and thus maybe he could sneak in a provision to earn the rights to everything above the Massive, including what he really wanted—the Eutaw. Gulf took the bait and granted Stewart the farmout. He set about to turn his deal.

He walked into the office of Hilton Ladner and Robert A. Lee, who worked close-in drilling deals and ran a map service called Mississippi Subsurface

Map Company. Hilton Ladner already had a reputation as a crackerjack subsurface geologist. "I walked in, not knowing what I was doing," Stewart said. "They looked at it. They were very active in that area. They were flabbergasted that I had the thing and that they didn't know about it. They said, 'What do you want for it?' I said, '$5,000 and one eighth carried interest to casing point.' They looked at each other and said, 'Wait.'

"They took it next door to Slim Allen, who had piles of money, and shared an office with them. They sold Allen half. Then they came back and said, 'Okay. It's a deal.'"

The group drilled the well and found oil in one Eutaw sand and gas in another. They drilled a second well and got 17 feet of pay in the Massive. There was a pipeline right on top of them. It was Stewart's first success.

Then he conjured another deal. He found a well Larco drilled in the Maxie Field that was plugged and abandoned but looked very good on the logs. He assembled a land package on his idea and went back to Ladner and Lee. "They said, 'What do you want for it?' I didn't charge them enough last time, so I said, 'You're not buying it for $5,000 this time. I'm not taking a cent less than an eighth and $7,500.' They said, 'Wait here.' They walked next door to Slim Allens's office and sold him half, then came back and said, 'It's a deal.'"

The group got another producer. It made two and a half million cubic feet a day, and Stewart had an eighth of it. "Hell, I thought I was rich!" he said. They told him that the well would last 15 years because there wasn't anything draining it, but then came the first of many setbacks—the Alaskan earthquake.

"The earthquake registered in Mobile—I don't know how much. The pumper called the next morning and said, 'We've got a problem. There's no pressure on the well.' We thought the cement had collapsed. We block-squeezed it twice but we never got the well back. It was making two million cubic feet a day before the earthquake. And apparently there was enough of a tremor that it broke our cement job to where we never could get it back. That was it."

Things got tough for Stewart after that. Everything he touched turned sour, and he had started a family. He couldn't sleep or keep food down under the pressure to find a deal to turn. The family doctor told him he needed to dump the worry or else plan on getting sicker. "I walked out of there and kicked myself in the rear end and started getting with it."

A couple of weeks later opportunity reared its elusive head again. The old Flora Field, located 20 miles northwest of Jackson, had been dormant for decades, but Stewart learned that a man named Ben Edwards had decided to make a saltwater disposal well out of one of the old producers. When Edwards perforated the well so saltwater could be pumped into the formation he got a huge surprise. It came in flowing almost 1,500 barrels of oil per day. He had to call in bulldozers to dig pits for the oil, a practice allowed only in an emergency today. "When I heard about it," Stewart said, "I called my wife's uncle who owned some land right up there by the well, and I asked him if his land was leased." Part was not. When Stewart checked the courthouse records, he found a huge lease only 600 feet from a second well that Edwards had put down, which was making 150 BOPD. He sprang into action again. "I went to Hilton Ladner. Bob Lee was gone. I said, 'There's 1,820 acres of Anderson lease open 600 feet from the well that is pumping 150 BOPD and another one flowing 1,000 BOPD. I took a sample in this pickle jar, and it's all oil. There's no saltwater!'. . . . I asked the Miller Oil truck driver and he said they had four trucks running in and out of there hauling oil as fast as they can. And they've been doing it for a month and a half.'

"'Let me check it some more,' he said. He called me back the next morning and said, 'Jim, come up here.' I went up there and he said, 'This is a gut cinch. It'll make a well! Not only that, but it'll make a bunch of wells! Show me exactly what's open.'"

The problem was, there were 95 different mineral owners under the tract. When Edwards found out Stewart and Ladner were trying to get those leases, he reportedly laughed at them, but within 60 days the leasing was completed and the two turned a drilling deal that resulted in a 150 BOPD well. Ten more producers followed without a dry hole.

"That's more or less how Hilton and I got thick," Stewart said. The two would work many more close in deals in the Wilcox, Eutaw, and Lower Tuscaloosa, but perhaps they made their main mark a few years later when they were among the first explorers open up the treasures of the Black Warrior Basin.

A Down-hole Tug of War

As Stewart and Ladner did at Flora, two larger companies decided in 1963 to experiment with finding some new pay in an old field, but they ended up in a tag team wrestling match thousands of feet down. Possibly inspired by Triad's graben successes, Texaco tested the graben in the old Pickens Field and found oil in the Selma Chalk (Upper Cretaceous).

Cities Service Oil Company then drilled on the 40-acre unit next door to Texaco and lost mud circulation in the chalk. Cities proceeded to dump cottonseed hulls, peanut hulls, shredded plastic, gravel, and other material down their hole, in a common practice to plug the voids in the chalk. If successful, they might regain normal circulation and continue drilling.

Soon thereafter, Texaco began producing cottonseed hulls, peanut hulls, and plastic in its well. The junk had migrated through the reservoir and killed the oil production in Texaco's well. On the other hand Cities was delighted because their technique succeeded. They regained circulation and completed the well as an oil producer. Texaco reworked their well and also reestablished oil production.

In the end, all was for naught, as neither well paid out, though the companies gained valuable technical knowledge for the future. They had shown that the Selma Chalk could be so fractured in places that bulk foreign materials under sufficient pressure migrated horizontally through the reservoir rock.

Light Activity in Alabama

Exploration in the Black Warrior Basin was negligible during the sixties. The basin is primarily a natural gas province, and due to artificially low Federal price controls, operators considered gas hardly worth the effort and expense. Still, Shell Oil attempted a couple of deep tests in the small Siloam Field in Clay County, Mississippi, which Carter Oil, Inc., found in 1953. One well bottomed in the Ordovician below 11,000 feet. They found weak gas production in two Pennsylvanian-age sands. The same year McLean and Hill found a small oil well in a Mississippian sand in Monroe County, Mississippi, which they dubbed the South Amory Field.

A few other dry holes yielded some useful information for the Black Warrior's future. Among them was the No. 1 Lee, a Pickens County, Alabama, test by SONAT (Southern Natural Gas Company) and Geochemical Surveys, Inc., that reached a total depth of 10,250 feet. That well was originally permitted to 7,000 feet and was by far the deepest well in the Alabama portion of the Black Warrior Basin up to that time.

Farther north, Gulf Oil drilled a stratigraphic information test well on a topographical feature known as Wiley Dome in north Tuscaloosa County in 1962. Originally permitted to 5,500 feet, the hole was drilled to 11,060 feet, starting in Paleozoic Pennsylvanian-age rocks and going through Mississippian, Devonian, Silurian, and Ordovician-age strata. It found the top of the Knox section at 5,705 feet and bottomed in the Cambrian. Geologists gained valuable information about the nature of the deep rocks, some of which, like the Knox, produced in other regions of the country.

Elsewhere in Alabama the Continental Oil Company tested small amounts of oil from the Smackover in their No. 1 Trice well in 1963. The well, about a mile north of the Gilbertown Field in Choctaw County, was abandoned after testing but it encouraged more Smackover exploration in the region.

The following year Mississippi recorded its third Smackover discovery, the Barber Creek Field in Scott County. Pan American Petroleum tested over 200 BOPD from the Smackover below 15,000 feet. Previous Smackover discoveries in the state were the Loring Field, which was mostly CO_2 gas, and the single oil well Bienville Forest Field. Like the first two Smackover finds, the Barber Creek Field was not a significant strike. Only three wells were completed in the field and a bit over one million barrels were produced through 1999, but Barber Creek kept Smackover hopes alive in the wake of a steady stream of failures across the region.

A discovery in Florida turned some heads that direction in 1964. The Sunshine State saw a long dry spell after its first oil discovery in 1943, the Sunniland Field.[10] Sun Oil Company made the new discovery, which flowed over 400 BOPD from the Sunniland limestone/dolomite (Lower Cretaceous) below 11,000 feet. The State of Florida named the new find Sunoco-Felda Field. Humble also completed a Sunniland Field well in 1964 that flowed at 736 BOPD, a Florida record.

Over the next three years Florida completed only ten successful wells and 24 dry holes. Florida operators were disappointed, and few if any could predict the strike in that state that stunned the North American oil business a few years later.

The Million Dollar Letter

Among the Smackover seekers in Mississippi in the mid 60s were two big sisters who weren't on speaking terms. Skelly Oil Company had something Shell Oil wanted—leases. Shell had something Skelly didn't—seismic data that showed a prospect on those leases. Shell suspected that if they asked Skelly for a farmout, Skelly would suspect Shell knew something they didn't know and refuse it, so Shell decided to get the farmout on the sly. For that, they needed a middleman. Chesley Pruet was the perfect choice because he had gotten many farmouts from Skelly.

"Shell's landman in Jackson called me and asked when I was coming to Jackson. I told him I could come any time," Pruet recalled.[11] The Shell people showed Pruet some Amoco seismic work done near the town of Bay Springs. How they got the Amoco seismic is not clear, possibly the seismic shoot was a joint program. Shell was aware of Pruet's close relationship with Skelly. They proposed an interesting deal.

The plan called for Pruet to obtain a checkerboard farmout from Skelly to drill a Smackover test. If Pruet got the farmout, he would assign it to Shell. In return, Shell would give Pruet the drilling contract, as well as an interest in the well. Pruet agreed, and Shell prepared a letter for him to send to Skelly. Skelly granted the request, and Pruet conveyed it to Shell.

Then it got complicated. Another big sister got into the act—Amoco, the company that shot the seismic. They found out that Pruet had the farmout they were considering asking for themselves. Amoco's Joe Hildebrand in New Orleans called Pruet and said he (Hildebrand) was in big trouble. The head office in Tulsa suspected that the seismic information had been leaked to Pruet. Pruet disclosed that the scheme was Shell's, because he wanted to remain in good stead with Amoco. That forced him to tell Shell that Amoco was privy to the deal.

Amoco and Shell cooperated, and Shell made good on their promise and gave Pruet an eighth interest plus the drilling contract. Pruet spudded the well one mile east of Bay Springs in Jasper County in January 1965. The early results did not look good.

Shell geologist Stew Welch was assigned to sit the well. When they ran the logs, the Smackover looked marginal, but Welch remembered that the samples he saw uphole in the Cotton Valley at 14,500 feet had weak shows. "It had a little asphaltic show in the upper 15 feet," he said, "and that was about it—no fluorescence or cut. The problem, as it turned out, was the sand was like loose beach sand. . . . They [the crew] were literally washing all the oil out of the samples. The sand grains were so loose the oil wasn't sticking to the outside of the grains."[12]

That hunch led Welch to order sidewall cores to be shot in the Cotton Valley. (Sidewall cores are about the diameter of a nickel and an inch or so long. They are obtained by shooting small core barrels horizontally into a selected rock interval and recovering them on the surface for analysis.) "We got all kinds of oil show. But it was lower resistivity than it should have been, so we still weren't that excited about it," Welch said. In a last ditch effort to find something before declaring it a dry hole, Shell perforated the Cotton Valley in a sand section that became known as the Bay Springs Sand.

They tested almost 600 barrels of oil per day of sweet light crude. The pressure was high, and the pay sand thickness was nearly 70 feet. "One like that will make a believer out of you," Stew Welch said.

Prior to the Bay Springs discovery the only Cotton Valley production in Mississippi came from a deep test at Soso drilled in 1958 as part of an agreement with the landowners to sign the Soso unitization agreement. That well was not good enough to cause excitement over the Cotton Valley.

The Bay Springs Field was a different story. It eventually produced over 35 million barrels from 31 wells covering about 1,200 productive acres. At a time when oil was still selling for three dollars per barrel, Chesley Pruet sold his one eighth interest—that he got writing a letter—for over one million dollars.

Bay Springs seemed to be a lucky break for Pruet but he regarded himself as a hard worker who earned his luck. He told Dudley Hughes, "I'll tell you something, and I firmly believe this. Ed Hudson told me that one hundred per cent of what a man accomplishes in life is luck." Hudson, a close friend of Pruet's, was a successful oil man who owned enormous blocks of stock in Amoco and Halliburton. "I said, 'Mr. Hudson, I find that the harder I work the luckier I get.'"

Hudson said, "You're just lucky you were born with the genes that make you want to work!"[13]

Pruet proved he had the genes. As the turbulent sixties drew to a close, he stayed busy flying from one southern oil city to another picking and choosing deals as he went. Another opportunist was also busily shopping for deals. His pickings were smaller, but his involvement was noteworthy since he was not really an oilman. He was a brain surgeon.

Gotta Make a Livin'

Charles Neill came to the Millsaps College campus one day and saw a drilling rig going up. The college sat right on top of the Jackson Gas Field. With growing curiosity he watched it drill ahead day after day. Finally it struck gas with a roar that rattled the windows in the college's buildings. Neill was hooked.

He took some geology courses and announced his intention to become an oil professional, but his grandfather, C.R. Ridgway Sr., patriarch of a prominent Mississippi oil family, advised a more cautious approach. "You can get rich in the oil business, but you must first have a way to make a living."[14] Neill took his advice. He followed two uncles into the medical field. After schooling at Millsaps, Ole Miss, and Cornell, and serving in the Army Medical Corps during WW II, he opened practice in Jackson as a neurosurgeon, but he never forgot his early fascination with petroleum, and when he got back to Mississippi the oil fields were popping with excitement.

One of Neill's uncles, "Preacher" Ridgway, who bought and brokered thousands of acres of minerals and royalty, mentored the young doctor and convinced him that his grandfather was right—you could get rich in the oil business. Neill invested with Lyle Cashion in the 1950s and made money he used to drill his own deals. He fell in with J. Willis Hughes and Dave Gammill in 1959. They began sweeping through the McComb area buying leases. As Sun Oil developed the new McComb Field, it ran into the group's leases at nearly every offset. They bested Sun at its own game—blockbusting. Neill ended up with interest in 15 wells at McComb.

He succeeded in Mississippi and Louisiana while keeping up a thriving medical practice. At one point he was president of the Southern Neurological Society. Dr. Neill participated in Mississippi oil deals into the 1990s, long after he retired from medicine. He was one of a rare few who loved and succeeded in two challenging and fascinating professions simultaneously. But an astute eye for opportunity was not limited to crafty individuals like Chesley Pruet and Dr. Charles Neill. Some big corporations also had sharp eyes.

You snooze, you lose

The mid sixties saw a gas discovery in extreme southern Mississippi that didn't seem terribly exciting at the time. In the summer of 1965 Humble found the

Waveland Field in Hancock County. Only a few miles from the coast, it became the southernmost significant petroleum discovery in Mississippi. The discovery well tested good gas flow rates from two Lower Cretaceous zones.

The second well also succeeded, though with the low price controls on natural gas Humble did not consider the discovery an economic success. Still, the two wells produced with practically no pressure decline for ten years. When the government let the price of gas rise to competitive levels in the 1970s, Phillips Petroleum and Saga Petroleum began snooping around Waveland and saw what Humble apparently did not—that the wells were evidently draining a huge reservoir.

Then Phillips' landmen reported that Humble let thousands of acres of leases around the two wells expire. The two companies promptly leased that acreage and developed a field that covered 20,000 acres (over 30 square miles) with 37 wells on 640-acre spacing and produced a staggering 160 billion cubic feet of gas.

In the summer of the Waveland discovery Phillips scored with the deepest production yet in the southeastern United States. Their No. 1 Josephine "A" in Perry County tested 1 million cubic feet of gas per day from Smackover at a depth of over 20,000 feet. The high bottom hole pressure of 14,500 psi and temperature of 366 degrees F were among the highest recorded in any producing zone at the time. The gas, however, was comprised of 76% hydrogen sulfide. They named the discovery the Black Creek Field.

Phillips figured the field would be profitable for its sulfur content and sold half interest to Pan American Sulfur Company. A second produced similar results. Keeping the tubing open was a problem because the sulfur tended to plug it. Phillips had to order costly specialized tubing. Soon thereafter the price of sulfur dropped, and the operators abandoned their plans.

While Phillips struggled with their H_2S problem, Texaco tapped into a nice gas find in Walthall County, Mississippi. They tested dry gas from two Paluxy reservoirs, discovering the Darbun Field. The well flowed a total of seven million cubic feet per day from 13,000 feet. Future development of the area saw the Knoxo, Kokomo, and Darbun fields become one large dry gas field producing from multiple zones in the Paluxy and Washita-Fredericksburg formations and oil from the Lower Tuscaloosa.

Exciting things happened in the early sixties in Mississippi, where there was much new production. Explorers made notable advances in understanding the dynamics of Lower Cretaceous oil traps. Extensive drilling by major oil companies and aggressive independents fueled an exponential rise in geologists' subsurface knowledge, which in turn spawned more ideas, more deals, and more strikes.

Chapter 10

A Winning Team Falls Apart

The mid sixties saw the dissolution of one of the period's most successful companies. By the end of 1964 Triad Oil and Gas had found and developed four significant fields and several minor ones and was operating over 60 wells producing almost 7,000 BOPD. The small company's achievements were phenomenal.

Success, however, divided the partners. Dudley Hughes described the growing rift. "Carroll Jones, the partner who at first wanted to take no financial risk now wanted to become another Humble. He gave the partners an ultimatum that he would run the company with no interference or we would split up. In 1965 we split the company and divided the assets."[1]

The news upset the Vaughey brothers, Triad's silent partners. They liked being on a winning team and expected a long-term relationship. Beadie Noel sold his share of production and retired financially well off. Jones took the office space and the employees plus his quarter of the production. He kept the Triad name, hired a geologist, and with Tom Aitken handling the operations, attempted to expand the company. Hughes said, "Within six months they went broke. Tom Aitken took over Triad and turned it into a commercial operating company with no personal ownership interest in the production being operated. My secretary, Marge Edwards, left Triad to become my only employee, and I started over as Hughes and Hughes, Inc., with a two-room office in the Petroleum Building [in Jackson]."

The Hughes brothers turned their attention to Canada, where they became involved in a major natural gas discovery in the Peace River area of Alberta, but Dudley stayed in Mississippi and continued to look for oil lurking within the salt structures. He succeeded again in 1965, finding a west fault segment in the MaGee Field, Simpson County, which resulted in four wells.

Mississippi also achieved a new depth record in 1965. The Shell-Placid No. 1 W. P. Barnes was plugged at a total depth of 20,970 feet, eclipsing George Vasen's old record of 20,450 feet, but Shell's record didn't last long. The very next year Phillips Petroleum's No. 1 Zellerbach "B" reached 21,052 feet in Simpson County, but it was also dry.

For Mississippi operators who preferred discoveries over depth records, 1966 was a banner year. They brought in 31 new fields. By far the most active trend in Mississippi that year was the Wilcox, with 19 new field discoveries.

One of the best of the new Wilcox fields was Hazlet Field in Wilkinson County, where Germany-Gulman gauged 120 BOPD from the Walker Sand. The field produced over four million barrels.

Germany-Gulman scored again in Adams County with the discovery of the Cotton Valley Field (not to be confused with the Cotton Valley rocks of Jurassic age), which flowed 157 BOPD from the McKittrick Sand. The field, a mile south of the prolific Quitman Bayou Field, made over three million barrels.

The Germany family was involved in oil exploration for many years in Texas and other Gulf Coast areas. They drilled 25 to 30 wells per year for 25 years and are still at it. Norman Germany said, "The Wilcox was more fun than anything."[2]

There were other plays in Mississippi. In 1966, Hughes & Hughes sold a deal near the town of Satartia in Yazoo County, based on an old surface map done by the state after the Tinsley discovery. The effort yielded 77 BOPD from Rodessa perforations at nearly 10,000 feet. The initial pressure and size of the Satartia Field was not impressive, but it was located in an area that had failed up to that time to yield any production in the Lower Cretaceous. The field made seven wells in four Lower Cretaceous reservoirs and one in the Cotton Valley. It was eventually waterflooded and produced over three million barrels, but to the disappointment of many, very little Lower Cretaceous production in the area northwest of Jackson was found in the years following Satartia.

In the same year as the Satartia discovery, the oil community was saddened by the death of Buzz Morgan. Founder of Dixie Geological Service, Morgan was one of the pioneers in the oil industry in the southeastern United States. After graduating from Texas Christian University with a degree in geology, he went to work for Gulf, surface mapping in Mississippi and Alabama in the late 1920s. He drilled the discovery well at Pickens Field, Yazoo County, Mississippi, in 1941.[3] That same year he founded the Dixie Geological Service. Information was exploding, and the industry needed it. Through Dixie, Morgan put it all together in a sensible format and kept it up to date. Many companies used the vital shared information Dixie provided in their exploration. Before his death, Morgan sold Dixie to Petroleum Information, Inc.

While explorers brought in one success after another in Mississippi during the early sixties little happened in Alabama, and when a strike finally came, it did not exactly make headlines. "After ten lean years without a discovery,"[4] as Don Moore of the Alabama Oil and Gas Board grievously expressed it, a strike was finally logged in November 1965, 27 miles north of Mobile in Baldwin County on a broad low relief domal structure. There, operator Robert A. Lee found oil in the Paluxy at 8,300 feet, but the new field, named Tensaw Lake, produced only 165,000 barrels. Two more lean years passed before Moore could get excited again.

Another Big Cotton Valley Strike

Mississippi's Jurassic play was coming into prominence by 1966. While the Smackover discoveries were disappointing, some Cotton Valley fields were excellent. Shell's prolific Cotton Valley production at Bay Springs Field in Jasper County, discovered in 1965, kicked off large scale Jurassic wildcat activity especially on salt anomalies. Although only four new Jurassic fields were found that year, many exploratory wells were drilled and geophysical activity abounded. Together, those two factors provided what was lacking in the Jurassic Trend—a lot of new and important subsurface information.

One of the most significant new Jurassic fields was Tallahala Creek Field, found in 1966. Merrill Harris, who discovered and helped discover some important Lower Cretaceous fields in Mississippi, had a hand in finding Tallahala Creek. By then he had a very powerful financial ally as a partner. "Our first association. . . was in the mid sixties," he recalled. "Thanks to Bob Hearin, I made the acquaintance of Mr. Leon Hess, and he was looking for someone to find him some production. They didn't have an exploration office or anything. His wants were not that simple because he wanted to find production right along the pipeline." Shell had it [the leases on the Tallahala Creek prospect], and we farmed it out after buying some stuff that was open. Hess ended up with about half of it and Shell had about the same."[5]

Shell drilled the well in eastern Smith County, six miles southwest of the town of Bay Springs and seven miles southwest of Bay Springs Field. In August 1966 the No. 1 Mary James tested nearly 1,000 BOPD through Cotton Valley perforations below 15,000 feet. By 1994 the field had produced over 20 million barrels and almost 40 billion cubic feet from multiple pools in both the Cotton Valley and the Smackover. Tallahala Creek is a complexly faulted structure, more like the salt structures of South Louisiana than those of Mississippi and Alabama. Merrill Harris' association with Hess ended after the Tallahala deal, and Hess merged with Amerada to form the giant Amerada-Hess, Inc.

Harris and his partners weren't the only independents to team up with a giant. Two gentlemen from Meridian, Mississippi—Field Chisholm and Jack Stack—formed a partnership called the Brandon Company and took drilling deals. One was a proposal to drill a Smackover test in Clarke County about 18 miles south of Meridian near the town of Quitman. The two bought the deal and headed to Texaco's Jackson Office seeking a farmout or some form of support from Texaco on its acreage in the area.

Most independents recoiled at the thought of asking Texaco for a farmout. The company was notorious for refusing to make deals on its mineral holdings, even where there was no activity. Chisholm and Stack asked anyway.

True to its reputation, Texaco did not give Stack the time of day, much less a farmout, so Stack switched to his back-up plan and asked for a $75,000 bottom hole contribution. Texaco agreed but counter-offered with $50,000. They saw it as a cheap way to evaluate its leases in the area.

The partners agreed to the compromise and went to Jackson to tie up the deal, but then Texaco decided to press for a better deal. They lowered the offer to $40,000. The infuriated Stack told Texaco's district landman, "No! But I will give *you* $50,000 and *you* drill the well!"[6] Their bluff called, Texaco relented and agreed to pay the $50,000. Brandon Company drilled the well and discovered Quitman Field.

In October 1966 Chisholm and Stack's well flowed over 500 BOPD from the Cotton Valley below 11,000 feet and had oil shows in the Smackover as well. After the Quitman discovery the Brandon Company retained Dudley Hughes to help develop the field and evaluate other deals. The company deepened some of their Cotton Valley development wells to test the Smackover and eventually completed several wells in it. That afforded Hughes an opportunity to study the dynamics of Smackover entrapment, much as he unraveled some of the mysteries of the Lower Cretaceous during the Triad days.

He and others interpreted the field as a faulted salt structure along the northern *hinge line* of the Salt Basin. The hinge line is best visualized as a regional line along which the sedimentary beds begin a steeper plunge toward the center of the basin.

Hughes remembers the work as another important educational advance. "I learned that thin, low relief salt structures may provide the best Smackover traps. The salt was too thin along the hinge line to form large domes—only low relief anticlines, which may be several miles in length." To date Quitman has produced over of 22 million barrels from one Smackover pool and six Cotton Valley pools and almost a million barrels from the Lower Cretaceous.

While Hughes and the Brandon Company partners continued to study the Smackover and test it where they could, Continental Oil Company (Conoco) took a crack at it in the state's oldest and most famous oil field, Tinsley in Yazoo County, the third attempt to tap the Smackover at Tinsley. They encountered about 200 feet of Smackover porosity with good oil shows. The well tested over two million cubic feet per day and 25 barrels of oil per day from a Smackover interval near 13,000 feet. A laboratory analysis of the gas indicated that most of it was methane but 19% was hydrogen sulfide.

A Big Disappointment

In 1966 Texaco made one of the most frustrating and geologically mystifying discoveries of the decade in Scott County, Mississippi. While drilling a 13,800- foot Smackover test, they discovered a tremendous gas field in the

Hosston at 11,000 feet. The No. 1 Wade well tested nearly three million cubic feet of gas per day. There was only one problem: the gas was 67% carbon dioxide (CO_2), the common gas used in carbonated drinks. Geologists scratched their heads over that, finally deducing that the CO_2 migrated up through a fault zone from the Smackover and took refuge in the porous Hosston sands. But how, they wanted to know, did it get into the Smackover? A possible answer came.

By the end of 1967 there were several more CO_2 discoveries in an area that included parts of Rankin, Madison, and Scott Counties. Underneath the region is a huge, deep-seated anticline, fifty miles long and at least twenty miles wide. The CO_2 gas zones were sometimes hundreds of feet thick with enormous reserves. As more information became available observers advanced a theory. They suggested that the ancient volcanic activity that produced the Jackson Dome caused chemical alterations in the surrounding deep source rocks, resulting in a proliferation of CO_2 gas throughout the area.

For many years, companies hoped they might use the huge reserves of CO_2 they discovered in central Mississippi in tertiary recovery efforts (gas flooding) in other oil fields. Eventually Shell built a CO_2 pipeline to Little Creek and McComb Fields and on into Louisiana, but when oil prices dropped below $2 a barrel they suspended CO_2 operations. Denbury revived CO_2 flooding in 1999.

A very timely and important lecture presented at the Mississippi Geological Society meeting in December closed 1966. Marvin L. Oxley of Lone Star Producing Company presented a paper entitled, "A Study of the Jurassic Sediments in a Portion of Mississippi and Alabama." Co-authors were E.D. Minihan and Julius M. Ridgway. The benchmark paper took some of the mystery out of the Jurassic sequences and advanced the predictability of Smackover reservoir rocks.

The highest oil prices in a decade ($2.91 a barrel) fueled a frenzied exploration business in 1967. A year after its great find at Tallahala Creek, Shell logged an important strike in Rankin County, Mississippi, 22 miles east of Jackson. There they drilled a deep test in the old Pelahatchie Field, which had produced small amounts of oil from various Lower Cretaceous sands since 1962. Although the Smackover was undoubtedly Shell's target, they found oil instead in the deeper Norphlet Formation, the first such find in Mississippi. The *Rankin County News* printed a gigantic aerial photograph of the well with the caption "She's a Big 'Un, Boys." The paper reported that on an initial one-hour test, the well flowed "a barrel a minute."[7] More precise tests later brought the rate down to a more believable 500 BOPD (merely a nice 'un) from perforations below 17,000 feet, the deepest oil well in the state.

The Norphlet is commonly sandstone and lies immediately below the Smackover. Shell successfully petitioned the Oil and Gas Board for 160-acre spacing and an allowable of 1,000 BOPD for the new zone. The field, however, never produced significant volumes of oil or gas, and the hunt for more Lower Cretaceous and Norphlet production in southeast Rankin County proved disappointing.

Another noteworthy discovery in 1967 was Nancy Field in Clarke County, where Placid Oil Company tested over 500 BOPD from Smackover perforations below 13,000 feet. The high initial flow rate delighted Placid and its partners, because the zone had not yet been pressure treated with acid solution. Placid's engineers concluded that the limestone reservoir was probably fractured naturally giving it more effective porosity and permeability than the core analysis indicated. Nancy Field grew to 17 wells spaced over 640 acres and has produced about seven million barrels from the Smackover and Norphlet pools.

A notable Wilcox discovery made news in 1967. Wyatt E. Craft and Richard MacRay brought in the Tom Branch Field in Franklin County. MacRay's company was Raymac, a reversal of his name's syllables. They drilled three dry holes before they discovered the field, which has produced about four million barrels from six Wilcox reservoir sands with 28 wells covering about 600 acres.

A Guiding Light

A young Jackson geologist named Vaughan Watkins worked with Raymac, one of the many geologists produced by the excellent geology school at the University of Oklahoma, but he was also a native Mississippian. G.W. Terry, a landman who lived down the street where he grew up, kindled his interest in the oil business. Terry told Watkins, "You could be a landman or an engineer, but the people who really know what is going on are the geologists."

After college Watkins worked with Mobil and then consulted for his father's law firm, which dabbled in the oil business. The firm's interest in Summerland Field gave Watkins an opportunity to serve on the field's unitization committee, a break that launched his career. "I had so much confidence with that [the unitization work] that I felt I could go down the road and prospect." He went to Hilton Ladner to get advice on getting started. Ladner told him that, although he might be called an independent, in reality he would be very dependent on other people throughout the oil industry and that the controlling factor in an independent's career was the ability to work effectively with people. "Hilton was a guiding light," Watkins said.[8]

Armed with technical skills and Hilton's wisdom, Watkins partnered with a landman, Benton Vernon. Richard MacRay put up the seed money for them. "Our biggest concern was to not lose much of his [MacRay's] money," Watkins said.

Watkins remembered one day when Benton did some mapping on his own and came in with a prospect. Watkins didn't think much of it. He spotted a flaw. He told Benton not to pursue it. Benton partnered with another landman, Jimmy Clements, and put the prospect together. Watkins warned them again, but they sold the deal.

Watkins played golf rather than go out to witness the log run. When he finally got to the rig they were running pipe. The two landmen discovered a million barrel field. Watkins' hat was off to them. "So it turns out that a good landman can draw a good map. If he has a lot of common sense and pays attention to what is going on, I really think he can." Watkins continued to hunt with success in the Wilcox and he did some important work in deeper exploration in the 1970s. While Watkins worked the Wilcox, one of the most important alliances in the petroleum history of the Deep South was formed to explore the deeper targets of the Lower Cretaceous.

Despite his successes since the break-up of Triad, Dudley Hughes felt handicapped without a staff. Furthermore, he was not happy with using contractors for production operations. He needed to get back into the hunt with more powerful economic weapons. He looked around for an aggressive partner with a proven knowledge of operations and a solid track record of fund raising. He didn't have to look far.

A Hell of a Ride

Dudley Hughes was in for the ride of his life in more ways than one. "I had only met Chesley Pruet once or twice before 1967," Hughes said. "He knew of my past activity and I knew of his. As I recall, I called his office one day in the spring of 1967 and suggested that we get together. I had some prospects and some investors. He had a landman and was staffed to drill and operate wells."[9]

Pruet had an able landman in Emmett Gathright and an equally good engineer, Herschel Lane, but he had no geologist. He mulled Hughes's suggestion over for a couple of days then called him from the King Edward Hotel in Jackson where he and Gathright were staying. "I went down and had a few drinks with him," Hughes recalled. "We agreed on a fifty-fifty deal where we would split any interest and profits that we made on deals. We also agreed that either of us could buy into our deals but had to pay the same promoted price that any other investor would pay. Nothing was put in writing. For the first two years we had only a handshake deal. It was kind of a natural fit. But I will say this—I learned to defend my interest with him because he was a heck of a trader."

Pruet clearly remembered his first impressions of Hughes. "He had good business sense and dressed very well. He always went first class in everything he did."[10]

As they prepared their first prospect to sell, the quiet, unobtrusive Hughes was about to discover that his partner was a swaggering, impetuous, race-horse of a dealmaker. Pruet picked Hughes up in his plane, and they winged to meetings with potential investors in Ft. Worth, Houston, and New Orleans. Hughes vividly remembered that first whirlwind trip. "On landing [in New Orleans] Chesley said, 'It's too late to see anybody here, but we can catch the last three horse races at Evangeline Downs.' Chesley rushed up to a betting window and asked the clerk what was a good horse to bet on. The clerk suggested one. Chesley said, 'Give me $200 on the nose.' He did the same on two other races, winning two out of three and picking up $3,000. He gave the clerk $100. . . . Whichever city we were in, he would end up at a racetrack if it was open—and usually won."

Such trips were standard routine. Pruet's prowess in deal-making amazed Hughes. Pruet spoke with a "strong, slightly husky voice, always smiling, but with a rough charm," Hughes noted. "He could be disarming when he was negotiating a deal. He was a very tough trader. People he outwitted may not realize they had been bested, mesmerized by his frankness." In casual settings, Pruet dominated conversation, always joking.

Harry Spooner, a geologist who came to work for Pruet and Hughes, remembered the unsettling feeling Pruet cast over him. "For some reason, you were really concerned about what he thought about you . . . more than you were concerned about what most people thought about you. I was talking to a friend of mine in El Dorado, who was also a friend of Chesley's. I told him I couldn't figure out why I am so concerned about what he thinks. He said he was the same way. . . . He [Pruet] had a real influential personality."[11]

Pruet had an abrasive side as well. He rented a car everywhere he and Hughes went, rarely taking a cab. He insisted on driving and usually drove like "he was going to a fire," Hughes said. A cab once pulled out in front of them in New Orleans, infuriating the impatient Pruet. "Chesley said, 'I'll teach that son-of-a-bitch,' and rammed the cab. The driver jumped out and Chesley jumped out, both shouting obscenities at each other for several minutes. Then we left with Chesley saying, 'This car is insured, so what the hell?'"

The discovery of Verba Field in Jasper County, Mississippi, in August 1967 was the partnership's first success. The small field produced about two million barrels from several wells in a number of Lower Cretaceous sands, but it was just a warm-up compared to what was to come for them.

Success Revisits Alabama

Tom Joiner, Alabama's state geologist 1977–81 and successor to Phil LaMoreaux, gave geologist Ed Minnehan credit for opening Smackover production in Alabama. "Ed kept thinking that Alabama should have some

Smackover production. . . . And he kept working and working until he discovered the first Smackover production here in the state."[12]

Minnehan was with Placid Oil Company when they and others sank a couple of dry holes in Choctaw County. Those wells led to a discovery in April 1967. E L. Erickson, Chesley Pruet's former partner in the Zach Brooks Drilling Company, was the operator. Erickson brought in a marginally commercial well in Choctaw County about five miles northeast of the old Gilbertown Field. That minor discovery, the Toxey Field, was a Smackover reservoir atop a simple salt anticline that surprised most geologists because it was north of the supposed updip limit of the Louann Salt. Another surprise was that it was north of the Pickens-Gilbertown-Pollard regional peripheral fault system. From then on, the hunt for Smackover north of the peripheral fault zone would be referred to as the *Updip Smackover*, a term which became a veritable battle cry for explorers in the 1990s. Erickson's well tested 147 BOPD of low gravity oil from perforations just below 10,000 feet. The small field produced only 1.8 million barrels and had to be pumped from the outset, but at least the Smackover was now officially a producer in Alabama. Minnehan later went independent. "Other people may give others the credit, but I give the first credit to Minnehan," Joiner said. "He chased the Smackover."

Toxey was a disappointment, but it drew wildcatters' attention to south Alabama. What got Dudley Hughes' attention was a couple of previous failures in the Gilbertown area. Conoco drilled a 12,000-foot Smackover test which was dry but had Smackover shows. Conoco then farmed the lease block out to Woods Petroleum of Oklahoma City, which earned 50% with a 12,000-foot test of their own. That test, one mile south of Conoco's, was also dry.

Pruet and Hughes took a farmout from Conoco and Woods to drill a Smackover test halfway between the two dry holes. They retained Dick Brewer, a geophysical consultant from Houston, to interpret Conoco's poor quality seismic records, which added very little to the subsurface evaluation. Hughes thought the prospect looked similar to the Smackover structure at Quitman, Mississippi, some 20 miles northwest. The prospect was what geologists dubbed a *look-alike*, but the real question was, would it be a produce-alike? As usual, there was only one way to find out.

As the well neared target depth, Hughes got a scare. His correlations were running low to the Conoco dry hole north of them. More often that not, that meant impending failure, but when they examined the cuttings, they found shows in the Smackover and decided to run a DST at 12,000 feet. The test spewed nice 40 degree gravity oil high over the crown block. They knew they had a significant Smackover field. The well cut 30 feet of dolomite and granular limestone, usually high quality reservoir rocks, and tested at 840 BOPD.

The Alabama Oil and Gas Board, in keeping with naming fields after nearby towns or landmarks, moved to name the new discovery Water Valley

Field in honor of a nearby community. Chesley Pruet objected vigorously. He was "somewhat superstitious," according to Hughes, and was afraid the name might jinx the new production, turning it to water. The Board capitulated and made a rare exception, naming the new find Choctaw Ridge Field, after a Bobby Gentry song popular that the time.[13]

Over the objections of several other independents and landowners, the Board also granted Pruet & Hughes' request for 80-acre spacing. Until that time all oil produced in Alabama was on 40-acre spacing. The field was very profitable and approached four million barrels by 1997. More significantly, it caused many heads in oil circles to turn east again. While Choctaw Ridge was being developed, lots of work was underway back in Mississippi where a corporate newcomer was trying to get a foothold.

"We found oil in spite of management!"

Matt Lutz was a good company man. He was loyal and stuck around. Upper managers liked his type, but Lutz was no yes man either. When he got an idea in his head he didn't hesitate to buck the company's conventional wisdom. They didn't like that part of him, because at times it left them with dry holes and other times embarrassment.

Lutz, a Louisianan, took his geology degree to Tidewater Oil Company in 1956, and they put him to work mapping the Gulf Coast. In 1968—the year Lutz and his contemporaries dragged Tidewater management kicking and screaming into some serious oil-finding—J. Paul Getty decided his company was finally worth having his name on it. He changed it to Getty Oil Company.

Lutz was scouring the Mississippi Smackover that year, hoping to find an opportunity for Getty. He befriended a Canadian who transferred from Getty's Calgary office to New Orleans, Russell Check. Check's knowledge and influence channeled Lutz toward a risky but fascinating concept, apparently still untried in the Salt Basin. Lutz didn't hesitate to give Check credit. "He understood how carbonates developed and where they developed and where reservoir type rocks developed, and he imparted a lot of that to me before he left Getty. Then it became my chore to say, okay that sounds good, but where do I practically apply this?"[14]

Lutz began by integrating subsurface mapping with gravity data, a common starting point for most serious geologists in those days. He looked for a high spot in the Jurassic zones. So did everyone else. Most had already been drilled, but his association with Check gave him a different perspective. "A place to look for good carbonate rocks, like in the Smackover, would be places where you had a shallow water high-energy environment." Wave action would have developed Smackover porosity.

He developed a theory that the high energy zones where Smackover porosity was good might not necessarily be the highest point on a structure. If that were true, then many dry holes drilled atop the various structures beneath central Mississippi may have narrowly missed significant oil pools. Lutz guessed that finding good Smackover might not be a matter of simply drilling on the top of a salt structure. The important point, he theorized, was where the crest of a given structure was at the time of Smackover deposition, not where it is today.

Basinal tilting became Lutz's mantra, as he developed a plan to revisit the structures drilled unsuccessfully before. Oil explorers knew that the Salt Basin sagged continually as more and more sediment poured in at the top. That caused the strata on the basin's flanks to become more inclined, or to *dip* steeper, as geologists would say. Over time, as the basinward side of a dome-shaped structure subsided more than the updip side, the dome's crest migrated toward the updip side, while the thinnest part of the Smackover migrated toward the downdip side.

Imagine holding an umbrella straight up and observing the top of the umbrella from directly overhead. Tilt the umbrella to one side, the apex moves. The original highest point moves downward and is no longer the highest point. In the case of the Smackover in that particular part of the basin the best rocks were on the side of the umbrella, not at the current highest point. Figure 11 illustrates basinal tilting.

"So we concentrated our efforts in Clark County," Lutz said. "There was a well drilled by Southwest Gas. No one had that log. It had never been released and nobody could get the information. We had an old seismic map that showed that the well was drilled right on top of an old structure. But we didn't know what the well had encountered."

As Lutz worked to develop his ideas, he mentioned to friend that he was working on an interesting area and wished he could get the log on the old Southwest Gas well. To Lutz's astonishment, the man said he had the whole well file. Lutz tore into the file and found not only seismic maps, logs, and test data, but also actual core chips. "I examined those core chips under a microscope and saw that they were all oolite development, but in between the oolites was a sparcalcite infill that completely blocked the porosity and permeability. So, while the rock had shows, it was tight. And what I had learned from this old geologist out of Calgary was that if you found sparcalcite in the rocks, you were very, very close to a high energy depositional environment."

Lutz decided to reverse the basinal tilting process conceptually. He had to determine where the crest of the structure was 170 million years earlier. For the answer he turned to his geophysicist Bill Reeves and asked him to make an isopach map, which contours points of equal thickness. The point where the map showed the Smackover rocks were thinnest should be the original high point, or *paleo-high*. Reeves used seismic data from the Southwest file and made the map. Lutz smiled when he saw it. Sure enough, it showed thinning south of the dry hole Southwest Gas drilled.

"So I drew the conclusion that as the Mississippi Salt Basin began to fill up with sediment after Smackover time and on into the Cretaceous, it downwarped to the south and rotated those old Smackover structures, so that the crest of the original structures pulled to the south."

Next, Lutz faced the hard part—convincing a conservative management to drill what was essentially a stratigraphic trap in rocks they were unfamiliar with. He worked up two prospects, one based on the Southwest well, another nearby with similar geology. Predictably, the bosses balked. "Back then," Lutz said, "very few people had done carbonate work. Everybody just drilled on top of structure." Lutz's theory fell on deaf ears, and the people in the New Orleans district office who helped him develop the prospects were despondent.

Jim White, a landman in the district office, told Lutz he was sick and tried of not being able to sell management on anything. He quit. White called Lutz two weeks later with an interesting proposal. He wanted to assemble some acreage on Lutz's ideas and sell it, but he was afraid of a conflict of interest.

Lutz told him, "You can put the deal together with the understanding that when you get it together you offer it first to Getty. They won't have any complaint. They can take it or not take it. If they don't, then you've done all you can do."

White secured a farmout from Shell, who owned most of the leases and approached Getty with the deals. Getty's upper management still didn't like the ideas, but they finally relented and took half of them—to avoid embarrassment, in case oil was found, Lutz thought. It wasn't the first time a company took an outside deal originally generated by its own in-house geologists and rejected, and it wouldn't be the last. Management cultures in oil companies change continually with frequent reversals in perceptions, attitudes, and biases. Lutz knew that and though he didn't like it, he learned to live with it.

One of Jim White's first stops to raise funds was at Mosbacher Energy in Houston. Bob Mosbacher respected no boundaries when hunting for oil and gas, but he had a fondness for Mississippi and Alabama, partly because of his good pal Chesley Pruet. He liked White's ideas and bought in to them. Mosbacher noticed White admiring a couple of his waterfowl paintings. "I'll give you that one if we make a discovery." Mosbacher told him.

"What if we make two discoveries?"[15] White asked.

Mosbacher grinned.

Love Petroleum of Jackson also got into the deal, and Mosbacher operated both wells. They spudded in early 1968. Both were logged on the same day and Jim White got both of Bob Mosbacher's bird paintings.

One discovery became the Pachuta Creek Field, with four productive zones in the Smackover at about 13,000 feet, that eventually expanded to 65 wells covering 4,400 acres. It produced 55 million barrels, making it the largest Smackover field in Mississippi. At least 16 of the wells have produced over a million barrels, and one produced over three million. The other discovery became the East Nancy Field, with Smackover pay at 13,600 feet, and has produced about 11 million barrels from twelve wells.

The two fields established Getty as the major Smackover oil producer in Mississippi and yielded a nice bonus. The second well at East Nancy found 40 feet of oil sand in the Norphlet. The combined Norphlet production at East Nancy made almost three million barrels and was the first commercial Norphlet field in Mississippi. The Norphlet never became a sweetheart oil producer in Mississippi, but it was destined to put Getty Oil Company in the national spotlight in Alabama a few years later.

Lutz and company continued to hunt for the subtle Smackover stratigraphic traps into the 1970s. In February 1969 they logged another good strike on a prospect west of East Nancy. "We cut four 60-foot cores," Lutz said, "that were all oil-bearing—240 feet of core! And when we pulled out the first core it was just loaded—a beautiful oolite section, very porous. We took a cigar from the mudlogger, Bob Legate, and blew smoke through that full core, it was so porous."

Getty's No. 1 McCoy Unit 6–10 gauged a staggering 2,600 BOPD from Smackover perforations at almost 14,000 feet. The new find became the West Nancy Field and has produced over 19 million barrels from 15 wells, for a remarkable average of 1.25 million barrels per well.

Lutz wasn't the only geologist pondering the basinal tilting/paleo-structure theory. Dudley Hughes recognized the Pachuta Creek structure's potential and tried to get the Shell farmout on it. He and Pruet were too late, but they did get the drilling contract and an eighth interest from Mosbacher.

Nevertheless, Lutz and his co-workers at Getty first put the basinal tilting concept to the test and turned it into a resounding economic success. They bucked management and the odds and made it happen, and that's what counts among oil people. And they weren't done yet.

While the Getty people worked to bring their ideas to fruition, Inexco found two nice pay zones in Clarke County. They tested almost 3,000 BOPD from the Smackover and nearly a thousand from the Norphlet. The combined flow of almost 4,000 barrels a day was one of the best potentials ever encountered in Mississippi. It became the Prairie Branch Field and has yielded about nine million barrels from eight wells covering 520 acres, for an average of over 17,000 barrels per surface acre and 1.25 million barrels per well.

Another significant strike in 1968 occurred in Wayne County, Mississippi. In August Mobil Oil brought in the South Cypress Creek Field into being.

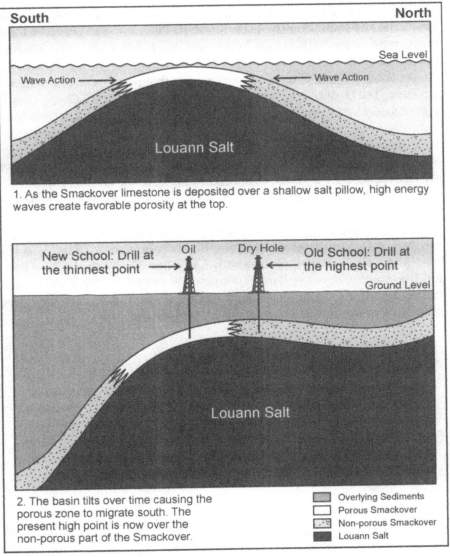

South   North

Sea Level

Wave Action →

← Wave Action

Louann Salt

1. As the Smackover limestone is deposited over a shallow salt pillow, high energy waves create favorable porosity at the top.

New School: Drill at the thinnest point →

Oil   Dry Hole

Old School: Drill at ← the highest point

Ground Level

Louann Salt

2. The basin tilts over time causing the porous zone to migrate south. The present high point is now over the non-porous part of the Smackover.

- Overlying Sediments
- Porous Smackover
- Non-porous Smackover
- Louann Salt

Figure 11. Diagram of Basinal Tilting Concept

They found two Smackover zones below 14,000 feet, both of which tested better than 700 BOPD. The field has produced almost 12 million barrels from 11 wells.

Mississippi enjoyed several other minor discoveries in 1968. As an operating company, Triad established Smackover production at Harmony Field in Clarke County, another of the tilted umbrella type traps. The field expanded to nine wells, producing almost two million barrels.

The most prolific well in Mississippi was drilled in 1968 in the Tallahala Creek Field in Smith County. Texas Interstate Oil & Gas and Union of California tested 1,300 BOPD, 1,344 BOPD, and 384 BOPD from three different Cotton Valley zones in a single well.

Another well that year was a poor producer but caught a lot of geologist's attention. The Double Creek Field in eastern Clarke County, Mississippi, made only 116,000 barrels from a single well, but it was not on a salt structure. Rather than salt, a swell in the igneous basement—the floor of the sedimentary basin—formed the trap, proving that Jurassic oil could be found in structures unrelated to salt tectonics. After that geologists knew they could expect Smackover porosity updip of the northern limits of the Louann Salt.

As one discovery after another in Mississippi's Smackover trend hit the headlines, Humble Oil and Refining Company lost its resolve. Latecomers, they couldn't get enough acreage in the trend to launch a significant Smackover program. A few mid-level geologists in the company were confident that the Smackover play extended southeasterly. Their appeals fell on skeptical ears, but they wouldn't give up. Finally, Humble's managers relented and turned its geologists loose on south Alabama and northwest Florida. The slow pace of life in that region was about to change profoundly.

PART III
Mid 60s to Early 70s

Chapter 11

"A real fouled-up situation"

"**I** told this story to the Houston Geological Society," Charlie Meeks drawled, "and it made the guys at Humble mad as hell."[1] Meeks, a burly Texan, went to work for Humble in 1951 immediately after collecting his geology degree from the University of Houston. "It was a real fouled-up situation." It turned out to be the kind of foul-up no oil stalker would mind getting into.

Meeks was Humble's zone manager and worked for Harry Owens, the district manager. "During that time," Meeks said, "we were looking for Smackover in Clark County and Jasper County, Mississippi. We had two crews shooting in there. Our boss called us in and said, 'We can't get any acreage in here. It's all taken up.' Harry Owens said, 'I think if we go own down the trend there's a possibility that we can find some dark shales [source beds] and we could continue the Smackover trend.'"

Meeks, Owens, and Dave Brassfield went to Houston to try to convince Humble's management to jump ahead of the crowd and explore for Smackover far to the southeast. Brassfield, the group's stratigrapher, was especially excited about the idea, but the pitch failed. "They [Humble's management] wanted to just get out of the Smackover trend," Meeks said. "They said it was all gone and they really didn't want to spend any more money on the trend."

The three didn't give up. Brassfield prepared a more persuasive proposal, and they went back to Houston. They were partially successful. They got authorization to shoot seismic and buy acreage. Their strategy was simple: key off of the old production at Pollard field. The Lower Tuscaloosa oil there must have had a deeper source. Pollard was a good place to start. "We already knew where Pollard field was. It was an old producing structure and old salt structure. We just bought acreage around Pollard field. Shot all around it. We bought a lot of acreage."

The seismic data showed a deep closure against a fault, and on the strength of it they got money from management to drill a well. On October 18, 1968, Humble's No. 1 Bernice Wessner well in south central Escambia County, Alabama struck gas-condensate, but not where they expected it. The Smackover beds were tight. The Norphlet sands were porous and packed with gas, but it was extremely sour.

Tom McMillan Sr. and his consultants, geologist Dudley Hughes and log analyst Ed Kendrick, watched the test from a hill a half mile away. The wind carried the gas their way and made them mildly sick.

The high H_2S content—the state's first such well—got the Alabama Oil and Gas Board's attention. Staff engineer Gene White remembered the Board's keen interest in the test procedure. "A bunch of us from the Oil and Gas Board went down there to watch that completion. They gave us all kind of information. They told us to move back up the hill, a great distance away, near where they had set up a hospital in a trailer. They sent two men in there tied to each other. The H_2S was nine to ten percent, which will kill you instantly. They spaced them out where one was on the side and the other was on the well to open the test. Both those boys went in there and opened that well up with no problem whatsoever."[2]

The discovery well for the Flomaton field tested 7,500 MCFD and 436 barrels of condensate from the Norphlet at 15,400 feet, but the Humble people rubbed their chin when they ran the economic analysis. Gas was selling for 20 cents per MCF and oil at $3 a barrel. With those prices and the need to build expensive facilities to treat the gas and extract the sulfur, the field didn't look lucrative. "We were real happy," Meeks said, "until we found out that the Smackover was tight, and the Norphlet had 30 or 40 percent CO_2."

The easternmost extension of Jurassic production had been extended 75 miles to the southeast of the recent Smackover discoveries in Choctaw County, a colossal jump, but it was not the coveted Smackover production explorers hoped for. Still, Humble, Louisiana Land and Exploration Company (LL&E), Amerada, Chevron, Sun, and others began adding to their acreage positions in south Alabama and the florida Panhandle areas they thought were on trend with Humble's new Norphlet discovery.

Because of the time required to build the production facilities, the Flomaton Field did not go on production until 1970, but when it did, Alabama's gas condensate production rose phenomenally. In 2003 the field was still one of the state's top five gas-condensate producers, having made nearly 15 million barrels of condensate and 248 billion cubic feet of gas, plus great amounts of commercial sulfur.

Bernice Wessner, on whose land the discovery well was drilled, became something of a legend. A story circulated for years that in the early stages of leasing she ran oilmen off with a shotgun. Gene White thought that was a plausible story. She called him frequently. "She would call me at three in the morning and tell me that the oil companies were trying to kill her, and that I needed to make arrangements for her safety."[3]

Most of the residents of the peaceful farmlands of south Alabama and northwest Florida were more normal and began to feel the excitement and urgency that gripped Citronelle 13 years before. But if they thought the Flomaton discovery disruptive, they couldn't imagine what was to come only a couple of years later. Charley Meeks, Dave Brassfield, Harry Owens, their still hesitant employer—Humble, and a few other risk-takers were a couple of years away from astonishing the entire American oil world.

Smackover fervor in Mississippi continued into 1969. Shell opened Smackover and Norphlet production at Goodwater field in Clarke County. Conoco discovered the Davis field, also in Clarke County, a monster discovery that has produced 21 million barrels from 29 Lower Cretaceous pools and one Smackover pool. Average production per well was over 600,000 barrels.

Other minor discoveries made in Wayne County in 1969 included Winchester field (Pruet & Hughes with LL&E) and Robinson Junction (Pruet & Hughes). At Winchester, Pruet & Hughes completed a Smackover well and later added a dual zone Cotton Valley well, flowing 400 BOPD and 200 BOPD below 12,000 feet. Robinson Junction was the southeasternmost Lower Cretaceous oil found in Mississippi. Also in 1969, Pan American found the northernmost Smackover production in Mississippi at the Tchula Lake field in Holmes County.

Some noteworthy activity was underway in 1969 farther north into the next basin. With the ink still wet on their Shell Oil Company resignation letters, partners Fleming Browning and Stewart Welch fell to the task of renewing the languished hunt for gas in the Black Warrior Basin.

Just a Decimal Point Off

"We wanted to do something with Siloam Field, which I was very familiar with," Welch said. "I could see other possibilities with the field that Shell never did pursue."[4] Siloam Field, discovered by the Carter Oil Company in 1953 and developed by Shell, was 10 miles northwest of West Point in Clay County, Mississippi, and was one of the largest commonly known subsurface geologic structures in the Black Warrior Basin. If it were a topographical feature, it would look like an elongated mountain over 1,000 feet tall and 10 miles long, lopped off on the northeastern side by a fault plunging down over 1,000 feet. Unfortunately, the common Mississippian-age producing sands across the structure are generally tight and sporadic, limiting productive capability, but the structure's enormous size captivated the imagination of many geologists who envisioned vast reserves locked in its depths. Stew Welch is the foremost among them.

With the limited finances of a new start-up company, geologist Stew Welch and landman Fleming Browning restricted their efforts to find more production at Siloam to the known shallower sands. "We thought we were going to buy Siloam Field," he said. But they [Shell] didn't want to sell to ex-employees."

Undaunted, the upstart pair acquired other leases and drilled three holes on the structure. The third, the McFadden well, hit a Pennsylvanian sand with shows, and the partners ran a DST. The test lasted most of the day before a small flare developed. "We were disappointed," Welch said. "We went to a little café to eat. We were thinking about plugging it. But then the DST man came in and said it had over 500 pounds pressure on it."

Welch rushed to the phone to order production pipe. After the pipe was run and cemented, they discovered that the DST technician had misplaced a decimal in his calculations. The pressure was 50 psi, not 500, but now it was too late to back out. They perforated and fracced. The result vindicated the DST man's blunder. "We gave it a frac and, lo and behold, after it cleaned up, it made over a million cubic feet a day." It was a shot in the arm for the partners' new company and helped launch them into prominence as Black Warrior Basin explorers.

Browning and Welch's next endeavor was dropped in their laps. Two men who put together a lease play in the Williston Basin in North Dakota that made them a great deal of money came to town. They were looking for place for a repeat performance and had a tip that the Black Warrior Basin was a candidate. A local oilman in Jackson referred them to Stew Welch, one of several geologists specializing in the basin.

"They asked me to work up some regional geology, and they would organize a lease play," Welch recalled. "I worked up a set of maps. It was a lot of fun. We showed it around and got somebody to go on it. By then they had already started on the leasing. Most of it was in Alabama." The leases were turned to various companies, notably Terra Resources out of Denver. Terra and others drilled many discoveries in the years to come based on Welch's original geology and the leases that resulted from it.

The alliance took Browning and Welch back to the northeast in shallower areas of the Black Warrior Basin where the sands were better, but the partners kept an eye over their shoulders at the deeper regions of the basin, expecting astonishing deep discoveries there and hoping to take part in them.

Fatal Attraction

Browning and Welch's efforts at Siloam sparked a new wave of activity in the Black Warrior Basin, overshadowed as usual by the much more exciting and profitable exploits in the Salt Basin. While Flomaton electrified landowners and explorers in south Alabama, central Mississippi enjoyed some high-profiled Jurassic excitement of its own. Although the independents did the lion's share of exploration work in Mississippi, they knew some work was simply meant for the lions. Early in 1969 the independents stood back and watched as Shell Oil Company's New Orleans Onshore Division stepped up to take on the deep Smackover in Rankin County.

Charlie Blackburn had been promoted to the division's general manager a year earlier. An Oklahoman with a degree in engineering and geophysics from OU, Blackburn was no newcomer to big, tough production operations. The Thomasville Prospect 15 miles southeast of Jackson was just another challenge for him and the other members of Shell's exploration team. They expected sour gas, like Humble found at Flomaton, and they were prepared. Or so they thought.

The Thomasville structure was a huge, low-relief, deep-seated salt feature on the southeast flank of the Jackson Dome. Shell completed its leasing and spudded the No. 1 Garrett in 1968 and reached a total depth of 20,450 feet in April 1969. They sought to keep the results of the well *tight* (confidential) but rumors spread that Shell found good shows of gas-condensate with CO_2 and H_2S. The rumors were true.

Blackburns' engineering team found the going tough and proceeded cautiously. The reservoir pressure was extremely high, and they knew if anything went wrong hell would come to breakfast. The careful testing resulted in a flow rate of nearly 10 million cubic feet of gas and 1,000 barrels of condensate per day at a depth of over 17,000 feet. The tubing pressure was said to be 13,000 psi. The rumor mill estimated the H_2S at 11%. That proved false. It was 35%.

The strike was big and exciting, but unlike Humble's Flomaton discovery, rural and far from population centers, Thomasville sat only 12 miles from Jackson. Shell mobilized its vast resources and began building extensive facilities to treat the deadly gas. A large facility that could process 10 million cubic feet of gas per day soon arose among the pine forests. Shell prepared a detailed contingency plan and coordinated with the state and local governments to respond to emergencies if the pressure got out of control or if an H_2S leak erupted from the plant.

Thomasville field was indeed big. Since 1969 it has produced well over 400 billion cubic feet of gas and created tremendous wealth for Shell and Rankin County. In October 1970 Shell awarded a contract to build the largest sulfur recovery plant in the United States in the county. The complex was costly but immensely successful. Some of Shell's managers wanted more Thomasvilles, but others—like Humble's managers in the Flomaton case—dissented. Blackburn recalled, "We had a hectic time. There was a lot of debate over whether we should even be pursuing that kind of thing because of the H_2S."[5] The lions won the debate, and Shell looked around for another Thomasville. That was an ill-fated decision.

From Electric Blankets to Electric Logs

Soon after their Choctaw Ridge discovery in Choctaw County, Alabama, Pruet & Hughes took a farmout on another structure in the county. In contrast with the poor quality shooting at Choctaw Ridge, they procured quality seismic records that bolstered their confidence. When the test well reached target depth below 12,000 feet, Hughes called Schlumberger out to log the well.

He was delighted to see Ed Gamrell, an old friend, come out as the logging engineer. Gamrell's father was the principal landowner in the Summerland field that Hughes found with Triad in 1961. Gamrell, an electrical engineer working with the Sunbeam electric blanket company, came out to observe the logging of the Summerland well. The well and the electrical logging operation that Hughes explained to him intrigued him. The next day Gamrell quit Sunbeam and joined Schlumberger, becoming a logging engineer. Eight years later, Hughes's mentoring of Gamrell into the oil business paid off for Hughes and his partners.

Although the logs on the test well didn't look very encouraging, Gamrell determined that the well should produce from just seven feet of a low resistivity and low porosity section in the upper Smackover, but Pruet and Hughes were not enthusiastic about his calculations. They suspected they had a dry hole. Still, they ordered a DST because the sidewall cores exhibited some shows. To everyone's disappointment, the DST recovered only salt water. Gamrell stood his ground, insisting that well would produce.

The partners had a tough choice to make. Gamrell, a Schlumberger employee, was relatively inexperienced in the oil field and had no financial stake. Going on his advice would be risky. After much deliberation they ordered production pipe. It was the right choice. The well came in water-free at 324 BOPD. By 1997 the field, Turkey Creek, produced over three million barrels from only four wells.

The Turkey Creek field was also notable in that it was located on a federal game preserve along the Tombigbee River. That forced the operators to erect their tank batteries, treaters, and pumps outside the preserve, a mile from the wells. Yet the well was an environmental and economic success. The Alabama Oil and Gas Board granted 160 acre spacing to reduce environmental exposure, the first such spacing granted on oil wells in the state.

As Alabama's oil industry steadily grew, the Mississippi scene was hot. The city of Jackson gained another major company in 1969 when Union of California reopened an exploration office. Howard Samsel was district geologist and district superintendent. Pat Foster handled land operations. In just a few years, they captured some great prizes for Union and some lucky south Alabama landowners.

More drilling records fell before the sixties ended. Lone Star Producing Company deepened the No. 1 H.G. McFarland well at Bryan field in Jones County to 21,105 feet. The well, originally projected to drill to 17,000 feet, set a new drilling depth record for the state, knocking off Phillips' No. B-1 Zellerbach at 21,052 feet. It didn't last long.

Shell regained the depth record with its No. 1 Shell-McNair in western Hinds County at a total depth of 22,738. That time, at least, Shell got a producer with their record-setter. The well was completed in the Sligo at 13,300 feet flowing five million cubic feet per day. It became the Learned Field and has produced 15 Bcf.

Paging Mr. Benke

As the decade drew to a close, the Gulf states east of the Mississippi were awash in oil people, oil companies, and oil deals. Many made bold advances to sell their ideas and establish their place in the swelling petroleum business. Roy Benke was one of them. A Jackson geologist, Benke constructed a set of subsurface maps on the Tuscaloosa horizon extending from Delhi Field in northeastern Louisiana to Mobile, Alabama. Rinehart Oil and Gas Reports published them as reference material to supplement its reports. To sell his deals, Benke put the maps on a table at the Petroleum Club with a sign reading "Free Maps." The club manager thought the Petroleum Club should not be a forum for free advertising for Mr. Benke and asked him to remove the maps. That didn't stop the innovative Benke from calling attention to himself. When the King Edward Hotel was a gathering spot for the petroleum fraternity, Benke often had himself paged in the lobby.

The sixties paid off handsomely for vigorous and persistent people like Benke. It was the decade of a maturing Wilcox play and a dominance of the Lower Cretaceous. The Jurassic proved itself a powerful economic factor for the future. State governments in the Deep South established a sensible and cooperative framework for the responsible exploitation of mineral wealth.

Overall, they were a good stretch of years, but oil people in the South didn't spend a lot of time looking back. They made maps, leased land, raised money, and kept the rigs drilling ahead. Most who pondered the next decade, their busiest ever, could not predict the crucial changes that were about to happen in the energy industry.

Chapter 12

The Peak

The 1970s opened with rampant inflation which President Nixon attempted to restrain by imposing wage and price controls. To the government's surprise, the measures failed to slow escalating oil prices. Industry people understood the inadequacies of Nixon's economic tactics. There was a shortfall in domestic producing capacity, and demand for oil exceeded supply. In his highly acclaimed book, *The Prize: The Epic Quest for Oil, Money, and Power*, Daniel Yergin described the turning point: "By 1970 only a million barrels per day remained [of excess production capacity], and even that number may have been overstated. That was the year, too, that American oil production reached 11.3 million barrels per day. That was the peak, the highest level it would ever reach."[1]

The Nixon administration was alarmed. High oil prices were not the problem; diminishing domestic supply became the compelling issue. Nixon had to abolish import quotas in April 1973. A flood of relatively cheap foreign oil came in, and Nixon knew this would damage the U.S. domestic oil industry and make the country even more dependent on imported oil. In August 1973 he instituted a compromise solution he hoped would encourage new exploration while keeping prices moderate.

A two-tiered price ceiling resulted. Oil was classified as *old oil* or *new oil*. New oil prices were uncontrolled and free to fetch the market price, set by the commodities and futures markets. Old oil was pegged at the May 15, 1973, price plus 35 cents. In addition to newly discovered oil, new oil also included the amount of crude produced monthly in excess of production on a particular property during the same month of 1972.

There was still another incentive category: *released oil.* For every barrel of crude an old field made above the old oil change-over date, a producer could sell a barrel of old oil for new oil prices. The measure aimed to boost not only new discoveries but also to increase production of older fields. Most people scratched their heads over the regulatory puzzle, but oil professionals saw the potential immediately. The new law encouraged investment in certain older fields suitable for costly unitization and secondary recovery operations.

There was yet a fourth category. Wells that produced fewer than 10 barrels a day were called *strippers.* To keep those puny wells alive (and there were tens of thousands of them), the new law let stripper oil sell at whatever price the market would bear.

Just as oil people started laying plans to take advantage of the new incentives, another Arab-Israeli war broke out in October 1973. The U.S. supported Israel and the Arab oil producing countries cut production back and eventually embargoed exports to the U.S. Crude prices soared. Operators moved quickly to find not only new production but also to increase established production to take advantage of *released oil* prices. In the Deep South, Pruet & Hughes joined the frenzy.

"There was a scramble to release old oil from regulation," Dudley Hughes recalled. "In the Turkey Creek field in Alabama, we unitized the field, then drilled one new well. The *new* oil from the new well created an equal amount of *released* oil, which enabled us to get market prices for almost all the crude produced. We had similar success with unitization and adding wells at Choctaw Ridge and Womack Hill [Choctaw County, Alabama]. In other fields, such as Giles Bend [Adams County, Mississippi], we had pay sands behind pipe which we drilled twin wells to get the released oil."[2]

The measures increased Pruet & Hughes' revenues and allowed them to expand the company and invest in more exploration. Many other companies that took advantage of new and released oil enjoyed similar gains. One presented a scheme to Pruet & Hughes to take advantage of the new regulation.

Bart Chamberlin, the Mobile operative who bought the Citronelle Field when Gulf sold out, approached Pruet & Hughes with a clever plan. He knew that in 1973 Pruet & Hughes barged 12,000 to 15,000 barrels of crude per day from its Choctaw County, Alabama, fields from a loading dock on the Tombigbee River to a refinery in south Louisiana. Chamberlain's idea was to load the Choctaw County and Citronelle crude on ships in Mobile and transport it beyond United States territorial waters, then bring it back to sell in the U.S. as uncontrolled imported oil. The scheme was based on ambiguities in the new Federal regulations, but his lawyers assured Pruet & Hughes it was legal. "Fortunately, we did not go along," Hughes said. "He made a lot of money but a few years later the government came after him. He fled the U.S. to Switzerland where he has resided ever since, to the best of my knowledge."[3]

While the complex pricing scenario played out in Washington and the Middle East during the early 70s, Pruet and Hughes and their contemporaries in the Deep South continued to hunt for the prize Daniel Yergin wrote about 20 years later. Of them Shell was the only one interested in going after the extraordinarily deep and dangerous prizes beneath Rankin County.

Hell Comes to Breakfast

To say that the seventies started off with a bang in Mississippi is an understatement—at least to Charlie Blackburn. Shell's New Orleans On-shore Division Manager had worked on the company's deep Smackover discovery at Thomasville in Rankin County, Mississippi. The discovery was extremely dangerous with its high bottom hole pressure and H_2S content. Blackburn didn't relish the idea of tackling another Thomasville, but Shell's top management was insistent. They drilled another deep Smackover prospect six miles south of Thomasville. They called it the Piney Woods Prospect. "It looked at least as big as Thomasville, which we thought was several hundred Bcf," Blackburn said.[4]

"We were very comfortable about the well because we had managed to set a 7-inch steel liner at a real good [position] and had gotten to the top of the Smackover and were . . . coring some shows that we had seen. Everyone thought the well was completely under control." But at 8:30 on the morning of March 25, 1970, came a phone call that Blackburn would never forget. "Dean Cox said that there was a problem on the Cox well up at Piney Woods. He had always been proud of that well because it was his namesake and he always contended that it shouldn't be a dry hole."

Indeed the news coming in from Cox's pet well was unsettling. As the crew pulled out of the hole with a Smackover core, they started gaining drilling mud. Something was pushing it up. They continued to pull out and at 10,000 feet they had 6,000 pounds of pressure. The blowout preventers activated, shutting the well in. Engineers scurried about the office in Shell's New Orleans tower, gathering information. Soon Blackburn was on the phone to his boss. "We have a real bad situation at Piney Woods."

Blackburn turned and looked at Cox. "Dean had gotten off the phone by then and he was pale. He had the information . . . and sure enough, we had 6,000 psi at the surface on the preventers. More than likely, we had already ruptured the 9 5/8" casing at some depth between the surface and T.D."

Reports came in that a man was down at the location. He was wearing a gas mask, but he was unconscious. They picked him up and carried him off the location and tried unsuccessfully to revive him with oxygen. He was airlifted to a hospital but did not survive. An autopsy determined that the gas got into the man's body through a perforated eardrum.

Blackburn called his staff together and began selecting a team of experts. They called Otis Engineering to send a team to the well and come up with a plan to kill it. Blackburn then briefed his boss while a plane was chartered to carry the Shell team to Jackson. Then another call came, one he dreaded. The crew, who had abandoned the location, heard an explosion and could see the well burning. Within half an hour, an emergency became total disaster.

Shell called famed oil well firefighter Red Adair and asked him to start for Jackson. Blackburn assembled an emergency team and consulted Phase II of Shell's emergency plan for Piney Woods. They notified Civil Defense and the Highway Patrol and monitored the evacuation. The evacuation plan provided a map of all residences within three miles of the well. Another call reported that police were evacuating 350 children from the nearby Piney Woods School.

Especially equipped trucks from Chemtech Labs hurried to the area to monitor the atmosphere. More quick meetings and responsibilities were assigned to various personnel. Then Blackburn tapped several of his specialists and headed for the airport.

On the way in they circled the well. "It looked like a volcano," Blackburn said. "It looked like a crater." State Troopers met them at the town of Star and took them to another site 4 miles north of the blowout. Blackburn was appalled to see National Guard troops and the Governor of Mississippi waiting for him. There were news reporters too.

"I began trying to access the situation," Blackburn said. "The Governor wanted to know what was going on. He had been in a helicopter and flown over to look at the well. He said, 'Boy, that was some fire. What's happening?' We told him that we had evacuated all the people needed. Also, we showed him the curves on what we expected the toxic gas concentration to be. I told him that the gas was on fire. It wasn't nearly as dangerous on fire as it would be if it were not burning. He asked if Adair was coming. I told him that he was on his way. This seemed to satisfy him."

More unsettling news came before nightfall. Oil workers reported smelling sulfur dioxide as they were driving through in the town of Brandon, 15 miles north of the well. Blackburn saw that the southerly wind was blowing the plume north toward Brandon's vicinity. He sent a team with a portable monitoring device to Brandon to measure the H_2S component in the air. Happily, it was nil, but he needed to make sure the escaping gas stayed lit. He stationed men with flare guns around the blowout with orders to re-ignite it immediately if it went out.

Blackburn settled in for what he knew would be a long night, but one thing still nagged him. The Chemtech trucks had not arrived. So far, the only information he had on air quality was from small, less reliable hand-held monitors. At 7:00 P.M. the Chemtech trucks arrived and Blackburn deployed them at critical spots downwind of the plume. Then, more bad news.

A weather report forecasted a big wind shift at midnight with gusts of 50 mph. "I got to worrying," Blackburn said, "[whether] all the people had been evacuated south of the highway, particularly around Grady's Corner, since a northeast wind would blow directly to Grady's Corner. I asked a patrolman, 'You guys did evacuate all the people in the [three mile] circle didn't you?' He said, 'No. We didn't evacuate anybody south of Highway 49. They are still out there.' I said, 'Oh! I was told they were all evacuated. We are going to have to do something about that because the wind is going to change to the north.' They started evacuating."

The burning well was easily visible from downtown Jackson. John Richart, Howard Samsel, and the employees at Union Oil monitored the blowout from their office windows in the Petroleum Building. "You could look out the window and clearly see the smoke plume 25 miles away," Richart remembered.[5]

About a week into the crises, the wind shifted dangerously, and the rotten egg smell of H_2S reached Jackson. Blackburn's reassurances to local authorities that the danger was slight, narrowly averted a frantic evacuation of Jackson. "That would have been a real nightmare."

With the immediate danger at bay, Shell laid plans to kill the blowout. They decided to drill a relief well down to the reservoir to a point near the bore of the runaway well. Then they would pump mud into the reservoir and reduce the pressure so the uncontrolled well could be shut-in safely.

But the plan was not feasible. Blackburn explained: "We couldn't directionally drill into the Smackover and pump into it because it was 18,000 feet deep. So what we did was directionally drill to intercept the casing of the first well. It was very difficult." Blackburn and his team learned that the key to an interception is to home in on the magnetism of the casing in the hole. As the relief well neared the casing of the blowout well, they brought in a mathematician and a crew with a special tool to measure disturbances in the earth's natural magnetic field. The tool sensed the nearness of the casing, and a successful intercept occurred at 10,000 feet.

After hitting the casing, they ran a perforating gun down the relief well and perforated from the casing in the relief well into the blowout well, which by then had bridged over and was blowing out underground. With the well bridged, some residents returned to their homes, but the situation was still dangerous. Shell began drilling dozens of monitoring wells around the blowout to monitor the fresh water sands. Some produced gas.

It took exactly a year to kill the well, plus millions of dollars and an extraordinary engineering effort. Finally Shell developed the field to recover some of the enormous expense, but in the end the field was disappointing. It was nothing like Thomasville, as they hoped. "Big structure, little field," Blackburn lamented.

For all its initial thunder, Piney Woods was a dud, but the disaster did not deter Shell from trying again five miles southwest of the crater. In December 1974 they opened Smackover sour gas production at their No. 1 Ridgway Management, testing over 33 million cubic feet per day below 22,000 feet. The new field was named Southwest Piney Woods and at the time of its discovery was the deepest producing zone in Mississippi. The well also encountered the world's highest bottom hole pressure, more than 22,000 psi. To date the field's two wells have yielded over 100 billion cubic feet of gas.

Damned Near Starved

While Shell fought to tame the Smackover at Piney Woods, other companies found it housebroken and affable. In Clarke County, Mississippi, sixty miles southeast of Shells'work, Inexco found oil in both the Smackover and Norphlet in the Prairie Branch Field. The dual completion below 14,000 feet flowed at a combined rate of 3,800 barrels per day, one of the best potential flow rates ever discovered in Mississippi.

Another noteable discovery came in 1970 in Walthall County. Miss-Tex Oil Producers, Inc., and the company they turned the deal to, Ada Oil of Houston, tested oil from the Lower Tuscaloosa below 10,000 feet in what became the Dinan Field. It was a nice oiler, making nearly six million barrels from 19 wells, averaging about 300,000 barrels per well.

The field was significant because Miss-Tex found the edge of the play. They didn't know it at the time, but Dinan became the easternmost occurrence of the Lower Tuscaloosa stratigraphic type fields. This was bad news to small explorers with no access to lots of seismic data. The big Lower Tuscaloosa fields back to the west were found mostly on gravity data and subsurface mapping using well control. That era was about over.

But the two men who formed Miss-Tex were not through. Ralph "Stogie" Hines, a Texan, got his geology degree from Texas Tech and went to work with Gulf Refining "in their land department! Geology jobs were pretty skinny then."[6] He worked his way into the geological section and was transferred to Mississippi. He worked for other oil companies but eventually resigned and formed Miss-Tex with his brothers-in-law, Bob and Harold Moon. Dinan, which they showed over 50 times before finally selling to Ada, was their biggest success. They found oil and gas in and around several other fields in south Mississippi.

Hines remembered how hard they worked sell their first gas reserves. "We sold it to a paper mill. They laid a 16-mile pipeline and amortized it out of what they were paying us, 18 cents per MCF. It wasn't all that bad. . . . We survived on it. Damn near starved to death one time. The papermill workers went on strike. We had to shut our wells in. Fortunately, we had some sympathetic bankers who stayed with us."

In 1971 the partners dissolved Miss-Tex, and Ralph Hines and Bob Moon went into business as Moon & Hines, Inc. Their aggressive drilling earned them a coveted "Wildcatter of the Year" award from the Mid-Continent Oil and Gas Association. The pair went on to discover a great deal of gas in the Black Warrior Basin. Bob Moon, one of the best-liked men in Mississippi's oil business, died in 1993, but Ralph Hines and his sons remain active.

While Mississippi wildcatters big and small probed for the mysterious Smackover, other bold venturers were eyeing south Alabama and the Florida Panhandle, hoping to find Jurassic treasure there. Some focused their attention on the sister Escambia counties—one in Alabama, the other in Florida—which shared a border. But explorers first had to charm the favor of a single family.

A Turkey Hunter's Vision

Dr. Walter B. Jones, the third man named Alabama State Geologist and the first state Oil and Gas Supervisor, was a dedicated proponent of oil and gas exploration and conservation. He understood the realities of the game. In 1927 he wrote: "The chance of making a killing in the oil game sets the average citizen wild with excitement, as nothing else will. When the cold facts are analyzed, it will be seen that more fortunes are lost than made."[7]

Despite that warning, Doc Jones was a tireless visionary who trekked Alabama from border to border, talking up the state's petroleum potential to anyone who would listen. "He constantly kept legislators aware of the mission of the Geological Survey of Alabama and oil and gas potential in this state," wrote Alex Sartwell, historian of the Survey. "During critical periods of legislative activity, Jones would even sleep on a cot in the upstairs halls of the state capitol. Doc Jones had a personal commitment to insure that the mistakes that had been made in the past by other oil and gas producing states would not be duplicated in Alabama as a result of inadequate oil and gas laws."[8]

Dr. Jones succeeded in getting responsible laws passed in 1939, but he still didn't have any oil to regulate. Those who knew him were keenly aware that he was no ordinary civil servant. A fire burned inside him for his state and his profession. He loved Alabama, geology, and hunting.

His passion for people, rocks, and the outdoors took him into the coastal plains of south Alabama where he developed a friendship with an Escambia County attorney. Tom McMillan Jr., of Brewton, remembered how his grandfather, Ed Leigh McMillan, caught oil fever from Dr. Jones. "Somehow he got to know Dr. Jones. They were both big turkey hunters. I can remember him having Dr. Jones drive down to discuss what he thought about the [oil] potential. . . . My father [Thomas E. McMillan Sr.] became an oil and gas investor soon after that."[9]

The oil and gas enthusiasm he infused into his turkey-hunting friend was just what Dr. Jones wanted. In 1950 Ed Leigh, a Brewton lawyer, became the president of the T.R. Miller Mill Company, one of Alabama's largest family-owned timber companies. The company owned 200,000 acres of timberland in south Alabama, most of it with mineral rights. "We're a timber family from the late 1800s," said Tom Jr. His grandfather was "one of those who didn't just cut and move on to the next tract and sell the land and move on to another tract and sell out. He built a company. He started buying land and holding on to it. . . . And through that ownership we always had a keen [interest] in minerals."

Ed Leigh's enthusiasm spread down through the generations. His only child, Thomas, caught it when the Pollard Field was discovered in Escambia

Miss Winnie McGlammery, the unsung heroine of Alabama's geological knowledge

Fred Mellen, consultant and Mississippi State Geologist (Miss. Geological Society 1958 Photo Directory)

Dr. Walter B. Jones, Alabama State Geologist

Robert Womack (Miss. Geological Society
1958 Photo Directory)

Bud Norman (Miss. Geological Society 1958
Photo Directory)

Wil Knight (Miss. Geological Society 1958
Photo Directory)

Walter E. Sistrunk Sr. (Photo courtesy
Walter E. Sistrunk Jr.)

J.P. Evans Sr. (Photo courtesy
J.P. Evans III)

Dale Myers (Miss. Geological Society 1958
Photo Directory)

Carter Oil Co. No. 1 Mattie McFadden, discovery well of the Siloam Field, 1953, Clay County, Mississippi (Courtesy Walter E. Sistrunk Jr.)

No. 1 Moye-Franklin, April 1952, discovery well of Pollard Field, Escambia County, Alabama. Oil sprayed into the derrick on DST (*The Brewton Standard*, 1951)

John and Sim Callon, circa 1945
(Courtesy Callon Petroleum, Inc.)

Fred Mellen, Dr. Walter B. Jones, and operator Harry Cullett at Hamilton Field, Marion County, Alabama, circa 1952. (*The Petroleum Engineer,* 1954)

L-R, James Evans, Emmett Vaughey, Alex Brunini, Robert Hearin, Bill Vaughey

George Vasen No. 1 Tung Tree Corporation,
Stone County, Mississippi, circa 1950

No. 1 Sanders blowing wild in Monroe County, Mississippi, in 1951. It was the discovery well for the Muldon Field, the first significant discovery in the Black Warrior Basin.

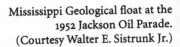

Desk & Derrick Club float at the Jackson Oil Parade, 1952, Mississippi's first and only oil parade. (Courtesy Walter E. Sistrunk Jr.)

Mississippi Geological float at the 1952 Jackson Oil Parade. (Courtesy Walter E. Sistrunk Jr.)

Shreveport geologist Everett Eaves,
discoverer of the Citronelle Field, Alabama,
1955

Conference at the Donovan well, Citronelle, Alabama. L-R Mayor Dewey Wyatt,
Z.B. Skinner, Sam Hester, John Donovan (*Saturday Evening Post*, 1956)

The Zach Brooks Drilling-Everett Eaves No. 1 Donovan, discovery well of the giant Citronelle Field (*Saturday Evening Post*, 1956)

Phil LaMoreaux, Alabama State Geologist, 1961–1976

Independent Jim Stewart with a well that launched his career in the Maxie Field, Forrest County, Mississippi, 1962.

Choctaw Ridge discovery blowing out. Derrick man coming down in a hurry,
Choctaw County, Alabama, 1967.

Triad Oil and Gas, Inc. L-R Dudley Hughes, Beadie Noel, Carrol Jones, 1961
(Photo Dudley Hughes)

Dudley Hughes during the Pruet & Hughes era, 1967–1978

Chesley Pruet (center) and Dudley Hughes (right) receiving the
"Wildcatter of the Year" award from Hilton Ladner

The signing of the huge Miller Mill Company lease, 1970, Brewton, Alabama.
Sitting L-R Tom Neal, John R. Miller, Tommy McMillan. Standing, Dick Stephens,
Ed Leigh McMillan. (Courtesy Tom McMillan Jr.)

On location in the quadruple giant Jay Field, Florida. LL&E's Richard Stephens (L) and John R. Miller Jr., Pres. Miller Mill Co. Circa 1971. (Courtesy Tom McMillan Jr.)

L-R Bob Moon, Ralph Hines, and Jim Furrh at the discovery of Dinan Field, Walthall County, Mississippi, 1970 (Photo Jim Furrh)

North Choctaw Ridge discovery, Choctaw County, Alabama, 1972

Kelton Corporation's Tom Sylte helped discover much Smackover oil in south Alabama. (Photo Tom Sylte)

Discoverer of the Greens Creek Field, Jeff Davis County, Mississippi, Larry Boland (1976). The field was the biggest in the Deep Hosston Play.

Pruet Oil Co. Exploration Manager, Dave Cate, who helped explore the Deep Hosston

King of the wildcatters, Chesley Pruet, at a speaking engagement in Boca Raton, Florida, 1976

Consultant Tom Joiner, Alabama State Geologist and Oil and Gas Supervisor, 1977–1981

L-R Oil finders George Vockroth, Dan Herlihy, Hilton Ladner, and Marvin Oxley, circa 1980

Mississippi geologist Harry Spooner

William "Bill" Tucker,
founder of Warrior Drilling &
Exploration, Inc.

Geologist Les Aultman and Log Analyst
Ed Kendrick on a well in south Alabama

A pumping unit on one of 5,000 wells in west central Alabama, removing water
from coal seams to produce methane gas

Paramount's Trimble discovery, Smith Co., Mississippi, 1988
(Photo courtesy of Paramount Petroleum Corporation)

Geologist Bob Schneeflock at his Frisco City, discovery in 1988, Monroe County, Alabama

Paramount Petroleum's Robert Chaney (L) and Bob Schneeflock at their
North Frisco City discovery, Monroe County, Alabama, 1991

M.B. "Duke" Rudman, oil investor who risked millions to support exploration in the Deep South

Geophysicist Robert Gaston

Geophysicist Charles Morrison

Black Warrior Basin pioneers Fleming Browning (L)
and Stewart Welch, who sparked Mississippi's
Selma Chalk Play in 1989

Bean Resources 29-7 Beard, Wayne County, Mississippi, 2001.
The rig was lost when the Smackover blew out.

County in 1952. He too was a lawyer, but Pollard fired his imagination and mobilized him to learn as much as he could about the science and the business of oil. He never started a company, preferring to work on his own leasing and buying minerals, and investing and promoting interests in wildcat wells. Still, he and everyone else in south Alabama gradually became despondent. It seemed to them another Pollard was not to be. For sixteen years, dozens of wildcat wells found only dust or water in search of more Lower Tuscaloosa oil. Humble's Norphlet discovery at Flomaton in 1968 revived hope.

It's Coming Our Way

Thomas McMillan's oil passion flared again with Flomaton, as did every other mineral owners' along the Alabama-Florida state line. "After that it got really hot around here," Tom Jr. said. "All the big companies came in looking for leases and putting together their plans. Humble opened an office here in Brewton. The Oil and Gas Board opened a field office here. Brewton was a boomtown for a while."[10]

The McMillan family and other heirs of T.R. Miller watched as the Smackover play in Mississippi marched toward them. "Everybody got really excited," Tom said. "We thought, if it comes this way [toward their 200,000 acres], it could hardly go around us."

Oil companies began to court the vast T.R. Miller and related land interests that included the McMillan Trust and the McDavid Lands—250,000 acres all told, much in the immediate vicinity of the Flomaton discovery. Securing such a lease would be a coup of major proportions. Everyone wondered who would get it.

John Appleyard, historian of the T.R. Miller Mill Company, wrote that a small and relatively new oil company decided to go to Brewton to talk with the Miller group. The Louisiana Land and Exploration Company (LL&E) invested with Dudley Hughes and Chesley Pruet in the Jurassic play of Mississippi and were encouraged by those successes. They took a negotiating team with them from their New Orleans headquarters. John R. Miller Jr. headed the owners team, which included Tom McMillan Sr. and other family members, plus members of the Douglas, Foshee, and Huxford families, all large landowners. Several meetings led to an agreement. LL&E leased the lands for a one-year geophysical option of one dollar per acre, with attendant lease selection rights of five dollars per acre. The royalty reserved for the landowner group was a staggering, almost unheard of 25%.[11]

Observers speculated that LL&E's advantage over other oil companies in the negotiations was its ability to talk landowner to landowner. The company owned over 600,000 acres of land in Louisiana, which it used in agriculture, forestry, and recreation, as well as oil and gas. Appleyard wrote that the unique rapport between the two companies stemmed from their mutual understanding of the rights and expectations of multiple land use and conservation.

Tom McMillan Jr. put it this way. "We felt like they [LL&E] would take care of the land. That was important, too. We had seen some environmental problems at Pollard. The timber still hasn't grown back where they allowed saltwater to flow out onto the ground. We didn't want to turn our forests into an ugly eyesore. So we felt like LL&E would do a better job of looking after the rights of the property owner. . . . It worked out great for us."

LL&E enjoyed another advantage; many of the competitors were concerned that the vast majority of the Miller acreage was north of the Foshee fault, which played a major role in the geology at Flomaton. Lands north of the fault were not considered geologically attractive, Appleyard explained. "LL&E . . . the newcomer on the block, was not as bound as most others by this geological dogma. They also had the foresight to realize that the Miller group wanted to lease to a single company for a comprehensive exploration program over the entire 250,000 acres, not just the generally considered more attractive 15,000 acres south of the Foshee fault."[12]

Meanwhile, Humble acquired a very strategic lease south of the Foshee fault from St. Regis Paper Company and commenced extensive seismic operations on and around it in 1969. LL&E conducted similar but more focused seismic surveys on selected areas north of the fault. As a result, Appleyard noted, "Some felt that Humble could just wait out LL&E's seismic option [on the premise that LL&E] would probably choose to relinquish most or all of their options south of the fault, as they had no seismic information upon which to intelligently base a lease selection. The only 'chink in the armor' in this scenario was that, because of the extensive nature of the group's holdings, LL&E would have the right to extend their seismic option rights for an additional six months beyond the initial 12 month term by making an additional pro-rata option payment of 50 cents an acre."[13] The extension provision proved to be LL&E's salvation as events rapidly unfolded in the following months.

"It was our last hurrah."

While LL&E wrapped up its deal with the Miller group, Humble's Charlie Meeks, Harry Owens, and Dave Brassfield went back to Houston in the wake of their Flomaton discovery. Meeks' insider version of Humble's attitude toward its south Alabama-Florida Panhandle play contrasts with John Appleyard's account. Despite the company's leasing and seismic work in the area, Flomaton and its H_2S infested gas was not popular with Humble's managers. "They chewed Harry out unmercifully," Meeks said, "for wasting Humble's money."[14] Meeks and Owen told them they wanted to drill another wildcat in the area. Their bosses initially said no. Meeks and Owen still had some exploration money allotted to their district, though it was only enough to drill half a Smackover well. They figured that was enough for a start.

Meeks created a structure map from the seismic data Humble shot across the area. The quality of the data was not good, because the shooting in the river bottoms was more difficult than anticipated and produced poor records. But Meeks did his best. His map showed that the Foshee fault, against which the Flomaton Field was trapped, extended southeasterly into Escambia County, Florida. His contours showed no north dip into the fault, and the separation between his prospect area and Flomaton was iffy at best. That was a serious weakness, because his proposed location appeared to be structurally low to Flomaton. Meeks knew that the Smackover was tight at Flomaton and formed a barrier against any migrating Smackover hydrocarbons—if the Smackover was porous at his intended drillsite. That was another very big if.

"We went back to Houston and asked for enough to drill the well," Meeks said. "Kind of our last hurrah." The Humble managers looked at the poor data, shook their heads, and showed the geologists the door, but Meeks and Owen had an idea.

Although they were employees of a giant oil company, they mounted a deal-hawking campaign that would do an independent proud. They sent their district landman, Jack Robbins, to some potential partners—W.R. Moncrief and Marshall R. Young—asking if they were interested in joining Humble in the well. Both wanted a quarter each, which would leave Humble with half, the amount that Meeks and Owens had remaining in their exploration budget. They took the plan back to Houston and got it approved. By then they were in deep land trouble. The St. Regis leases were expiring, and they couldn't find a rig.

Meeks had to scramble. "I went to LL&E and showed them my map. We didn't have very much good data. We showed it to their geophysicist, Jim Landrum. He was about as crazy as me. He said, 'I'll take it to my boss, J.O. Banks.' J.O. took it, agreeing to 30% of the well."

Moncrief and Young wanted Humble to operate the well. Humble agreed but it wanted to reduce its risks further. In his history of the T.R. Miller Company, Appleyard explained that Humble sent a negotiator to LL&E and proposed a risk-sharing unit "encompassing 3,840 acres southeast of Flomaton, on which Humble and LL&E would each have 35%. That would give each of them a dry hole exposure of about $100,000. Humble shared its seismic information with LL&E as an inducement. After evaluating the data LL&E agreed to the deal. Soon, other leaseholders within the unit (Moncrief & Young, Amerada, Chevron, and others) agreed to join. A few companies got jittery at the risk and economics of sour gas and farmed their interest out to the participators."[15]

LL&E's Richard B. Stephens thought that those companies had good reason to opt out. "The latter group's position [those who opted out] was understandable as the general attitude within the domestic oil and gas business was pessimistic. Low pricing, increasing imports and numerous voices in Washington calling for the reduction/limitation of the depletion allowance were all factors collating to pinch oil companies' exploration budgets in the late 1960s. Many of the old pros in various organizations pointed out the extremely high risk nature of the test, both from an H_2S sour gas and CO_2 standpoint, as well as the fact of its being in an untested area and fault block. Clearly, prudence directed sitting this one out, at least until the overall environment for oil and gas showed some improvement."[16]

Prudence also paid off for a few savvy independents who didn't mind bucking Doc Jones's old warning. Two years earlier Chisholm and Stack of Meridian, Mississippi, earlier looked at a 2,000 acre Lower Tuscaloosa property submittal located about six miles southeast of Flomaton. They didn't like it much but called on their consultant, Dudley Hughes. Hughes didn't like the Lower Tuscaloosa idea either, but he recommended Chisholm and Stack take the deal for its deep potential. Hughes, wary of sour gas prospects, was not interested in any of it for himself. On his advice they took the deal and drilled a 7,000-foot dry hole, earning the deeper rights. Little did they realize that this small venture that resulted in a dry hole would save their company from bankruptcy and make them fabulously rich. Two years later those leases were under Humble and LL&E's bullseye.

A Real Mess

LL&E's Stephens described what happened when the joint venture well finally got started. "In spite of the formidable odds against it, the Humble-LL&E No. 1 St. Regis Land Company [two miles south of the AL-FL line] . . . was spudded during the first week of March 1970. As drilling ensued, results were anything but encouraging. As the well began to enter the Jurassic formation, intermediate logging and geological correlation found the well running discouragingly low to the original geophysical/geological prognosis. Some of the more creative geophysical mapping at the time even traced some newly recognized faulting in the vicinity of the drillsite in anticipation of explaining the forthcoming dry hole to management."[17]

As the well neared the Smackover, Humble's Charlie Meeks picked a coring point and sent Ed French down to monitor the coring operation. Meeks was in his office when French called. "Ed said, 'We've got a real mess down here. We've got oil everywhere! The core is black. It stinks. What do you want me to do?'" Meeks recalled his veteran geologist, Dave Brassfield, from vacation and sent him to the well. "Dave called and said, 'Charlie, we've got 400 feet of pay in this well!'"[18]

Richard Stephens recalled that day with metaphoric flair. "Then lightning struck and the forest trembled—while drilling at 15,428 feet the well entered the Smackover formation, heretofore not productive within 80-100 miles of the Flomaton area, and began coring operations on what proved to be almost 100 feet of Smackover pay. After this unexpected but dramatic encounter, the well continued drilling through its primary objective, the Norphlet section, which unfortunately proved to be 'popcorn dry' to a total depth of 15,984 feet. It was later completed on June 11, 1970, testing at a rate of 1,712 barrels of Smackover oil per day."

Stephens' dramatic account notwithstanding, no lightning strike could ever shatter the stillness of the Gulf Coast like that well did, nor could the forests of the Florida Panhandle tremble as did the oil people who watched the epic discovery unfold. The strike was far grander than any of them imagined. Meeks, Owen, and Brassfield had found one of the biggest onshore oil fields in the lower 48 states since Dad Joiner discovered the East Texas Field in 1930.

As development wells were put down in the new Jay Field, which eventually covered 22 square miles, the geological information they revealed was fascinating. Meeks and his contemporaries found that a saddle of only 100 feet separated the Jay structure from the higher Flomaton structure. They found also that they were wrong to predict no north dip. The structure had several hundred feet of dip reversal into the Foshee fault. As information came in, the field's structural contours began to resemble a jagged witch's nose coming down out of Alabama and pointing southeast.

The Smackover dense micritic limestone in Flomaton changes to porous dolomitized grainstones—ideal reservoir rocks—on the Jay structure. Development drilling delineated a permeability barrier that forms an inverted "V" shape with the apex sticking up into Alabama, though the main body of the reservoir lies in Florida (Figure 12). The average pay thickness of the wells is 98 feet, with an average porosity of 15%. One well, the St. Regis 5-2, had an astounding permeability of 8,000 millidarcies. The rock was a veritable sponge.

The oil in the Jay Field contains 10% H_2S, which necessitated building nine plants to sweeten the crude at the rate of 91,500 barrels per day, at a cost of $50 million. The gas separated from the oil was dehydrated, compressed, and sent through a pipeline for sale to Florida Gas Transmission Company. The oil was piped to Mobile and the sulfur was trucked in a liquid state and sold.

LL&E's Stephens described the strike's amazing results. "Jay was a true Cinderella story. Subsequent drilling proved Jay to cover over 14,000 acres and to have an estimated reserve of 737 million barrels of original oil in place. This obviously turned out to be a company-maker for both the T.R. Miller Company group and LL&E."

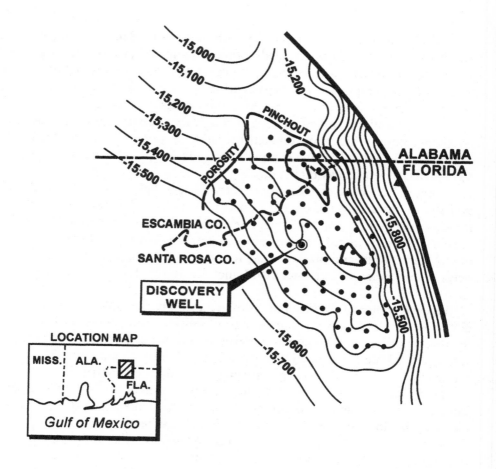

Figure 12. Structure Map—Top of Smackover, Jay Field, Escambia County, Florida after Ottomann, Keves, and Ziegler, Transaction—Gulf Coast Association of Geological Societies, Vol. XXIII, 1973.

Through the end of 2003 Jay had produced an equivalent 413 million barrels of oil. Gas production reached over 500 Bcf—halfway to giant gas field status.

Most Floridians thought of oil as something they put in their automobiles. They didn't know enough about petroleum to realize what a monumental piece of history the strike was. It absolutely astounded the petroleum world, and the timing could not have been better.

The wells could not be produced until the H_2S processing plants were built, a lengthy delay, but while the Jay operators waited it out, the government installed its tiered price system. The delay caused the Jay oil to fall under the "new oil" classification. Thus, not only did the operators find a quadruple giant, they found it just before oil prices quadrupled or more.

Jay represented the best the oil business can be. At its peak, Jay oil flowed at over 100,000 barrels a day.

Humble was an able steward of the field, applying its vast resources and expertise with state-of-the-art technology to maximize production. It was the first company to discover oil in South Alabama at Pollard in 1952. Flomaton followed in 1968. "We consider ourselves to be old corporate citizens of this state," said R.G. Parse, Humble's district manager. Local citizens tended to agree. They became familiar and comfortable with their corporate neighbor.

Humble and the field's other operators—along with a host of companies watching on the sidelines—launched aggressive new leasing campaigns throughout the area. *Business Week*'s July 8, 1972, issue noted that Jay touched off the same type of exploration enthusiasm as Texas' famous Spindletop Field in the 1920s.[19] The Florida Division of Interior Resources issued temporary allowables of 1,000 barrels a day per well in the field. It was only a precaution. Humble had been in the business too long to jeopardize the field with ill-advised excessive production rates.

The three men who peered down through 16,000 feet of rock and visualized the Jay Field—Charlie Meeks, Harry Owen, and Dave Brassfield—met both frustration and elation in 1972. They made plans for a new beginning as independents. Meeks remembered the Jay days with the cynicism of an eager employee collared by big company bureaucracy and the realism of a streetwise oil finder. "Well, if we had listened to Humble's management we would never have discovered Jay Field. Someone else would have, because there's a structure there and wherever there's a structure, some idiot's going to drill it. I really believe that. The guy that found Jay Field was Harry Owens. He stuck to it. He wouldn't let it go. Harry and Dave Brassfield did the stratigraphy, and they believed in it."

The minor players also gained immensely from the big strike. Despite earlier successes in Mississippi, Chisholm and Stack owed a great deal of money. They were close to bankruptcy. The First National Bank of Jackson, of which Bob Hearin was president, called a creditors' meeting. Hearin was responsible for bringing Amerada-Hess to Mississippi and served as a director on their Board. While the creditors were meeting with Chisholm and Stack, a landman from Humble walked into Hearin's office and offered a staggering price for the 2,000 acres of leases Chisholm and Stack owned (from drilling the shallow Lower Tuscaloosa well) two miles south of the Jay discovery. Hearin thanked him and said he would let him know. Then he called Leon Hess and told him of Humble's offer. They agreed to try to get the acreage for Amerada-Hess.

Hearin took Chisholm and Stack out of the creditors' meeting and offered to take over all their debt and properties. Chisholm and Stack would get back half their interest after Amerada-Hess got their money back. They accepted. The deal eventually produced several hundred million dollars of income for the two companies, since the 2,000 acres of leases became part of the Jay Field. Reflecting on the deal, Bob Hearin said, "A good deal is a good deal for everybody."[20] In the case of Jay no truer words were spoken.

More words, true and embellished, inundated the area's newspaper readers and spread the fever further. The Tri-City Ledger's "2nd Annual Oil Issue" (circa 1973) heralded the following banner across the top of the front page: "The Oil Center of the South: The Tri-cities of Flomaton, South Flomaton, Century, and Jay."[21]

Few readers noticed, perhaps, that there were four cities, not three, and the fact that they were more like hamlets than cities was immaterial. In the hopes of many growth minded citizens, they might soon become cities. Interestingly, in a small piece buried in a corner of the special edition—surrounded by columns of hype, scuttlebutt, and commentary—the Ledger warned its readers that petroleum was "only a near term answer" to the nation's insatiable energy appetite.

The T.R. Miller Company was a big advertiser in the Tri-City's special oil issue. The company flourished as never before with the influx of production revenue, turning the money back into its operations, building more infrastructure, and hiring more employees. The McMillan family kept a close watch on the oil field operations that spread across their holdings and saw that the land remained clean and mostly undisturbed. Brewton and the local economy boomed. The Old South Restaurant in Brewton became the preferred eatery and social spot for oil field people. The Colonial Inn, next to it, housed the many out-of-state workers. Ben Strain, then the president and manager of MD&S Mud Sales said, "From 3:00 A.M. until past midnight, the Old South served as a reference point, watering hole, and kitchen for all oil field personnel. To find anyone connected with the field, one needed only go to the Old South and ask Mae, who would tell them what time any individual was in the restaurant."

Strain's most vivid recollection of the Jay boom days is a vision that rouses oil seekers. "Probably the most famous spot in the oil patch was the Double Bridges, a spot on Highway 29 between Flomaton and Brewton where two bridges cross the Escambia River. At one stage of development, from the bridges after dark you could see the lights of 28 drilling rigs in full operation."

The Smackover boom would continue for a while. More strikes came, but few as big as Jay anywhere onshore in the lower 48 states. Through it all, the creeks ran clear and undefiled, the forests teemed with wildlife, and the oil facilities were so well managed that a stranger driving through the area would likely not know he was in a major oil producing region.

The Escambia County courthouse was awash with landmen and lawyers, and out in the countryside tall derricks rose above the pines and sent their bits spinning toward the deep Jurassic rocks. Oilmen still hoped to extend the trends that began in Mississippi into Alabama. Back to the northwest, rural Washington County, Alabama, was about to join the producers' club.

Chapter 13

Landman to the Rescue

Working for Phillips Petroleum Company's land department out of Jackson, Lloyd Tankersley enjoyed meeting the people who made the oil business possible—landowners. He knew it took a special kind of poise to work with them. They wanted respect, honest talk, and sometimes even emergency help.

A recently widowed woman, unaccustomed to doing business without her husband, was reluctant to sign a lease. Another landman had failed to sign her. Tankersley was asked to give it a try. He found her looking hysterically up into a tree where a snake was about to devour a nest of baby birds. The mother bird flapped helplessly. Tankersley borrowed a shotgun from a neighbor and dispatched the snake as it was about to make its breakfast selection. In no time he had a signed lease in hand. "I will always wonder if I had hit the birds rather than the snake would I have gotten the lease."[1]

On another occasion Tankersley walked into a real crisis. He arrived at a prospective lessor's house about 30 minutes after a woman suffered a heart attack. The husband was trying frantically to call an ambulance. It soon became obvious to Tankersley that the ambulance might not come because the people were poor and likely could not pay. Tankersley got on the phone and told them he was an oilman there to lease the couple's property and that they'd better get their butts out there on the double. The couple's credit rating instantly went up, and the ambulance arrived shortly.

Tankersley's most memorable project was his role in Phillips' attempt to get in on the act in Alabama. Geologists had known for years about the large salt structure in west central Washington County, about five miles from the Mississippi line. It had been drilled twice, by Humble in 1949 and by Coral Drilling Company in 1978. Both ventures were dry, as was a re-entry attempt. All but two of Phillips' geologists wrote off the structure.

Dick Strahan and Ed Schuett concluded that Humble and Coral never reached the Louann Salt, as assumed previously. They convinced their management that the structure needed more seismic data. Tankersley was sent to acquire seismic permits but ran into opposition by a Jackson independent who owned some of the leases. Still, he found a sufficient number of leases open to justify a leasing program. His boss, Henry Tyler, convinced company management to buy the leases first and then shoot the seismic survey—a gutsy gamble. Tankersley and his team went to work buying at $25 an acre but soon were stonewalled by the Scott brothers, big owners in the area. The Scotts wanted $50. Phillips' management said no. Such a high bonus would inflate lease costs across the county. Tankersley haggled with the Scotts for weeks until Shell hit gas in the Norphlet six miles west in Mississippi, which became the small State Line Field. Tankersley said, "I knew my game of cat and mouse with Howard Scott was over." Phillips caved in and paid the asking price for the 1,720 acre Scott lease.

They tried to keep a lid on the big bonus, but the word spread like wildfire. Tankersley remembered hearing the news. "While I was checking leases in the courthouse, Ed Turner, a local lawyer, came into the record room and called across the room to [an associate], 'John, the oil business has come to Chatom! I just saw a check to Howard Scott from Phillips for $86,000!'" The cat was most assuredly out of the bag.

Even after acquiring the difficult lease, Tankersley's troubles were not over. Phillips engineers were moving faster than the land department could secure the remaining leases. The prospect was ready to drill before Tankersley could sign a critical farmout from the Jackson independent who stonewalled them on the seismic permits. He had a verbal agreement with the independent, but the guy was busy and out of pocket much of the time. By the time Phillips spudded their Williams AA No. 1, he still had not signed a written agreement on the critical farmout. "Dick Miller and myself were way out on a limb on this matter," Tankersley said, "and if he [the independent] had not been a man of his word I probably would have not reached retirement with Phillips."

The well hit big, testing almost 1,000 barrels of gas-condensate per day and over four million cubic feet of gas per day from over 100 feet of Smackover pay beginning at 16,000 feet. The gas was sour and a plant had to be built. The field, named Chatom, went on production four years later in 1974. It was unitized in 1976 and by 2000 it produced over 16 million barrels of oil and 188 Bcf from nine wells. Chatom was a remarkable example of good geological investigation and clever landwork.

Amoco hoped it would find a Chatom of its own when it spudded a wildcat four miles northeast of Phillips' big strike. They found porous Smackover below 16,000 feet on a small salt pillow and named it Copeland Field. The field produced only 14 Bcf from the Smackover and a small amount of oil from the Norphlet. Washington County, Alabama, saw a few additional small strikes in later years but, with the exception of Chatom, it has remained curiously barren of large accumulations of commercial hydrocarbons. That is especially disheartening to Washington County landowners since they are sandwiched between producing counties north and south.

Although no one knew it at the time, 1970 was a climactic year for Mississippi. The state reached its maximum oil production, producing 65 million barrels, coinciding closely with the peak oil production in the United States. Like the nation's, Mississippi's production would decline steadily in the years ahead (Figure 13).

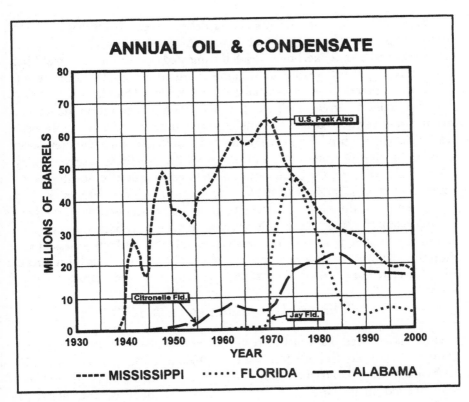

ANNUAL OIL & CONDENSATE

Figure 13. Annual oil production

Alabama had not yet reached that somber peak. Operators like Humble were busily trying to find more Jay-like Smackover production in southwest Alabama. Much to the T.R. Miller Mill Company's delight, it succeeded. Humble brought in the Miller Unit 32 in Escambia County, Alabama, testing nearly 500 barrels a day from the Smackover below 15,000 feet. The Oil and Gas Board granted 160 acre spacing for the new discovery, which it named the Little Escambia Creek Field. Geologically, the Little Escambia Creek Field was the portion of the Jay Field that extended northward into Alabama. By the mid 1990s the field had produced over 31 million barrels of oil, four billion cubic feet of gas, and 300,000 long tons of commercial sulfur.

On the heels of Chatom and Little Escambia Creek came two small strikes by a newcomer to south Alabama, Getty Oil Company. Emboldened by their Smackover successes in Clarke County, Mississippi, in the late 60s, Getty marauded into Alabama precariously near the Smackover's updip limit, but the gamble did not pay off as well as they hoped. In December 1970 Getty discovered the Uriah Field in southeastern Monroe County. Three months later they drilled five miles southeast and scored again, discovering the Vocation Field.

Both fields found porous Smackover draped over a basement anticline below 13,000 feet. The Louann Salt was absent. At Vocation, the Smackover thinned over the anticline, but at Uriah it truncated against the basement high point, forming a combination stratigraphic/structural trap. Vocation turned out to be another dreaded one-well field, but it produced handsomely, making over two million barrels of oil and five Bcf. Uriah was an economic failure, making only 300,000 barrels. Both fields were significant only in that they extended Smackover production farther north in south Alabama than previously thought feasible. Despite disappointment with the two fields' reserves, Getty refused to give up on the Smackover and turned its attention south toward Mobile, where it scored one of the South's best strikes a few years later.

In distinct contrast to the excitement of the Smackover play, an enterprising group of oilmen began toiling antlike in the mushy backcountry north of Mobile, hidden, ignored, and overshadowed by the flashy business of exploration. They were an innovative group, convinced there was more profit to be harvested in an old field most people avoided like the plague.

"Oil people wouldn't go in there!"

Charlie Haynes had just finished his Ph.D. in petroleum engineering at the University of Texas and was looking for a challenging sort of job—back in Alabama, he hoped. A friend of a friend got him in touch with Henry Belden, who needed an Indiana Jones type to lead an expedition into some of Alabama's most remote swampland to do some additional development in a cantankerous old oil field—South Carlton. The weak and feeble-hearted need not apply.

Humble discovered South Carlton in 1950, atop an expansive salt-supported structure 5,000 feet below the Alabama River in north Baldwin County, but Humble had been disappointed. They found oil only in the Massive Sand of the Lower Tuscaloosa, and it was very low gravity: 15 degrees API, the consistency of molasses. The crude had to be heated once it reached the surface or else it would solidify. It was a messy, expensive operation made worse by its location in the remote, swampy region. Humble developed the field nevertheless and later sold it to Patrick Petroleum.

New technology and rising oil prices caused opportunistic eyes to swing toward the old field, among them Belden & Blake of Canton, Ohio, interested in diversifying from its Appalachian operations. In 1971 Belden & Blake bought South Carlton and some additional leases around it from a Houston broker. Charley Haynes arrived in the swamp a year later, after the company's operations got underway.

Haynes, who had some oil field experience from several years at Shell prior to his graduate studies, tackled the challenge but quickly found he had much more than he bargained for. Transportation into and out of the remote field was a major problem. From the get-go he found himself playing as much the role of civil engineer as petroleum engineer. "I was riding into the field on the back of a bulldozer just to drill the wells. It was so impassable; that's the way you went in to the field and you just sat there until they brought you food or a way out. . . . What I noticed when I went down there is they didn't have any idea of logistics in preparing for the wet season.

"You learned to live with the idea that you could actually die on your way to work in the winter, because you couldn't drive into the field but had to go on that river at high water. It sent a message to you." There was no solid ground when the river was at flood stage in winter. "You could fall out and grab a treetop, but what have you got then?" Several times barges full of casing overturned in the river. "I immediately put the operation on a schedule where we drilled in the summer and then laid in all of our supplies in the fall—the dry season—and then just stayed there as if we were on an island. This simplified things until the sticker shock when we found out how much we had to buy. It was a very remote area."[2]

Early on, Haynes had let some wells to go under water during the wet season, but he worked out a plan to keep South Carlton's feet dry. "I ran a line of levels from a benchmark about 20 miles south of the field. I brought the line in and established to my satisfaction where sea level was. Then I started backfilling 25 feet above that. I thought that would take care of the 100-year flood. So we drilled on the swamp floor in the summer and set surfacing casing about 25 feet in the air. It looked strange. And then we would backfill the pads and build all our roads."

Road building in the swamp was another headache. "People take stone for granted. In the swamp there's no stone, so no matter what you build, it's out of squishy, fine-grained swamp material. I heard about this fabric from some civil engineering buddies. We put geotech fabric down and backfilled on that, and it just stabilized the heck out of the roads. When the weather came in we were all set. I found out a lot of this after a long time of trial and error."

With the flooding and roads problems solved, Haynes focused on production and drilling operations. When he came on the scene, Belden & Blake was conducting directional drilling operations. From a six-well pad, one was vertical and five were directional, or slanted in different directions. Directional drilling's advantage was the ability to drill from a surface location hundreds or even thousands of feet horizontally from the intended target point below the surface, but it was very expensive.

Belden and Blake's directional drilling was successful, but the mechanics of bringing the heavy oil up a sloped hole were troublesome. "The hydraulic pumps didn't work," Haynes said, "so we did some experimenting and tried rod pumps in those wells—some of them inclined up to 35 degrees. And we managed to whip the engineering problems associated with rod-pumping directional wells."

Finding experienced personnel to work the field was also a problem. "Oil people wouldn't go in there. For example, we had to change the rod pumps, and you had to have a rig to do that. You couldn't call one in from Laurel. Well, you could, but it wasn't good practice when you saw the bill. So we had to buy a pulling unit and train people from outside the oil patch. . . . We took auto mechanics, cops, and people like that and tried to make oil field hands out of them."

Haynes' learning curve shot up steeply those first months. Often he was the most experienced hand in the field and learned as he went. "I would sit out on a stump or can and go through dry runs of just latching onto sucker rods and tubing and finally got up enough nerve to have them lower it into the well."

Finally, production operations on the new wells began, and with it more headaches. "It comes out hot," said Haynes, "at about 110 degrees with a lot of water—say 90% water. So you're okay getting to a tank battery. The oil would separate from the water very nicely. But then when you put it in the tanks it solidified. The tanks were all steam-traced—with coils around them. And so when we decided to ship, we'd get 10,000 barrels ready and the barge would come. We would have to heat the stock tanks in order to be able to pump the oil over into the barge." South Carlton's 15-degree gravity crude was a semi-solid below 100 degrees. They had to heat it to 120 degrees to pump into the barges.

The energy source for heating the oil was steam. They used diesel fuel to generate the steam. "It got pretty expensive." Haynes looked for a way to cut heating costs and saw a unique opportunity when the government instituted the tiered pricing system. Most operators focused on "new oil" to get high prices, but Haynes was delighted with finding sources of "old oil" for his steam boilers. "I checked around and found I could get condensate from Bassfield, Mississippi, as old oil. We spent $6 a barrel for this natural crude oil versus $1 a gallon for diesel. Quite a difference in costs—42 gallons equal $42 versus $6. . . . I tested it, and it appeared to be like a natural diesel.

"Now here's the fun part. We made the decision to buy 500 barrels of that condensate to use as boiler fuel. That stuff looked like water in a glass—very clear, beautiful stuff!

"Well, the guys were scared of it. They thought the boiler would explode. I said, 'Look, here are the specs for diesel—gravity, viscosity, and so forth—all you really have is ultra-clean diesel.' That's all it was. It had practically no sulfur in it. I mean, I didn't go into this thing blind. I had a lab check it. I knew what I had. They [the crew] still wouldn't buy into it. So, I did the ceremonial lighting of the boiler. I walked up there and lit it and, poof! It lit. I said, 'Okay guys, get back to work.' I couldn't let them see my weak knees. I had to play big shot. I staggered around behind the tank battery."

But the expense of heating didn't stop there. "The barge was also traced [heat-coiled]. So when it got to the refinery they'd hook up a steam generator to the barge and heat the oil and pump it off."

Haynes had little trouble finding a market for the oil. "I sold it every where from Exxon on the Mississippi River all the way around to Tuscaloosa at Black Warrior Refining. I sold it wherever I could."

Haynes' knack for economizing didn't stop there. Later he was a part-time professor at the University of Alabama, where he gave his students a project to keep as much heat in the South Carlton tank batteries as they could. "They put all kind of stuff down there and probably saved us 10-12% on fuel costs."

The field was also an environmental success. "We worked hard on environmental issues at South Carlton," Haynes said. "It was a wetland, and was very beautiful. So I made myself the 'swamp czar' with a mandate to keep the place as unspoiled as possible. Actually, seasonal flooding carried everything loose to Mobile, so we had a 'giant enema' each spring."

Belden and Blake later decided to diversify into other mature fields. "Belden had taken a heavy licking on start-up and on the learning curve at South Carlton," Haynes said. "So someone said what we ought to do is buy more operations in Alabama and spread out this overhead. Dave Grubbs and I evaluated Gilbertown for them." Dr. David Grubbs was an exploration geologist teaching petroleum engineering at the University of Alabama. "Grubbs had a special talent for finding candidate wells, and we reentered a lot of them in South Carlton and Gilbertown on the basis of his work."

Gilbertown was Alabama's first oil field, found in Choctaw County in 1944. Grubbs and Haynes called Glenn Blake to report that Gilbertown could be bought for about $1 million dollars but that the wells made great amounts of water. "Blake, a wonderful man but very profane, cussed us out in a conference call because of the high water production. After he finished his tirade, Dave, in his quiet, elegant manner, just said, 'Glenn, I suppose that this means you don't want Gilbertown. I do, and I have raised the money to buy it. Could you wire us your official refusal so that we can get it?'" They heard Blake muttering in the background, and finally he committed. "Gilbertown repaid the $1 million dozens of times between 1976 and 1989. It was the company-builder that Belden & Blake had sought but could not find in South Carlton."

The lack of other Lower Tuscaloosa oil fields like South Carlton, Pollard, and Gilbertown across south Alabama at first puzzled geologists and mineral owners, then challenged, then frustrated them. Haynes felt all those sentiments a few years later when he participated in an attempt to find another Lower Tuscaloosa field. "Belden drilled the Ferguson well at Little Bear Creek in Baldwin County with Don Fish, geologist, and me as driller," Haynes recalled. "There was a big fault that ran through there that we had seen on old 2-D seismic. We drilled where we thought the Lower Tuscaloosa ought to be behind it and cut 20 feet of Massive sand, oil bearing. I thought we are rich beyond our wildest dreams." It turned out to be a dry hole.

The noticeable absence of widespread Lower Tuscaloosa oil production in the region, according to Tuscaloosa geologist Mike Epsman, was the problem of displacement on the faults. "The key," Epsman said, "is getting the marine shale on the down-thrown block in juxtaposition with your sands on the upthrown block. Porous sand thrown against porous sand will not form a seal; sandstone needs to be thrown against shale or other impermeable rock to trap oil."[3] A fault that might trap oil down deep in the Smackover commonly would not trap the Lower Tuscaloosa. "The oil had just kept on going," Haynes lamented. He and Fish had found only traces of oil that had leaked through the fault.

In 1989 Belden and Blake sold South Carlton and Gilbertown to Ladd Petroleum. From its discovery in 1950 to the beginning of Belden and Blake's operations in 1971, the field produced steadily at a rate of about 10,000 barrels per month. After 1971, production increased to about 12,000 barrels per month and held steady at that rate until the present, at which it has yielded a cumulative total of over eight million barrels, not a lot by the standards of some of the Gulf Coast's other fields, but a remarkable example of how energy sources can be managed more efficiently with innovative engineering and proper price incentives.

Haynes went on to become president of Belden & Blake in the 1980s. The company was sold to the Texas Petroleum Group in 1997.

More Action in Florida

Other than the Jay area, there was light activity elsewhere in Florida in the early 70s. Florida's first oil field, Sunniland Field, a Lower Cretaceous discovery in 1943 in Collier County south of Ft. Meyers, grew to 26 producers, and its production neared 13 million barrels.

Humble reentered a dry hole drilled in 1969 and found oil in the Sunniland zone at about 11,000 feet. It was named the Lehigh Acres Field and was the first production in Lee County. Another Norphlet discovery, Mt. Carmel, was added in 1971 in Santa Rosa County, just east of Jay. Also that year the governor denied Getty Oil permission to drill a Smackover test in east Pensacola Bay. Despite Getty's assurances and attempts to educate a skeptical public, the governor cited "environmental factors" in his decision. In 1972 Humble's

Florida successes continued with the Bear Island Field three miles southeast of Sunniland in Collier County, which has made almost 12 million barrels.

The headlines about the big companies and the thrill of the Smackover strikes of the early 70s overshadowed the little companies' daily struggles, but careers were formed, then, that had significant impact in the long term.

Charlie Meeks finally decided luck would never pay him a visit as long as he stayed on Humble's payroll, no matter how hard he worked. He had security there, but he wanted a piece of the action. As the development at Jay got underway, Meeks—Jay's co-discoverer—had a carrot dangled in front of him. "After the third well was drilled [at Jay], a guy came to me and said, 'We want you to go to work for us.' The guy's same was Ashley Prillion with Sabine, Inc. So I resigned from the Humble company. I really got mad at Humble, because after they drilled their third well they told me, 'Boy, you've done a wonderful job, but you're primarily a geophysicist. We're going to turn this over to another guy to develop.' And they were right, but at the time it made me furious. I was not a development geologist, but at the time I thought I was everything. So I just quit. I was really hacked off. I left and opened a little office in New Orleans. . . . Harry Owens, said 'Charlie, you got room for a partner? I'm going to quit, too.' I said, 'Great!' I took him up to meet Ashley Prillion; then the landman quit who put it all together, Jack Robbins. The Humble company didn't miss us. Hell, they just assigned some other men."[4]

Soon Meeks and Owens had uncovered a new lead, which they showed to Sabine, the company that retained them to generate new prospects and screen outside deals. Sabine bought acreage on the lead a few miles southeast of Jay in Santa Rosa County and drilled. They found Smackover and Norphlet and named the new strike the Blackjack Creek Field.

Blackjack Creek was a significant find. It produced over 58 million barrels by 2000, but it became a somber marker for explorers in the years to come. Meeks lamented over the sad significance of his discovery: "And this is the end of the Smackover trend, as we know it. We never have been able to find anything to the south." Meeks worked with Sabine for 14 years, making additional discoveries in the Hosston, Lower Tuscaloosa, and Smackover in Mississippi and Alabama.

With the Florida discoveries of Jay and Blackjack Creek at its southern doorstep, exploratory action in south Alabama was firmly established in two focal points which people hoped would work toward each other and merge into a great trend. Those points were southcentral Escambia County—kicked off by the Jay discovery—and south central Choctaw County, which was the trend extended from Mississippi. The gap in between was over 80 miles long.

Hits, Misses, and Head-Scratchers in Choctaw

Pruet & Hughes, preferring to work the northwest end, provided the next excitement. After their successes at Choctaw Ridge in 1967 and Turkey Creek in 1969, both in Choctaw County, they wanted more. They made a deal to work Amoco's seismic records in the area. They mapped several untested structures, based on the data. Two were promising, and the third was poorly defined and did not inspire much confidence; but Pruet & Hughes sent their brokers out and secured blocks on the prospects.

They drilled the first two structures, the ones that looked good, and found nothing. Some of their investors lost heart and dropped out of further drilling. They were replaced, and the group drilled the third prospect, the one north of Turkey Creek that did not look as good as the other two.

The result was one of the best discoveries of the Pruet & Hughes era—Womack Hill Field, an elongated salt anticline oriented northwest/southeast, four miles long by one mile wide, faulted along its southwestern flank. The average net pay thickness was 56 feet with a very high porosity of 18%. The new strike tested 600 BOPD from the Smackover below 11,000 feet. The field has produced over 30 million barrels of oil and 18 billion cubic feet of gas from 14 drilling units of 120 acres each.

After that Hughes saw that the Choctaw County play was bigger than he could work alone. He needed help. A promising young geologist working the shallow gas provinces around Monroe, Louisiana, had just turned down a job with Carroll Jones, Hughes's old partner at Triad. Hughes met with him, and soon Harry Spooner was onboard with Pruet & Hughes and helping with the Womack Hill development program.

Spooner was from Arkansas, born and raised in a town that sat atop a giant oil field. Consequently, he caught oil fever. "I worked in the oil field when I was about 17," Spooner recounted. "I was a roustabout, mainly working in the derricks because I was so light. I knew I wanted to be a geologist, although I never knew what a geologist did. The only ones I ever saw were the ones that sat on the well. I didn't really know what one did. There were about 400 kids in the whole 12 grades. We had one geology book in the high school library. I read that book and decided that was what I wanted to do."[5]

Spooner headed for the University of Oklahoma school of geology to satisfy his hunger for a knowledge of the mysteries of the subsurface, eventually emerging with a master's degree. He was tall and thin and spoke with a leisurely drawl.

Spooner came to Jackson in 1954 with Arkansas Fuels, Inc., and learned the geologist's trade under the tutelage of geologist Rex Hewitt. "Rex was good with regional maps," Spooner remembered. "He had the whole state mapped." He recalled that Rex mapped the Citronelle structure before it was discovered but was never able to persuade Arkansas Fuels to make a lease play there. After graduate work back at OU and several years with Chevron and Colorado Oil and Gas, then eight years as an independent in Louisiana, Spooner joined Pruet & Hughes. He was the "best geologist I have ever worked with, before or since," Dudley Hughes said.[6]

Soon after, another geologist, Les Aultman, who also had Hughes' respect, became Spooner's assistant. A Mississippi native, Aultman started out as a high-school football coach but became disenchanted. "I coached five years, and then I realized that I didn't want to be dependent upon 16-year-old kids for my living for the rest of my life."[7] He went back to the University of Southern Mississippi and earned a master's degree in geology. After a short stint with Gulf, he hired on with Pruet & Hughes.

"They had anywhere from 11 to 16 rigs running at that time. It was really exciting," Aultman remembered. He and Spooner were heavily involved in Pruet & Hughes' busy activity in Choctaw County, Alabama, in the early 70s. Both became thoroughly familiar with the Smackover Trend. Both later went independent.

Aultman recalls a particularly interesting pair of industry outsiders who came onto the Smackover scene, stumbling into success with their daring. They couldn't depend on their knowledge and experience—that was almost nonexistent. "Frank Kelton was a Yankee," Aultman said, hinting that Yankees were allowed to stay permanently if they showed the good judgment to marry into the Southern culture, as Kelton did. He established a lucrative soft drink bottling company in Pensacola and began to look for more interesting places to invest his considerable profits. The oil activity in southwest Alabama attracted him, and he began investing in shallow Eutaw drilling deals in the old Gilbertown Field in Choctaw County. After a while, he had enough of being promoted and sought to get in on the ground floor, so he began buying leases on his own. Kelton, his son Frank, and his son-in-law Tom Sylte formed the Kelton Company and bought leases they thought had Eutaw potential on trend with the Gilbertown Filed

Sylte remembered getting the leases himself and learning the landman's trade as he went. "On Saturday mornings I would go up to Butler, Alabama, and go to the courthouse and check the records and find out who owned the leases around there. Saturday afternoons I'd go around and knock on the doors, sign up the farmers, and come back home. Pretty soon I had assembled a block of about 600 acres in there."[8]

"But they [the leases] were in the wrong place for the Eutaw," Aultman said. A mudlogger who worked many wells in the area told Kelton and Sylte he thought the leases had Smackover potential. That excited them, and on the advice of a consultant, they arranged to have a seismic line shot across their block. Then they went to Conoco for a farmout on additional leases.

They weren't sure what to ask for; they just knew they needed the Conoco leases, but they came away with a farmout. Then they went to see Pruet & Hughes' landman, Dane Oliver, for a farmout. Oliver's terms were brutal.

"Dane saw that they were babes in the woods," Aultman said. He gave Kelton an exceedingly tough farmout—50% back-in after payout. Kelton took it without much fuss, believing he was getting a standard deal. "He [Oliver] felt so proud of himself," Aultman remembered.

Kelton drilled the hole straight up. "Straight up" meant putting up 100% of the cost, which amounts to taking 100% of the risk. That was a rare, gutsy move for any small company. It was a dry hole. Shortly after that Mr. Kelton died.

Although dry, Kelton's hole revealed information that suggested another test was in order. The dipmeter log showed north dip. Sylte, wary of drilling another costly well straight up, went out to sell the deal, but found the going tough. "Can you imagine an accountant from a bottling company going out to sell a drilling deal? It was naïve. Everybody laughed at me. No one would take me seriously except one person. That was Dudley Hughes."

"He [Sylte] came up and showed us these two seismic lines," Aultman said. "They were just what we were looking for . . . looked just like Womack Hill! Dudley and I were just drooling when we saw the lines." Hughes decided he wanted a farmout from Sylte, but in the oil patch, what goes around, comes around.

When Hughes asked for the farmout, Sylte replied, "Sure." He was glad to salvage something and have at least a chance to get in on a discovery on someone else's nickel for a change. When Hughes asked what terms Sylte wanted, he shrugged and said, "Same as you gave us." Hughes was not aware of the terms and didn't bother to ask, assuming it was a standard 60/40 or 70/30 deal. Hughes went to Oilver and told him to prepare a farmout agreement with Sylte. "What kind of trade did you make?" Oliver asked.

Hughes said, "The same trade you made them."

Oliver jumped up and shouted, "Oh, my God, you didn't make that deal, did you? We can't live with that!"[9]

But a deal was a deal. They had to live with it. Pruet & Hughes drilled in 1972 but found the Smackover faulted-out. The logs and dipmeter showed they were structurally high but about 300 feet too far south. They planned another try. Sylte laid 50% of his interest off on Robert Mosbacher. The group then kicked off uphole and sidetracked, aiming for a point at the Smackover 500 feet farther north. The sidetrack worked. They found Smackover pay at 12,000 feet. The discovery became the North Choctaw Ridge Field, grew to six wells, and produced over eight million barrels by the end of the century. Amazingly, two of the wells flowed at their maximum allowables of 300 BOPD for over 20 years.

Thereafter Tom Sylte was a regular player in the southeastern Gulf Coast oil business and participated in many wells. Summing up his career, Sylte said, "If you're persistent the first time around, it works a whole lot easier from then on."

As the buy-back of their own farmout showed, Pruet & Hughes wasn't above eating humble pie when the recipe was good. In 1972 they did it again. Jackson independent Vaughan Watkins assembled a block of leases in Choctaw County that Pruet & Hughes had allowed to expire. He shopped it around and eventually showed it to them. They took the deal and drilled it, discovering the Barrytown Field, which produced over three million barrels.

Pruet & Hughes continued to evaluate their North Choctaw Ridge Field by shooting seismic to define the structure's eastern portion more accurately. The work revealed another structure to the northeast. In 1973 they leased and drilled but came up dry. However a dipmeter on the hole showed a strong southerly dip. They moved a quarter mile north and drilled again, discovering the Sugar Ridge Field, which produced over four million barrels. At their height, Pruet & Hughes' Choctaw County operations reached 52 wells, which have cumulatively produced 55 million barrels of Smackover oil, averaging over one million barrels each. Some wells made over 3 million barrels.

With production from its Choctaw County holdings approaching 12,000 barrels a day, Pruet and Hughes evolved into a prolific oil company. They entered into enhancement deals with partners to increase yields. They built a gas processing plant with Placid and invested in storage facilities and barge docks on the Tombigbee River. "This made for a fine operation with the price of crude steadily increasing," Hughes said.

Tough Call on a Cold January Night

While Choctaw County sizzled, Mallard Exploration Company of Midland, Texas, jumped into the Smackover trend and drilled a marginal discovery— or at least they thought so. They nearly walked away from what would become a very lucrative strike.

Mallard's founders, Robert M. Leibrock and Charlie Marsh, obtained a couple of seismic lines across the west flank of the Flomaton anticline, but the data was not definitive. Still, they approached the owners of the leases in the area—Humble, Chevron, and LL&E—for a farmout, which was granted. The bigger companies had no confidence in the acreage, because the Smackover was tight in the Flomaton Field and in other wells drilled on the crest of the anticline. Undaunted, Liebrock and Marsh brought all their partners in on a ground floor basis and started a well.

In August 1971, Mallard spudded its International Paper *et. al.* Unit 2-6 No. 1. It encountered porous Smackover at 15,000 feet. They tested and produced a blue flame, which indicated a high CO_2 content. Marsh was exceedingly disappointed and became despondent. He urged his partners to plug the hole. Geologist Greg Halvatzis, who worked for Mallard, wrote, "Fortunately, Robert [Liebrock] and some of the other partners calmed Charlie down by walking him around the red hills near the well on a very cold January night until he agreed to continue the testing."[10]

The well was eventually completed in the Smackover, flowing six million cubic feet of gas and over 300 barrels of condensate per day. Tests in the Norphlet recovered small volumes of gas and condensate. The Alabama Oil and Gas Board christened the field Big Escambia Creek. Mallard immediately set about to build a processing plant and began to sell gas to an intrastate market. As Halvatzis points out, however, "Exxon, with only an interstate market, did not sell any product until about two years later because they had to build an interstate pipeline. As you can imagine, this caused some major problems regarding balancing and allowables.

"The result was an extremely complicated allocation formula worked out with the Alabama Oil and Gas Board and was used up until the last few years. This also created problems with Exxon's royalty owners who were not receiving income while their neighbors, the Mallard royalty owners, were receiving income.

"Even after Exxon started selling product there were still unhappy royalty owners, because Exxon was receiving a $1.25 per mcf on the interstate market and Mallard was getting $2.50 per mcf selling the gas to an intrastate market."

The Big Escambia Creek Field expanded to 19 wells and by the end of the century reached a cumulative production of over 57 million barrels of gas-condensate and nearly a trillion cubic feet of gas, rich in propane, butane, and sulfur.

The field boasts an unusual, even bizarre, evolution with respect to common oil and gas field development. Halvatzis, who worked extensively in the field through the years, described the surprise it hid for 18 years. "The First Energy Company's Booth 36-14 well drilled in 1989, 18 years after the field was discovered, is the structurally highest well in the field and has the most amount of net pay. Its location was overlooked by Exxon and the other majors in the field, to the benefit of First Energy."

Charlie Marsh was grateful that his partners took him on a cold walk and persuaded him to complete their doubtful discovery. But equally grateful were other keen observers who were convinced that the absence of Smackover porosity at Flomaton did not spell the death of Smackover hopes north of Jay and throughout south Alabama. Big Escambia Creek, or "BEC" as oilmen dubbed it, boosted their expectations, and they stepped up investigations across the region.

The result was another quick discovery. Humble netted a small find at the Fanny Church Field between BEC and Little Escambia Creek Fields. Like its big neighbors, the Fanny Church trap was a pinch-out of porous Smackover. The small field yielded a nice 12 million barrels.

While Escambia County was the object of most oil companies' affections in South Alabama, the resourceful explorers of Union of California studied their maps and rubbed their chins over an area everyone else seemed to have lost confidence in—the graveyard around the giant Citronelle.

Chapter 14

"It had 'time-growth' written all over it."

When Dudley Hughes made a speech at the 50th anniversary of the Alabama Oil and Gas Board, he poked fun at his old friends at Union of California. They were the newcomer on the block in south Alabama, and their insistence that there was more oil to be found in northern Mobile County was pure foolishness, according to many established oil players in the region. Hughes summarized the activity in Mobile County, Alabama, in the early seventies this way: "As a newcomer [to the Salt Basin], we did not give them [Union] much of a chance of succeeding. . . We decided that if Citronelle did not produce from the Smackover, certainly a [nearby] structure low to that would not either. But Union of Cal did not have our superior knowledge."[1]

What Union did have was some shakers and movers in the Jackson office: exploration manager Howard Samsel and senior exploration geologist John Richart. Samsel was a graduate of the University of Washington with a master's from UCLA. He his spent his entire career with Union, mostly in Jackson. His contemporaries agree that he was one of the most colorful characters in the big oil companies. His staff thought of him as eccentric, short-fused, and unpredictable, but possessing a peculiar sense of humor. Geologist Jim Files remembered when Samsel asked him to come into his office shortly after Files was hired. Samsel motioned him to come behind the desk. That unsettled Files, but he did as told and looked down into the desk drawer. It was full of uncashed company paychecks. Samsel—who had done well in the stock market—burst out laughing, telling Files, "It drives the accountants crazy!"[2] But, as Files soon learned, Howard Samsel also had the reputation of a sharp geologist.

"The thing that led us into this area [south of Citronelle Field] was our regional mapping," Samsel said. "We noticed that Citronelle—a giant by definition—was sitting off here by itself at least 75 miles from the nearest significant production. This is very unusual."[3]

"The thing that really rang my bell was Jay," said John Richart. "My God! That thing's unbelievable!" Richart's personality was the opposite of Samsel's. He was a slow talking, laid-back southerner who had gotten his training at the University of Illinois. Yet the two worked together well. "With Jay on one side of the Mobile Graben," he said, "you wondered, 'What about the other side?'"[4]

Richart said Union tried to get an acreage position in the Escambia County play, but they were too late and the price was too high. They turned their attention farther west. "You had the Wiggins Arch coming in from the west," said Richart, "and the Conecuh Ridge and Pensacola Arches coming in from the east. It looked like there just may be a platform in there similar to the Jay/Flomaton area. We were hoping for a couple hundred feet of oolitic peletal rock types, like at Jay."

Because of the absence of Smackover production at Citronelle, the Union team was wary about proposing such a risky idea to management, but they were convinced that the prospect they called "Bayou Sara" was a different ballgame. They thought the seismic information they shot showed that the Smackover section thinned across their prospect. On the Citronelle structure, it did not. That indicated that the Bayou Sara salt feature was growing during Smackover deposition, whereas the salt beneath the Citronelle structure began uplifting after the Smackover was deposited. The team figured the shallow water environment on the growth structure could create reservoir quality rocks. The early timing of the growth would create a trapping structure for subsequent petroleum migration.

Union's Houston managers jumped on the idea. "Bill Ramer knew it had 'time-growth' written all over it," Samsel said. "We had no dissidents."

They drew a huge buy outline, almost a township in size, and turned their landmen loose. Union acquired about 70% of the leases, most of which was International Paper acreage, which was easier than having to deal with highly fragmented small ownership.

In September 1973, Union spudded its test well, the International Paper Company 22-13. Five expensive months later, as the hole neared its target depth below 18,000 feet, Richart was on location to help pick a coring point. He observed several 5-10 foot *drilling breaks*. (A break is a point where the rate of penetration of the drill bit increases markedly, possibly indicating a porous zone.) At each break he ordered the rig to stop drilling and circulate the drilling fluid to give the gas detectors on the surface a chance to record any shows that might come up. The detectors sat dormant and the geologists' hopes fell. Finally, Richart turned to his colleagues and said, "Damn! We should have gotten it by now."

One of the other geologists picked up the interphone and called the rig floor to see what was going on. "They had shut the rig pumps down for 15 minutes to do some work," Richart said, "so we decided to wait another 15 minutes after they started them back up. And—oh boy!—in about five minutes the detectors started kicking off scale. It was just loaded! Everybody there went ape! It was one of those things you don't see very often."

They commenced coring operations and recovered 50 feet of Smackover pay, which they described as a dolomitized algal mat. The well tested a marvelous 1,158 barrels of gas-condensate per day. The gravity was 61 degrees API and the saltwater content was less than 5%. Furthermore—an unexpected and pleasant surprise—the production was relatively free from H_2S compared to the Escambia County production. The Oil and Gas Board granted 640-acre spacing and christened the new discovery the Chunchula Field.

The celebration had hardly subsided when the confirmation well was spudded in February 1974, but that well left Union and lots of others scratching their heads. The Smackover was tight and dry. Another attempt at confirmation was spudded in June 1974 and found good Smackover, testing almost 900 barrels per day. Subsequent development delineated five separate Smackover zones throughout the field. In 1981 the field was unitized. The cumulative production by the year 2000 was over 62 million barrels, putting Chunchula two thirds of the way to giant status.

Samsel, Richart, and the Union gang never found another Chunchula, though they tried. They did, however, find Tiger, Mt. Carmel, and McRaney, all in Mississippi. "We hit three out of every four wildcats," Richart said, "and that was damn good!"

In the 1970s Chunchula was Union's single most valuable holding, according to Samsel. Richart said, "The Gulf Coast was producing about 90% of Unocal's revenues and Chunchula was producing half of that. So we were 45% of the company's revenue."

"Union was a different company, for large companies," Jim Files said. "If somebody had a good idea, it didn't have to go through much red tape to get to the top."

Richart agreed, "And Bill Ramer was 90% of it. He had so much stroke and was such a sharp guy. He cut through the red tape. After he left it changed completely. Not mentioning any names, but when you get a guy who thinks he knows everything about running the show and he doesn't have a clue for exploration, the game's over. It wasn't fun anymore."

Howard Samsel and John Richart both opted for retirement in 1986 after more than 30 years with Union. Their legacy is Chunchula, and if the skeptics still couldn't see the time-growth factor written in Chunchula's geology, Samsel, Richart, and the others on the Union team rewrote it for them 62 million times.

While Union opened their treasure chest at Chunchula, another enterprising exploration staff battled bitterly with their company management over the possibilities right next door.

We had the last laugh.

After the brilliant discoveries of Pachuta Creek and East Nancy in Clarke County, Mississippi, and the disappointing ones in Monroe County, Alabama,

Getty's Gulf Coast staff fell to the task of finding something big again. They poked around the hot action in Escambia County but couldn't interest their management in it. Einar Pedersen, a staff geologist in Getty's New Orleans district office explained it. "We had mapped Jay and wanted to buy the leases, and they [the Getty management] wouldn't let us compete for the leases at what turned out to be the Jay Field. We had a chance to get some of the St. Regis leases, and our management said, 'You guys are crazy and way out of your league.' But we had the last laugh."[5]

Following the rebuff by management, they turned their attention westward and continued their investigation with subsurface work and residual gravity maps. Soon they had some leads. An area south of the old Citronelle Field caught their eye. Matt Lutz, orchestrator of Getty's Clark County, Mississippi, discoveries in the late sixties, explained the attraction. "A lot of folks at that time didn't feel like the Smackover/Norphlet had any potential that far south, because there was a deep Buckner/Haynesville basin just north of the old Citronelle Field. And they thought the rocks would continually deteriorate as you moved southward.

"Our concept was that that would not be true—that there was a paleo-shelf down there that was associated with the Wiggins anticline, and that there would still be a chance for some high energy rocks in the Smackover, and hopefully, some good Norphlet."[6] Union had the same idea at Chunchula, but the two companies were thinking and acting independently, even though their areas of interest were adjacent to each other and overlapped.

An old dry hole in the area drew Getty's attention, not because it had any profound shows, but just because it was there. "One of the things we liked to do back in those early days," Lutz explained, "was to look at old wells that were drilled by major companies that were abandoned as dry holes and had no shallow production. Our concept was that if a company such as Shell or Exxon or Gulf or what have you drilled a well, they must have drilled on an anomaly. And they were at that time looking for the shallow Lower Cretaceous. But when it turned out to be nonproductive, they just stopped. Our concept was that the anomaly was still there and maybe they didn't go deep enough."

Everyone understood the idea, but in this case those who believed the Jurassic rocks south of Citronelle were tight considered it a bad risk. That's why no one tried it, but Lutz and his co-workers did not accept the conventional wisdom.

The old dry hole Lutz mentioned was a Shell well drilled into the Lower Cretaceous and stopped short of the Jurassic. It was the basis for the outline Lutz and his colleagues drew for the exploration project. Their idea was the same as Union's growth concept. Lutz called it a paleo-structure, but unlike Union's smooth ride with management, Getty's New Orleans team ran into trouble with their bosses in California.

"The interesting part of this story," Lutz said, "is that not much of our management thought we had any sense. There was lot of resistance to moving that far out of the regular play—we were 30 to 40 miles from the nearest production." (Union had not yet drilled Chunchula, right next door.) Lutz believed Getty was working the idea before Union got interested in Chunchula, and Union believed *they* were first. Union beat Getty to the punch at leasing operations, yet a big lease offer literally dropped into Lutz's hands. He had to go way out on a limb to secure it for Getty.

Many oil people left for the fabled three Martini lunches on Fridays and didn't return. "I was one of the few people in that office that didn't imbibe," Lutz said, "so I was always left to hold the office down. There was only a landman in the office that day with me—Ronny Jackson. A guy came into the office by the name of Jay Aultmayer. Jay was a promoter/landman from the Mobile area and he had a block of acreage that he wanted to lease. Ronny got so excited he called me to his office. Ronny was a grunt landman, and I was a grunt geologist at that time. He said, 'There's a man here who has acreage all over the Chunchula area.' I said, 'Let's take a look at it.'"

When Lutz saw it he knew he had to take action. Aultmayer had options on several leases, with Creola Minerals the largest owner. The leases sat right on the paleo-structure Lutz was studying. On his own initiative he committed Getty to buying a checkerboard layout, every other square mile (640 acres) across a huge area that covered his prospect. The price was $15 an acre, a steal because most explorers thought it was goat pasture. The five-year leases gave plenty of time to drill.

After the successes in Clark County, Lutz didn't anticipate another war with management, but he was wrong. When the brass hats in Los Angeles found out about Lutz's unauthorized land commitment, they blew their stacks. "The exploration VPs in the Los Angeles office chewed my butt out real big time for buying acreage out in the boondocks—so far out in front of a play in an area that they thought had no potential. But we held on to it and with the help of our district geologist at the time—George Hingle—we fought real hard to keep the acreage. Then finally we convinced the company to let us do the seismic work over it. That was about 1971."

They shot seismic over the area and confirmed the structure. It was big, nine or ten sections. As more information poured in, it grew to 14 sections. Lutz saw that Union's Chunchula feature was a lower lying structure, spread out over a larger area, but not as prominent as the prospect he christened Hatter's Pond. The company finally consented to buy more acreage, giving Getty about a 95% interest in the Hatter's Pond Prospect. They also managed to get some acreage on the Chunchula feature.

When Union proposed to drill, Getty's Los Angeles management forced them to farm their Chunchula acreage out. "Obviously we were butting our heads against a brick wall," Lutz said.

Even after Union's enormous strike at Chunchula, Lutz said they still had trouble convincing Getty to drill Hatter's Pond. Einar Pedersen said, "We told them, 'Hey guys. What are you, crazy?' I think we embarrassed them into drilling it." Only when the Chunchula well began to look like a big discovery did Getty decide to drill Hatter's Pond.

Getty spudded the No. 1 Peter Klein 3–14 in 1974, scant months before the checkerboard leases expired. On the day the Smackover was cored, Lutz was at Getty's quarterly exploration meeting with his boss, George Hingle. He remembered the looks on the corporate managers' faces when the news came. "Each district had a presentation to make. I was at that meeting, and I remember George Hingle getting a phone call from the geologist out on the well. He said, 'We've got 60 feet of solid pay, and we're going in with another core barrel.' By the time the next district—the Houston district—was about to make their presentation the next day, George came in to break up the meeting, saying, 'We've got another 60 feet in the Norphlet. There's no water leg. It's continuous pay!' That went on for a week. We cored about 300 feet of solid pay, Smackover through the Norphlet. Talk about exciting! It was exciting!"

The No. 1 Peter Klein was completed in the Smackover at 18,000 feet producing over 2,000 barrels of condensate per day and over six million cubic feet of gas per day. It was also completed in the Norphlet below 18,000 feet, flowing at over 1,200 barrels of condensate and 3.5 million cubic feet per day. To date, the field has produced over 70 million barrels of condensate and 75 billion cubic feet of gas.

Especially satisfying to Lutz was that the discovery well was on one of the sections in the original checkerboard. That first buy developed into a major extension of the Smackover play in Mississippi and the largest Smackover field in Alabama at that time. The Norphlet, however, offered the biggest surprise. "I think everybody finally concluded it was eolian—a dune type of environment," Lutz said. "The Smackover deteriorated as you went southward toward Mobile Bay. In fact, what we liked about the Norphlet was that at East Nancy we had discovered the first commercial Norphlet production in the state of Mississippi. That's what led to the attraction of the Norphlet southeastward down into Alabama and Mobile Bay."

The Chunchula and Hatter's Pond one-two punch knocked the skeptics over backwards and brought Alabama back into the oil business mainstream. Yet even bigger prizes in Alabama's coastal panhandle awaited.

Chapter 15

"It blew sky high."

By 1970 so little had been done in Alabama's Black Warrior Basin that virtually no one in the oil business paid any attention to it. What had been accomplished was mostly the work of local promoters with little experience in the mainstream oil business. Between 1940 and 1970 only about 100 wells were drilled in the basin, and of those only two found small fields, Hamilton and Whitehouse, both in Marion County. They produced an insignificant volume of gas from shallow Mississippian-age rocks.[1]

In 1970 a series of events began to unfold near the hamlet of Detroit in northern Lamar County that profoundly changed people's lives in northwest Alabama. The man who started it was as gruff, as blunt, and as surly as any character the oil field could produce. Walter Sistrunk Sr. returned to the spotlight and found a permanent niche for himself.

Partnering with D. W. Skelton and Bob Tatum, Sistrunk conjured a hunch, bought leases, and drilled. To his surprise he hit oil rather than gas. The well pumped only a few barrels a day from a shallow sand of Mississippian age. The well—discovery well for the East Detroit Field in northern Lamar County—is still pumping today and has produced over 15,000 barrels of oil, but the little well turned very few heads back in the big oil patches. For Sistrunk it wasn't much; he found much bigger stuff working the Eutaw in Mississippi with Merrill Harris and J. Willis Hughes. Still, it warranted more drilling.

A year later Sistrunk sold Champlin Petroleum on the idea of drilling a couple of offsets to his well. On one, the rig stumbled into more pressure than they were prepared for. While they were attempting a completion the well blew out, spitting the entire tubing string out of the hole. The Alabama Oil and Gas Board's Gene White said the tubing looked like a pile of spaghetti. There was a major interstate power line only 50 yards away. "I'm surprised that tubing didn't get tangled up in that line," White said. "It blew sky high. It wrapped around trees like tying ribbons around them."[2]

Red Adair stopped the blowout. The well was eventually tested at 1.4 million cubic feet a day at a depth of only 1,500 feet. Due to the scarcity of pipelines in the area, the little field didn't go into production until years later when it eventually produced over 11 billion cubic feet of gas.

Compared to the big excitement in the Salt Basin's hot spots, the blowout in north Alabama caused little more than some spirited conversation over coffee at the Petroleum Club in Jackson, but the excitement at East Detroit captured a few geologists' fancy. One was Hilton Ladner.

Ladner was interested mostly in the Mississippi side of the basin, but the East Detroit blowout in Lamar County, Alabama, was very near the state line. Ladner was sure there was more gas in north Mississippi and north Alabama. He stepped up the hunt.

The Black Warrior's Crown Jewel

"That place is a graveyard!" Jim Stewart barked. That didn't surprise Ladner. He asked Stewart to check out a lease at a spot in north Mississippi that beckoned him. "Nobody's made any money up there since Muldon," Stewart told Ladner. "Besides, I checked out that same area for Harold Karges about a year ago," Stewart said, pointing to the spot on Ladner's map. "I couldn't put it together."³ Karges was a respected independent geologist and consultant in Jackson for decades.

Arguably, Stewart was right. Little was found in the Black Warrior since Howard Nason blundered into the rip-snorting Sanders Sand at Muldon in 1952. Federal price controls were still in effect, keeping gas artificially cheap, and the intrastate market situation was shaky at best. In north Mississippi the Maben Field in Oktibbeha County was the only commercial find in recent years, and it was small. In December 1970, Texaco tested a half million cubic feet per day from the Knox zone (Ordovician) at a depth of 15,000 feet—a Black Warrior Basin production depth record. The one-well field produced a little over one billion cubic feet before abandonment.

Ladner would not be deterred. He kept contouring Monroe and Clay Counties with the scant well control and rough seismic he had. But Ladner wasn't the only believer in the Black Warrior Basin's potential. Two partners out of El Dorado, Arkansas, Joe Baria and Richard Mason, were eyeing the basin as well.

Their company, Gibraltar Energy, garnered the financial backing of a New York oil and gas drilling fund. When Baria and Mason heard Hilton Ladner was working the Black Warrior Basin, they visited with him and struck a deal to assemble and drill a number of his ideas. Ladner had mapped a high area in Monroe, Lowndes, and Clay Counties, Mississippi, east of the old Muldon Field along the Tombigbee River. He called it the East Muldon Prospect. Well control in the area indicated the presence of a down-to-the-northeast fault with shows in flanking dry holes. Figure 14 is a reproduction of the original prospect map Ladner prepared for Baria and Mason.

The group put together several thousand acres on and around the prospect, eight miles southeast of Aberdeen. With the New York fund money behind them, Ladner-Hildebrand-Gibraltar spudded in early 1970, and in

February they brought in the No. 1 T.A. Richardson. The well tested 2.3 million cubic feet per day from the Sanders Sand below 5,000 feet and 1.2 million from a Pennsylvanian sand at 2,800 feet. The operators named the shallow sand in honor of the man whose unrelenting efforts opened Muldon's production twenty years earlier—Howard Nason. When they petitioned the Mississippi Oil and Gas Board for special field rules, Hilton Ladner's East Muldon Prospect became the Corinne Field.

The operators knew they had logged a good discovery but didn't know how good. They drilled a confirmation north of the strike that came in 20 feet low, and the results were disappointing, although they found some gas in the Nason. The next location would be critical. Richard Mason recalled the third attempt: "After drilling the north offset we decided to gut up and drill due east of the discovery. This was a make-or-break well for the field. I remember driving over to log the well and meeting Hilton out in a cotton patch near the well where we laid the log out on the hood of the car. It was obvious the Sanders was loaded and we were high to the discovery well."[4]

The Gibraltar group's big discovery turned many heads toward North Mississippi and bolstered the confidence of some who were there already. One was Bill Cleary, whose Cleary Petroleum Corporation worked the Anadarko Basin in Oklahoma successfully for years. Cleary liked the Black Warrior Basin because, like the Anadarko, it was largely a stratigraphic play, and Cleary was comfortable with that. He also liked the fact that he could still get 10-year leases there; the landowners were not yet streetwise to the oil business. He entered the northeast Mississippi/northwest Alabama area in the early seventies, acquiring between 80,000 and 100,000 acres.[5]

The stunning strike at Corinne compelled Cleary to expand its operations, and quickly. They decided that acquisition was the most expedient method, but while negotiating to buy the Gibraltar group out, Cleary stopped the talks to wait for the results of a step-out being spudded two and three quarter miles south of the discovery. They were confident the step-out would be dry and Gibraltar could be forced into a cheap sell.

The step-out was the work of R.L. Burns, another colorful player. "Dick Burns is quite an individual," said Richard Mason, who sold Burns the leases south of Corrine. They took the 30,000-acre lease package to Burns, and he committed to it before they finished their pitch. "He was the greatest risktaker I have ever run into in the oil business," Mason said.[6]

Cleary Petroleum watched anxiously as Burns' well bored toward the hard Mississippian sands, 5,500 feet below the Tombigbee River lowlands. Richard Mason summarized what Burns found. "This first Burns well drilled right into the middle of a major Sanders Sand channel. The Upper Carter, Lower Carter, Upper Sanders, and Lower Sanders all stacked up along with the Nason and Lewis Sands. We had over 220 feet of net micro-log pay!"

Burns wanted the world to know about his big success. He issued a press release to the New York Stock Exchange reporting that an independent engineering study placed net reserves in the well at more than 17 billion cubic feet of gas plus an undetermined amount of condensate.

The bold news release put the Black Warrior Basin and particularly Corrine Field in the spotlight. Cleary's opportunity for a bargain acquisition deal was gone. "When we arrived on a price for our reserves," Mason said, "all units offsetting the Burns well were considered proved with a very high dollar figure on each." Nevertheless, Cleary anted up. It wanted a piece of this unexpectedly big prize and bought Hildebrand, Ladner, and Gibraltar's interest. Within the next two years Burns drilled two dozen wells in the south area of Corrine while Cleary developed the north end.

By the early 80s Corrine operators had enough data to postulate that the structure extended southeasterly underneath Columbus Air Force Base. Richard Mason wrote, "Several companies tried to get it [the air force base] put up for bid. The government refused until a certain oilman with very good Republican connections got them to put up the base. I suspect that was Chesley Pruet. I don't know for certain."

A bidding war erupted in which Thomason-Monteith, a Black Warrior Basin newcomer, won by a huge margin. Proceeding under very strict environmental and operational restrictions, the company directionally drilled some very good wells underneath the base's runways.

As reservoir data came in from the development work, the operators estimated Corrine's reserves would exceed 200 billion cubic feet, which they did in 1997. Corrine became and remained the Black Warrior Basin's crown jewel. "Corinne Field made my partner and me a lot of money," Mason said.

In 1978 Cleary sold out to Grace Petroleum, a subsidiary of the W.R. Grace Company. Grace wanted a source of gas near its huge fertilizer plant in Memphis and intended to get it from the Black Warrior Basin. For a decade it continued to develop and explore the vast acreage blocks Cleary acquired in northwest Alabama and northeast Mississippi, but it never used any of the gas for the Memphis plant. Sam Cerny, former president of Grace Petroleum, believed Grace's most significant contribution to the Black Warrior Basin was its leading role in bringing pipelines to the basin.

A Prudhoe Bay Look-alike?

Even before the big strike at Corinne, the 1971 blowout at East Detroit in Lamar County, Alabama, attracted the interest of another aggressive company—Pruet & Hughes. Dudley Hughes did some work in the basin years before for Union Producing Company. He was familiar with the area, and though East Detroit renewed his interest, he had no time to work it. Hughes remembered a timely proposal that fell into his hands. "Chesley Pruet had a nephew, Ronald Pruet, teaching at the University of Southern Mississippi. He became associated with Bob Thomas, another professor at Southern, who was a geologist with many years of West Texas experience. Together they approached Pruet & Hughes with the proposal that we furnish them with logs and maps so they could make a study of the Devonian possibilities in the Black Warrior Basin. In exchange they would give us exclusive use of their work, but we would pay a small fee and a small override for any prospects drilled of theirs."[7]

In 1972 Pruet and Thomas finished their report and gave it to Hughes. By then, Harry Spooner had joined Pruet & Hughes, Inc., and Hughes assigned him Black Warrior Basin responsibilities in addition to his Smackover work in south Alabama. Hughes and Spooner looked over the maps and cross sections and decided there was a significant trend play to be made in north Monroe County, Mississippi. They projected the fault at East Detroit across to Okolona, Mississippi, about 50 miles west, although well control was sparse and seismic almost nonexistent.

"I worked on it with Bob Thomas," Spooner said, "and we came up with an idea. What Bob liked was the Devonian porosity, because it was a good producer in West Texas and his experience was with that. He was always pushing the Devonian."

The Devonian is the geologic time that occurred 360-400 million years ago, but geologists in the Black Warrior Basin commonly used the term to mean the cherty rock layer of that age that lay just beneath the Chattanooga Shale, which is also Devonian in age. The Chattanooga is a thin, oily shale that was deposited over the chert after a period of erosion had truncated the chert. Spooner's theory was that the chert's high porosity could accommodate enormous volumes of oil, and the tight Chattanooga Shale that truncated it could not only provide the source for the oil but also seal it from further migration updip. Geologists called the type of contact between the two rocks units an *angular unconformity*. It was a look-alike to Prudhoe Bay, Alaska, discovered in 1967, where the same contact trapped billions of barrels of oil.

Interest in the Devonian was strong among all the Black Warrior Basin players. Jackson geologist Marvin Oxley reported that Walter Sistrunk took a piece of a Devonian core and stuck it in a bucket of water, and it sucked the water up like a sponge.[8]

Hughes and Spooner picked a location along the north-south highway north of Amory where the Texas Eastern gas line crossed the road. Although Texas Eastern was an interstate line, they hoped the increasing demand for gas would cause the Federal Power Commission to raise prices. They planned a 3,300-foot well and contracted with Jack Daniels to drill it. "Jack Daniels was acting as tool pusher on the well," Dudley Hughes said, "and he made it a practice to call me every morning when he went into Amory for breakfast, to relay the drilling report before I left for the office.

"One morning the phone rang. I answered it only to find that it was the mud-logger rather than Jack. He said the well was blowing out—I could hear the roar in the background. Luckily the drill pipe was still in the hole but all the mud had been blown out. A moment after I hung up, Jack called. I could hear him picking his teeth after a big breakfast, and he gave me a routine drilling report that the well was drilling ahead at 1,700 feet. I let him finish then calmly asked, 'What about the blowout?' He said, 'What blowout?' I said 'Don't you know the well is blowing out?' He panicked and hung up. Later they killed it by pumping in heavy mud."

The Devonian theory evaporated. The porous tripolitic chert was water saturated, but the hole penetrated two fine Carter gas sands. It was completed January 3, 1973, and named the Four Mile Creek Field. Pruet & Hughes eventually drilled four wells on 320-acre spacing and sold some short-term gas to Mississippi Valley Gas, Inc., but found no permanent market before selling the field in 1975. Since then, the field has produced over 14 billion cubic feet.

Six months later, Pruet & Hughes sought to stretch their luck. Moving along the same fault, Spooner picked a location ten miles east of Four Mile Creek, almost to the Alabama state line. They set up a three-well deal. "As fate would have it, the first two wells were dry," Spooner said, "but the third test found gas in thick Carter sands similar to those in Four Mile Creek. The well was completed July 1973 at a depth near 1,800 feet. This was a larger field with 18 wells on 320-acre spacing."[9]

The new discovery became the Splunge Field but it also had no market outlet. Splunge and Four Mile Creek were the best fields in the northern fault trend that started with the East Detroit Field. Others were found, but none produced as much as those two. "That's usually the case," Harry Spooner said. "When you go into a new play the best fields are found first." Splunge eventually produced 36 Bcf.

Mule Skinner Skins Oil Men

With Splunge and Four Mile Creek discovered and Corinne expanding, Hilton Ladner teamed again with Gibraltar and found the Strong Field, west and downdip of Corinne between Corinne and Muldon. That field eventually produced almost two billion cubic feet from the Carter, Sanders, and Lewis sands.

Jim Stewart knew his work was cut out for him when Ladner asked him to try to put together a 1,400 block in Hamilton in Monroe County, Mississippi. "It was a bunch of town lots," Stewart said, a landman's nightmare.

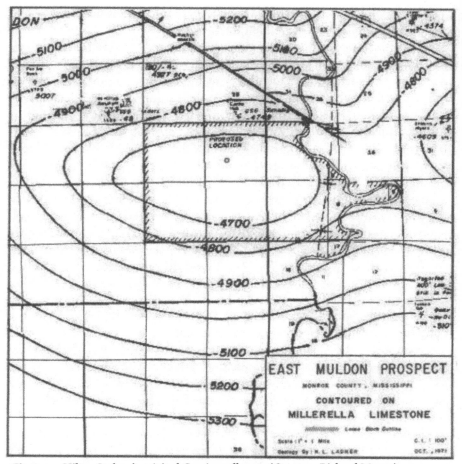

Figure 14. Hilton Ladner's original Corrine sell map. (Courtesy Richard Mason)

Richard Mason had assured Ladner, however, that Gibraltar would take the deal if they could put it together. Stewart got the necessary farmouts from acreage still under lease from an earlier dry hole in the area, but he was a seasoned landman and knew how to handle the town lot problem. He found a local insurance salesman, Ed Benefield, who knew almost everyone in town and hired him, fed him the lot information, and turned him loose. The pair leased about three quarters of the town. "Leasing somebody's house for $5 is kind of hard to do, but we did it," Stewart boasted.[10]

The tedious work paid off handsomely. The group completed the No. 1 Nevins, finding gas pay in the Lewis Sand and in a new Pennsylvanian sand, which they dubbed the Nevins Sand. The discovery was the McKinley Creek Field, which produced over 15 billion cubic feet from four Pennsylvanian sands, five Mississippian zones, and even some from the Devonian chert.

Richard Mason and Joe Baria's Gibraltar had a marvelous string of discoveries, with the aid of Hilton Ladner, but the extensive landwork was overwhelming their landman, Joe Hildebrand. When Mason asked him to buy two sections of leases, Hildebrand hired outside help—Mr. Howard Nason, the former mule skinner, moonshiner, and boiler operator whose claim to fame was his reentry well that blew out and discovered the Muldon Field. "Howard had no trouble buying the leases for $5 an acre," Mason said, "and we paid the drafts, which went directly to Howard. But when Howard signed the leases, he kept a one eighth overriding royalty interest for himself. We screamed like hell, but Howard kept the override. It cost us over a million dollars.

"Howard Nason was, without a doubt, the most interesting fellow in the entire basin," Mason said. The old man was obsessed with the idea that every plugged and abandoned well in the basin had bypassed shallow pay uphole. Over the years he squandered much of his fortune from Muldon by reentering dry holes around Aberdeen. "Some he filed reports on," Mason said, "and some he just never got around to permitting. He never found any shallow gas. If he caught you on a well he would spend hours going on and on about passed up gas."

The Bee in Tom Joiner's Bonnet

Richard Mason's assertion that Howard Nason was undisputedly the most interesting fellow in the Black Warrior Basin would be arguable to the players on the Alabama side of the basin, where Walter Sistrunk Sr. enjoyed that dubious honor. Yet Sistrunk contrasted with Nason in that he was a respected self-taught geologist and oil field engineer.

Tom Joiner, former state geologist and Oil and Gas Board supervisor, remembered his stormy but affable relationship with the temperamental Sistrunk. "Walter Sistrunk was a smart man. And he was a good geologist, even though he wasn't an actual geologist—he had come up through the college of real geology. What a character! He was the hardest guy to control that I've ever seen. He had his idea on how to do things, and if it didn't fit the regulations, then the regulations were wrong!"[11]

Joiner remembered the run-ins he had had with Sistrunk over the years, but he also respected him, because Sistrunk was not above backing off apologizing when he knew he had pressed too far. After Joiner left the Oil and Gas Board and started his own consulting firm, Sistrunk was his client, but Joiner found out that he was just as feisty a client as he was an adversary. "Walter was in all kind of trouble. Tom Watson was his attorney. They were having a hard time getting the Board's cooperation on a matter. Walter came over one day and said, 'Tom, would you be willing to represent me? If I go over there, I get mad, and they get mad.' I thought about it and said, 'Walter,

I will if you'll promise me that you'll sit back and be quiet while Tom Watson and I handle matters.' And he said, 'I will, I will.'

"So we got to working on a problem, and the Oil and Gas Board staff was really trying to work with us. Walter had drilled a well that he really didn't want to do anything with at that time—he had his own reasons. This was when Earnest Mancini was Supervisor. Mancini asked me, 'Are you going to do anything with this well?' Walter bounds up in the back and yells, 'What kind of a goddamned question is that? [Sistrunk didn't think that was any of the government's business]'

"We left that meeting and were driving back to my office and I said, 'Walter, you promised me you were not going to do that kind of thing. He was just asking a question.' He said, 'I'm sorry, I'm sorry. It won't happen again. If he kicks me in the behind, I won't say anything again.'"

When Joiner was state geologist he revolutionized the way the Alabama Oil and Gas Board operated. He struck a balance between professionalism and familiarity by reversing the informal communication roles of industry and the government that regulates it. Instead of going on wild game hunts sponsored by companies (something that today might be interpreted as conflict of interest), the Alabama Oil and Gas Board invited company officials to go hunting with them.

The hunts were held at the Sportsman's Lodge near Livingston. No money came from public coffers other than the staff's own expenses. Joiner and his staff provided a program to review the Oil and Gas Board activities. The company people paid for their own lodging and meals. In the relaxed atmosphere of the lodge, the Oil and Gas Board staff and company people discussed problem areas candidly and established a working relationship rarely seen in government/industry affairs. "We wanted to find out if there were things we were doing that were causing problems, and to let them know if things they were doing were problems for us, so we could handle them in a nice way. We did that for several years."

The informal get-togethers were effective and untainted by conflict of interest issues. But Joiner did run into trouble with one company man who didn't get an invitation—Walter Sistrunk. "After one lodge meeting, Walter came into my office one day, and he said, 'Tom, I don't dress as fancy as some of these folks, but I'm still a part of this oil industry. And I didn't get an invitation!' He really cut me to the quick," Joiner recalled, "because I would never have hurt his feelings by intentionally not inviting him. He got invitations to the others.

"We did a lot of work with Walter. We really got to know and love the man. Once you got to know him personally, you found out that he had a heart as big as the outdoors. And he was just a teddy bear for children. . . . He supported a missionary and supported one of the children's homes in

Mississippi [Sunnybrook Children's Home]. He never made a big deal out of it. He was a very complex man that you had to know. We were friends right on to his death [in January 1987]."

Sistrunk never scored big in the Alabama portion of the Black Warrior, but he did very well for himself. His most significant work was showing that the area was a lucrative hunting ground for natural gas and maybe oil. His accomplishments centered mainly in Lamar County, Alabama. He wasn't interested in regions to the east. Neither was anyone else—except for two men who had a dream and wouldn't let go of it.

Chapter 16

Little Old Man and a Big Dream

Prior to 1972, the activity in Fayette County didn't amount to much. Most operators and promoters thought it promised little. Cleary Petroleum found small fields at Davis Chapel and Hubbertville, northeast and east of the county seat of Fayette, but they were shut-in, lacking a pipeline and a market. Cleary looked for an exit. The mainstream oil industry paid scant attention to successes in the county, but profound change was in the making.

Two men who might rival Howard Nason and Walter Sistrunk as the Black Warrior Basin's most interesting people got excited about Fayette County, Alabama. One, like Nason, was poorly educated and unrefined. He was an elderly layman, an outsider with virtually no practical knowledge of the oil game but with an enthusiasm for it that knew no bounds. The other was exactly the opposite, an insider and a highly trained professional. They formed an unlikely association, in which the older man's optimism consumed the pragmatic professional and armed him to make history.

Sometime after the turn of the twentieth century a twelve year-old boy came to America from Russia and found himself in a bizarre place called Tuscaloosa, Alabama. His father distilled vodka for the czar. When the czar business in Russia went bad, the family moved to the United States where the lad joined his uncle as a backpack peddler, carrying merchandise in a pack and walking from farmhouse to farmhouse, selling needles, thread, and such. When they couldn't sell, they bartered. That evolved into a wagon operation, and the wagon evolved into a store. Eventually they had a department store. They were well suited for the American way, and people who knew him said the boy got his name changed to something that sounded more American.

As the years went by, the young Russian immigrant, known as Louie Hodges, acquired the biggest department store in Fayette, Alabama—a three story building. He arrived in Fayette about the time the old Fayette Gas Field was discovered. The gas fueled the city's streetlights. The gas sellers convinced everybody to buy gas stoves and gas water heaters, but the gas quickly depleted. The observations of modern oil professionals reveal the reason. The drillers of old didn't use cement; they wrapped a burlap bag around the bottom of the pipe string and jammed it down the hole. The field simply bled to death.

Hodges was impassioned with the idea that raw energy could be tapped from the earth, like water. Methodically, he put his energy fascination to practical use. A lot of his customers in the 20s and 30s didn't have money for clothes and household things. He bartered their minerals, though never more than half. He would not let them sell their whole mineral estate; he took half and gave them credit in the store. Eventually he owned lots of minerals and was delighted when anyone showed interest in drilling in the county.

Occasionally during those years someone popped a hole down and Hodges invariably put money into it. He traveled frequently to find oil investors for his adopted home county. He said he once met a Texas geologist who frequently went home to his birthplace near Florence, Alabama. Hodges convinced the gentleman to stop by Fayette and took him out to the old Fayette Gas Field and showed him the little spring there where natural gas still bubbled to the surface. The man told him he had some work to do in Texas and would come back to Fayette when he finished. The geologist went out to Texas and drilled the No. 3 Daisy Bradford—the discovery well for the super giant East Texas Field. The world renowned "Dad" Joiner never came back to Fayette. But Hodges didn't give up.

The discovery at Citronelle excited Hodges and he went down there to be among the oil crowd and to glean what information he could about the ways of the business. He hoped to bend a few ears about Fayette while he was there. He decided to stop first at the newly opened field office of the Alabama Oil and Gas Board. That turned out to be the choice of destiny.

Hodges got off the bus almost in front of the Board office. He gathered his crude maps and papers, bundled them under his arm, and went in. A man looked up and got up from his desk. Hodges' eyes swept upward, following the enormous frame that rose above him. The man towered over him like a derrick, the broad shoulders casting an imposing presence. Thick, black hair crowned a jutting forehead and penetrating eyes. A massive hand reached out to take his. The nervous Louie Hodges shook the hand of the perfect man to orchestrate his dreams.

A Good Place to Start

Bill Tucker watched Hodges get off the bus. "He knocked on the door and came in," Tucker remembered. "He had heard of my appointment and that I was supposed to be a 'hot shot' oilman from Louisiana and Texas. He wanted to tell me all about the oil and gas prospects in Fayette County, which he did for the next six hours."[1]

Tucker was born into an energy-minded family. His grandfather invented the Alabama gasoline tax law that paid for highways. "I don't know if he's a hero or not for that, but he had the idea that motor vehicle usage should pay for the roads, and rightly so." Tucker's dad subscribed to a magazine called *The Lamp*, because his initial business was in lamp oil. He remembered that all the illustrations were in watercolor. "There were fascinating pictures of dinosaurs, fossils, and reptiles, as well as diagrams of geologic deposition, swamps, and coal formation." He remembered reading the theory of how oil was formed. At only ten years Bill Tucker could hardly wait for that magazine to arrive each month.

"My father worked with Standard Oil of Kentucky. He was a terminal supervisor on one of the pipelines that ran from Baton Rouge to New Jersey. And you could look down the pipeline right of way and see the big tanks on the terminal, and I had a great curiosity of where all that stuff came from. . . . So somewhere in my early teens I began to think that this was a field that I would be interested in pursuing."

His grandfather told him about the oil wells in Gilbertown and knew there were gas wells in North Alabama. "We were not poor but just middle class people. And some of the romance of the industry was that it was a way to make lots of money. It was like a treasure hunt—a way that you could take a few dollars and expand it into lots of dollars. So it had some intellectual interest and also some monetary interest."

Alabama didn't have a petroleum engineering school then, and the geology school focused on coal and iron ore. The nearest school offering petroleum engineering was LSU. Tucker packed and headed to Louisiana. In his freshman year he interviewed with Halliburton who hired him for the summer of 1952 and sent him to Texas. "They told me I was going to be in the logging department," he said. "I thought, all these derricks are made out of trees and wood, so I guess they cut trees and make logs, and lumber for these oil derricks. Steel derricks, of course, had replaced [wooden derricks by that time.] Lo and behold, I got on the job, and they had all this electronic gear and I ran electric logs down in wells. That's going from a neophyte to learning things very quickly."

He worked for Halliburton each summer during college, then went full time, working offshore after graduation in 1956. Occasionally a job came up in Mississippi or rarely, Alabama. "And every young man likes to think that he can come home and get involved in a successful business at home. My goal was to come back to Alabama."

In 1959 a job opened with the Alabama Oil and Gas Board. He applied and was appointed field agent in Citronelle, not the job he wanted but one that would teach him more about the industry. He visited wells during the drilling and completion operations, making sure that the sites complied with state regulations.

Louie Hodges was delighted when Tucker transferred to the Oil and Gas Board's main office in Tuscaloosa; he could visit his new friend frequently. He wasted no time in urging Tucker to go with him to the old Fayette gas field. They rode out, and Hodges told Tucker about the streetlights they left on 24 hours a day because it was cheaper to do that than to hire somebody to turn them on and off. He told him about the gas stoves and heaters everybody bought. He told Tucker there was even an excursion train that came over from Birmingham bringing visitors to see the curious new gas field. They built a picnic area on the edge of town near the spring that burned bubbling gas, but Hodges reminded Tucker that the gas ran out in just two years, and all the stoves and heaters were useless.

Tucker remembered visiting the old wells with Hodges. "There were two or three wells we went to that had 800-900 psi on them. They were shut-in—drilled by some promoter that had left the country. We would open them up and let them whistle a little bit and shut them in. He and I developed a real good friendship."

The Board let Tucker attend graduate school at the University of Alabama while he worked. He earned a master's degree in mineral engineering with a petroleum option. All the while he stayed in touch with the inquisitive little old fellow most others avoided politely but with whom he was beginning to share a compelling dream. "As was the custom in those days, merchants closed their stores on Wednesday afternoon. I could usually depend on Mr. Hodges to come to Tuscaloosa and keep me hyped up on all the gas potential of Fayette County. We spent many enjoyable hours talking and sharing his dreams, and capturing me into those dreams. . . . Over the years we had a wonderful experience with each other. He liked to smoke cigars and I liked cigars. We liked to go to roadside cafes and eat steaks and smoke cigars and sit there and talk."

Although Hodges became Bill Tucker's special friend, the rest of the Oil and Gas Board staff only tolerated him. H. Gene White, another staff engineer, remembered him. "Louie would come into my office and sit down, and I'd be trying to get ready for a Board hearing. He'd sit and watch me and make a few comments, then I'd have to excuse myself to go to the hearing. When I got back, several hours later, he'd be sitting right there, holding his cane!"[2]

After he transferred to Tuscaloosa, Tucker had an epiphany in his quest to get into the hunt for oil. It came in the guise of an environmental project. During the late sixties, part of his job as chief of research at the Oil and Gas Board/Geological Survey was to investigate using deep wells to dispose of industrial waste. Many states were interested in the concept, and under State Geologist Phil LaMoreaux's leadership, Alabama took an active lead.

The state allowed three industrial companies to drill test wells for disposing of waste, with the stipulation that Tucker's department supervised the drilling. He and his team intended to research the disposal concept feasibility. They supervised drilling in Mobile County at the Ceiba Geigi Corporation and at US Steel at Fairfield near Birmingham and drilled a hole at the

Reichold Chemical plant near Tuscaloosa, all using conventional oilfield drilling rigs and techniques. The companies financed the operations with grants from the Environmental Protection Agency (EPA). As operator, the State of Alabama was essentially in the drilling business, and Bill Tucker was the supervisor. The rig personnel shared a great amount of experience with him. His learning curve about drilling operations rocketed upward. "It was a classroom in itself," he said. "I learned a lot about it. I was on a rig in a trailer 24 hours a day. So, I had a cram course."

His assignment was fascinating enough, but what he found at Fairfield changed the direction of his life. "One of the requirements was that we were to find zones that had permeability. Then we would take water samples out of those zones and test compatibility with the waste they were going to put in there. The US Steel well in Fairfield was in the Possum Valley fault system. We had located a zone that would take the waste. We set a packer and swab-tested it to see what kind of fluid it would make. We set it up just like a regular perforation. Then we hit it with about two licks with a swab, and the well came in and cleaned up and burned about a 40-yard flare. I really got excited about that.

"I went tearing off to US Steel headquarters and told Mr. Jim Davis, head of the project for them, 'It looks like the disposal is trying to be a gas well!' He said, 'Great! We use 90 million cubic of gas a day in that plant out there. I'm going to call Pittsburgh and tell them this good news. You go back over and watch the well.'

"About an hour later he drove up and said, 'Pittsburgh said that was a disposal well, and it is going to remain a disposal well.' So we shut it in and killed it and made a disposal well. But as far as I was concerned, the seed was planted there. I was thinking of getting into the [oil] business as quickly as I could."

Tucker had the passion to search for petroleum a long time and the EPA project gave him the knowledge of drilling he needed. The sight of burning gas at Fairfield—gas he found—gave him confidence and direction. Still, his education in the oil industry at the Oil and Gas Board seemed boundless. He learned even more about the human part of the business as a promoter of Alabama's petroleum potential.

He conceived an idea to promote the state's potential to commercial investors and initiated the effort with the approval of State Geologist Phil LaMoreaux, who needed no convincing that the state had a duty to encourage outside investors to come in. When visitors came from out of state to look for oil in Alabama Tucker put on a presentation for them. "Soon I had a pretty good song and dance routine that I could go into, as soon as somebody arrived on the doorstep, about all the virtues of drilling in Alabama, especially in Fayette County. My audience was somewhat inappreciative. You have to realize that gas was selling for 12 to 16 cents [per mcf]. There was not a pipeline there anyway, so what difference did it make? Gas was considered during that time period more of something you had to deal and cope with rather than a valuable resource. By 1971, nobody was believing my story. I decided that, if I could not convince anybody else to get into it, at least I convinced myself to do it."

Tucker thought the time to go after Black Warrior Basin gas was ripe for several reasons: first, national gas reserves declined every year, and gas use increased every year. That spelled a shortage, and a shortage meant an increase in gas prices. Second, the industry was developing innovative well-stimulation techniques, especially acidizing and fracturing, whereby an operator could increase the gas production rate from relatively tight, impermeable gas sands like those in the Black Warrior Basin. And third, as he remarked in a speech at the Alabama Oil and Gas Board's 50th anniversary celebration, "Everybody accused me of having access to all the secret records at the Oil and Gas Board, and I am here today to confess that it was true."[3]

Tucker's inside information was a matter of public record. The Alabama Geological Survey and the Oil and Gas Board had accumulated a wealth of data. Yet the heart of Tucker's secret wasn't a bunch of data—it was a person, the unsung heroine of geological science in Alabama. "What most people do not realize is the secret was, from about 1931 to about 1961, there was one lady that read every sample from every well in the state. She described those samples and put them in typewritten documents. When I began to do my geological work in the basin, these sample logs were the only continuous records that had a great deal of continuity from one well to another, and mainly it was because of this lady, Miss Winnie McGlamery.

"She loved to use the Alabama names for all the rock units and because of the early establishment of the geological survey, she had personally named many of the formations. . . . That was the great secret I enjoyed. I took those well descriptions and plotted strip logs and correlated the sands in Fayette County with the new discovery at East Detroit."

Studying Miss Winnie's logs and Walter Sistrunk's work at East Detroit Field in Lamar County, Tucker developed a plan. "I realized that [what McGlammery observed in Fayette County] was the Carter sand. So I finally had a name on something. . . . I wasn't doing original work. People like Stewart Welch already knew all about the Carter sand. But I thought, that's the same sand I see in this entire area in old cable tool drilled wells drilled in Fayette County. It's just as good and as thick there as it is at East Detroit. This is a good place to start."

He swallowed hard and went in to see the supervisor. "When Bill came in to resign," Phil LaMoreaux remembered, "he said, 'I don't know whether I'm doing the right thing or not, going out on my own. But I've got to try it.'"

LaMoreaux told Tucker he was irreplaceable and would always have a job if he wanted to come back. "That big guy sat there and cried up a storm," LaMoreaux recalled.[4]

As often happens in the oil business, Bill Tucker had a vision and no money. His break came through an acquaintance he developed in Montgomery. A group of 12 professional people agreed to put up enough money to seed his business, which he called Warrior Drilling and Exploration, Inc.

Subsurface information in Fayette County was scarce but he had a map showing a strong magnetic anomaly just west of Fayette. That indicated a possible swell in the basement rock which in turn might mean that the sedimentary rocks over it arch into an anticline. It looked on his map "like somebody took a lid off a mayonnaise jar and drew a circle with it," he said. In time, geologists learned that magnetic anomalies in the Black Warrior Basin had little to do with trapping petroleum, but for Tucker it was his place to start.

He bought a few leases on the circle and acquired a farmout from Lone Star Petroleum, who owned some of the acreage. Next he had to find an operator. The Montgomery group gave him $60,000 for half interest in the test well. "I got on the phone and wrote some letters to drilling contractors and asked for bids to drill this well. And they said moving a rig to Fayette, Alabama, would cost $40,000 plus $60,000 to drill the hole. The $40,000 covered getting the rig there and back, because they knew there wouldn't be any more holes. They knew it would not be successful." His budget wouldn't allow it. He had to find another way.

Finally, a friend found a rig for him at a little town south of Monroe, Louisiana, but it wasn't readily available. The local sheriff had seized it drilling at 9,000 feet. The owner ran of money, and his creditors attached a lien. The sheriff walked up and gave the cut signal. The driller set the brake, and the crew went home. A year or two later, the sheriff took the engines to a warehouse. The derrick stayed there upright for nine years and was such a permanent feature of the landscape that crop dusters used it for a visual navigational aid. The desperate Tucker figured it was the only chance he had to get his program started.

He bought the rig from the sheriff for $8,000 and found a mechanic to help him start the engines. The drill pipe, still in the hole, was stuck. That forced him to spend more to hire specialists to jar the pipe loose with downhole explosives, just like hitting the pipe with a big hammer. The first attempt failed, but Tucker knew he had to have that drill pipe. "I had $80 in my pocket, and my mechanic had $40. I told the guy I had $120 cash and offered him that to shoot it one more time. He said okay. So he went in and shot it around 9,000 feet."

The second shot worked. They recovered 9,100 feet of valuable drill pipe, which was in surprisingly good shape after its nine-year subsurface sleep.

They laid the derrick down and hired a trucking company to move the rig to Fayette for $10,000.

The whole thing took four months, but it was worth it. Tucker's rig was a big one by Warrior Basin standards. It was a triple—meaning it could hold stacks of three connected joints of 30-foot pipe in its upright derrick for a total stand length of 90 feet. The rig was capable of depths to 12,000 feet, much more drilling power than he needed.

"I felt like James Dean in the movie *Giant* putting that rig together. You have to put this operation in the proper context to appreciate the magnitude. . . . Experienced labor did not exist [nearby]. The only people I had were a driller and a derrick man. The three of us trained every pulpwood cutter we could find on how to work on a rig. I was the driller on the three till eleven tour. Only collectively did we have the experience of one good man. Total disaster was seconds away at any time, but we finally got the well drilled.

"We shot the Carter, and it tested at about 400 mcf per day. And we were about two miles from the city of Fayette gas pipeline. The city didn't need it, but they had a line that went to an asphalt plant. I went to them to see if they wanted to buy the gas for that line. They said they would pay 58 cents per mcf, which was an unheard of high price. It even made the Oil and Gas Journal."

The new discovery was the No. 1 Hollis-Collins, and the field was designated the West Fayette Field. They wasted no time getting the gas to the waiting market. "So they laid a pipeline over to this asphalt plant," Tucker said, "and we got it all hooked up and turned the well on. That plant had to heat all this tar and sand to make asphalt. When those burners turned on, it sucked that well down so fast . . . that pressure went to zero in 30 minutes time. So I said, this is not going to work. We put a frac job on it, and sure enough, it tested about 2.5 million a day. That ran the plant. And it saved us."

Tucker's first well was a success, though highly unusual. Ready-made markets like the asphalt plant were rare for the early Warrior Basin explorers, and Tucker's fledgling oil company was not out of the woods. The asphalt plant didn't operate year round, only in the road paving season. The gas sales revenue was not steady, but Tucker kept drilling, adding five development wells to the Hollis-Collins.

While Tucker operated in Fayette County, Walter Sistrunk was busy developing a nice strike at Fairview Field in Lamar County, where he found gas-fat Carter Sands at only 2,500 feet. This news thrilled Tucker because it was close to Fayette County.

By the time Tucker proved himself an able operator, a wave of further discoveries washed across Lamar County to the west. In 1974, Cleary's extraordinary discovery at Beaverton Field in Lamar County found pregnant gas sands at only 2,000 feet.

The following year, Terra Resources, Inc., of Denver found the biggest Black Warrior basin field in Alabama to date. Their No. 1 McDonald, discovery for the Blooming Grove Field, found an enormous gas load in the Carter at only 2,700 feet.

That year Terra also was the operator in Fayette County's biggest strike, Musgrove Creek, a stratigraphic trap just northeast of the town of Fayette. It grew into an enormous field by Black Warrior Basin standards—10 miles long with 39 wells.

All the discoveries were in primarily stratigraphic traps until Gibraltar and Stewart & Welch drilled a prospect in southern Lamar County in 1975 and found the lucrative Star Field in a fault trap.

Tucker scored additional discoveries in Fayette County and began to lease in Lamar County. So many different companies banded together in each Alabama Black Warrior Basin strike that virtually all of them were involved in every discovery. In addition to Warrior Drilling and Engineering, other major players were Browning and Welch, Ensearch, Grace, Gibraltar, Moon and Hines, Pruet & Hughes, Terra Resources, and TXO.

One company discovered a small field in northwest Lamar County and named the wells after characters in the book *Gone with the Wind*. When the Alabama Oil and Gas Board assigned special field rules and considered a name for the field, the company asked that it be named the Tara Field. In keeping with its practice of naming fields after nearby landmarks, the Board refused and named it the Wesley Chapel Field. The company was embarrassed when the Board told them *Gone with the Wind* was set in Georgia, not Alabama.

By 1977, billions of cubic feet of gas in Lamar and Fayette Counties lay behind pipe, practically worthless. Walter Sistrunk found a limited local market for his early Lamar County finds, but that market couldn't handle the huge volumes of gas that were discovered. The Warrior Basin operators needed cash flow. Investors were getting itchy and banks impatient. Bill Tucker's young, perilously capitalized organization was more vulnerable than the rest. With the help of the other operators, he took the lead role in finding that outlet.

Through his friend Dudley Hughes, Tucker made contact with a representative of some European investors interested in helping get his gas to market. "I think the company had about $6,000 left to its name," He said. "I went down to my banker and said, 'This man in Europe thinks he can raise money to build a pipeline.' And the merchant banker in Mobile said, 'If you'll raise a million dollars, we'll lend you a million dollars.' He was the cosmopolitan, world traveler type. He said, 'Bill, I don't have much hope that you can raise the money. But I think everybody needs to see Europe one time.'

"Two weeks later I walked into his office. I had two checks. One of them for a million dollars and one for a million six. The million six was for our drilling program. So that's kind of when we got into high gear."

Tucker negotiated a sales contract with Alabama Gas Company (Alagasco) and started building a pipeline from a gathering point in Fayette County to a tie-in point with Alagasco's system near Moore's Bridge in Tuscaloosa County. Later they tied in with Southern Natural at McConnell Station. Finally, with a gas market in place, other operators started drilling across the region. Tucker's company expanded dramatically. A totally self-contained company doing all its own drilling, production, and marketing, Warrior Drilling and Engineering, Inc., flourished, growing to over 400 employees with five drilling rigs, five work-over rigs, great fleets of trucks and tractors, and an assortment of equipment yards.

With the new pipelines in place, other fields came on line and began paying off. Sistrunk's Fairview complex produced nearly 18 billion cubic feet and 600,000 barrels of oil by the century's end from a depth of only 2,500 feet.

The Beaverton Field in Lamar County came on line and produced over 45 billion cubic feet of gas. The Blooming Grove Field, north Alabama's biggest conventional gas field, made almost 70 billion cubic feet. Fayette County's big one, Musgrove Creek, made 44 billion.

No one thought much of Cleary Petroleum's early discovery at Davis Chapel in east Fayette County until the pipeline reached it, but it was a sleeper that grew to 15 wells and produced 18 billion cubic feet. All of those highly profitable fields produced from depths of less than 3,500 feet.

The Star Field produced over 38 billion cubic feet of gas and 162,000 barrels of oil from eight horizons, ranging from the Pennsylvanian to the Devonian, and a depth range from 1,700 to 4,800 feet.

The Walking Stick

Bill Tucker's plate was full with managing a growing company, working with industry partners, and building pipelines, but he never forgot his old friend Louie Hodges, whose health was failing. Shortly after the first discovery in 1973, he picked up Hodges and drove him out to the first offset to the Hollis-Collins. They had just fracced the well and tested it at over three million cubic feet of gas per day. They laid two joints of tubing from the wellhead to the reserve pit and staked it down securely. They placed a half-inch choke in it and lit a flare pot at the end of the line. The crew waited for Tucker and his frail guest.

They arrived at the location, and Tucker helped Mr. Hodges from the car. Shriveled and hunched, the man ambled toward the well with his cane, an exotic hand-carved stick he had bought in Mexico. When they got as close as Tucker dared, they stopped, and he signaled the crew to open the wellhead valve.

The ground trembled as the massive blast of gas exploded from the tubing and ignited. The flame thundered out across the reserve pit and lifted skyward, orange flames billowing upward. They felt the wall of heat and smelled the sweet odor. For the first time in years, Louie Hodges straightened. His face, awash with the glow of the flare, lifted upward. His eyes widened. He smiled. Then Tucker watched in awe as the old man lifted his walking stick high. Twenty-six years later, Tucker said with wet eyes and a breaking voice, "He threw that stick toward that flame."

As the stick arched toward the flare, Bill Tucker realized that two men's visions had become a reality. It was a defining moment. The Black Warrior Basin had come of age.

PART IV

Late 70s

Chapter 17

Smackunder?

In 1975 Jay Field passed its first hundred million barrels, officially becoming a giant. Its owners and those of the other recent Smackover discoveries scrambled to unitize. Although unitization had been in use for decades, it became even more attractive in the 1970s as a way to recover additional oil.

Inspired by the additional revenue possible with "new oil" and "released oil" pricing, Pruet & Hughes quickly unitized all their fields. Many royalty owners opposed it until they understood they would not only recover more oil but also fetch a higher price for it. Some never understood.

Most of the Smackover field-wide units established in the 1970s were in Choctaw County, Alabama. Alabama required all wildcat oil wells to be permitted on 40-acre drilling units. If a Smackover discovery happened, the Oil and Gas Board held public hearings to establish appropriate spacing for the new field, usually 120 or 160 acre producing units. The initial wildcat unit expanded, and future wells in the field were drilled on the larger spacing.

The problem with expanding a square 40-acre unit was that some landowners who expected to be included would inevitably be left out. A 120-acre unit, for example, could be built with three 40s in a row, but which way should the row run—north-south or east-west? It was a vital question to those who land stood to be included or left out.

Tom Watson, the Board's attorney, described some producing units as having a lot of goat pasture. "You could always tell when there was a hearing related to Choctaw County, because there wouldn't be a parking place around the Board. The people from Choctaw County poured out because the Board was setting units, and in some cases reforming units based on developing [information from additional wells]. So we tried to form variable size units, and people had a fixation that they were entitled to 160 or 120 acre units, and if you tried to do anything different they thought you were cutting them out. They thought the oil companies were riling them, so they would just pour out [for the hearings]."[1]

Watson remembered J.D. Morton, an elderly gentleman from Silas, Alabama. Mr. Norton owned a lot of land in Choctaw County, and he drove his black Fleetwood Cadillac up to Tuscaloosa for the hearings, often attending in overalls. During one hearing, at which the Board considered a motion to reform a production unit, his confusion and anger exploded. In one of the most profound statements ever uttered before the Alabama Oil and Gas Board,

Mr. Norton jumped up and shouted, "I don't care whether it's Smackover or Smackunder, I just want my oil!"

Although unitization wars in Choctaw County made Watson and his associates want to pull their hair out, at least oil was a readily marketable commodity. Not so the gas. Producers were scratching their heads because they could not sell their gas for a reasonable profit. To them, government price controls were an impediment to the stability of a free market. They were sure supply and demand would eventually prevail, but until then they had to find a way to survive. Some serious brainstorming was in progress in the Pruet & Hughes camp.

Take or Pay

Two years after its 1973 discoveries at Splunge and Four Mile Creek in Monroe County, Mississippi, Pruet & Hughes still had not found a suitable market for the gas reserves. Fifty billion cubic feet languished behind pipe in the two fields. The only ready markets were the interstate pipelines, regulated by the federal government. To connect its wells to those lines, the company had to commit to a 20-year contract of only twenty cents per mcf. By contrast, in Texas the intrastate markets were bringing around $1 per mcf. Pruet and Hughes came up with a novel idea: if there was no intrastate market in north Mississippi, they would create one.

They determined which industries needed large volumes of gas and decided that Monroe County was short one brick plant. Brick-making required large nearby clay deposits. The company called in geologist Fred Mellen to locate a suitable clay deposit near Amory. Fred found one and arranged for it to be cored. It contained a 100+ year supply of brick clay. Pruet & Hughes hired a Boston firm to conduct a study which concluded that a brick plant would be feasible but risky. Pruet & Hughes bought the property with the clay deposit but decided against the plant.[2]

They pursued another idea. Someone referred them to two investment brokers in Europe, David Reese and Lance Cone, looking for investment opportunities in the U.S. Hughes approached them with the idea of building an ammonia plant, another industry that required lots of energy. Reese and Cone pondered the idea for several months but finally abandoned it. So Hughes floated another idea.

He sent the brokers to Tuscaloosa to talk with Bill Tucker about marketing his shut-in reserves in Fayette County. Pruet & Hughes participated in many of Warrior Drilling and Engineering's ventures in north Alabama and stood to profit if Tucker could get a market. The effort was successful. Reese and Cone were the European connections that helped Tucker finance a pipeline to join Alagasco's system.

Pruet & Hughes, Inc., still had the problem of their own shut-in wells at Splunge and Four Mile Creek. If they piped the gas across the state line into Alabama to put into Tucker's pipeline the gas would come under federal price controls. Patience and a long, cold winter up north in 1976 solved the problem. Northern industries closed due to gas shortages. In response Congress passed legislation allowing higher prices on newly found gas marketed across state lines. Industry responded immediately.

Mississippi's natural gas industry turned around in 1976. A 20-year decline from a height of 250 Bcf in 1956 to only 80 Bcf in 1976 frustrated producers, but the government's pricing initiatives energized them and they opened the valves. Reserves behind pipe were developed and gas exploration vaulted. Annual gas production in Mississippi doubled within two years and rose every year for the next twelve.

Dudley Hughes heaved a sigh of relief. "We were mighty glad we didn't get into the brick or ammonia business."

"We set 'em on fire."

In 1970 Chesley Pruet sold all but two of his seven drilling rigs, but by 1972 the demand for rigs soared again. He added two more. Customers teemed at his doorstep. Many were major oil companies. The partners' hard work established them as one of the hottest independent drilling and exploration programs in the country. Their success attracted more investors than they had room for. After several Wall Street firms suggested they go public, the company selected Kidder-Peabody to orchestrate the transition. Pruet and Hughes headed for New York.

They hired a cab for the ride from the airport and Pruet insisted on taking the front seat. Hughes and Gathright sat in the back and listened as Chesley barked commands to the driver. He gave the taxi driver an exceptionally hard time, according to Hughes. "Turn here! Don't go that way! You're just trying to run up the fare! Speed up, we don't have all day!" Finally, he ordered the driver to stop while he dashed into a liquor store. The driver turned to the guys in back and said, "Wouldn't you hate to work for that son-of-a-bitch?"[3]

Kidder-Peabody's first step was to have Milt Capsimalis in Houston evaluate Pruet & Hughes, Inc. After evaluating the favorable report, Kidder suggested that a merger or sale might be better than a small public company.

Pruet and Hughes hit the road with a proposal that took them into the headquarters of a number of large companies in New York, Chicago, and California in late 1974 and early 1975. One company showed serious interest—Aquitaine, a French oil company which later became Elf Aquitaine. The partners spent a month negotiating the deal. In the end Aquitaine paid Pruet & Hughes $25 million, an enormous sum in 1973.

The sweetheart deal for Pruet & Hughes was a great deal for Aquitaine as well. Not only did the value of oil and gas triple in the next five years, but also the wells produced 50% more than the reserve report predicted. Chesley Pruet and Dudley Hughes paid off a $3 million debt with the Bank of Mobile, paid Kidder-Peabody their half-million-dollar fee, and split the rest. They formed a Pruet & Hughes Partnership, a three-year, 50% joint venture with Aquitaine to explore in Mississippi, Alabama, and Montana.

Pruet & Hughes was reasonably successful between 1975 and 1978. The exploration work with Aquitaine yielded discoveries at Silas, Zion Chapel, and West Mt. Olive. In Choctaw Country, Alabama, Silas found 2 million barrels in the Smackover. West Mt. Olive, in Smith County, Mississippi, was a teaser. Hughes thought they found a huge Lower Cretaceous gas field, but it produced only four Bcf before depleting.

While Pruet & Hughes blazed away with their sweep of Smackover discoveries, Florida's Jay Field quietly passed the 200 million barrel mark. It was a double giant. Few noticed. Everyone was too busy trying to find another Jay.

Pruet & Hughes' successes in Clarke County, Alabama, inspired geologist Vaughan Watkins, tired of the Wilcox and Lower Tuscaloosa and wanting in on the hot Smackover play. He involved the Roy Guffey family and their wildly successful Texas family company named Midroc. Watkins' deal with them was the standard grubstake. "They put up the money for leases and I came up with some ideas where we could buy acreage and drill.[4] After drilling a string of dry holes, he asked Dudley Hughes what he was doing wrong. "Nothing," Hughes said. "You're just not drilling enough wells." Watkins went back to the mapping table.

He mapped two high features north of a Pruet & Hughes dry hole in the Gilbertown area of Clarke County, Alabama. He put the two prospects together and sold them to Pruet & Hughes. Both were discoveries—Mill Creek and Barrytown.

Hughes thinks the most profitable fields the company found during the late 70s were in the Black Warrior Basin. Although they weren't involved in the big strike at Corinne, Pruet & Hughes joined the hunt for more big reserves in north Mississippi to add to their earlier finds at Four Mile Creek and Splunge. They didn't find another Corinne, but they discovered some other good fields.

In June 1977 they found Maple Branch Field in Lowndes County, followed two months later by Buttahatchie River Field in Monroe County. Hilton Ladner gets the credit for discovering Buttahatchie River, but Pruet & Hughes controlled most of the acreage. Caledonia Field in Lowndes County followed in August 1979. Maple Branch produced 12 Bcf and almost a million barrels of oil from 44 wells. Buttahatchie River produced 38 Bcf from 11 wells, and Caledonia produced 17 Bcf from 17 wells. As prices climbed toward $4 per mcf, Buttahatchie River became one of Pruet & Hughes' most profitable properties.

After the Aquitaine sale Dudley Hughes and Chesley Pruet began to think along different tracks. Each had his idea of what he wanted to accomplish in the oil business, and the different concepts became harder to harmonize. When the participation agreement with Aquitaine expired in 1978, the two decided to follow different paths.

Looking back, Dudley summarized their tremendously successful run. "We made all our money in the downturns, not the upturns. I think the only time we actually lost money was during that boom period."[5]

Pruet had a more concise summary of Pruet & Hughes' success. "We set 'em on fire!"[6]

The two parted amicably and remained good friends. Chesley founded a new exploration company, Pruet Oil Company. He also acquired Pruet & Hughes' operations structure and renamed it Pruet Production Company. He assigned the overall company's management to his sons-in-law, Rick Calhoon and Randy James, who divided the business among contract drilling, exploration, and production.

When James took over operations, his father-in-law told him that any time a man did something dishonest in the oil business, everyone in Houston would know it in 24 hours. "He [Chesley] came up in an era when a handshake was as good as a contract. He truly believed that a man's word was his bond.[7]

The exploration team went with Hughes, which left Pruet Oil Company with no explorers. They needed an exploration staff and prospects—fast. Pruet acquired a number of properties from the R.L. Burns Company, mostly prospects and undeveloped leases in the Alabama portion of the Black Warrior Basin. A technical staff headed by geologist Jim Smith came with the deal. The Black Warrior, plus others generated by Smith's staff, provided numerous profitable wells over the next few years.

Pruet, Calhoon, and James knew they needed to expand their exploration beyond the Black Warrior Basin to keep the new company growing. They did it in two ways. Chesley teamed with Bob Mosbacher, his old friend in Houston, to form a drilling company in the Rocky Mountain region. He negotiated a separate deal with another long time friend, Jack Bowen, at Transco in Houston, making Transco the lead investor in a group of financial backers for an exploration program in the Southeast and lower Gulf Coast regions. Various companies invested during the life of the program, but Transco was a steady and supportive participant until the mid 1980s when it decided to build its own exploration staff.

In 1979 Pruet Oil Company hired Bill Wooten as exploration manager. Wooten, a landman by training, was independent for a few years after leaving

Amoco but wanted to get back into a corporate environment. Pruet gave Wooten his marching orders. "I found out after I got there," Wooten said, "that my job was to go out and find some more investors in addition to keeping the program together. We had to put together a finite amount of prospects per year, for which the investors put up an amount of overhead to cover the cost of operating the company."[8]

After Pruet negotiated the Transco deal in Houston, he told Wooten, "Well, we got 'em going. I told them we would produce 20 prospects."

"My God, Chesley, I don't even know where 20 prospects are!" Wooten responded. Wooten and the staff had to work hard trying to keep up with their fast-paced boss.

On the operations side of the house, Dudley Hughes' departure didn't slow the Pruet companies down. They expanded their drilling fleet, and Pruet Production Company became "probably the largest independent operating company in the southeast," said Randy James. Their rigs worked continually, most noticeably in south Alabama where the Smackover was still running hot.

A new fire was about to heat things up over in south Mississippi as rising prices fueled renewed interest in gas. With a suddenness that took many explorers off guard, a deep gas play in the late seventies swept through south Mississippi like wildfire. Geologist Dave Cate, Pruet Oil Company's exploration manager, found himself in the thick of it.

No Gas South of U.S. 84?

"I came down here in '69," Cate said, "and I've been here ever since, except for nine months. But there was an old saying starting back in the late 60s and early 70s that there wouldn't be any Hosston or Lower Cretaceous gas found south of highway 84. And 84 runs right straight across the south part of Mississippi. That was one of those geologic 'facts.'"[9]

Cate started with Skelly Oil Company when he came to Mississippi after a brief stint with Texaco. He was in on Skelly's Hosston gas discovery at South Williamsburg in Covington County, not a very exciting find but a few miles south of Highway 84. He remembered how people were longing for a new play. "The Smackover play up north had petered out. It was mature. Jay had been discovered. So there was need for a new play to develop."

A small, almost unheard of gas pipeline company kicked off the real excitement. Florida Gas, Inc., was having trouble finding gas for its pipelines. Gas was in great demand, and prices headed toward nine bucks an mcf. Pipeline companies competed aggressively with to secure contracts with producers. Realizing they had a rare seller's market, Florida Gas conceived the idea of feeding its own pipeline and formed Florida Gas & Exploration, Inc., to do just that.

Florida Gas hired a start-up staff of geologist Elwood Ruhl and geophysicist Ed Andress. Thinking the modest strike at South Williamsburg might prove that Highway 84 was not a geologic barrier, the Florida Gas team turned to Shell for clues. Cate, who left Skelly to join Florida Gas, said, "If you've ever seen a Shell seismic coverage map, you see Mississippi is black with their lines." Along with the lines, Shell had leases—lots of them. Although the Shell data showed many interesting structures in the Jefferson Davis/Covington County area, Cate believed Shell had no confidence in the stratigraphy. Simply put, they thought the Lower Cretaceous rocks were too tight to produce oil or gas.

Shell's skepticism did not deter Florida Gas. They analyzed Shell's seismic data, took farmouts from Shell, and began drilling in March 1974, in Jefferson Davis County. The result rattled the industry.

The discovery well, the Florida Gas No. 1 Booth, tested at a combined open flow rate of 6.5 million cubic feet per day and nearly 200 BOPD from Hosston perforations at 16,000 feet. The production came from two new Hosston sands, the Booth and Harper. The astounding strike was named the Bassfield Field. It blossomed into an enormous field, producing over 100 billion cubic feet of gas and 1.4 million barrels of oil.

Bassfield's depth was especially important. To encourage expensive deeper drilling, the government exempted gas found below 15,000 feet from federal price controls. Gas produced below 15,000 often fetched over $10 per mcf, a far cry from twenty cents per mcf a few years earlier. With such an incentive, the hunt for the Hosston was on in earnest. Seismic and lease plays ignited and spread through Covington, Jeff Davis, Marion, and Lawrence counties (Figure 15).

The Mother Lode

Dave Cate left Florida Gas in 1976 and joined First Mississippi Corporation, where he worked in the sensational unfolding play of the Deep Hosston. First Mississippi was a fertilizer company then and needed gas for its plants in Louisiana. "The idea," Cate said, "was to initially drill some natural gas wells arranged so that they could swap out production and get the gas to their plants. But that soon went by the way. They began to just look at it as a profit center. Eventually they spun off First Energy Corporation and set it aside as a separate oil and gas entity."

The Deep Hosston geology was a no-brainer, according to Cate. "They were really simple structures—*four way closure.*" (Four-way closure is a subsurface structure on which the contours "close" upon each other in a pattern resembling a bullseye, though often elongated rather than round.) The Deep Hosston prospect maps were clean and simple. Everyone in the company and everyone interested in investing could understand them.

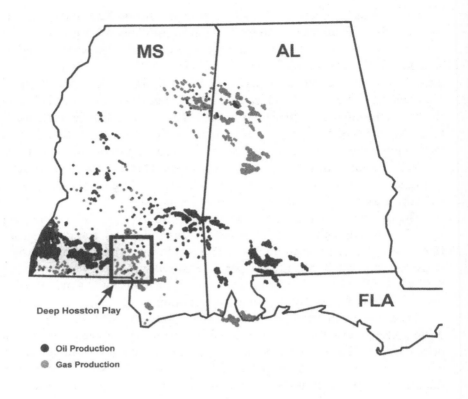

Figure 15. Map of Deep Hosston Play.

As Cate settled in at his new job at First Miss the Deep Hosston started to sizzle. After Bassfield in 1974, the second strike was Seminary Field six miles southeast of Collins in Covington County. In March 1975, Florida Gas Exploration Company tested over four million cubic feet of gas and nearly 500 barrels of condensate per day from Hosston perforations below 14,000 feet. Despite the initial thrills, Seminary was an insignificant field, producing only 3.5 Bcf and 350,000 barrels from six wells. At the time of its discovery it looked good, however, and it defined the easternmost edge of the play.

The next strike came in May 1976 right in the middle of the play at McRaney Field, eight miles southwest of Collins in Covington County. Howard Samsel's team at Union of California tested almost 400,000 cubic feet and 170 barrels per day below 15,000 feet. The field grew to eight wells and made 17 Bcf, plus a half million barrels of oil. It was Union's only major effort in the play.

A year went by before another hit. In May 1976 Louisiana Production Company opened production 10 miles south of Collins with a test of nearly three million cubic feet per day below 15,000 feet. The Bowie Creek Field eventually made 10 Bcf from eight wells. As companies got their financing together and retail gas prices soared, the Deep Hosston play boiled over.

A short month after Bowie Creek, Inexco struck at Monticello Field, named after the town in Lawrence County. The initial test was two million cubic feet per day and 80 barrels of condensate. The field marked the western edge of the play and produced 44 Bcf from 23 wells.

A month after Monticello, Florida Gas logged Hosston pay at Clear Run in eastern Jeff Davis County, but it was a disappointment. As 1977 closed Forest Oil got into the act and logged a strike at Carson Field in Jeff Davis County, but that also fell short of expectations.

Those discoveries, both big and small, marched the Deep Hosston play steadily southward. Many geologists grimaced at the idea that the Hosston sands would hold up in that direction with good reservoir-quality porosity. Some recommended going no further south.

One who did go south was Larry Boland. Boland studied logs of dry holes and developed a lead in south central Jefferson Davis County, another risky step-out farther south. He convinced the Harkins Company that retained him to purchase some seismic lines which transformed the lead into a viable prospect.

People who knew Larry Boland thought he was special. He had gone to the University of Kentucky, where he had played football. Tall and broad framed, Boland was a down-to-earth family man, generous and sentimental but quick tempered. His weakness was tobacco, which killed him.

Boland spent much of his career with Amerada Petroleum before going independent and picking up a retainer with the Harkins Company. Geologist Jerry Zoble, a consultant for First Mississippi Corporation, had an office next to Boland's, and they were close friends. Taking his deal to Zoble was a natural first step for Boland.

Zoble was from Wyoming and worked with Amoco and Occidental before going independent. He thought Boland's prospect looked good and convinced First Miss to take a quarter of the deal.

Geophysicist Charlie Morrison, who had just joined First Mississippi, remembered the difficulty Boland had convincing other people. "He had a hard time selling it because it was down south past everybody's 'zero-sand' line. Nobody wanted it!"[10] Boland called it the Dry Creek Prospect, which probably didn't help his marketing.

Finally Boland sold the rest to his old employer, Amerada. He told Jerry Zoble, "They never would do much with my recommendations when I was with them, and now they decide they like something I put together!"[11]

The group drilled on school board land 11 miles northwest of Columbia, Mississippi, near the Jefferson Davis-Marion County line. Dave Cate monitored the well for First Mississippi. He remembered when Boland called and told him they had hit the mother lode. "They had mud log shows from here to there. Booming shows in several sands."

As the well was prepared for logging Cate went down to the location and found Boland and some of the crew in the mudlogging trailer. "They all had a pained look on their face," Cate said, "and I said, 'What's going on?' And Larry said, 'Some son of a bitch stole the mudlog sheets!'"

Just as Cate arrived they discovered someone got into the mudlogging trailer and stole the sheets with vital information describing good shows. The men were digging around in drawers, trying to find them. "Man, you talk about getting a sick feeling," Cate said. The operators were holding the well *tight* or secret. "The mudlogger was dumbstruck," Cate said. "He was white in the face. He figured somebody was going to lynch him. He knew he was the first one they would point to."

An investigation ensued but implicated no one. The companies tried to keep the theft under cover. Cate thinks a lot of potentially good leases might have been lost to the information leak.

The electronic logs confirmed the stolen mudlog's predictions. "It was a beautiful looking log," Zoble recalled, "the sort of thing that makes your heart beat faster. When that log came out of the hole—boy, I'm telling you what—there was some interesting partying going on."

The No. 1 Board of Supervisors 16-8 indeed found the motherlode. The well was completed in two sands at nearly 16,000 feet. One tested at five million cubic feet per day and the other at almost four million. They named the enormous discovery the Greens Creek Field.

To date, Larry Boland's discovery is the premier Hosston gas-condensate field, having produced over 140 billion cubic feet of gas and over a million barrels of condensate from 15 wells. Dave Cate will never forget the empty feeling of seeing the oil business' worst dregs pilfer the hard work of true professionals.

"Larry was interesting and funny, an extremely generous man," Jerry Zoble said. "After his death we started the Boland Scholarship Fund for Mississippi geology students."

The Deep Hosston Play took off with Bassfield in 1974, but Greens Creek lit the afterburner. "It was crazy down there," Cate said.

Oil and gas attorney Walker Watters remembered when several out-of-state clients burning with Hosston fever told him, "Mississippi is the hottest place in the country now because of the shortage of natural gas."[12]

After a disappointing find at Newsom Field (Marion County) in February 1977, Florida Gas hit big the next month. The strike was Oakvale, 12 miles north of Columbia, in a deal put together by Rex Hewitt. Florida Gas tested almost seven million cubic feet a day from the Harper Sand at 16,000 feet. To date the field has produced over 100 Bcf from 21 wells. Oakvale and Greens Creek showed that there were good Lower Cretaceous rocks farther south in the Salt Basin than previously thought. Dave Cate and others concluded that the Hosston sands were deltaic in origin.

On the heels of Oakvale came Holiday Creek, an oil strike. The discovery well tested 324 BOPD and about 1 million cubic feet. The field produced only about a million barrels and 40 Bcf from 34 wells. "It wasn't much," Cate said, "but it did show that there was some oil down there. That was a Phillips deal. Burt Rosson and Dee Layman got it together, and we took it at First Miss and drilled it."

First Miss was now on a roll. In May 1977, they hit again at Columbia Field, just north of Columbia in Marion County. That field produced 10 Bcf and a quarter million barrels of condensate.

In October 1977, Sun Oil attempted a step-out to the southeast and scored a nice Hosston discovery at Tatum's Camp, just south of the Midway Salt Dome in central Lamar County. Sun, Amoco, and Exxon developed the field into 11 wells that eventually produced 21 Bcf and nearly a million barrels. The field was an isolated outpost of Hosston gas production. That same month, System Fuels logged an insignificant strike that became Whitesand Field on the west edge of Jeff Davis County.

Newcomers to the play, Robert Mosbacher and Pruet & Hughes got into the act in May 1978, scoring a strike eight miles west of Mount Olive in Covington County, which became the West Jaynesville Field and produced 12.5 Bcf from five wells.

That same summer Sunmark opened Hosston gas at Improve Field, five miles northeast of Columbia. Their discovery well tested a nice five million cubic feet per day and eventually produced over 7 Bcf from eight wells.

No more discoveries came until the following winter. In March 1979, Tomlinson Interests made a dual completion in what became the East Morgantown Field, six miles northwest of Columbia on Board of Education land. They tested over six million cubic feet per day from two Harper sands below 16,000 feet. The field grew to 15 wells and made 50 Bcf, plus a million barrels.

Though the Deep Hosston gas play petered out in the early 80s, small strikes were scored at Hooker and West Oakvale. Petroleum Corporation of Delaware opened Hooker Field in Lawrence County in April 1980, eventually making 5 Bcf from five wells. Tomlinson found West Oakvale Field, which produced 11 Bcf from the Hosston, Rodessa, and Sligo. A short, thrilling, and profitable era came to a quick end, but operators had no problem finding good markets for their new reserves.

As the Hosston excitement spun down, another play emerged 100 miles to the southeast, but it was profoundly different from all that preceded it.

The risks were enormous, and so was the entrance fee into the new game. There was no precedent; the rest of the oil business sat back and watched in awe as a major oil company with deep pockets and patience Job would envy, took on an indecisive government, an aggressive environmental lobby, and some very long odds. The royalty owners, the citizens of Alabama, had to cope with the consequences for years to come.

Chapter 18

The Sand Sea

The Appalachian Mountains looked a lot different 165 million years ago from how they look today. They towered perhaps as high as today's Rockies, with jagged, sharp peaks and steep, stony precipices. To the south the land was dry and windswept, a stark contrast to today's lush, humid climate. Ice, water, and wind clawed at the towering mountains, sending endless bedloads of sand into the dry lowlands. Strong winds swept the sandy plains, pushing, redistributing, reworking the sand, and piling it into enormous dunes 200 to 400 feet high over expansive salt plains that would one day lie deeply under the coast of Alabama and the Florida panhandle. The formidable desert was a veritable "sand sea."[1] Geologists know it as the Norphlet.

A few million years after the last sand grain settled, the sea rose and deposited layers of carbonate material across the desert, the layer known as the Smackover. Over the eons the sea rose and fell repeatedly, each cycle leaving hundreds of feet of sediment until the sand sea sagged five miles below the surface under the weight. The salt below the dunes redistributed itself under the increasing overburden, creating high and low areas in the dunes over it. Heat and pressure squeezed hydrocarbons out of the oily Smackover and into the porous Norphlet dunes below.

By the time Admiral Farragut dodged the Confederate mines in Mobile Bay, the deeply buried dunes were pregnant with hydrocarbons. During the 1951 surge in drilling associated with the Korean War, Gulf Oil Corporation sank a pair of 10,000-foot Lower Cretaceous tests in the upper Bay but came up dry.[2] When 1969 arrived, men were still shouting and shooting at each other, but a few undistracted geoscientists were shooting seismic lines instead of guns and saw the salt bulges below the bay in the reflections.

The explorers still knew little of the great desert four miles below; they saw only a huge bullseye at the mouth of the bay, just west of the Fort Morgan Peninsula. As they prepared bids for leases in the State owned waters their attention turned to an event 2,000 miles to the west that profoundly affected the chances the bullseye would ever be drilled.

In the afternoon of January 29, 1969, Union Oil Company's Platform "A" was tripping out to change a bit six miles offshore of Summerland, California. The hole, over 3,500 feet below the ocean floor, lost mud and blew out. The crew regained control and shut the well in, but pressure built up in the subsurface and crude oil erupted from the ocean floor near the borehole.

Crews fought the leak for eleven days before shutting it off, but the discharge fouled many square miles of surface water and several miles of beaches. The United States Coast Guard estimated the spill at 100,000 barrels.[3] Engineers later determined that Union had not set enough surface casing, although they were in compliance with current Federal offshore regulations.

Birds, seals, and dolphins covered with crude oil washed ashore. Globs of gooey tar marred beaches. Union sustained huge losses cleaning up the mess and paying damages. The oil industry's image suffered immeasurably.

A few days after the spill, activists in Santa Barbara founded "Get Oil Out" (GOO) and urged the public to cut down on driving, to burn oil company credit cards, and to boycott gas stations associated with offshore drilling companies. The organization gathered 100,000 signatures on a petition to ban offshore drilling. They were partly successful. Offshore California drilling was banned for 16 years, until the Reagan Administration allowed it to resume under severe restrictions.

Several small oil releases subsequently ignited another round of anti-drilling fervor. The June 2003 *AAPG Explorer* reported that an average of 28 barrels of oil spilled annually from offshore activities in the Santa Barbara Channel after the big spill in 1969, less than seeps into the channel from natural sources in a single day. The *Explorer* quoted a frustrated oil industry executive: "The industry has done an incredible job improving what we do. But the environmentalists still point to the pictures of the spill more than 30 years ago and say, 'This is what you guys are all about.'"[4]

The environmental lobby doubted the offshore industry would police itself. They mobilized a serious and lasting campaign against offshore drilling. In addition to GOO, Greenpeace came into existence in 1969, the first "Earth Day" occurred in April 1970, and Congress created the Environmental Protection Agency the following year. An abundance of State and Federal legislation, such as the National Environmental Policy Act, the Clean Water Act, the California Environmental Quality Act, the California Coastal Initiative in 1972, and the California Coastal Act of 1976 was quickly drafted and passed. The new laws required companies to comply with extensive and costly provisions to protect the environment.

When the activists heard that Mobil Oil Corporation, through its subsidiary Mobil Oil Exploration and Producing Southeast, Inc. (MOEPSI), had won four tracts at the mouth of Mobile Bay, they turned their attention to the Heart of Dixie. The exploration staff at Mobil knew they could not have picked a worse time to drill in the shallow offshore waters of Mobile Bay, but they were determined.

The SOBs Attack

In January 1971, a family that owned a waterfront home on Mobile Bay gathered around the table after reading in the local news that Mobil had won leases in the bay. The announcement upset them profoundly. One of the daughters asked, "Can't someone stop them?" Myrt Jones, a nurse, blurted out the answer to her daughter's question: "Yes!"

"That day, I became a concerned citizen and a fledgling gadfly," she wrote in her autobiography, *A Gadfly's Memoirs.*[5] Jones proudly quoted the dictionary definition of *gadfly*: An intentionally annoying person who stimulates or provokes others, especially by persistent irritating criticism. An Alabama state senator gave her the label and it stuck. She claims the company of Socrates, another gadfly.

Mrs. Jones joined forces with the Mobile Bay Audubon Society (MBAS), of which she was elected president, and began a decades-long battle against what she saw as an assault by the forces of "dirty oil" on Mobile Bay's natural environment. She also joined a group called Save Our Bay, or SOB, which formed earlier to oppose dredging the bay. She influenced SOB to turn its attention to the proposed bay drilling. "Now we had people power," she proclaimed, but she wasn't through mustering her forces yet. She connected with environmentalists active in Santa Barbara, California, and put together her own GOO group. Organized, funded, and motivated, Jones and her fellow gadflies were a force far more powerful and daunting than the oil industry anticipated. The second battle of Mobile Bay was under way.

While the oil companies and the state authorities they worked with were aware of the growing opposition, they did not anticipate the intensity of the fight to come or the tactics the opposition would use. Their first order of business was to award the leases and put some new regulations in place to address environmental issues associated with offshore drilling.

Alabama awarded many lease tracts in Mobile Bay during the 1950s and 60s but only Gulf actually attempted to drill, and got two shallow Lower Cretaceous dry holes in 1951. All the other lessors allowed their tracts expire. Some tracts were leased two and three times over, and some went for as little as two cents an acre. Pan American Petroleum paid the highest bonus between 1951 and 1969, $39,409. In October, 1969 Mobil bid for and won four blocks totaling nearly 20,000 surface acres for a total bonus of $78,882, or about $4 an acre.[6]

Former Alabama State Geologist Tom Joiner, now a consultant, said, "Mobil picked up those four tracts at the mouth of Mobile Bay at a time when there wasn't a lot of interest in drilling offshore."[7] That was due in part to the Santa Barbara Channel incident and its resulting environmental fracas, still fresh in the public mind. Companies weren't keen on taking on the environmental lobby, but Mobil liked what it saw in the seismic reflections and it was not deterred.

When the leases were awarded, red flags went up in Montgomery. According to Joiner, Governor Albert Brewer called Phil LaMoreaux, state geologist at that time, and asked him if the state had any offshore rules and regulations. LaMoreaux said it did not. Alabama's strict, thorough rules were land-specific. At the governor's request "they set up a committee," Joiner said, "which was comprised of industry people, federal people, agency people, and conservation people, such as the Water Improvement Commission, the Mobile County Wildlife Federation, etc." Nine months later in March 1971, the committee finalized new offshore rules and regulations and circulated them for public review.

William Wade, Jason Plater, and Jacqueline Kelley, authors of *History of Coastal Alabama Natural Gas Exploration and Development* (1999), published under contract for the U.S. Department of the Interior, wrote, "Drafting the rules turned out to be the easy part; the challenge became getting them adopted."[8] The authors contend that the new state rules were based on the U.S. Department of Interior's rules for the outer-continental shelf, some of the toughest rules in existence. When other Alabama and Federal agencies lined up to pile on their pet requirements, Joiner said that's when "the flack started."

Mobil spent the rest of the year in meetings and hearings about the proposed rules. Many in the company wondered if the project was worth the hassle. While Mobil's attorneys and engineers lugged documents from hearing to hearing, its geologists added to their database, reevaluated the proposal, and headed to the management suite to propose a change. In October 1971, two years after filing its original drilling application, Mobil amended its application. They wanted to drill even deeper to test the Norphlet at 21,500 feet. "Mobil changed the target from Smackover to Norphlet," Joiner said. "If they had stopped drilling at the Smackover we probably would still not know today what we had missed." The decision to go deeper was critical.

Mobil suffered a setback when a powerful politician, Alabama Attorney General Bill Baxley, weighed in against them. Baxley sided with Jones and the National Audubon Society. He told the news media, "Oil wells in Mobile Bay would present an unacceptable risk to the ecology of the bay.... A runaway oil well would spell ecological disaster for the Mobile Bay."[9]

Mobil mustered its public relations personnel and resources to extol its industry-leading safeguards against such accidents, but Baxley and his staff turned a deaf ear. "He had tapped into a politically popular issue," Wade, Plater and Kelley reported. "The fight was drawn."

The environmentalists were delighted with their new ally. "A politician had seen the light," Myrt Jones proclaimed in her book.

Baxley may have seen a different light from Jones. With his popularity as a messiah come to save the public from Big Oil surging, he began planning an unsuccessful campaign to move into the governor's mansion.

The *Mobile Press Register* described Baxley as "a young gentleman who has gone far in the field of politics, climbing on the bandwagon occupied by zealous environmentalists."[10] In January 1972, Baxley sought to block the project by asking the U.S. Army Corps of Engineers to deny Mobil's permit to move a submersible rig into the bay. The Corps took it under advisement. Tom Joiner said that Baxley wanted to "give the money back to Mobil and take the leases back." Baxley did not have the full backing of the Alabama legislature, many of whom were in favor of drilling, but the powerful Attorney General prevailed into the mid-seventies.

In Mobile in August 1972, the Alabama Oil and Gas Board opened public hearings on the proposed rules that lasted until October. The principal advocates at the meetings were the Board's own Boyd Bailey, touting the toughness of the proposed rules; Assistant Attorney General Henry Caddell, who emphasized Baxley's position of total prohibition; and Mobil's Ed Bell, pitching the industry's technological safeguards.

Myrt Jones saw it differently. "The Board quickly put together a very weak bunch of regulations that had large gaping holes in them. There was no safeguarding of our human resources or protection of human life and health."[11] Her book did not identify the "gaping holes."

Groups and individual citizens were also allowed to voice their opinions at the hearing. Waiting eagerly in the audience were Jones and a guest she had flown in. State Geologist and Oil and Gas Board Supervisor Phil LaMoreaux opened the proceedings, planning to present the new rules and call for comments. Mrs. Jones would not stay silent so long. ("I didn't trust LaMoreaux," she wrote.) As LaMoreaux called the hearing to order and addressed the first item on the agenda, she jumped up and accused him of violating Roberts Rules of Order by not addressing old business first. She later wrote, "I had obviously shaken up this 'giant of a man,' but I felt GREAT!" [caps hers].[12] Tom Joiner, the assistant supervisor, doubted Jones or anyone else could "shake up" LaMoreaux, an accomplished public speaker and debater. More likely, Joiner thought, LaMoreaux deferred courteously and let the lady speak her piece.

Jones introduced her guest, Dr. Norman Sanders, a professor of coastal geomorphology from California, and a favored GOO speaker, urging him to "Go get them." She wrote, "Norman told everyone that Big Oil could not be trusted and drilling should not be allowed in Mobile Bay. The media gave him full coverage."

Wade, Plater and Kelley wrote that Sanders "delivered a lengthy testimony about [potential] spills in the Gulf of Mexico, claiming that, 'Red Adair would be on welfare... if oil well drilling technology was as well developed as the oil companies say.'"[13]

Tom Joiner recalled the Oil and Gas Board staff's frustration trying to keep the discussions focused on facts rather than emotional appeals and unsupported assertions. "They brought in this guy from California who had been highly active and vocal in the Santa Barbara situation. They had him showing slides of the Santa Barbara spill, saying, 'This is what your bay is going to look like.' I don't know whether you can say they don't play fair. But they don't have to. If we say something we have to justify it. If they say something, they don't. .... They were just firm in their belief that we were going to get everything all screwed up."

Joiner remembered that the hearings got emotional and personal. Mrs. Jones invited the Board members to go for a boat ride to view the Bay's ecology, saying, "Mr. Cook, I'd like to get you out in a boat with me." Drexel Cook, the Board's chairman said, "Ms. Jones, you'll never get me out in a boat with you!"

Jones wrote in her book that a "petroleum individual," which she did not identify, approached her after the meeting and asked how much money it would take to shut her up. "I told him he didn't have that much money."

Ralph Hellmich, the Board's Southern Regional Supervisor, thought Jones was interesting. "She is as consistent a person as I've ever known in my life. But she can also be the most frustrating person, because she can ask you a question, and before you can answer it she's already accusing you of something else. .... Facts didn't normally get in the way of her arguments."[14]

Jones and her supporters also worried about the new industry's effect on the culture. She warned in *Business Week* about the snowball effect on Mobile's laid-back lifestyle. "As you have more producers, you have more pipelines and more chemical industries coming in. That means more housing, more schools, and more law enforcement. Our lifestyle is going to change for the worse. We do like a slow pace of living."[15]

As multiple hearings dragged on, Mobil suffered another setback. The five-year term leases were into their third year. At the rate things were going Mobil would not have time to start drilling operations before the expiration date. Mobil asked the Alabama Department of Conservation to extend the leases until the drilling permit was approved. Under pressure from Baxley the Department blocked it. Mobil sued in U.S. district court and got the leases extended four years.

The Oil and Gas Board adopted the new rules in January 1973. They were satisfied with Mobil's application, but they did not approve it until other state agencies had a chance to weigh in. During that process Mobil began preparing the environmental impact statement it filed in October 1975.

Two months later the Alabama Water Improvement Commission (AWIC) broke ranks with Baxley and voted to certify Mobil's application to drill. Baxley argued that the State should have a single cohesive position and recruited an ally on the AWIC, one who owned a house on Dauphin Island at the mouth of the bay. The two turned the Commission's opinion, and Mobil's permit was rescinded. Mobil applied again in April 1976, presenting exhausting technical testimony to the Commission, and was again rebuffed.

A month later Mobil went back to federal court for an injunction against the AWIC. Baxley's forces argued that the matter should be considered in state, not federal, court. The court ruled in favor of the attorney general. Mobil filed in state court. Negotiations began and continued for the next 15 months. It looked as though a bit might never pierce the great bullseye nearly five miles beneath the mouth of the bay.

Uneasy Truce

Finally, a settlement came. The oyster beds in the lower bay concerned local oystermen and environmentalists like Jones, who kept the Audubon Society on center stage during the talks. The breakthrough came when Mobil agreed not to discharge fluids or solids of any kind into the bay—not even water. That became known as the 'zero discharge policy.' "Nothing goes overboard," Wade, Plater and Kelley wrote. "No drill cuttings, mud, or wastewater may be discharged into Mobile Bay. No galley waste, sanitary waste or cooling water waste may be discharged."[16]

"They put up a huge bond [$55 million]," Tom Joiner recalled. He emphasized the cooperation of industry, government, and community interests as the driving force that established the ground rules. "The regulations were about as strict as any, anywhere."

Mrs. Jones, however, contends the rules were developed around her kitchen table. "We [the Mobile Bay Audubon Society] sat around the table discussing the issue and we eventually came up with suggested conditions that actually became a part of the permit."[17]

After another public hearing, the settlement was signed in February 1978. Wade, Plater and Kelley said a Mobil spokesperson described the rules as "the most stringent ever adopted by any state—much stiffer than federal rules." Shortly thereafter the Corps of Engineers gave their go-ahead, and on May 18, 1978, Tom Joiner, who replaced the retired LaMoreaux as State Geologist, signed the most significant drilling permit in his term of office and the most consequential in the state's history.

Finally, Mobil Drills Ahead

On November 17, 1978, almost six months after Joiner signed the permit, Alabama Block 76-1 was spudded two miles east of the eastern tip of Dauphin

Island with a submersible rig. A submersible rig floats on gigantic pontoon-like structures which are flooded after the rig is towed to the desired drilling location. The pontoons rest on a prepared shell bed sea floor, leaving the operating decks well above the sea. Once the well is completed, the pontoons are pumped out and the rig re-floated. Since they must rest on the sea floor, submersibles operate in relatively shallow water.

Trouble broke out almost immediately. Before it reached 6,000 feet the well developed technical problems and had to be plugged back to 2,500 feet. In January 1979, Mobil kicked-off and started a sidetrack hole and drilled to 14,659 feet. There they stopped, plugged back, and kicked-off again. The drilling continued late into the year with no significant shows of oil or gas and finally reached the Smackover at 19,400 feet below sea level. As they progressed down through the formation, Mobil's exploration team shook their heads in disappointment. The evaluations were dismal. The Smackover was tight. Only one target remained, but before they reached the Norphlet, Mother Nature tested them with all her might.

One of the worst Gulf Coast hurricanes on record, Frederic, hit Mobile Bay dead center aimed precisely at Block 76-1. That was a crucial test for drilling advocates. Everyone who participated in the debate on both sides of the argument braced for the impact. If the submersible rig foundered or was structurally damaged, it was reasonable to expect future production platforms might also fail, endangering the environment.

The storm struck with fury. Winds gusted to 145 mph. The storm surge reached 15 feet. Five people were killed ashore, and the destruction totaled $2.3 billion. A quarter-mile section of the Dauphin Island causeway, only one mile from the rig, was swept away. When the wind died, the rain stopped, and the visibility lifted, the giant submersible and its tall derrick were still there, undamaged. Drilling soon resumed.

A month after Frederic, Mobil's geologists confirmed that the drill bit had entered the Norphlet formation. The gas detectors on the surface went off scale and sounded the alarm. Drilling stopped ten months after it began at a total depth of 21,113 feet. Mobil ran an eleven hour test November 27–28. Gas flowed at the rate of more that 12 million cubic feet per day. The total productive interval was nearly 300 feet with porosity as high as 20%. Everything about the well was huge, including the cost: over $20 million, $7 million more than projected originally.

Mobil's chief geologist, Roy Roadfier, called the discovery "remarkable." *The Oil and Gas Journal* called it "awesome."[18] Jurassic production had been extended 50 miles south of Hatters Pond in one giant leap, but there was a big problem. Nine percent of the gas was H_2S. The corrosive, poisonous gas required building expensive facilities—but that would have to be dealt with later. First, the new discovery had to be evaluated and developed.

In November 1980, Mobil appeared before a state agency again, but under circumstances that put smiles on their faces. The previous confrontations were worth it after all. Mobil's F.T. Musson and Joseph Fryer, who worked on the project from its inception, presented the technical testimony, and the Oil and Gas Board approved the company's proposal for a new field. Mobil's CEO, Raleigh Warner, requested his wife's name be included in the field name. In a rare departure from its strict custom of naming fields exclusively after local geographic features, the Board consented and named it the Lower Mobile Bay-Mary Ann Field.

Mobil sank two more successful wells in 1982, one of which required 18 months to drill. Well 94-2 was drilled from the same surface location as the discovery well to minimize the number of production platforms in the bay and avoid the ship channel. The hole was deviated to the south underneath the neighboring lease block.

Tom Joiner summarized the methodology that led to the discovery and the development that followed it. "At discovery time they had [only] 2-D seismic. They saw the 'high'—they drilled the high, and they were lucky they hit some good porous Norphlet. It was still kind of a luck thing as they went ahead with the next few wells in development, because we weren't understanding at that time exactly what the Norphlet was like down there. It was only after they started using 3-D seismic and additional subsurface geologic data from well bores that we could see what the Norphlet looked like within the structural high that was mapped."

Joiner explained that once the advantages of 3-D seismic data became available, operators targeted the highest points of the enormous dunes, which were not recognized and adequately mapped on the original structure map. That was totally new. The northwest-southeast trending dunes were mapped in intricate detail. "That started making a lot of difference on the success ratio. They completed some wells in the dunes that tested 80 million cubic feet a day and one we thought would test at 100 million a day. That's a lot of gas coming out of a little hole in the ground."

The Mobile Bay-Mary Ann discovery was Alabama's third commercial Norphlet discovery, coming eleven years after Flomaton in Escambia County, 75 miles to the northeast, and five years after Hatters Pond in north Mobile County. The Alabama Oil and Gas Board initially estimated the reserves under the bay to be between 5.7 and 6.5 trillion cubic feet (Tcf).[19] If the federal waters are included, the recoverable reserve estimate is nine Tcf. Mobil's discovery was a nine-fold giant.

A Cash Madness

The waters off Alabama's dazzling white sandy beaches erupted in a lease feeding frenzy for the big boys of the petroleum industry, among them Amoco, Conoco, Exxon, Getty, Gulf, Phillips, Shell, Sohio, and Union. A few smaller fish, such as Hunt, Louisiana Land & Exploration, Naptimes, and Pennzoil joined in the fray. The high stakes bidding war spread south beyond Alabama's three-mile offshore limit into federal waters, where the companies hoped the Norphlet production extended.

By March 1981, Alabama had awarded leases totaling over 55,000 acres on 13 of its blocks.[20] The bonus money paid for those blocks amounted to nearly a half billion dollars. The state reserved royalties from 25% to 28%. It rejected bids on 22 blocks. Wade, Plater and Kelley wrote that when Department of Conservation commissioner John MacMillan was asked why the state rejected bids on the other 22 blocks, he replied, "With nearly $450 million in the bank—more than we ever imagined—we simply rejected all the bids below $2,000 an acre." The total of the bids for the rejected blocks would have added only 11% to Alabama's total take. The business move was a risky but smart. The 22 blocks brought much higher bonuses later after the estimates of the field's size increased.

The federal government cashed in too, netting nearly one quarter billion dollars on 17 blocks. The feds didn't drive as hard a bargain as the State, reserving only 16.67% royalty.

The influx of wealth into one of the nation's poorest states in terms of tax revenue created a cash madness in Montgomery. From the governor's mansion to the legislative chambers, politicians smacked their fiscal lips and bellied up to the pork barrel. "We've struck oil!" Governor Fob James told the press. Wade, Plater and Kelley pointed out that, "The bonanza couldn't have come at a better time because interest rates were at record highs. The money was invested in 90 day time deposits earning about 14% while the governor and State legislators decided what to do with the bonanza."

Governor James proclaimed the windfall "a once in a lifetime opportunity to solve the majority of the problems facing the State." On the governor's shopping list were prisons, roads, and bridges. Controversy over the proposed spending flared. Everyone wanted a piece of the pie, but cool heads prevailed.

Alabama finally took the high and smart road. Mobile's Senator H.L. "Sonny" Callahan proposed to set the principal aside and invest it, spending only the interest, so future generations would continue to benefit. The *Birmingham Post Hearld* said the governor had serious reservations about Callahan's proposal; but he relented, and he and the legislature created the Heritage Trust Fund, the first of its kind in oil politics.[21]

Interest from the fund and royalty revenues are used for a variety of purposes, including roads, bridges, landfills, public utilities, and government buildings. Other beneficiaries included a biomedical research facility at the University of Alabama-Birmingham, the State Docks in Mobile, and the Forever Wild Land Trust. Revenue has also paid debt service on Alabama Public School and College Authority bonds.

Some of the money became part of pricey incentives to entice industries like Mercedes, Hyundai, and others into the state. Tom Joiner, now free from the verbal restraints of public service, spoke with a hint of sarcasm toward the state he once served. "No 'Mercedes' type incentives were extended to the companies who brought about this development," he said in an address at the 50th anniversary of the Alabama Oil and Gas Board. "They paid their money . . . just for the opportunity to drill to see if something was there. They came to the State in the face of relentless opposition and at enormous financial risk."[22] One wonders if Mercedes, which accepted lucrative financial incentives to locate in Alabama, would have come to the state under the circumstances Mobil faced. Joiner opined that without Mobil's tenacious resolve, the payoff and its inevitable trickle-down effect on Alabama's economy would never have materialized.

Double-Crossed

On Friday, June 18, 1982, Mobil's local manager got a call from an attorney who had received an anonymous phone call claiming that a rig in the bay turned its lights off and dumped liquid waste into the bay. Mobil sprang into action, launching an investigation and disclosing the matter to the various state and federal agencies concerned. MOEPSI president Ken Keller testified about the incident at a hearing. "I received verbal reports that I can best describe as shocking." He said fluids had been dumped into the bay from a hopper barge used to collect rig liquids and solids.

The Attorney General, the Alabama Water Improvement Commission, the U.S. Coast Guard, and the Oil and Gas Board all ordered investigations. Mobil hired a retired FBI agent to interview the rig crews. Keller further testified that the discharges were not accidental and that they took place at night to avoid detection over a 15-month period. The nature and quantity of the fluids were unknown. Keller attributed the act to a "few individuals trying to save time and money by sending less waste to the approved disposal sites."[23] Mobil told the regulators that the personnel responsible for the dumps were accustomed to drilling in other waters and had never encountered such stringent requirements, that they were disobedient lower echelon employees who thought the rules were unnecessary. That was undoubtedly true, but the state authorities did not get out their crying towels.

Mobil paid a $2 million fine and fired 15 people. They assigned higher management level employees to supervise all drilling activities personally. The corrective action was positive and swift, and the incident was the only black mark on the entire Alabama offshore undertaking.

Another mammoth lease sale took place in 1984. Nineteen state blocks totaling more than 75,000 acres were awarded, bringing $350 million more to the state coffers. Bids on six blocks were rejected.[24]

As more bonus dollars rolled in, the legislature and then-governor George Wallace created another fund, the Alabama Trust Fund, similar to the Heritage Trust Fund. The two funds merged into a single one, the Alabama Trust Fund, in 2001.

Mobil and Exxon drilled 11 straight successful wells after the first discovery. By the end of 1984, they had discovered an additional five Norphlet reservoirs. By the end of 1985, Mobile Bay operators had discovered eight Norphlet fields. Exxon had four, Mobil three, and Chevron one. Between then and late 1985 five more fields were added: Mobil's West Dauphin Island Field, Exxon's Block 867 Field (estimated to contain a trillion cubic feet), Exxon's Northwest Gulf, and North Central Gulf Fields, and Chevron's Block 861 Field. Development in the federal waters to the south also found huge reserves. Between 1985 and 1989, Exxon, Chevron, British Petroleum, Conoco, Shell, Texaco, and Union added seven more fields and between 1990 and 1993 two more, then another two by 1997. That brought the total to 19 in federal waters. The Mobile Bay complex became one of the biggest gas-producing provinces in the United States.

The first production began from the first field discovered—Lower Mobile Bay-Mary Ann—in 1988. A complex network of pipelines connected the production platforms to shore facilities that processed the sour gas to make it safe for sales pipelines. Mobil, Exxon, and Shell built gigantic onshore processing plants south of Mobile.

As more leases were sold and more wells were added to the bay and offshore waters, more records fell. Exxon's Block 112 No. 3 well south of Dauphin Island tested at an astonishing rate of 127 million cubic feet of gas per day, establishing a new production rate record in the entire Gulf of Mexico region. As astounding as the record-breaking flow rate was, it could have been much higher. The well could not flow at its maximum potential rate during the test due to limitations in the capacity of the production platform. The well was opened to only about 50% of capacity.

The fields produced gas at fabulous rates through the 1980s and well into the 90s, fluctuating as market forces and plant capacities dictated. The State of Alabama and the federal government shared the royalty revenues according to the boundary agreed to in 1983, but in 1993 the feds got greedy and tried to snatch some waters from the state.

The southernmost point in Alabama is Sand Island, a bar off Ft. Morgan occupied only by a lighthouse. The three-mile line that defined the boundary between state and federal waters extended from Sand Island. In the late 80s and early 90s, the sand eroded leaving the lighthouse standing on its foundation in the water. The federal government asserted that a piece of Alabama now no longer existed and took legal action to move the three-mile boundary closer inland, taking 4,300 acres away from the state and giving it to the federals. The state put up a fierce fight and won. Alabama got $2 million held in escrow pending the outcome and tens of millions more on production royalties thereafter.[25]

The Oil and Gas Board's Ralph Hellmich said the bay's production peaked between 1994 and 1996, when it reached over 235 Bcf per year. It has since dropped to around 200 Bcf. He said production is a function of market forces and plant capacity. "The driving force is keeping those plants full. . . . The drilling rate slowed when Exxon and Mobil merged."[26] By 2003 the onshore facilities were processing 600 million cubic feet per day from state and federal waters.

The Norphlet dune complex extends southeasterly from Mobile Bay into federal waters off Pensacola, Florida. The trend passes just offshore of Alabama's lucrative tourist beaches in southern Baldwin County, where some geologists believe there are more huge gas reserves. In 1996, under pressure from tourist interests, the U.S. Department of the Interior banned all offshore drilling in federal waters nearer than 15 miles from the Alabama shore. The tourist industry did not want the unsightly rigs within sight of the beaches. Governor Fob James and the state legislature sided with the tourist industry and the local communities and adopted a resolution banning all offshore drilling in state waters off Baldwin County.[27]

The Norphlet complex also lies over a huge geologic feature 40 miles south of Pensacola, known as the Destin Dome. Hellmich estimated it contains enough gas "to run every home in the State of Florida for 16 years," but those homes will never see that gas until the federal government lifts a drilling ban within 100 miles of Florida's coastline. Florida's governor, Jeb Bush, who requested the ban, reportedly had a brother high up in the government in Washington.

Swell of Spirit

In contrast to the Floridians' fears of environmental disaster, Alabama forged ahead to convert its resources to wealth while establishing environmental quality control standards for the entire world. Constant monitoring and testing has shown the bay free from pollutants historically produced by the petroleum industry. Hellmich said that other pollutants found in the bay, such as mercury in fish, are consistent with those found in the fish in the fresh waters that feed the bay, and other areas of the Gulf where there are no platforms.

Of the platforms themselves, Hellmich said they will leave when the gas depletes. "They are easily moved," he said. "We require them to plug the wells and cut everything off below the mud line. They'll cut the pilings off and the risers on the pipeline. Then they go in with divers and sidescan sonar for a sight review to make sure there is nothing left."

One non–oil related business that benefits from offshore production platforms is the fishing industry. Fisherman catch great quantities of fish that school around the platforms along the western Gulf Coast, but in the late 1990s the conservation department began getting reports that the fishing around the Mobile Bay platforms was poor. That raised fears that something detrimental to fish, and possibly humans, was being dumped. The department investigated.

"It turned out," Hellmich said, "that it was so clean under the platforms that there was no habitat for the fish. So now the conservation department is putting crushed limestone next to the platforms to enhance the fish environment, because nothing is being thrown over from the platforms. Everybody got a big kick out of that."

Hellmich credited the gadfly for much of Mobile Bay's environmental success. "What Myrt did accomplish, is that she raised the bar. . . . She made these companies so nervous of the public forum that it kept their attention focused. In fact, the companies, over the years, have used this [Mobile Bay] and held it up as a world class environmental project."

Hellmich represented the Alabama Oil and Gas Board at a Caspian Sea drilling conference in Kazakhstan to explain the Mobile Bay success story. The president of Exxon also attended, explaining how Mobile Bay could be an example of environmental stewardship for the Caspian.

One unsightly impact on the environment could not be avoided. The lower Mobile Bay area and the shores around the residential community of Dauphin Island are studded with towering steel behemoths beyond the breakers. At night clusters of offshore lights spoil the meditative gazes of beachcombers who long for views of vast, empty seas. Mobile Bay Audubon Society member Dianne McGee understood energy needs but lamented over what she will probably never see again. "I remember visiting Dauphin Island when the Gulf horizon was a pure line of sea and sky; when staring out from the sands you could still experience that swell of spirit you feel when met with a seemingly endless ocean. I remember the shock of the first lights of the first drilling rigs, and the beach there has never been the same since."[28]

Future beachcombers will see that unbroken horizon again but probably not in Dianne's lifetime.

Chapter 19

The Burning Water Well

By 1978 annual oil production in Alabama peaked out at 12 million barrels and began decreasing with occasional upward spikes as additional fields were discovered. A year later Alabama's annual gas-condensate production also peaked at 13 million barrels and began a steady decline. Those unhappy milestones were hardly noticed in the wake of the great Norphlet gas discovery four-and-one-half miles deep under Mobile Bay.

The enormous strike electrified the big boys of the petroleum industry and sparked a hunt that migrated onshore. One of the first major companies to search for the Jurassic onshore in the wake of the bay activity was Amoco Production Company. Amoco picked a spot near Foley, Alabama, in Baldwin County, and prepared to spud a 20,000-foot stab.

Morton Wakeland, an Amoco geologist, was assigned to sit the well. He remembered doing his homework before going out to the site and seeing some interesting features in dry holes around the area. "I reviewed lots of old e-logs and saw these large resistivity spikes around 1,500 feet."[1] He discussed the spikes with his boss and others in the office. Some suggested the spikes were coal seams. Others agreed with Wakeland that it could be gas. They decided to log the shallow zones before setting surface casing.

On his way to the site, Wakeland, who doubted the coal interpretation, stopped at a tourist shop and saw something that tickled his curiosity. "I was looking at post cards and noted one had a picture of a water well on the Fort Morgan peninsula that burned." Other geologists knew of the well, but Wakeland went to see for himself. He wondered if the gas in the water well could have migrated up from deeper gas-bearing sands.

Amoco spudded their Smackover test and paused to log the shallow section before setting surface casing. When Wakeland saw the strong gamma ray deflection he suspected sandstone, not coal, and when he saw that the neutron and density curves crossed one another exhibiting a classic "gas effect," he was certain they had found a shallow gas sand. The rest of the New Orleans staff agreed. Amoco amassed "a bazillion landmen," Wakeland said, to invade south Alabama and lease the shallow rights.

The Jurassic test was disappointing. Amoco plugged back and completed in the shallow sand, which flowed a million cubic feet per day. They called it the Amos Sand, and the Oil and Gas Board named the new discovery the Foley Field. The Amos was Miocene, only a few million years old, while the Smackover and Norphlet were almost 200 million years old. The new strike kicked off the Miocene Play.

A new kind of hunt started in south Alabama. Getting at the Miocene gas cost only a bit over $100,000, versus tens of millions to get at the Norphlet. Besides, Miocene gas was sweet—it had no pesky H_2S and was almost ready for market the moment it came out of the ground. The independents took notice. That was their kind of game.

The question of just how to about finding a Miocene field didn't stop many independents. The shallow structure maps geologists hurriedly put together across the region showed almost no structure. That meant the gas was in stratigraphic traps, which are difficult to find. While many independents began chasing the Miocene by random drilling, Amoco took a different tack. They noticed an oddity in the seismic records that coincided with Miocene gas accumulations. They called them *bright spots* and thought that was the key to finding the shallow pay.

As it developed the Foley Field, Amoco drilled other bright spots in southern Baldwin County with great success. Some independents who could afford seismic programs followed suit. The play eventually went into the bay and spread westward into Mobile County. To date, the Miocene trend in south Alabama has produced nearly 80 billion cubic feet of gas with 60% coming from a single field, the North Dauphin Island Field. "It [the field] was projected to produce about seven years," the Alabama Oil and Bas Board's Ralph Helmich said, "and it's still producing 15 years later. In fact they're looking at it now for a gas storage field."[2]

The companies that used bright spot technology enjoyed great success and those who chose other exploration means peppered the coastal counties with dry holes. Helmich thought some of those companies may not have been too interested in success. "Because the beach was so nearby it just turned out to be a nice tax deductible reason to get away, for some of them. They set pipe on everything they found. Back in the 80s the rules of investment and the tax structure were quite different. There were quite a few companies that came in here, and if they found gas they probably would have been in big trouble."

Helmich went out to one particular wildcat well when it was logged and found dozens of local people eating picnic lunches and watching in lawn chairs. "They had bought into this, at like a $1,000 a pop. . . . The log looked like a pair of railroad tracks. I felt sorry for them."

Morton Wakeland's doubts about the coal seam idea helped lead to a short-lived but exciting gas play where no one ever suspected it would happen. The Miocene Play across south Alabama faded in the mid 1990s after discovering only 60 gas pools. Many thought the shallow gas wells would number in the thousands, an independent's dream, but for all its initial excitement, the Miocene was only the clown juggling in the circus parking lot. The deep Norphlet was still the Big Top.

$125/Barrel Oil?

As the 70s closed, things started happening for the Miocene players and other gas seekers. Hard, cold winters plagued the North in 1978-79. Gas use shot upward and shortages developed. Many businesses shut down and the economy slumped.

Finally, Congress passed legislation that gave producers relief from the price controls, without eliminating them completely. Newly found shallow gas in North Mississippi and Alabama soon fetched around $4.50 per mcf. At that price shallow gas wells became gold mines, and a new round of exploration kicked off in the Black Warrior Basin.

Bill Tucker's Warrior Drilling and Exploration, Inc., led the charge, discovering fields at an astonishing rate. What he found in 1979 at North Blowhorn Creek in Lamar County, Alabama, stood the oil business on its ear. He hit oil—not just a show of oil or a little oil associated with gas production, but crude in abundance. Tucker and his group found the 33 degree gravity oil in the Carter Sand at a depth of just 2,600 feet.

Hughes and Hughes, Inc., took over operations and developed the field into 52 oil wells. Unitized and water-flooded, it produced over seven million barrels by 2003. The field's gas cap has produced 26 billion cubic feet.

Many oilmen have scratched their heads over finding significant oil in only one place in the entire Black Warrior Basin. Jackson geologist Stewart Welch suggested, "There is a black shale that develops in that area that is between the Carter and the Bangor lime below. I think it's a local source rock that you don't have elsewhere. It is apparently a marine black shale that isn't all that thick—maybe ten to fifteen feet. I think that's the reason."[3]

For Tucker and his investors, the oil couldn't have come at a better time. The government's energy initiatives allowed the gradual decontrol of crude oil prices over a 21-month period. It also set up a windfall profit tax on crude oil and put conservation regulations in place. President Carter's energy advisors told him the world was about to run out of oil and prices would soon reach $125 a barrel. Companies began to evaluate the future value of their reserves at figures from $80 to $125 a barrel. Even after oil rose to $35, it was still considered cheap. Dudley Hughes wrote, "Huge funds were raised to buy while it was cheap. Companies expanded their personnel and hired every geologist, geophysicist, and landman available at unheard-of salaries."

Raising great sums of money, investor groups bid each other up on oil properties offered for sale. Hughes said, "Sales were bid to ridiculous heights. Large companies were formed almost overnight from these purchases. Everyone wanted to get into the act. Money poured into the business. Lease costs were driven up. No farmouts were available. All the best trends were leased up. Drilling costs skyrocketed and rigs were hard to get. A pipe shortage developed. Competition was fierce."[4]

Driven by the influx of money, nearly 50 fields were discovered on the Alabama side of the Black Warrior Basin in the late 1970s, most of them in Fayette and Lamar Counties. In Mississippi's Black Warrior Basin, nearly 40 new fields and pools were found during the same period.

Activity in the Interior Salt Basin also surged. One of the most active years in south Alabama was 1979. While a few major oil companies were still poking around Alabama's southern counties, the independents were carrying the play. For one independent, a casual question over lunch with a friend led to a rich oil strike.

"There was a pony in there somewhere."

Midroc's Les Aultman was having lunch with Union of Cal's Howard Samsel. He asked Samsel what was going on in the Union camp and Samsel told him about a prospect that they had just put together in Alabama. The leases had been secured so he invited Aultman to look at it. It was four miles north of Jackson in Choctaw County. "It was a big structure," Aultman recalled."[5]

But Samsel was having trouble with his company's engineers. They were telling him that the proposed location was in rough terrain and would be costly to prepare. The engineers won the argument and moved the location into a flat pasture. Their Jurassic test came up dry.

Aultman looked at the logs and his mouth fell open. "They had 100 feet of beautiful dolomite!" he said. "But not one breath of a show. When we saw that dolomite we knew there was a pony in there somewhere." He and Vaughan Watkins, Midroc's operatives in Jackson, tried to get a farmout from Union but were politely refused. Union was still considering another test on the prospect.

Some time later Aultman was riding with Harry Spooner to a tennis court and Aultman mentioned that he had asked Union for the farmout. Spooner and Aultman were friends and had been co-workers at Pruet & Hughes. Spooner now had his own company, Spooner Petroleum. Spooner looked over and said, "I just got that farmout!" That angered Aultman but Spooner calmed him down by inviting Midroc to join him 50/50 in the deal. The group put the deal together but had trouble selling it because it was so far out from known production. The distance between the Clarke County Smackover trend and the Chunchula Field to the south was almost 60 miles and they were right in the middle of that gap.

After a struggle finding investors they finally got it a drilled. It was dry with very little show. They analyzed the new data from the dry test and moved to a new spot to try again. The second time worked. "We had 20 feet of solid oil saturation," Aultman said. "We got 300 feet high to the Union of Cal well by drilling their original location [the one Union's engineers didn't like]."

The new discovery became the Stave Creek Field. "It wasn't nearly as big as we thought but the well paid out in 40 days. We were getting $40 for the oil." It eventually made over three million barrels.

Midroc wasn't so lucky with its other deals. "When I went there they already had three prospects and then we generated a few more and that made a ten well package," Aultman said. The prospects were thoroughly seismic supported and were spread through Clarke County, Mississippi, and Choctaw County, Alabama. They turned the package to Tenneco. "I had this concept back then that there's no way you could drill ten prospects and have ten dry holes. Just the law of averages would work for you. All ten of them were dry! And I think the guy with Tenneco that took the [package of deals] got fired."

They didn't give up. Watkins and Aultman generated another package of three deals. The one Aultman thought least likely to hit, did. On the closing week of the decade of the 70s Midroc found Smackover oil at West Bend Field in Choctaw & Clarke Counties, Alabama. It wasn't a monster but it paid out, making a million barrels.

Aultman, Watkins, and the other explorers and producers in the Southeast again turned a jealous eye toward northwest Florida in 1981 as Jay Field passed the 300 million barrel mark. Now it was a triple giant. None other like it had yet been found. But they continued to work hard chasing the elusive Smackover in south Alabama. Meanwhile some innovative thinkers upstate were putting together a revolutionary idea. It was simple in concept but it needed the latest technology to succeed. And, succeed it would, even to the point of causing governments and energy organizations across to world to look to the Heart of Dixie.

An Unconventional Idea

The idea's roots go back to 1968 in Farmington, West Virginia, when a coal mine explosion took the lives of 78 miners. The blast was caused by methane gas that came out of the coal and filled the mineshaft. The problem had been widespread in the mining industry for centuries and had been dealt with in various ways, mostly by using venting fans to draw the gas from the shafts. The Farmington explosion compelled the U.S. Congress to find a better method of "degassifying" coal mines. The task fell to the U.S. Bureau of Mines and in 1975 it initiated an experimental project. It found a willing industry partner in U.S. Steel Corp. in Birmingham, Alabama. Thus began a new saga in the evolution of fossil energy technology. The era of coalbed methane (CBM) production had begun (Figure 16).

U.S. Steel's project engineer, John Wallace, and his team knew that coal beds were replete with natural fractures, which in effect increased the surface

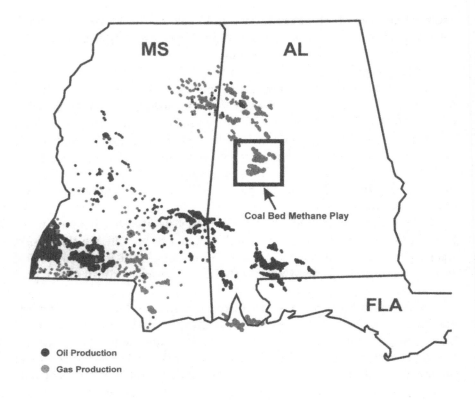

Figure 16. Map of coal bed methane play.

area of the coal. They also learned that because of this vast surface area coal beds can store six to seven times more methane gas than the equivalent rock volume of a conventional gas reservoir.

The gas methane molecules are held in place on coal surfaces by a force known as adsorption. The team postulated that in order to "desorb" the methane and free it they would need to reduce the pressure on the coal. They discovered that the most expedient way to reduce the pressure and release this vast volume of gas was to lower the hydrostatic pressure on the coal seam. In simple terms, they needed to pump out the water surrounding the coal to release the gas. But the disposition of the water became an immediate concern.

Water produced from shallow coal beds is generally not as saline as water produced in conventional oil and gas operations, but its variable chloride content raised valid environmental concerns. These concerns brought the Alabama Department of Environmental Management (ADEM) into the permitting process along with the Oil and Gas Board. Working with the U.S. Environmental Protection Agency ADEM established guidelines for produced CBM water and set up monitoring programs. Waters with chloride content below a determined level could be discharged directly into local streams. Waters with higher chlorides had to be disposed using conventional subsurface injection procedures. ADEM set up testing stations in selected streams and closely monitored the salinity and water quality of the Black Warrior River, into which all the local streams drained. Wherever chloride concentrations increased ADEM placed additional restrictions on the operators discharging in that stream system.

The CBM extraction process began by drilling a pattern of wells around the coal seam and installing pumps to remove the water. Robert "Jerry" Sanders spoke about the process at the 50th anniversary celebration of the Alabama Oil and Gas Board, explaining, "As the pressure surrounding the wellbore is reduced gas is desorbed from the coal and flows to the well. Wells are generally completed in a configuration where the water is removed through the tubing, and the gas is produced up the space between the tubing and the production casing."[6] The Oak Grove project was so successful that a second one began in 1981 at the Jim Walters mine at Brookwood, Alabama. These projects would come to employ both vertical and horizontal wells to collect the gas, and both would be the only coalbed methane projects in Alabama established around actual underground mines.

A year later the Jim Walters mine became the first of its kind in the world to commercially produce "gob" gas, which is the methane captured directly from coal mining operations. Sanders explained, "This is gas that, unless it is captured, would be mixed with mine ventilation air and vented out through fans into the atmosphere." The Jim Walters company reaped a double benefit from the degassification project. Not only could it rid itself of the dangerous nuisance it could actually sell it.

In 1982 other ambitious programs began at United Gas' Cedar Grove Multi-seam Project and TRW's Deerlick Creek project. While those projects were in progress, the University of Alabama Mineral Engineering Department, in cooperation with the U.S. Department of Energy, drilled two experimental wells on university property at the edge of the campus. Information from that project led to the establishment of the Coalbed Methane Forum where industry, education, and government came together to share and discuss technology. Many new ideas from the forum were put to test. While the focus of the campus project was technology development, the University relished the possibility of future CBM revenue from its many acres of endowed land in the coal basin. Those hopes eventually became reality.

One of the main problems the forum addressed was the low volume of gas produced by CBM wells, typically only a few hundred cubic feet per day—hardly economical. At the same time a debate over national energy policy to enhance CBM economics was going on in Washington. In 1980, in Section 29 of the tax code, Congress gave tax credits to industries that produce energy from "unconventional" sources. Among those sources was CBM.

The Alabama Oil and Gas Board knew the CBM industry would be more than a passing experiment and enacted special rules to govern it in 1983, the first such rules adopted by any state and a model for other states. Even with the tax incentives, CBM became an attractive energy investment on a par with conventional oil and gas only in 1987. "Mike Chambers, Bill Hurt, and their company, the River Gas Corporation, began developing the Deerlick Creek and Blue Creek areas," Sanders said. "Their success with controlling development costs opened many eyes to the potential for economic development of coalbed methane resources."

Even Wall Street cut its eyes at the CBM industry, which was still confined to Alabama. The developing technology, along with the Section 29 credits, ignited a "phenomenal development in coalbed methane that occurred between 1989 and 1990," when over 4,000 wells went down in west Alabama. It was the CBM boom. Sanders pointed out that the Brookwood project alone had produced over 100 billion cubic feet by the time the boom started.

The boom spun off thousands of jobs in local support industries and got major oil companies such as Amoco, Chevron, and Sonat involved. The largest producer of CBM in the state is an Alabama company, Taurus Exploration. "The coalbed methane industry as it exists in Alabama is a 'homegrown' product," Sanders bragged in his speech. He said that another Alabama company, River Gas, headquartered at Northport, developed the largest single coalbed methane project in the world. Other home grown companies developing the trend were Torchmark and Black Warrior Methane.

CBM companies have spent over $2 billion in a four-county area of west central Alabama. Sanders compared that to the $350 million initial investment Mercedes made at its automotive plant at Vance. Yet the CBM industry drew virtually no media attention as Mercedes did and remains almost unrecognized in Alabama's socio-economic framework. Sanders noted that "this all happened without a whole lot of fanfare—at least none from the industry." Indeed, the conventional oil and gas industry hardly noticed as CBM production overtook and exceeded the entire conventional gas production in the Black Warrior Basin in Alabama.

Today, Alabama produces CBM at a rate of nearly 116 billion cubic feet per year or approximately 30% of the state's total gas production. Almost 6,000 CBM wells have been drilled in the state to date, and the cumulative production is now more than 1.4 trillion cubic feet. Total reserves of coalbed methane for the state may exceed three trillion cubic feet, almost half the estimated six trillion cubic feet the prominent Alabama offshore conventional industry is expected to yield.[7]

"In either case," Sanders observed, "both of these discoveries of gas [CBM and Mobile Bay] represent some of the largest energy discoveries in the United

States in the last 25 years. At least six of the fields in the Alabama Warrior Basin coalbed methane fields are listed in the top 100 producing gas fields in the U.S.—quite significant!"

Tuscaloosa, Alabama, is the undisputed coalbed methane capital of the world. The city hosted many CBM symposiums attended by representatives from around the globe. The CBM industry promotes its accomplishments proudly. It maintains it has made mining a safer occupation and by extension allows the recovery of more coal reserves. The recovery and marketing of methane, furthermore, reduces the amount of gas that escapes into the atmosphere from mining operations and improves air quality. Methane burns clean, and its impact on the environment may be less when it is burned than when it is freely released.

The end of Section 29 tax credits was not the death warrant some in the CBM industry feared, but it slowed the industry's explosive growth. Still, given the volume of coal in Alabama's Warrior Coal Basin, if the return on investment holds up, the state's coal bed methane industry should provide clean abundant energy for many decades.

PART V
1980s into the 21st Century

Chapter 20

Berserk

S tarting with a boom, the eighties epitomized the industry's historical boom and bust cycle. An Islamic revolution swept Iran and overthrew the West-friendly government that had let western oil companies develop its vast reserves. The new government shut in the wells. An immediate shortage developed in world oil markets, and OPEC took advantage of it and doubled prices. U.S. domestic oil prices followed the market upward.

President Jimmy Carter responded by declaring the "moral equivalent of war" on the nation's energy problems. In 1977 he created a new cabinet level agency, the Department of Energy, and appointed James R. Schlesinger secretary. Soon thereafter a prominent Mississippian who was very familiar with the affairs of big government got a call from Washington.

Emmett Vaughey responded to the call enthusiastically. However he wasn't asked to solve petroleum supply problems, as he did when President Truman appointed him Director of the Petroleum Administration for Defense (PAD) in 1952. The government wanted his advice and counsel only. He was glad to offer them. He prepared a background paper for Secretary Schlesinger, describing how he ran the PAD during the Korean War.

Charlie Williams and several others in the Mid-Continent Oil and Gas Association helped Emmett with the presentation. Williams remembered what happened. "Emmett told me when he was shown into Schlesinger's office that, before he could inform the Secretary of how he had run the PAD with 17 major oil company experts [all working for a dollar a year], Schlesinger expounded on his grand plan to build one of the largest departments in Washington."[1]

The new department was responsible for many energy initiatives other than petroleum production, but Emmett saw at once that the Secretary was neither interested in enhancing oil resources nor open to advice from the industry. According to Williams, Emmett concluded that the secretary was interested mainly in building a government empire. Emmett told Schlesinger that if that was the idea, "the new energy czar would not need his [Emmett's] advice, so he politely left the office without further comment."

Carter's next move was to levy a Windfall Profits Tax (WPT) on domestic oil production. The WPT was a federal severance tax based on the gross value of oil at the wellhead. The WPT aimed to prevent domestic oil producers from profiting from prices influenced by foreign imports. In fact, producers scaled their operations back and the nation became even more dependent on foreign oil. Carter lost his re-election bid in 1980, and his successor, Ronald Reagan, trashed his energy policy and lifted all price controls on oil and gas.

With market forces in control, principally the commodities markets, the value of oil went up and with it went the rig count. The decline in domestic drilling, which began in 1977, reversed immediately. In 1980 a boom started. Over 91,000 wells were drilled in the United States, a new record. Profit margins soared, which encouraged more exploration and the discovery of more reserves. Consumers responded to the higher costs by conserving. An energy glut resulted, and a bust started.

The industry's tax woes were far from over. In November 1981, Mississippi's Governor William Winter announced his intention to fund educational reform campaign promises with an increase in the state severance tax on oil and gas. The Mississippi petroleum industry objected to the governor's plan. The impact of the severance tax increase depended on how one looked at it. The governor pitched it to the citizens as an increase of only 3%, from 6% to 9%. The petroleum industry saw a 50% increase and began preparing for a long, hard fight over being singled out unfairly to bear the financial burden of a broad-based government program.

Charlie Williams, president of the Alabama/Mississippi Division of the Mid-Continent Oil & Gas Association, organized all segments of the industry, including major oil companies, independents, oil service companies, refineries, and marketers into an effective voice. Others such as geologists, geophysicists, engineers, landmen, attorneys, accountants, landowners, royalty owners, and business leaders also recognized the negative impact of increased taxes on the gross value of Mississippi oil and gas at the wellhead.

Governor Winter waged an aggressive grass roots campaign, hammering the industry, claiming it was money hungry and included some of the greediest people he had known. He rallied the public with media support and said the industry's slogan was "Oil against education in Mississippi."[2] Williams and the activists knew that was far from the truth. The industry, comprised of highly educated scientists, engineers, technicians, and business personnel, certainly knew the value of education.

Williams' group countered with a campaign to educate the public about the industry's value to the state, by showing that it contributed to the state's economic well-being by paying severance taxes, excise taxes, sales taxes, income taxes, and fees; creating jobs; and taking risks to find and develop valuable natural resources to the state's benefit.

The funding brawl plagued the legislature for three years and was the main agenda item in both regular sessions and special legislative sessions. Industry stressed its contributions to the state and objected to being singled out as the primary tax source for a broad-based program which benefited everyone. Williams and company argued that everyone should pay a fair share for the education program. They cautioned further that if a bust started, the education reform would go unfunded to the detriment of all citizens. The legislature finally arrived at a funding method that did not single out one industry but was shared fairly. The governor signed the bill and ended a period of rancor.

Three years later, in 1986—as Charlie Williams was resigning from Mid-Continent Oil & Gas Association to join Bill and Emmett Vaughey as General Manager of Vaughey & Vaughey, Inc.—the wellhead price of oil and gas did in fact collapse. Many in the American petroleum industry—especially independents, service companies, and suppliers—were ruined. But consumers were delighted.

Problems with Moonshiners

As the decade began, the bust was not yet in sight. The oil industry hustled and bustled with enterprise and enthusiasm. The demand for natural gas and refined products was increasing. The government was deregulating oil prices. Optimism ran high among petroleum professionals. Oil companies hired every geologist, engineer, and landman they could find. Money poured in from investment sectors. Drilling companies flourished. The times were the most exciting any oilman could remember.

"In 1980 everything was going berserk," Les Aultman remembered, "and everyone who could spell oil was in the oil business, and some who couldn't."[3] The younger ones thought the feeding frenzy over leases and prospects was the norm and swaggered ahead as if it would go on forever. The older ones told them not to get too cocky; the downturn would come, as it always did.

One of those veteran oilfinders was George Vockroth, who had just become an independent. After collecting his master's in geology from Harvard, Vockroth spent 26 years with Chevron before deciding to have a go at it on his own.

One of his first assignments with Chevron was the unitization of the Brookhaven Field, discovered during WW II. As was the case with many young geologists, the unitization work provided an education like no other. Vockroth emerged with a keenness for mapping subsurface fluvial channels (sand deposits in ancient stream systems).

He formed Vantage Oil Company with partners Larry Kennedy, Don Williams, and Jim Cummings and set his sights on the Mississippi Wilcox. "We worked the Wilcox because you didn't need seismic,"[4] he said. In 1980, a few months after forming the company, he found a prospect, put it together, and sold it. It was a discovery—the East Rosetta Field, which found 12 feet of oil in an Armstrong Sand channel.

The field was in a rural area of Wilkinson County. Vockroth and his part-ners discovered they were losing the copper tubing off of their heater-treat-ers. A little investigative work revealed that moonshiners were appropriating the tubing for their stills. Guarding the wells around the clock would have been costly. Vockroth came up with a clever alternative. He visited the local Baptist minister and asked him, "Would you mind putting out a notice to your congregation that those treaters are dangerous devices that can blow up on you." The minister put a stop to the thievery with a pointed sermon.

Soon thereafter Vantage discovered East Junction City Field. Later the partnership dissolved, and Vockroth became the sole proprietor. He discov-ered other fields and extended or found new pools in many more. In several the confirmation well came up dry or ran into costly trouble, prompting Vockroth to advise, "Your second well in a discovery is the most dangerous one [economically]. You want to sell and get out after the first one." That was advice many independents wished they had heeded.

In 1982 Vockroth and others in the Wilcox club mourned the death of D.A. Biglane. He was one of Mississippi's most renowned independents. Biglane's rise from café cook to wildcatter inspired many gamblers to try their hand at the Wilcox roulette table. At the time of his death, Biglane's brother Noland and his partner Joe Fortunato were still actively selling Wilcox deals and drilling wells. Their company, Big Joe Oil Company, was one of the few remaining Wilcox explorers, but they continued to attract a small cadre of investors interested in the Wilcox's low drilling cost. For about $65,000, you could roll the Wilcox dice and rake in a quarter million barrels or so, with luck. In 1982 over 600 Wilcox wells were drilled, though with a wildcat success ratio of only 5%.[5]

Unlike Vantage and Big Joe, whose MO was generating and selling deals, other companies preferred a mix of deals generated in house and others they bought into. Sometimes one led to the other. Les Aultman remembered an opportunity that popped up soon after he went to work for Midroc. "Some guys out of New Orleans brought us this prospect and we condemned it," he said, but Aultman saw a *lead* on the edge of the prospect map. When he in-corporated the lead with other information he had in his files on that area, a new idea was born. "In the process of condemning it, we found this other prospect that really didn't have much to do with the original idea except it was nearby." Midroc leased it and drilled, discovering the East Magee Field in Smith County. They gave the guys who showed them the initial deal an over-riding royalty interest in their discovery.

Elsewhere in Mississippi, Adams Exploration found Cotton Valley pro-duction at the Newman Field in west Hinds County. The Newman structure is one in a series of salt swells that march southwest from the Jackson Dome, the giant volcanic feature that dominates the subsurface of Hinds and Rankin

Counties. Its presence probably accounts for the scarcity of petroleum accumulations in those two counties, except for the west edge of Hinds and the east side of Rankin. Newman has produced 24 billion cubic feet from the Cotton Valley since its discovery in 1984.

Other explorers looked in the deeper parts of the Salt Basin where the costs were much higher. One of them, Placid Oil, ignited hopes of another big gas play in 1982 by discovering gas in the Cotton Valley ten miles northeast of Vicksburg in Warren County. The Bovina Field also found gas in the Hosston and Rodessa, but the field produced only about 16 billion cubic feet. The big play didn't happen, but later in the 1980s small Lower Cretaceous gas fields were found elsewhere in Hinds County at Utica, Learned, and Edwards.

In 1985 Mosbacher Energy established the deepest production in Mississippi at Collins Field in Covington County. They opened production from a Cotton Valley sand at 18,400 feet with a test of nearly 300 BOPD. The Collins Field, discovered by Pan American Petroleum in 1962, had produced steadily from many Lower Cretaceous zones.

Those and many other new gas strikes began to load the market with more gas behind pipe than it wanted. In early 1982 some interstate pipeline companies started buying gas only from sellers with whom they could negotiate favorable contracts. On the surface that sounds like natural free enterprise, but many small companies and investors who rejected the purchaser's offer, suddenly found their in-ground gas drained without payment. Gas fields, like oil fields, are rarely 100% owned by a single oil company or investment group. Ownership commonly includes both an operator, and non-operators as well as the mineral owners who leased their rights to them.

Typically the operator installs the physical equipment to gather and meter the gas and get it to the buyer, the pipeline company. The non-operators are people or companies who own an interest in the field and who pay their share of the expenses the operator incurs. The operator distributes the revenue from gas sales proportionally to the non-operators. In some cases the operator owns no interest and is merely a contractor.

A problem arose when Transco, a gas pipeline company, began buying gas only from selected operators and non-operators, leaving the rest with the possibility of having their gas drained with no revenue. Julius Ridgeway, owner of Coastal Exploration in Jackson, filed a petition with the Mississippi Oil and Gas Board to enforce rules on the books to protect royalty owners from actions like Transco's. The "ratable take" law is designed to protect the co-equal and correlative rights of owners who share in a common pool and to ensure that each receives his fair share of revenue for the oil or gas produced from that pool.

Transco pressed their case before the U.S. Supreme Court and won. The high court opined that Mississippi's ratable take rule required purchasers to buy more gas than they were contractually obliged to do, and that interfered with federal authority by raising consumer prices.

Ridgway counterattacked. He formed a coalition of companies and royalty owners called the Mississippi Independent Producers and Royalty Owners Association (MIPROA). He found allies in the Mississippi legislature who agreed that the high court "missed the point." He said, "The State of Mississippi did not require Transco to purchase any gas at all, but whatever amount of gas it took, was to be without discrimination in favor of one owner against another."[6] The legislature responded by passing the Mississippi Natural Gas Marketing Act, which allows each owner to "elect" to market his gas with the operator if he chooses. No owner would be left out and risk having his gas drained unless he chose. The act also protected the purchaser by extending the terms of the operator's gas purchasing agreement to all non-operators. Thus, a non-operator who elected to have the purchaser take his gas couldn't negotiate a deal tougher than the operator's. That satisfied owners, the buyer, and the courts, and kept the hunt for more gas reserves at a fast pace.

Oil and gas-condensate were still the focus in southern Alabama, where in 1980 Shell stepped out to the northwest of the Escambia County Smackover trend and drilled in northeast Mobile County, discovering the Blacksher Field. It disappointed them, and they left. A couple of years later Midroc's Vaughan Watkins determined that the field still had potential. He and his partner, engineer Billy Powell, studied the Shell well, put acreage together, and sold a quarter of it to Dudley Hughes. Then they found another company that wanted all or none. Watkins took his dilemma back to Hughes, who told him he didn't have a dilemma. Hughes would take the whole thing.

"What will I tell the other people?" Watkins asked Hughes.

"Offer them a quarter.?"

The group drilled to the Smackover and laid out the logs. They didn't like what they saw. Some of Hughes's employees were there, but he was traveling. Watkins called him and said it didn't look good. The calculations suggested the Smackover was water saturated. Hughes replied, "Well, I know you didn't get what you wanted, but let's run pipe anyway."

"Everybody in the room looked at each other," Watkins said. "We got out of the room, and I saw that Billy Powell looked pretty worried. Billy said, 'Tomorrow I'm going to lay off [sell] some of my interest.' I thought that was a prudent thing to do, so I did that myself. It turned out to be a pretty good well. [Hughes made that decision] strictly on intuition and experience. Logs weren't everything."

Hughes was betting on the Smackover, but some people thought he had a sixth sense for finding oil. Wildcatter Bob Schneeflock summed up the way most oil people who know Hughes regard his ability: "There's a little piece of genius in there that sometimes doesn't travel into other phases of his life. But it's something that no one else has got."[8]

Smacking of Success

Shored up by high oil and gas prices, dozens of small prospects like Watkins' Blacksher deal were put together across the Interior Salt Basin. Charlie Meeks, one of the Jay heroes, had another success. He found a salt swell along a fault below the swamplands of the Alabama River 30 miles north of Mobile and 15 miles east of the Citronelle Field. The rig had to be brought in by barge. Because of the wetlands around it, the hole was drilled under strict offshore standards for environmental protection, which made it costly. The well, operated by Superior Oil Company, found oil in the Smackover at 17,000 feet and was christened the Movico Field. It tested almost 2,000 barrels of oil per day and set off a hectic lease play. Movico was disappointing, however, producing barely more that 100,000 barrels. No other commercial Smackover fields were found in far north Mobile County.

Shortly after the Movico disappointment, a series of modest Smackover discoveries began in Escambia County in 1982. Texaco brought in the Huxford Field, which produced three million barrels, and later the Appleton Field with almost three million barrels. Inexco found a few million barrels in the Norphlet at Chavers Creek.

In 1984 Dudley Hughes formed a new company, Hughes Eastern, and began buying into south Alabama deals. One of their best early finds was Hall Creek in 1985, which made over four million barrels. That same year Shell Western found a similar amount of oil at Gin Creek.

More Smackover strikes were logged through the 1980s, prompting *The Oil and Gas Journal* to write, "The Updip Smackover trend of southwest Alabama and northwest Florida has emerged into one of the hottest areas of exploration and drilling activity in the country. During the past year 19 wildcat wells were drilled . . . of which eight resulted in new field discoveries, for an outstanding 42% success ratio."[9] *The Dallas Morning News* said the south Alabama oil industry was "smacking of success."[10]

Explorers called the Smackover exploration play updip of the peripheral fault system the Updip Smackover. The Louann Salt there is thin or nonexistent. The trapping mechanisms are paleohighs, more commonly called "bumps," in the basement rock. Some geologists believe the bumps are an extension of the buried Appalachian Mountains. Good reservoir rocks usually occur where the Smackover thins across the bumps.

In 1987 one Smackover test yielded a highly unexpected result. It was another idea born at a Les Aultman/Harry Spooner lunch. Aultman was working with the Kelton Company, headed by Tom Sylte out of Pensacola. He was examining a piece of seismic data owned by a major company "as independents are wont to do," and saw a lead northwest of Jay on the upthrown block of a fault in the Pickens-Gilbertown-Pollard fault zone. There were no look-alikes for it elsewhere in Escambia County. In Choctaw County, however, there were plenty.

"Harry Spooner and I were having lunch one day, and I just casually mentioned it to him," Aultman said. Spooner thought he had a couple of seismic lines to add to Aultman's information. "It was sort of like the boy and girl who said I will show you mine if you'll show me yours."[11] When the pair combined information, they saw that there might be a play along the fault system. "We went in there from those two or three lines and we drew a series of bumps—Choctaw County look-alikes, Smackover and Norphlet plays on the upthrown sides of the fault."

They got a lease on a 6,000-acre block owned by a consortium of paper companies and sold the deal to Hughes Eastern. The group drilled three exploratory wells, but all were teasers. "All of them had something wrong with them," Aultman moaned. "They were tight or something. None of it worked worth a darn. I was up to my nose in debt." Then their luck turned.

Aultman thought he noticed a relatively high resistivity zone uphole in the Massive sand of the Lower Tuscaloosa on one of the Smackover tests. At first he thought the high resistivity was due to drilling fluid invasion. He compared other wells in the area and saw that the Massive had lower resistivity in them. He convinced Hughes, Spooner, and the others to get the logging truck back out to the well before they plugged the hole. They shot sidewall cores in the Massive and determined that they had 35 feet of oil column. They drilled an offset and found 95 feet. The Oil and Gas Board named the new strike the Foshee Field. The year was 1987, and the discovery was the first in the Lower Tuscaloosa since Pollard in 1952. Thirty-five years had elapsed since Dale Myers led Stanolind and Humble into the Lower Tuscaloosa at Pollard.

"We drilled on, following the fault," Aultman recalled, "and went downthrown and picked up another fault block, and that became West Foshee Field." The two fields made a handsome six million barrels of oil from a depth of 6,000 feet. "That saved me," said Aultman. "The bank would have cut me off if we had not have found those fields."

Whistling Dixie

The Lower Tuscaloosa and Smackover successes in south Alabama prompted one wildcatter to resurrect his hopes for Bullock County where he drilled a few dry holes in the mid 70s. Bullock is between Montgomery and Columbus, Georgia, far from the oil patch. The Alabama Oil and Gas Board's Assistant Supervisor Jay Masingill remembered when the stranger came in for a permit. "I thought I was familiar with the oil and gas producing counties in the state and Bullock County was just not registering with me."[12] Masingill knew Bullock County had only a thin sedimentary cover over the granite basement and was well east of the depositional limits of the Louann Salt. He and fellow staff member Richard Raymond helped the man with his application. When they got to the question that asked for distance to nearest production, the wildcatter replied, "about 120 miles."

The man planned to drill 20 feet into the granite and set production casing. He told Masingill and Raymond, "If I can just get below that granite cap rock, this well will blow so hard it'll whistle Dixie." The two geologists managed to hold back their chuckles while they helped the man with his permit. Predictably, the tune of Dixie was not heard from the granite beneath Bullock County, but the man's zeal was typical of the way oil fever compelled many highly motivated amateurs to join the hunt.

While Williams poked at the granite, the Updip Smackover sizzled, and explorers stayed busy in south Alabama. Foshee was a big surprise but an even bigger one was coming—the result of a partnership that was beginning a slow, risky rise to prominence.

Chapter 21

"We wanted to be the next Pruet & Hughes."

B ob Schneeflock was one of those dreamy kids who liked dinosaurs, and like most dinosaur freaks he had a rock collection. Sometimes he went riding with his dad near his Alabama coastal plain hometown of Foley to gaze at the drilling rigs. Once they met a geologist at a rig. "He looked like he was having a lot more fun than I was on the dairy farm," Schneeflock said. That clinched it. His future would be in geology and oil.[1]

Schneeflock started off with a BS in geology from Southern Mississippi in 1969 and joined Chevron in New Orleans. In 1972 he moved to Tuscaloosa and earned a master's at Alabama, after which he served stints with Tenneco, Hunt Energy, and Clayton Williams. While with Tenneco he knocked off an economics degree at Cal State. In 1981 he hung out a shingle in Jackson, called it Schneeflock Corporation, and made a snowflake his logo.

His learning curve was brutal. He sold a big chunk of his first deal to AGIP, the Italian national oil company. "When it came time to prepay the drilling costs," he said, "AGIP wouldn't prepay and refused get out of the deal. They considered prepay as an affront to their integrity." He met with his drilling contractor, Chesley Pruet, and explained the impasse with AGIP. He hoped Pruet would take the AGIP's IOU. Pruet eyed him with his glass eye and asked Schneeflock if he would stand good for AGIP if they didn't pay. Schneeflock shrugged and said he would if he could, but he didn't have that kind of money. Pruet glared at him. "Don't worry, son. I know how to get it out of you." The hole turned out to be a duster but AGIP paid their share. "I didn't know what Chesley had in mind," Schneeflock said, "but I didn't doubt him."

He got excited about his second deal. Using a bit of seismic and some subsurface information, he mapped a big nose in Franklin County, Mississippi with thick, porous Lower Tuscaloosa sands downdip and a shale-out higher on the nose. It was big stratigraphic trap, a potential "elephant." He sold a quarter to legendary Texas wildcatter M.B. "Duke" Rudman, a quarter to Mid-American Oil Company, and the rest to others, but Mid-America placed a condition on the deal. They wanted to survey the controlling wells and the proposed drilling location to confirm the elevations. Schneeflock wasn't worried. He had a topographic map, logs, and scout tickets to back up his prospect's subsea values.

When the results of the survey came in, Mid-America called Schneeflock and told him there was an elevation bust. They wanted out.

The rookie wildcatter wondered what to do next. He had spent a lot of money on leases. Overhead was eating into his personal finances, and because of the elevation correction, his second prospect was marginal at best. He was at the intersection of Eating Street and Ethics Avenue. He already had several other companies committed. He could look the other way and pretend he never discovered the elevation bust. He might even get lucky and hit something.

He swallowed hard, called the partners, and told them about the bust. Most, including Rudman, got out of the deal. He finally sold it at a fire sale price. It was a dry hole, but Duke Rudman and his exploration manager, Jim Trimble, knew honesty when they saw it. From then on Bob Schneeflock had an audience with Rudman and Trimble any time he went out to sell a deal.

Rudman was one of the most successful independent oilmen of all time. One of the original East Texas wildcatters, he was in the oil business for more than 60 years and drilled thousands of wells all over the country. He was one of the industry's most successful prognosticators. He was also one of the business' all time most colorful characters. Rudman was a health nut, an anti-smoking crusader, and a gourmet chef. His white suits and broad-brimmed feathered hat became his trademark. At speaking engagements he preached his "15 Steps of the Ladder of Success."[2] Among them were, *integrity, full disclosure, hard work, study*, and *knowing the business*. What motivated Schneeflock were Rudman's admonitions to *do your homework and know it well*, and *play the big shot until you have made it, then low profile it*.

Schneeflock and other Rudman disciples wove the 15 steps into their professional and personal lives. They became his protégés and earned his trust before they found him oil. Some became wealthy and powerful in their own right. Schneeflock hoped to join that club.

He worked like a man possessed in his shop in Jackson with the help of a draftsman and his wife, Susan, who kept the books and answered the phone. He set up several drafting tables and worked on geological ideas on each, shuffling from one to another as he gathered data. He always had a deal in the making, even while he drafted another one for the sales brochure. He had an abundance of ideas at various stages of development and the intuitive ability to sell them. At length he realized he needed a partner who knew where the money was and how to woo it, who could put together big land and seismic deals. Yet he wanted no ordinary business partner. There were plenty around who would have loved to join him. He needed someone with a burning, tenacious resolve, someone with a compelling dream to match his own. The perfect person was about to walk through his door.

Robert Chaney was all of 24 years old when he left Kilroy Company in Houston, where he was joint ventures manager. His performance in bringing companies and resources together prompted Edge Petroleum to invite him in as a partner.

He came from west Texas oil stock. His father was a landman and scout, and oil seeped into his blood early. A born entrepreneur and salesman, he constantly experimented with new business ventures as a kid and turned into workaholic. "I was always looking for a new crusade to embark on."[3]

While working on a degree in petroleum land management with minors in geology and engineering at the University of Texas, Chaney started his crusade. As a college junior he worked full-time as a landman with an Austin company. After graduation in 1980 he joined Kilroy's land department in Houston but quickly showed management he was capable of higher responsibilities. As Kilroy's joint venture manager, he racked up such an impressive track record that the aggressive Edge Petroleum lured him away to orchestrate even bigger deals.

In 1984, while with Edge, an idea hit him. "One day Bob Schneeflock comes into town. I had met him when he had shown me a deal at Kilroy in 1981." Chaney remembered the polished, professional, thorough presentation. Then he went to Jackson to see Schneeflock's set-up. It changed his life.

"I noticed he had three drafting tables, and there were these odd-looking bookcases, or kind of rack things against the wall. They were about 7 feet tall. . . . I finally realized what it was, and this convinced me that Bob was the most prolific geologist I had ever seen in my life."

Schneeflock's use of portable tabletops, which he slid into the racks Chaney saw, was an innovative way to move unfinished projects off the drafting tables temporarily while he waited for more data. Schneeflock would replace one portable tabletop with another one and kept working. "He had so many ideas going that he had to have three drafting tables going at the same time. And whenever one of them would come to a stopping point—waiting on a seismic line, log, or whatever—he would pick the top up with all the data, go over, slide it in the rack, pull out another one, set it down, and start working on it. That did it for me. I knew I had to work with this guy."

Chaney invited Schneeflock to work with Edge Petroleum Corporation on retainer status. Schneeflock accepted because Edge had the funding to make his ideas reality. They were also located in Houston, the heart of the oil business, where his prospects would be marketed.

Schneeflock worked the prospects up and Chaney did the leg work, lining up potential buyers—always oil industry insiders—and seeing that the land and legal matters were seen to. Schneeflock concentrated on the Cretaceous trends of southern Mississippi and southwest Alabama's Updip Smackover. One after another, the deals got sold, got drilled, got plugged. Some were marginal producers, and others were engineering failures, a term geologists use when engineers botch a completion attempt.

In 1985 they put together a relatively small block of acreage nine miles southwest of Monroeville in Monroe County, Alabama. Their target was a basement bump. They sold the deal to a number of investors, including their old devotee, Duke Rudman. Zinn Petroleum operated. In December 1986, as they were approaching target depth, Schneeflock got a 3:00 A.M. call from George Craven, the mudlogger, reporting a tremendous mud log show in a sand, not the expected carbonate. He ordered a core.

At 3:00 A.M. the next day the core came out. "Everything seems to happen at 3:00 A.M. in the oil patch," Schneeflock said. The core had good cut and odor but lacked an analytic quality known as fluorescence, which worried Schneeflock. At 3:00 A.M. the next day, the logs were out. The sand appeared to be water saturated. When Schneeflock and the other geologists representing the various partners correlated the logs, they saw they were looking at Haynesville, not Smackover. The Smackover was not present, and the Haynesville did not produce within a hundred miles.

Craven said that certain high gravity crudes he had seen elsewhere exhibited no fluorescence the human eye can see, which made Schneeflock think there was still hope. He ordered a DST and took some heat from the other participants because of the additional cost on what was apparently a dry hole. When they ran the DST, the ground shook when a stream of fire shot across the pit with a force that made a crater in the embankment on the far side. Fire fighters in the nearby town of Frisco City got worried and showed up with their trucks. Later, Schneeflock overheard a man in a drugstore say there was a whole lake of oil under the town.

Zinn tested over 200 BOPD and nearly half a million cubic feet of gas per day from the Haynesville, which is Jurassic in age and younger than the Smackover. Schneeflock, Chaney, and the others were astounded. *Oil and Gas Investor* called it a "lucky accident." Schneeflock recalled one of Duke Rudman's rules: One ounce of luck is worth one ton of brains.

The Alabama Oil and Gas Board named the strike the Frisco City Field. Development showed the field was complex. "It was very difficult to unravel the structure," Chaney said. "We drilled six wells to make three producers." Ultimately, the field was determined to be a structural/stratigraphic trap with a permeability barrier near the top of the structure. What popped into every geologist's mind who followed the discovery was, how did oil get into the Haynesville, with no Smackover to source it? In a cooperative study with the Alabama Oil and Gas Board, Schneeflock and others concluded that oil from the surrounding Smackover migrated through possible faults and fracture zones along the face of the basement structure and into the porous Haynesville sands.[4] Schneeflock urged the Oil and Gas Board to name the new sand the Fambrough Sand in memory of his friend, geologist Robert Fambrough, but the Board stuck with convention and named it the Frisco City Sand.

Frisco City Field is not significant for the two million barrels of oil it produced but rather the new play it started and the new strain of affliction in oilmen's brains—Haynesville Fever. Explorers took a fresh look at the region and hoped that Frisco City wasn't a fluke. They also hoped it had a big sister lurking somewhere. It did.

Schneeflock and Chaney finished their contractual obligation to Edge and left to kick off their own company on December 31, 1985. "We didn't care if we had raised five million dollars or five dollars," Chaney said. "We were leaving to pursue our dream. I think that commitment—which we decided on with a blood oath that we were going to live up to—is part of what drove us. You can always find reasons not to end up pulling the trigger, but we decided that we were not going to let that happen. We wanted to be the next Pruet & Hughes."

Chaney's admiration for Pruet and Hughes was cultic. "They were our heroes. We saw what they had done for the Southeast together and separately in their own companies afterwards. That was our goal—to emulate them. We wanted to dominate the region as they had and to be the top wildcatter in the country. We wanted to find a monster field."

They also wanted to build the biggest prospect generating company ever. "We planned to do what Henry Ford did for the automobile industry. We wanted to take a mom and pop, haphazardly done thing and turn it into a finely tuned, mass produced, state-of-the art type approach. And, we wanted to get filthy rich."

Chaney came up with a corporate name and went out and raised money. The economic outlook was good; West Texas intermediate crude was at $31.75 per barrel, its highest price in recent history. Their timing looked perfect. On January 1, 1986, Chaney and Schneeflock became Paramount Petroleum, Inc.—just in time for the bust.

The OPEC countries bickered and broke into a frenzied discount selling. It was a crude oil buyer's market, and shortly after January 1986, the price fell to $10 a barrel.⁵ "We watched as our newly created baby almost died." They narrowly avoided bankruptcy.

They survived by selling deals at bargain prices, but they hit dry hole after dry hole as their losing streak extended to 10 in a row over a period of two long years. "We couldn't find oil at a service station," Chaney said.

Their luck changed in late 1988 with the Northwest Range Prospect in southwest Conecuh County, Alabama. Paramount acquired the concept from Dick Lee, a Jackson geophysicist, put it together, and sold it in three days. The discovery tested over 1,000 BOPD from the Smackover. Paramount's standing in the business vaulted and pulled more buyers to their door. Production from Northwest Range fell off rapidly, but their next strike did not disappoint.

In 1987, Jackson geologist Phil Cook, working with Endevco Producing Co., showed them a Mississippi prospect he and Stan Theiling, another Jackson geologist, had worked up. At first sight it was not inspiring, but as the Paramount partners dug deeper into it they began to see it could be a company-maker.

Cook called Schneeflock's attention to a situation in Gitano Field in northwest Jones County, Mississippi, an old field producing from the Lower Cretaceous since 1957. The current operator, Ultramar, planned to use the Wilcox as a saltwater disposal zone, but the EPA (Environmental Protection Agency) blocked it, saying it was too shallow and might damage freshwater acquifers. They told Ultramar to find a deeper zone to inject the saltwater.

The deeper Eutaw was a good bet because it looked porous and wet on the logs and had only one-half ohm resistivity, a value thought too low for hydrocarbons. Ultramar perforated it and the well flowed at two million cubic feet of gas a day. They stumbled into a new gas pool while looking for a place to dispose of their saltwater.

Gitano Field is one of a series of small structures sitting on a huge salt ridge running through Jones and Smith Counties, which every geologist in the region knew about. Cook postulated that if the Eutaw produced at a half ohm at Gitano, then it should also produce on other structures where it was thought to be wet. Cook showed Schneeflock a likely candidate northwest of Gitano with two dry holes on it with and a resistivity slightly less than 1.0 ohm in the Eutaw. Cook guessed that operators of those two dry holes had overlooked the potential of Eutaw gas. Schneeflock and Chaney agreed, knowing that if the Gitano experience was common for the region instead of just one spot, the structure Cook picked should be a monster gas field.

Paramount took Cook's idea and ran with it. Chaney and company attorney Billy White assembled a 3,500 acre lease block, later expanded to 6,000, in southwest Smith County about halfway between Jackson and Hattiesburg. They learned later that they beat another company to the ground by just one week. They prepared a deal package, called it the Southeast Magee Prospect, and calculated a whopping 30 Bcf potential.

It was a scary, gutsy move. "You can't think of a harder deal to sell," Chaney said, "than one where you're going to twin a dry hole, because the people in the corporate bureaucracies think that, not only could I drill another dry hole here, but I could look really stupid."

Duke Rudman was no bureaucracy. His exploration manager, Jim Trimble, saw the potential and took a quarter of it. Others followed. Cobra Oil and Gas, Inc., was the operator. The drilling in the soft rocks went quickly, and on December 18, 1988, Schneeflock, Chaney, and their partners got a Christmas present. Cobra brought in the No. 1 Purser at almost three million cubic feet of gas per day from 70 feet of net pay in a section of the Eutaw called the Stanley Sand. Schneeflock and Chaney convinced the other partners and the Mississippi Oil and Gas Board to name the field in honor of the man who stuck with them through their stormy, dry-hole studded start-up period—Rudman's Jim Trimble.

Trimble Field grew to over 22 wells with no dry holes and has produced nearly 50 Bcf to date, 20 Bcf more than the sales brochure estimated. At its peak the field produced over 50 million cubic feet per day. "The reservoir turned out to be better than anybody could imagine," Chaney said. When they sold their interest, engineers had raised ultimate recoverable reserves to 100 Bcf. Chaney and Schneeflock had found their monster.

Paramount showed the deal over 30 times, but after the discovery, Schneeflock said, "I couldn't find anyone who would admit that they had seen it!" Phil Cook and Stan Theiling get the credit for the discovery with strong assistance from Schneeflock and Chaney. Arguably, the EPA deserves some credit too.

The year 1988 was eventful for Mississippi's natural gas industry, not only for the Trimble discovery, but also for a more sobering reason. Another profound decline began. Gas production across the state reached 230 Bcf, twenty less than its previous peak in 1956. Annual decline continued for 11 more years.

Trimble Field was indeed a company-maker for Paramount, creating the cash reserves on which to build a large exploration program and strengthen their credibility. "We went from dry-hole kings to great oil and gas finders," Chaney said. "I think we just out-worked and out-hustled everybody else."

The McParamount Burger

As the nineties arrived, the most active drilling area in Mississippi was the Eutaw gas play Paramount ignited with Trimble. More than 60 wells in the trend were drilled that year. As in the Eutaw play, almost all the activity in the state was done by independents, but at least one major company was doing pioneering work.

Amoco opened the decade with a Mississippi milestone. They completed the state's first horizontally drilled well. In a horizontally drilled hole, the well bore turns up to 90 degrees to travel through a reservoir parallel with the rock strata. Under the right conditions, the method can let one well drain a much larger area. In Franklin County, Amoco's USA-McKenna penetrated 300 horizontal feet of Wilcox sand in the Clear Springs Field and tested over 300 BOPD.

Several Alabama Smackover strikes were logged in 1990 in Conecuh, Covington, Escambia, and Monroe counties, none significant, and the Smackover had to move over for the red hot Haynesville Play Paramount started at Frisco City. The Haynesville explorers enjoyed some success, particularly in Covington County, Alabama, where they opened a second front in the play.

Sonat and Amoco lost interest in the Updip Smackover and made a deal with Paramount to use their seismic data in the area. From that data Paramount's Amigos affiliate—John Bush, John Marble, and Billy White, with consultant Bob Gaston—found a structure and put together a Smackover prospect called Boogy Hollow Creek in the southwest corner of Covington County a few miles north of the Florida line.

"We drilled it and, lo and behold, the Smackover was tight, and the Haynesville sand was loaded with oil," Chaney said. "And this is 50 miles east of the other one [the Haynesville discovery at Frisco City]. So again we get lucky."

The Jeffers 17-9 came in at nearly 500 BOPD and over 25 million cubic feet per day from the Haynesville at 13,000 feet. The well drew national media attention, and the landowner at the discovery location, Mr. Jeffers, told reporters the discovery "hasn't changed our lives much, but our bird dog hasn't been the same since."[6]

Boogy Hollow was the farthest east production yet found in the Mississippi Interior Salt Basin. The Oil and Gas Board again departed from Paramount's suggestion and named the field West Falco. It fell off rapidly and was never a significant producer, but it sparked exploration in southwest Covington County that led to several more discoveries.

Paramount grew rapidly as Schneeflock and Chaney evolved revolutionary methods of generating, packaging, and selling prospects. Unlike other companies that simply prettied-up certain maps and data and threw them at potential buyers, Chaney and Schneeflock decided to "treat prospect packaging as a very important part of our company—on par with geology, geophysics, and land. And we would take the professionalism of the process to a whole new level. And that would allow us to raise the capital we needed."[7]

The pair understood that deal buyers wanted documentation above all. A pretty airbrushed map was no better that the data that underpinned it. They knew that if the potential buyer had to do his own research to verify the data, he would likely put the package into a slush pile, assign it to an underling, or reject it outright. "An undocumented, airbrushed prospect is still a sorry prospect," observed the pragmatic Schneeflock. "There were no charlatans left in the deal screening process. 'Pretty' wouldn't sell anymore—you needed to doc-u-ment."

Chaney, the visionary, was always scanning the horizon. "We also realized something that very few people reflected on. If you look at things conceptually, an exploration company is really a manufacturing company. We thought we could take a Henry Ford approach to this. I think anybody who was ever over here [in our office] when we had several prospects in the packaging stage would have to say that it looked like a car manufacturing plant."

The pair even studied McDonalds' methods. McDonalds used a manual to standardize mass hamburger production. Schneeflock and Chaney decided they needed a manual too and put one together. All Paramount's employees who worked on prospect package preparation used it. The manual addressed quality, attention to detail, and clarity. They also added a Hollywood element. Chaney said, "When you're selling a prospect you're somewhat in the entertainment business. These people are looking at prospects all day and they get bored. You've got to make it interesting."

Chaney screened a lot of deals while with Kilroy. He knew how agonizing it was to absorb all the information about a deal at a sitting, then try to remember what the presenter said after he left. "As a buyer, you're looking at this prospect for the first time. It's very hard to keep up as you're going from the map to the seismic and back." The Paramount manual required, for example, that every fault have a single distinctive color in every exhibit in the package. The blue fault on the map was the blue fault on the seismic; it was the blue fault on the cross section; and on the logs.

Schneeflock and Chaney were painfully aware that they made many of their presentations to people who had no authority to commit to the deal but had to present it to their bosses themselves. The Paramount standard helped simplify the presentation so those people could be effective.

"Bob and I realized that there are two major factors in human nature that you've got to deal with when selling a prospect. Number one is the buyer's desire to not do a lot of work. We were willing to do all the work for them. You have to know the strengths and weaknesses of your prospect better than anybody else, and if you're showing a prospect and somebody surprises you with a question, you ought to be thoroughly embarrassed. There shouldn't be anything somebody can think of at the table that you haven't already gone through." Chaney was also a master at the age old technique of baiting audiences by dropping subtle hints that if they didn't move quickly, they would miss out. He let them know he intended to show the deal 20-25 times a week until it sold.

With their presentation methods firmly established and on par in importance with science and engineering, Schneeflock and Chaney took a hard look at their organization and their *modus operandi* and again made radical changes. They had imitated Henry Ford and McDonalds. Now they borrowed from the airlines and the real estate business.

Having seen enough of the classic pyramid management style in companies with upward of five levels of management, they decided to experiment with a new organizational scheme—the hub and spoke system. Taking the hugely successful Trammel Crow real estate firm as a model, they went out and found the brightest young explorers in the game and set up new subsidiary companies around them. Paramount—the hub—would provide essential services. They grew dramatically with the system and at the peak had 11 different spokes going out to affiliated companies. The system catered to the talents and abilities of high achievers who wanted to remain quasi-independent.

Chaney and Schneeflock knew that a few explorers find most of the reserves. "They're superstars. And we found that it is difficult to lure them away [from their employers] with just a normal compensation package." They knew that the high achievers wanted a chance to build on their own success but at the same time were reluctant to leave their employers and take the leap to independence in such a depressed oil business. So instead of hiring them, Paramount helped them "meet their dreams in a different way." The network of affiliates resulted.

Being a Paramount affiliate was indeed like owning a McDonalds franchise. Paramount provided accounting, finance, administrative assistance, engineering evaluation, prospect packaging, and helped the affiliate market their prospects. They hired a panel of top-notch specialists—processing geophysicists, petrophysicists, and workstation experts, their "advanced technology team," and made them available to the affiliates, most of whom could not afford such resources on their own. The team was a key to Paramount's success.

The arrangement attracted some of the best talent in the business. "At Paramount's peak, I think we had the most talented organization in the business," Chaney said. "We dominated. We had a structure that made us incredibly aggressive."

Paramount's 1990 budget was $20 million. Turning prospects in about six months, they turned the money over twice a year, giving them a $40 million budget for leasing, seismic, and overhead. Additionally, they raised many millions more for drilling. The company had almost 100 employees with 40 explorationists at its peak. Chaney called it a "monster machine" when it closed sales on 62 prospects between 1990 and 1991, raising over $100 million in a capital starved industry. "It was Patton's Third Army. We did everything we set out to accomplish."

Paramount's venture partners were excited about marching with them. Some participated in almost every deal. The legendary Duke Rudman's company examined nearly 1,000 deals in 1989 and trashed most of them—but they participated in almost every one Paramount presented. "Yes, I think we're going to make money in Alabama," Rudman told *Business Alabama Monthly*. "I became one of their [Schneeflock and Chaney's] insiders and drilling partners. . . . They are as good oil finders as exist in Alabama, Mississippi, and Florida."[8] The magazine added that the new breed of oilfinders in south Alabama "have more in common with Silicon Valley than the shoot-from-the-hip cowboys."

"We were the leading wildcatter in the U.S.," Chaney said. "We drilled almost 50 wildcats [in 1991], averaging 12-13,000 feet depth. It was everything we dreamed it would be."

Rocket Fuel

In 1990 the Blackstone affiliate composed of John Cox, Mike Harmount, Alan Rihner, and Mark Stephenson presented Paramount with another Haynesville prospect, a product of a Bob Gaston interpretation of a costly set of 2-D seismic bought from Texaco. Gaston mapped a basement bump five miles north of Frisco City, but the concept lost its luster after the company sold and drilled a dry hole nearby on a similar structure. Nevertheless Schneeflock and Chaney thought it deserved testing even if they did not think it was a high-quality prospect. They assembled the package, named it the Lufkin Prospect, and took it to the street. Like their Trimble deal in Mississippi, it was a hard sell.

But sell it they did and in early 1991 Torch Operating Company spudded the Sigler 25-6 and found Haynesville sand with porosity as high as 28% and an astounding permeability of nearly two darcies. Geologist John Cox, who was sitting the well, reported good shows, but he worried because there was no fluorescence. Remembering the lack of fluorescence at Frisco City five years earlier, Schneeflock consulted with the partners and ordered pipe.

The well came in at over 800 BOPD. The confirmation tested over 2,000 BOPD. The next four wells tested over 3,000 BOPD each. The Oil and Gas Board christened it the North Frisco City Field. Early reserve estimates were put at 18 million barrels. It was the largest oilfield discovered in the southeastern U.S. since the Bay Springs Smackover field in Mississippi in 1980. Schneeflock and Chaney found their second monster.

The influx of men and equipment and the sight of crude oil tanker trucks roaring through town astonished the local citizens. Rumors about who would become millionaires flew. Farmer Harold Lancaster, afraid the oil might not hold out, told *The Atlanta Journal*, "I'm going to wait a while before I go playing J.R." His neighbor, Mr. Sigler, on whose land the discovery was made, told the reporter he might quit agriculture, get a big screen TV, and just watch Vanna White spin the Wheel of Fortune." Another citizen said, "It's the biggest strike since Jed Clampett found a-bubblin' crude." The oil fervor flooding the town even made it to Peter Jennings' *World News Tonight.*[9]

The North Frisco City crude wasn't even close to what Jed Clampett found—not the common, slimy, black, gooey stuff. It was an *exotic crude,* according to Houston engineer Larry Tharp.[10] "It's much different than any Smackover crude in the Southeast. It's the only thing like it I've seen in the Gulf Coast." North Frisco City's oil was highly volatile at 59 degrees API gravity and loaded with gas. *Oil and Gas Investor*'s Louise Durham wrote, "Put this stuff in your automobile gas tank and you'd have something akin to rocket fuel."[11]

Reservoir engineers scratched their heads and geologists shrugged over the riddle of why the North Frisco City crude was so different from Smackover crude. Eventually they postulated that Smackover reservoirs lost some of their volatiles through leakage, leaving the oil thicker, while the Haynesville traps in the Monroeville area confined the lighter petroleum elements in the reservoir. Expensive state-of-the-art processing plants were built to stabilize Frisco City's "rocket fuel" and strip the liquids out of the gas.

As the plants went up, more wells went down, and Bob Gaston, the geophysicist who made the original prospect map, turned to a new tool to get a better picture of the beneath world—three-dimensional seismic, or 3-D. Three-D seismic was superior to conventional data. It had higher resolution and could be integrated with 2-D to produce three-dimensional images on a computer screen of selected blocks of the subsurface. Sophisticated software allowed geologists to *slice* an area mapped with 3-D by drawing a line across it with the computer mouse. They could then examine a profile view of the subsurface structure with a great deal of accuracy from any angle they wished.

Geologists and reservoir engineers found that 3-D worked especially well in developing a field found by conventional 2-D seismic, such as North Frisco City. "Three-D helps you locate the optimum position for the wells where structures have a small areal extent," Gaston explained. "Conventional seismic might miss part of the anomaly, but the dense grid with 3-D will cover the anomaly and minimize the risk in well location."[12] At the same time the Frisco City development work was going on, Mobil, Exxon and other major companies were enjoying tremendous success using 3-D to find the choicest spots to drill the deep Norphlet dunes in Mobile Bay.

North Frisco Field grew to nine wells, which have produced more than 20 million barrels of oil equivalent, outperforming the original reserve estimate of 14 million barrels and 17 Bcf. At its peak, it produced more oil monthly than any other field in the state. North Frisco City was one of Alabama's greatest discoveries, coming when the state's most exciting strikes were all but history.

7 Hectic Years

Many people contributed to the North Frisco City strike, but Bob Gaston's map put it over the top and made it a viable prospect. "A big discovery has many fathers," Bob Schneeflock observed. "It wasn't the best looking prospect on Gaston's map. It was a hard sell. But that's the point... you have to drill a lot of wildcats to find that really good field. Your 'A' prospects hit to some extent, but it's that one 'B-' or 'C+' prospect that comes out of nowhere that makes you all of your money."

More Haynesville fields spun off of North Frisco City. Paramount and its affiliates and investors found oil at Southeast Frisco City, West Huxford, and North Excel, while Pruet Oil Company found Haynesville oil at Meragel, and Harry Spooner scored at Hickory Branch in Escambia County.

In late 1990 Paramount received the prestigious "Wildcatter of the Year" Award from the Mid-Continent Oil & Gas Association, but midway through 1991 the Paramount machine began to lose steam. "We were at the top of the mountain," Chaney said. They were so busy selling their biggest deal ever—a 30-prospect drilling program and a 50,000-acre Austin Chalk play in Texas—they hardly noticed that gas and oil prices had started to collapse again.

Leveraged with about $30 million of debt, Schneeflock and Chaney watched two thirds of the industry's prospect buying funds dry up almost overnight. "We went into an environment the likes of which neither of us had ever seen, even in the downturns of 82 and 86." By 1992 the Paramount machine was struggling. "All of a sudden we realized we had a catastrophe on our hands. We had the biggest prospect inventory in the business and a crushing debt load." To make matters worse, the deals they sold just prior to the turndown were dry holes or marginal producers. "In just a few weeks we had gone from the greatest times of our lives to the worst. The Viet Cong were overrunning our perimeters." Paramount began the dreaded corporate retreat—downsizing.

The partners took a look at the state of the petroleum industry and determined that the oil business was undergoing permanent change. They realized the market place for prospects would probably never recover its previous level, the plays would be smaller, and pricey 3-D seismic would rule the prospect generation process. The Paramount model changed again.

Chaney thought the best course was to merge with a strong publicly traded company that needed an exploration arm. Just such a company was eyeing them, Houston's Nuevo Energy, which had bought in to several of Paramount's successful deals. The merger closed in March 1992, just in time to keep Paramount out of bankruptcy.

Following the merger, Nuevo began selling Schneeflock and Chaney generated drilling deals and finding new reserves. "They [Nuevo] let us run it just as we had run Paramount," Chaney said. In a little over a year Nuevo's stock tripled. Paramount paid off its debt, and investors realized a 30% rate of return.

In 1997 Schneeflock left Nuevo and was quickly offered the presidency of a large exploration company. The offer was tempting, but taking it would distance him even more from what he liked doing best—geology—and from Jackson's laid-back atmosphere and strand him in Houston's hectic clamor. "I went to see this old friend about what I ought to do, and he gave me some great advice. He said, 'Forget about what you ought to do, and go do what you want to do.' And it hit me like a bolt of lightning. I knew what I was going to do. I was going to start Paramount up again." The old friend was Robert Chaney.

Change was in the works for Chaney also. He got restless working with Nuevo and embarked on yet another crusade. "My first thought was to start another E&P [exploration and production] business, but I decided against it as I realized the Paramount experience could probably never be topped. That period had now passed." He founded Robert Chaney & Company and built it into a leading high-tech energy industry venture capital firm.

Following one of Duke Rudman's 15 *Steps to the Ladder of Success,* Bob Schneeflock decided to low-profile it, now that he had made it. He moved his equipment and his technical files into a warehouse in a Jackson suburb. He set up shop in a corner of the warehouse, hired a small staff, put on jeans, and brought his dog to work with him. Once more he was doing what he loved best—generating drilling prospects.

Although he reverted to his preferred relaxed style of living and working, Schneeflock didn't go back to the old ways of slipping logs and drawing contour maps. The guy who loved dinosaurs as a kid was determined not to become one himself. He knew he could cover much more ground with computers. He kept a critical eye on technological advances in exploration methods and usually knew what was coming down the pike before the pike knew it. He acquired the latest workstations and software and eventually steered his reconnaissance methods, prospect generation, and even marketing to a paperless mode. Building on the momentum of Paramount's earlier initiatives, Schneeflock marketed his deals via the Internet. He could call prospective buyers and give them a password to get into the prospect website where they could see a Power Point presentation. Schneeflock worked quietly through the late 90s and into the new century, generating deals across the South and selling them to old backers like Duke Rudman, as well as new ones who came and went.

The Paramount experience was phenomenal, the rival of anything the oil industry in the South had ever known. "The amazing thing," Chaney observed, "is that it all happened in seven and a half hectic years."

For the Deep South's oil community, the next 7 years were more lethargic than hectic, as oil and gas prices took an unpredictable rollercoaster ride that discouraged high risk investment in exploration. But discovery and excitement were still ahead for a few who persevered.

Chapter 22

Looking for Gas in All the Tight Places

"I want you to understand something; *we* started this."[1] The *we* were geologist Stew Welch and his landman partner, Fleming Browning, both keen opportunists. They went after gas wherever they could find it, and they were confident they had a few billion cubic feet cornered in a most unlikely place: the Selma Chalk in the old heavily drilled East Heidelberg Field, 12 miles northeast of Laurel in Jasper County, Mississippi.

Chalk, a carbonate, is a variety of limestone with a relatively high porosity that lets it hold large volumes of fluids and gas. Chalk also has poor permeability. Whatever is in its pores stays there. Over the years the Selma yielded only spotty production in a few places where it was naturally fractured. Usually explorers punched through it on their way to deeper objectives without paying much attention.

Browning and Welch achieved legend status with their work in the Black Warrior Basin, where they found very significant gas fields. Developing those fields, they helped pioneer hard rock fraccing techniques that sometimes tripled and quadrupled a reservoir's production rate. If anyone knew how to get gas out of a tight rock, it was them.

In 1989 Browning and Welch applied what they learned in the Black Warrior to their operations Salt Basin to Basin. They looked at some logs in East Hiedleberg, discovered in 1944, and saw the permeability was predictably low but in some logs they saw the classic *gas-effect*. They decided to try out a Warrior Basin-style frac job on the chalk. Unable to get any of the choice acreage held by deeper production, they edged in as close as they could to the old field and drilled a 4,000-foot test. The frac worked, coming in at a million cubic feet per day. Other wells followed. They moved on and did the same thing at Baxterville, another old Cretaceous field discovered during WW II. Browning and Welch later sold their chalk holdings to Denbury, but the play they started picked up steam.

In the early 1990s Paramount Petroleum looked for new ways to approach exploration. They needed ideas. Geologist John Cox of Paramount's Blackstone affiliate fell to the task. "We were challenged by Schneeflock and Chaney to look into new technologies."[2] The Selma Chalk was still virtually untapped. Cox and his team asked for advice from geologist Lindsey Stewart, who worked with Browning and Welch in their chalk initiatives. Stewart steered them to a widespread porosity zone near the top of the chalk, but they couldn't find open acreage on existing structures, except at one place, an old field discovered in WW II—Gwinville Field in northern Jefferson Davis County.[3]

Assembling the land package was difficult and selling the deal was even tougher, because oil and gas wellhead prices had collapsed again, and Paramount feared they might have to eat the deal. Title 29 came to the rescue. The company petitioned the government to classify the chalk as an unconventional energy source, just like the coalbed methane project in Alabama. Tax credits would help offset the huge expenses associated with fraccing.

Armed with that incentive, Paramount took the deal to the streets and found a buyer—Enron Oil and Gas (EOG) of Tyler, Texas (not the Enron that went bankrupt due to securities fraud). EOG forced a tough trade but Paramount was happy to sell.

EOG began drilling and fraccing the chalk in 1992, and by the end of the year Gwinville Field's annual gas production was up by 30%. The field vaulted in rank from tenth in Mississippi gas production to fifth. EOG's aggressive development program included drilling gas wells on 40-acre units and Gwinville's production rose another 30% by 1996. In 2000 it was the largest methane gas producer in Mississippi with an annual cumulative that year of almost 10 Bcf. The only field to exceed it in volume was South Pisgah in Rankin County, which made 18 Bcf, but that was noncombustible carbon dioxide.

Gwinville's success was one of a series of innovative efforts to find new methods to get at oil and gas previously thought economically unrecoverable. Alabama's coal bed methane initiative started the trend, and Browning and Welch's chalk play followed. Other thinkers were moving in on Mississippi to attack unrecovered reserves in a still different way. Their way began about 65 million years ago.

Pop, Fizz, and a Lot More Oil

The Jackson Dome formed when present-day Mississippi lay under water. The massive volcanic intrusion pushed upward through the sedimentary rocks and may have reached the surface. As the eons went by, the intrusive became dormant, and thousands of feet of sediment were deposited around and over the volcano. Today its top lies only 2,300 feet beneath Jackson. The heat of the intrusive influenced the subsurface geology and the occurrence of hydrocarbons in central Mississippi, and most geologists believe it caused chemical changes in the deep Jurassic rocks surrounding it and led to the formation of massive amounts of carbon dioxide (CO_2).

Chevron first found the CO_2 in large amounts. In 1967 it tested CO_2 at the Goshen Springs Field in Rankin County in the Norphlet. Not sure what to do with it, they left it there. In 1978 Shell hit CO_2 at the South Pisgah Field, also in Rankin County, that time in the Smackover at about 16,000 feet. A year later Shell found more of the stuff at two other sites in Rankin. In 1974 Shell got an idea about what they could do with their massive CO_2 reserves.

They banded with other companies to spread the enormous expense and laid a 183-mile pipeline to the Little Creek Field on the Lincoln-Pike County line. Shell discovered Little Creek in 1958 and unitized and waterflooded it in 1962. They thought that injecting CO_2 could squeeze more oil out of the field. The technique was not new but it was unusual; naturally occurring CO_2 was rare and occurred in only a few parts of the country beside Mississippi. Shell's method was called tertiary recovery.

The CO_2 acts as a solvent for the oil, which is removed from the formation and recovered along with the CO_2. Between 40% and 50% of the oil in a typical field can be extracted by primary and secondary recovery. More oil (approximately 17% at Little Creek) can be recovered by injecting CO_2 into certain wells and recovering the oil and the CO_2 from other nearby wells.

Shell's gas flood project was phased in gradually until it reached field-wide proportions in 1985, but in the mid 1990s, Shell lost interest in the project and sold Little Creek. A ready buyer waited.

Denbury Resources of Plano, Texas, operated a few wells in Little Creek and other properties in the Mississippi Interior Salt Basin. They were looking for an opportunity to expand in the region, and the Shell deal was their ticket. Denbury believed many of Mississippi's producing formations were excellent candidates for CO_2 injection and saw the acquisition as a chance to dominate a tertiary recovery niche. In 1999 they bought Shell's interest in Little Creek for $13.25 million, which boosted their working interest in the field to 99% (88% net revenue). They added more producing wells immediately and increased the number of injection wells, nearly tripling the field's production from 1,300 barrels per day to over 3,000.[4]

Denbury's success at Little Creek emboldened them. They wanted complete control of CO_2 sources in Mississippi. In February 2001, they acquired approximately 800 Bcf of proven producing CO_2 reserves in Rankin County for $42 million, a purchase that gave them control of almost all the discovered CO_2 supply in Mississippi, as well as ownership and control of the 183-mile CO_2 pipeline. The acquisition assured Denbury that CO_2 would be available at a reasonable, predictable cost.

The company added more reserves by drilling additional CO_2 wells and acquired more CO_2 prospective leases. In December 2001, they estimated their CO_2 reserves at about 1.9 trillion cubic feet. They believe there may be up to 12 Tcf of CO_2 reserves across Rankin County.

Denbury acquired several more mature fields after Little Creek: West Mallalieu, McComb, Brookhaven, Olive, and others, all producers at one time and all good candidates for CO_2 injection. Ultimately, the company expected to recover an additional nine million barrels from Little Creek and eight million from West Mallalieu. They believe CO_2 injection may recover up to 100 million barrels from southwest Mississippi's old Lower Cretaceous fields. Paramount's Bob Schneeflock observed that Denbury tapped into the equivalent of a giant oil field without drilling a single wildcat well.

Denbury also owns producing properties in southeast Mississippi, notably the giant East Hiedleberg Field, acquired in 1997. They plan to introduce CO_2 injection there and in other southeast Mississippi fields. Denbury is the largest oil producer in Mississippi.

On a smaller scale, another innovative Mississippi operator worked at squeezing more money out of old wells for many years. During the 1990s his business boomed.

I buy stuff.

John McGowan graduated from LSU in 1956 with a geology degree and wanted to get in the oil business—but no one was hiring. He tried his hand at hard rock mining in Mexico, but corrupt politicians siphoned his profits. He came back to the States and worked as a roughneck and a Core Lab technician. When that ran out, he considered giving it up and taking a job as a telemarketer, but his father told him to go out and hustle some leases around Little Creek and Brookhaven. He got pretty good at that but longed to get back into geology. Then a friend named Clyde Hutchinson persuaded him to buy an old well in Pickens Field making 700 barrels of water and 14 barrels of oil a day. Hutchinson told McGowan he could clear $400 a month. He could get the well for $5,000.

McGowan secured a loan from a reluctant banker, hired a pumper, and started operations. Three days later the pumper called and said they had a problem; a sucker rod had parted. McGowan said, "What's that?" He went back to the bank for more money to buy rods. "This was my entrance into the stripper oil business," McGowan said. "From that point, I started buying oil wells, and I learned how dear sucker rods were."[5]

He got experience by trial and error. He bought more old wells that mostly made a lot of saltwater. He bought both individual wells and large multi-well properties. "These were the ones no one else wanted. To this day, I buy stuff. I am the last person that will look at something, and when I get it and work on it [the property goes] back on production."

By 1998 McGowan's company had grown into a large, sophisticated organization with teams of engineers and field experts specializing in getting the most fluid possible out of wells. That, he says, is his modus operandi; he concentrates on total fluid movement and not necessarily increased oil production, although that's what often happens after he acquires and reworks a property.

McGowan grew the company to almost 300 wells producing about 6,000 barrels per day. Some make 2,500 barrels of saltwater per day and only a few dozen barrels of oil. McGowan's financial agility at balancing costs with expenses keeps his bustling company profitable even in the downturns—especially in the downturns. That's when other operators panic and sell the old fields at bargains. He gets them at his price or not at all. Often he has watched higher bidders take properties he was interested in, only to fail and offer them for sale again. Then he gets in on his terms and makes money. When oil was down to $10 a barrel near the end of the 1990s, he was making money. McGowan is yet another oilman who carved out his niche through hard work, hard learning, and smart money management.

Not everyone embraced the unconventional methods and mature field operations EOG, Denbury, McGowan, and others used in the nineties. Successful though those operators were, others preferred traditional exploration methods. In the early 1990s, some of them resurrected an old play that arose and died several times after 1960—the salt dome play.

Using successful strategies developed in Texas, wildcatters in the 1940s drilled on top of Mississippi's numerous salt domes, hoping to find petroleum in the domes' cap rocks. The strategy failed because the movement of Mississippi's domes occurred too late in geologic time to catch oil migrating through the porous rocks above them. In the 1980s, interest in Mississippi's domes surged anew as wildcatters used newly developed directional drilling technology to angle their holes underneath the domes' overhang areas and into deep reservoirs trapped against the side of the domes. Those efforts were more successful. Then in the 1990s, came the breakthrough that let geologists see salt dome structures in unprecedented detail—3-D seismic.

The new 3-D methods showed the complicated fault patterns around salt domes which older 2-D seismic could not discern with sufficient accuracy. With the new tool, salt dome explorers could drill directionally underneath the salt overhang and penetrate multiple reservoirs alongside the dome's vertical shaft (Figure 17).

One of the most active companies using the new approach to salt dome exploration was a Michigan company, Miller Exploration, that opened a district office in Jackson and hired Charles Morrison as exploration manager. Morrison's many years of experience as a Jackson geophysical consultant equipped him to lead the company's salt dome work. "We were going right up next to the domes," Morrison said. In earlier years operators were cautious about getting too close to the salt shaft, because inadvertent penetration into the shaft played havoc with drilling fluids and downhole tools. Many holes were lost. "This data [3-D], in conjunction with the reprocessing of older 2-D seismic, has significantly increased the success rate on the Mississippi domes."[6] Morrison said the reasons that drew Miller to Mississippi were: the possibil-

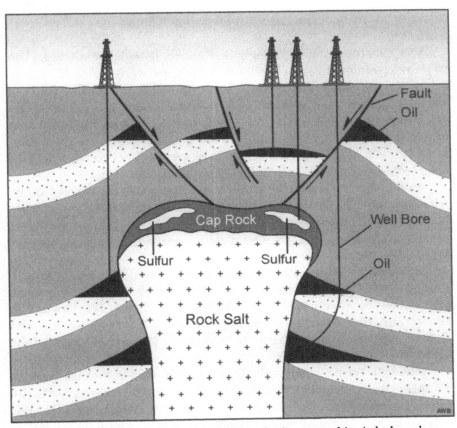

Figure 17. Salt dome diagram (depicts the faulting of sediment resulting in hydrocarbon traps; sulfur and gypsum are found in the cap rock).

ity of multiple pay zones associated with the salt domes; high sustained rates of production; and a 42% success rate with improved seismic technology.

With the new technology, discoveries came in steadily. Amerada-Hess scored at Covington County's Dry Creek Dome in 1993, testing nine million cubic feet and 165 barrels a day from the Lower Cretaceous at 10,000 feet. The field has yielded over 23 Bcf. The company hit again in 1995 at Midway Dome in Lamar County. That field has produced 36 Bcf from the Hosston. Later that year they hit another Hosston field at Prentiss Dome in Jefferson Davis County. That same year Torch Energy brought in a field at Brownsville Dome in Hinds County. In 1996 Fina hit at King Bee Dome in Perry County, and Stroud scored across the state in Warren County at King Dome. In 1997 Texas Petroleum found a large field at Oakvale Dome in Jefferson Davis County, which has made 18 Bcf from the Hosston. Other dome discoveries came at Moselle in Jones County and Maynor Creek in Wayne. Despite the many successes, Morrison maintained that Mississippi's domes were still relatively unexplored.

Still other conventional geologists in the 1990s thought the salt ridge plays were under-explored. A number of operators began using 3-D technology in an area in southern Wayne County, Mississippi, that had an abundance of salt features as defined by older seismic, a cluster of intermediate salt ridges oriented north to south. Only a few small Lower Cretaceous Fields had been found on them. The 3-D let explorers like Karl Kauffman, a former Paramount affiliate who joined Bean Resources, see subtleties on the ridges the older technology missed, such as the critical flank reflections.

Among the first results of the renewed emphasis on the Wayne County salt ridges was a Smackover strike in 1990 in the Chapparal Field, discovered in 1952. Weeks Exploration tested nearly 800 BOPD and 3.5 million cubic feet per day below 13,500 feet. The several additional wells have produced over four million barrels.

Jack Phillips logged a strike in the Cotton Valley at the Crawford Creek Field, discovered by Damson in 1976. In 1993 and again in 1998, a strike came in at North Clara in the Smackover. The later well, operated by Twister Gas Services, has made over a million barrels and five Bcf. Petro Corp. found Cotton Valley oil at Maynor Creek in 1995, in the Hosston in 1996, and the Cotton Valley again a year later.

While the Wayne County salt ridge play went on, Florida's Jay Field hit another grand milestone in 1996. It passed the 400 million barrel mark. The 1970 Smackover discovery that put Florida solidly in the producers club was now a quadruple giant. Would it make a half billion—a quintuple giant? At the current production rate—about 3 million barrels per year, assuming that holds—that monumental event is now at least twenty-five years away.

Warrior-explorers like Karl Kauffman wasted no time dreaming about somebody else's triumphs. They forged ahead to find more oil. In 2001 Kauffman and Bean Resources discovered Pine Grove Field in Jones County using 3-D technology on a salt ridge feature, finding Hosston production at 16,000 feet. The three wells have produced over almost 400,000 barrels of oil and a billion cubic of gas. Bean's next discovery was literally a barn burner.

"Balls of Fire"

In April 2001 the Bean Group drilled the flank of a salt ridge in Wayne County. Spooner Petroleum handled operations for the Bean Resources No. 1 Beard 29-7. "The rock looked a little tight," Karl Kauffman said, "but we thought we had a good discovery."[7]

It was just another routine day for Spooner's engineer, Ken Magee, who split his time between the Jackson office and trips to the field to monitor operations. Spooner's crew set an intermediate string of pipe to 17,000 feet in the Haynesville and drilled the well on to the Smackover at 18,500 feet. After taking care of duties at another location, Magee drove by the Beard well to check on the work before heading back to Jackson. He went into the company trailer and found no one there. He went up to the drill floor and saw men scurrying around. Something was wrong. He looked out at the shale shaker and saw mud spewing out at an abnormally high rate. He ordered the hole shut in and told the pusher, "This is not good!"[8]

When Magee went into the trailer to phone the company about the trouble, he heard an ominous noise. He looked back at the rig and saw joints of casing spewing up into the derrick. Roughnecks were fleeing the rig. The tool pusher closed the blind rams, which stopped the pipe ejection, then fled. Three joints of liner were jammed in the rams, sticking 90 feet into the air.

The drilling company ordered its personnel to stay away. The engineers were now the only people on the site. They called their insurance company and wild-well fighters, Boots & Coots, Inc. They also summoned Halliburton and called a mud engineer to prepare heavy mud to kill the well. Waiting for help, they monitored the manifold pressure, which stabilized at 2600 psi. Later that night Magee went out to check the pressure again and saw mud spewing up through the liner. They decided there were two things they could do: open the rams and let the liner fall back in the hole if the pressure allowed; or let the well blow it completely out so they could close the rams and get a clean shut-in. "That was the plan," Magee said.

Pat Rawson, a drilling foreman from an adjacent rig, came over to help. Everybody else was standing off at a distance down the lease road. When Rawson opened the rams for a short time, the pipe began to settle down into the hole, then stopped. Magee breathed a sigh of relief. Rawson opened them again and the pipe eased up and stopped. He shut it in again, then opened the rams a third time, and nothing happened. He tried it again. The pipe slammed upward and blew out of the hole. Magee watched the liner joints fly. "That liner was hitting that derrick, and it wasn't making sparks—I mean it was making big balls of fire." Finally it stopped.

Magee looked around. He couldn't see Rawson anywhere. He didn't know Rawson had fled. The personnel standing off up the road yelled for Magee to get away.

Although the danger of falling pipe was passed, the well was blowing mud and gas with an enormous roar. "Mud and stuff was going everywhere. It was pretty exciting!" The well had to be shut in and Magee was the only soul left to do it. He swallowed hard and went cautiously to the accumulator near the rig and started closing the valves. When he closed the blind rams, the flow died down. An eerie silence settled on the rig. "It was just a big fog up there; you could hardly see anything. I thought, 'We may have this thing under control.' But then it started again."

He backed away and watched the roaring gas geyser, recalling that some Smackover wells nearby had nearly 17% H_2S. Magee knew sour gas was much safer if it was burning. He decided to light the well and ordered the crew to fire flares into the plume. The gas ignited, and within 15 minutes the huge rig melted and collapsed.

Boots & Coots, Inc., and Halliburton diverted the well within ten days and snubbed in and killed it in twenty-one. When they could finally get a close look at the shattered wellhead, they found that a centralizer jammed the blind rams preventing them from closing completely.

After the clean-up Spooner brought in a fresh rig and drilled a sidetrack hole to the Smackover. The new discovery became the Ocean Forest Field, a name Ken Magee won't likely forget. The rig crew, who watched from a distance, won't likely forget Magee.

Karl Kauffman continued mapping the salt ridges looking for another barn burner. He noted that 3-D seismic cost was about $45,000 per square mile. A typical 3-D survey conducted over a 2-D lead could cost over $2 million. He and the other believers in the Mississippi Interior Salt Basin have no doubt that the remaining potential is tremendous. "We have thousands of square miles of Salt Basin without any 3-D. I have friends who work South Louisiana and South Texas. When I tell them that I can go out right now and justify over 200 square miles of 3-D shooting off of 2-D controlled prospects or leads in south Mississippi, they look at me and say, 'We don't have that. South Louisiana and South Texas have all been shot.'"[9]

Kauffman said there is a "serious prospect crunch" on the horizon, because companies are unwilling to put up the cost of 3-D. "They don't want to shoot the 3-D, but they want you to come to them with it all done." He joked sarcastically that at the next big prospect show he wants to put up a sign: *South Prudhoe Bay Look-Alike, Updip from Good Shows with 3-D for FREE!*

"You see a big change in our industry in that the people that work at these bigger oil companies are the guys who have come up through acquisitions. . . . They don't know how to prospect. And they don't know how to evaluate a prospect when it's brought to them." Kauffman hoped buyers would realize they must share some condemnation risk early in the generation process by underwriting 3-D.

Exploration's future in Mississippi and Alabama may not be tied solely to 3-D delineation of structures. One who believes it can be used effectively another way is Jackson independent Larry Baria, a specialist in clastic and carbonate stratigraphy. "We're getting more out of 3-D where there is minimum of low relief structures. And guys like me who are stratigraphically oriented, I hope, are going to have a significant impact on finding channels, looking at marine bars and really nitpicking the stratigraphy. Most of the drillable structures have been found, but there are a hell of a lot of classic unconformity plays to be made that show up beautifully on 3-D."[10] Baria may be right about the scarcity of undrilled structures in the Salt Basin, but in the neighboring basin to the north, there are plenty left.

Sleeping Giants Await Dummies

At the 2003 Spring Symposium of the Mississippi Geological Society, Stewart Welch stunned the audience with a prediction about the Black Warrior Basin. "Based on the early performance of the wells in Maben Field, and the potential for multiple objectives, ultimate reserves for the entire [Knox] play are estimated to be on the order of ten trillion cubic feet."[11]

His presentation included a report on the current operations of Fina Oil and Chemical Company's activity in the Maben Field in northwest Oktibbeha County, Mississippi. Texaco discovered the old field in 1970. The No. 1 Clyde Sheely tested 600 mcf per day below 12,000 feet from a section of the Knox. The one-well field produced slowly for 28 years, with a cumulative total of 1.3 Bcf. It didn't generate much excitement; no one was interested in going after a 12,000-foot zone that produced so little, especially in the expensive-to-drill hard rocks. Shallower sands on the basin shelf northeast of Maben lured most explorers, but Fina noticed something interesting about the Sheely well.

When it was shut in after all those years of production it built its original reservoir pressure back within a short period, a clue that perhaps a monster reservoir was down there somewhere. Fina figured that modern fraccing and completion techniques could coax that reservoir to produce at far greater rates than the Sheely well.

In 1998 Fina leased a large block and drilled a well near the Sheely, the No. 1 Sanders. After hydraulic fraccing, the well produced a whopping 6,500 mcf per day. Fina and others added nine more wells. The average initial production for Fina's wells is 7,500 mcf per day. The ultimate recovery is estimated to be 15 to 20 Bcf per well.

Curiously, Fina's success did not stir much interest in oil circles, although it did set off a lease buying spree. The lack of fanfare did not surprise Jackson geologist Marvin Oxley, an astute observer of everything that happens in the South's oil patches. "I've seen a lot of plays come and go. They [the industry in general] decided that the original Maben discovery is the only one that [is capable of producing] and that there's no other production around it." Oxley knew it was not uncommon for a company to make a discovery and drill a couple of dry holes around it, after which the industry loses interest. Then, he says facetiously, "Some 'dummy' comes in and figures something out and goes in and drills another well, and makes a well, and slowly the play evolves.

Well, right now in Mississippi, Fina—the 'dummy'—has gone in and extended Maben and made a couple of great wells, and yet nobody is excited! If the Fina offset had been the discovery well people would have been peeing all over themselves. But [in the minds of the industry] the play has already been killed, and everybody 'knows' it is no good. And here's Fina up here, just fat, dumb and happy, making these hellacious gas wells, and nobody's getting excited about it."[12]

Not everyone can afford to get excited. Clearly, the deep Knox play in the Black Warrior Basin is a big company's game; the average well costs $4.5 million. Still, that's a one year pay-out, which is something to get excited about. To date the Maben Field has produced over 30 Bcf.

Stew Welch described the Knox as a Cambro-Ordovician-aged dolomite and limestone with a total thickness of about 6,000 feet, equivalent to the Arbuckle Limestone of Oklahoma and the Ellenberger dolomite of Texas. Both are prolific producers. The Knox play in the Black Warrior Basin runs from Panola County, Mississippi, southeast to Sumpter and Greene Counties, Alabama—an area 130 miles long and 50 miles wide. With the basin's shallow shelf exploration maturing, the new, deeper, virtually unexplored play may be the lair of the South's next giants.

As the 21st century opened oil people were convinced that unconventional operations, tertiary recovery, and sophisticated 3-D exploration were the industry's exclusive new tools. The old ways were long gone, they thought. Surly in this day and age no one could raise funds for risky old-style exploring, much less find anything significant, even if they could. They were wrong.

Fourth and Goal

Barely a few months into the new millenium, Midroc Oil Company of Shreveport swaggered into south Alabama to drill a risky prospect few others would touch. It had no structural closure and poor seismic coverage, but it had one quality that would have inspired wildcatters 50 years earlier—it was updip of shows. In an age of extremely high drilling costs and a quirky oil market, it took nerves of steel to put scarce exploration funds into something as simple and risky as that, but Jim Harris tackled it. In fact, the art of tackling was old hat to him.[13]

Born in Terrell, Texas, Harris won a football scholarship as quarterback at the University of Oklahoma, where between 1953 and 1957 he led the team to a 31-game winning streak and two national titles. The Sooners never lost a game Harris started, and the record winning streak still stands.

In the summers of his youth, Harris roughnecked on a drilling rig for Roy Guffey. He found the oil business exciting and decided to major in geology. He was in the right place. Oklahoma University was not only a football powerhouse but it was also one of the country's top petroleum geology schools. After graduating, Harris was drafted into pro football and played with the Eagles, Rams, Dallas Texans, and Dallas Cowboys, but after four years he decided to retire and pursue a career in petroleum geology.

In 1962 he worked as a geologist with Guffey Oil Company in west central Texas. In 1964 he moved to Shreveport, Louisiana, where he worked the Wilcox trend of Louisiana and Mississippi. A few years later he teamed with Don Clark, a former California Company landman, and formed Midroc Oil Company with partners Guffey and Cowden. They scored early successes in the Wilcox trend.

In the mid 1970s, Midroc drilled a series of wells in Choctaw County, Alabama, which discovered Bucatunna Creek Field, Mill Creek Fields, Southeast Mill Creek, Chappel Hill Field, and Wimberly Field. Jackson geologist Vaughan Watkins, retained by Midroc, generated many of their prospects. The fields were small but were prolific Smackover producers, averaging about a million recoverable barrels per well.

After those successes, Midroc focused primarily on North Louisiana, exploring successfully for gas fields. In the early 1980s the company restructured and became the Midroc Operating Company. A following of investors financed much of their drilling. Exploring principally in North Louisiana, they kept their eyes on Alabama.

At the end of the 1990s, a particular well caught Harris' attention, a wildcat drilled by Hunt Oil Company in 1995 in Conecuh County. The well was completed as a small Smackover discovery named the Little Cedar Creek Field. The well was considerably east of the prolific Smackover wells in south Alabama, and most geologists thought it was out of the trend. Producing from only three feet of oil reservoir near 12,000 feet, the well flowed only about 30 barrels of oil a day. Hunt Oil tried to extend the field by drilling a well about two miles to the northwest. That well found the Smackover essentially pinched out. Hunt gave up, and in 2000 they put the well, still making 30 BOPD, up for sale.

Jim Harris got wind of it and recommended to his partner Don Clark that they buy the well. Clark's response was, "Why would we want to buy a well in the middle of nowhere?"

"Thirty barrels a day is a good show," Harris answered. Midroc won the bid and acquired title to the well and Hunt's surrounding leases. They bought more leases in the vicinity and drilled a well about a half mile to the north. That hole encountered a slightly thicker reservoir but still not enough to get excited about. Production settled down at about 75 BOPD, barely commercial for a one million-dollar investment.

Harris was not ready to punt yet. The company bought and shot a series of seismic lines across the acreage block, which indicated no structural closure associated with the producing wells—only a flat spot, at best. Midroc knew they were dealing with a risky stratigraphic trap, and when they insisted on another well, some of the investors headed for the lockers. Midroc had to find fresh ones.

Harris and Clark took their deal to NAPE, the annual exposition in Houston where operators exhibit their prospect to potential investors. There they found two risk-takers eager for a place on the line of scrimmage—Dudley Hughes and Hanson Petroleum of Roswell, New Mexico.

Harris' pass fell incomplete again. The step-out well was dry, with only a thin Smackover section. However, this provided more information to help them delineate the stratigraphic trap. Midroc wasn't yet ready for the shower.

They proposed another well a quarter mile east of the second well, the one that made 75 BOPD. More of the early investors hung up their jocks, but on fourth and long, Harris hit his man in the end zone. The well was a charm. In August 2003 the 20-12 well tested almost 400 BOPD. Despite that stunning score, the group wasn't yet sure they had the game iced. Before writing another million-dollar check, they decided to wait and see if production held up. It did, leveling out at 250 BOPD after several weeks. Don Clark expanded the acreage block to a staggering 20,000 acres, assembled under the direction of landman Charles Landrum. Then, what every oilman dreams about happened.

Drilling started in earnest, and well after well came in flowing. By October 2004, an additional 11 wells were drilled without a single dry hole—a stunning achievement in the updip Smackover trend. The field quickly grew to 14 wells covering 2,700 acres of a four-mile long area. The field continues to grow to the east. The Little Cedar Creek Field is becoming a significant Smackover field, already the largest oil field found in Alabama in the last 20 years. Ultimate production may average one million barrels per well with pressure maintenance—not bad for medium depth holes drilled on old-fashioned stratigraphic mapping and unshakable determination to stay in the game.

Jim Harris' Oklahoma winning streak continues with every well drilled in Little Cedar Creek. His hunch had no highly exalted structural closure and was so far from known good production the goats turned their noses up at it. Yet it was a magnificent success. Harris summed up the entire historical message of the lure of oil when he said, "Exploring for oil and gas is a great sport, especially when you're finding it."

Chapter 23

Is the End in Sight?

In 1956 a Shell research geologist, M. King Hubbert, made a bold prediction based on careful calculations: oil production in the United States would peak in the early 1970s and begin a gradual decline from which it would never recover. His prediction elicited some ridicule. In 1970 U.S. production peaked.[1]

In 1982 Hubbert published another paper using the same statistical methods to make another prediction. He estimated that global oil production would peak between 2001 and 2004. Some researchers challenged Hubbert's methods but his dire predictions raised a heightened awareness of impending energy shortages. Other think tanks also offered predictions. The U.S. Department of Energy's calculation of the peak in 2020 was the most optimistic. Others were earlier, averaging 2009 to 2010.[2]

Energy researchers believe when the world production curve begins its irreversible downward trend, demand for oil, which has traditionally followed the production curve, will rise, causing havoc in global petro-economics. The trickle-down consequence will affect everyone profoundly. The demand curve will come down as consumers conserve and switch to alternate sources, but those alternate sources may not be available before the cost of oil is painfully high, and then only after a long search for solutions.

The American economy is moving steadily away from production and toward service industries, making the oilman an increasingly rare breed whose aim is to create wealth. Service industries merely redistribute it. Somewhere on the far side of Hubbert's curve consumers may come to understand the importance of oil people's historical contribution to their standard of living.

There are not many young oil finders and few are coming in from the universities. Environmental geology is now the big attraction at the college level. The professors are advising geology and engineering students to steer away from petroleum; the oil companies are not hiring.

The youngest petroleum geologists are graying and having grandchildren. Still they are restless, wanting desperately to make something happen.

Karl Kauffman is one. He works like a man possessed, knowing he is as good an oil finder as any of the legendary prospectors, and fumes over the reluctance of dawdling purse-holders to convert his ideas into rip-snorting energy spouters. Laid-back Ed Hollingsworth low-profiles it and sticks with what he enjoys—mapping sand channels and hoping somebody will stick a well into one of them. John Cox is getting on past middle age. He enjoyed the sweet taste of success at North Frisco City, and he hopes the best is not behind him. Then there are the graying veterans who keep on keeping on.

Dave Cate sits in his office at Pruet Oil Company, two years after the death of its founder, Chesley Pruet. He once supervised a staff of geologists. Now he is the company's only geoscientist. He stares at his regional reference wall map, remembering the thrill of the Deep Hosston play, knowing he will probably never see that kind of excitement again. Like all exploration managers, he craves the sight of an exciting new prospect map and still looks at logs and seismic records between the obligatory meetings.

Phil LaMoreaux relaxes in Tuscaloosa and reads his journals. He offers occasional advice to the young men to whom he handed over the reins of his global consulting firm. He spends a lot of time just remembering the satisfying years he spent leading the professionals at the Alabama Oil and Gas Board and Geological Survey. Others like them served their states in Jackson and Tallahassee.

Ralph Hines still wipes a tear away when he remembers his brother-in-law and co-founder of his company, Bob Moon. He shakes his head and wonders where the next generation of oil finders will come from. None are being trained. He wrote a letter to Congress asking it to do something about the oil industry's brain drain.

Les Aultman hurries from workstation to drafting table and back again, spending little time gazing out over Jackson, the once proud oil center of the Deep South. He's got no time for nostalgia. He toils incessantly over his maps, looking for another "pony in there somewhere." Vaughan Watkins looks at Aultman's work station and shakes his head, then goes back down the hall to his office and pulls out his paper maps, sticking to the old fashion way to hunt the grease.

Bob Schneeflock scratches his dog Babe and maneuvers his computer mouse over an interesting seismic feature. His achievements have secured his future, but he isn't ready to quit yet. He figures there is at least one more monster field in his future. He has to; his kind has no choice but to expect it.

Then there's Dudley Hughes, the patriarch of Southern oil. If any oilman deserves to withdraw to a comfortable, carefree retirement, he does. He has enough outside interests to stay busy—travel, fishing, hunting—but Dudley refuses to give up the hunt he loves most, the hunt for oil. Even in the mature years of his immensely successful career he finds time to sneak away to a satellite office, away from the phones and secretaries and faxes, to a cubicle where he can slip logs and draw contours in peace.

All these men remember those who went before them with great reverence. Never will the oil world forget the venerable Chesley Pruet, the fiercest of competitors; always hustling up deals; always staking the ranch on a sure bet;

ever sharing hard-earned wisdom with his protégés; never showing his hand; never taking advantage of a lesser man—but his competitors knew they were fair game. Pruet was a mover and a shaker. He was motivator and a kicker. He was oil incarnate.

Many others made their mark. There was Wil Knight, always in the right place at the right time. Southern oil hunters will never forget the eternal optimist, Merrill Harris, who didn't have to find oil; it crawled to him and begged to be discovered. A few will fondly remember Walter Sistrunk, the clever loner many misunderstood. He was truly the last of a breed.

There were also unsung heroes, the guys who gave advice and counsel to the movers and shakers. Among them log analyst Ed Kendrick, who couldn't stay awake while driving; well-sitter Jack Henderson, always grinning and joking, always telling his clients the naked truth about the dirty secrets those drill cuttings harbored. Harold Karges helped a lot of discoverers better understand what they discovered. There are too many to mention them all. Many were not geologists but landmen and engineers who contributed immeasurably to petroleum legacy.

One man must be remembered in a special way, because he started it all. Fred Mellen pointed the way at Tinsley. He did it without expecting compensation or fame and went on to quietly work and study and serve his country and state. His pick falling against the rocks at Tinsley started the hunt. His words of encouragement inspired the kids coming along in his wake to persevere, the author among them. Fred planted the dream we chased. We all wanted to catch it and some did, but in the end it's the chase that counts.

Epilogue

Finally, the Author's Own Biggest Discovery

I clearly remember the day I switched the Ford's engine off and paused, feeling more than hearing. The car's frame shuddered every few seconds to the subtle humdrum rhythm of a thudding impact somewhere within the earth's breast.

Thump. Thump. Thump. Thump.

I sat for a while, listening to the thump, staring through the windshield at the rig. The ramshackle doghouse blocked most of my view of the aged contraption, except for the tall, rusted mask festooned with pulleys, cables, and guy wires. At the top a dirty, worn American flag hung listless in the humid air as if it were staring down, saddened.

All I could discern of the man I came to see was a huge hand grasping the steel cable. Up and down his gloved fist went—a few feet each way—clinging to the cable with a tenacious resolve. It was easy to imagine he was raising the heavy bit with the sheer power of his arm. But more likely, I figured, the strength of his character was commanding the bit to jump in its hole.

I sat in the car longer than I should, eager to meet him, yet heavy-hearted. Finally I opened the door. Immediately the thump got louder, with the harmonious chugging of a gas engine struggling to spin a heavy counterweight.

THUMP chucka chucka chucka THUMP chucka chucka chucka THUMP.

I walked past the doghouse, which was nothing more than a large metal shed, scuffed and rusting, where Oscar could lock up his tools or retreat from the elements. I suspected he had spent many a night in there, although normally he didn't work in the dark. I stopped next to the platform and watched him. With his back turned he didn't see me approach. His huge, khaki-clad frame stood like a human derrick on the wooden platform, mud-crusted boots spread apart, massive shoulders drooping from a humped back, the old rig singing its sorrowful rhythm as he worked. THUMP chucka chucka chucka.

The ancient, flanged metal hardhat atop his head tilted downward like a diving flying saucer in a 50's sci-fi movie. Down, into the hole his gaze plunged, eyes flashing, imagination running rampant.

Down: the direction of Oscar Hembree's aspirations.

THUMP chucka chucka chucka.

Yeah, his dream lay beyond the bottom of that hole. Not too far down. Three or four football fields should put him there.

Oscar had drilled here to almost 1,000 feet two years ago. But his partner gave up too soon, Oscar reckoned, and they were forced to plug and abandon the hole. And now Oscar was back by himself and determined to find the oil he was certain awaited the visit of his bit. "Why, just look at the driller's log of that old hole," he once admonished me. "Good shows! Real good shows!" Oil lurked down there, didn't I know? Yes, there was a good chance it was here. He knew oil.

THUMP chucka chucka chucka.

He spent many decades in the mid-continent oil fields, starting as a roustabout, then stepping up to roughneck, and on to driller. He watched some tremendous discoveries while orchestrating scores of drilling operations, and eventually the fever struck him. He took on a partner and turned independent. But the big strike eluded him in Oklahoma, Louisiana, and Texas. And the years were ganging up on him. There wasn't much time left. Nor money. Especially money.

He didn't have the bucks to hire a big, modern rotary drilling rig, complete with pusher, roughnecks, and roustabouts. And the luxury of a geologist to guide him was a pipe dream. Besides, he was a pretty damn good geologist himself, he chuckled. That many years in the oil patch taught a man a few things, didn't I know? And the leases—well, the sweet spots down in the Black Warrior Basin were about all leased up. Oscar couldn't afford them anyway. But up here in Marion County, where the big companies had no confidence, leases were still cheap.

Anyway, he allowed, he didn't have the business savvy to raise tons of money like the slick talkers down in Tuscaloosa and Jackson. And even if he did, he damn sure wasn't about to go out doctorin' and lawyerin.' It wouldn't look too good for an honest wildcatter to be doing that.

He knew how the rogue promoters worked. When they couldn't find professional oil investors to back their harebrained ideas, they sold "pieces of the action" for a few thousand bucks to unknowing outsiders, guaranteeing big discoveries and hefty returns on their investments. And he also knew how they inflated operating costs three and four hundred percent and how they lured unwary investors back again and again with their fantastic "discoveries." Yeah, some parts of the Black Warrior Basin could be an oil swindler's dreamland, he reckoned. Almost anywhere you could find a little natural gas and some spotty oil, but only in the sweetest areas were the reserves big enough to develop.

Oscar knew how some promoters shut their new wells in for a few days, letting the pressure build up enough to bring the investors out for a demonstration. They would light a rag at the end of the flare line and open the valve and WHUMP! A great blaze would lash out across the reserve pit with a savage roar and—as the investors passed out cigars and shook hands—the promoters would shut the valve off before the pressure dropped to a feeble flame. As time went by, token royalty checks would show up in the investors' mail boxes, but the bills kept coming as well. Big ones. And when they asked about their wells, they got complicated technical excuses and always more promises. Eventually the investors would walk away, burned, but there were more to be lured, checkbook in hand, by the telltale brownish stains reverently called shows in the oil field. Oscar Hembree would have none of that. He would find oil honestly and on his own, God willing.

But God must have played a trick on Oscar if He willed him this rig. The thing became obsolete in the 1930s. It belonged in a museum. Oscar knew it—he was no fool. The old cable-tool rig dug a hole by dropping a heavy bit down and picking it up, again, again, and again. It simply beat the hell out of the ground, forcing the hole deeper a fraction of an inch at every drop. Every now and then he pulled the bit out and lowered a bucket with a clamshell at the bottom to clean out the pulverized rock. It was too soon to expect the shows, but as he got deeper he would examine the cuttings carefully. He was only 300 feet down. A rotary rig could have drilled that much in a day. Oscar had been here a month.

He kept a careful log on the doghouse wall next to the copy of the log from the old hole, so he could correlate his progress against it. With each few feet of depth, he recorded his findings: gumbo, shale, sand. Eventually, Oscar predicted—around 1,800 feet—the log would read "lime, strong show of oil." He would clean out the hole, install valves, flow to the pits, and record the pressures. Then Oscar Hembree would call my office at the Oil and Gas Board to report his discovery. He would take his oil samples and his pressure data to his old partners and get re-capitalized. Then he would get a pump and a tank and maybe then hire a modern rotary rig and some men to develop the new field. And he would need a good landman to do more leasing, because the big operators down south would soon descend in search of that which dwelled not far below his bit.

THUMP chucka chucka chucka.

I waited for him to take his hand off the cable. He claimed he could tell what kind of rock he was going through by feeling the line when the bit crashed down. But he just stood, his back to me, staring down the hole, arm rising and falling, as much a part of the rig as the cable, mast, and engine.

THUMP chucka chucka chucka—Oscar Hembree's heartbeat.

I marveled at his steadiness. I admired his perseverance. I wondered what kept the man going. He was too old for this. Why didn't he just scrap this wretched monument to Rube Goldberg and go on home? Then, a frail voice called to me from behind, and I turned. I peered into the doghouse and saw why he didn't go home. Home came with him.

Mrs. Hembree, wearing a long, dark dress, looking like she just returned from church, sat in a rocker in the corner among the tools and equipment, knitting, rocking, watching. I stood, gripped, beholding the contentment from her tender eyes radiating like warm sunshine. Her stately, wrinkled face smiled as she welcomed me back to their rig, offered me iced tea, and asked about my family. On the windowsill was a wilted bouquet of wildflowers they picked near the rig. A fan hummed in the corner, gently blowing her thin hair, fluttering the gray strands like tiny searching tentacles. We might as well have been sitting on her front porch. Her rocker was carefully positioned so she could view the form of her toiling husband framed in the doorway. She hardly looked up from the needlework as she prattled. I strained to make her words out when suddenly his voice boomed above the rig racket.

"HELLO, STATE MAN!" He couldn't remember my name, but that was okay. I turned to greet him. Gratifying eyes, dimmed with age, beamed at me. The leathery red face, crisscrossed with creases like the faults and fractures of the rocks he drilled, grinned approval. Most drillers tolerated my visits politely, but I was Oscar's welcome guest.

He removed the greasy gloves and shook my hand, then ushered me to the drill log where his dusty fingers dabbed smudges on his scribbled notes. He had seen no shows yet, but he still had a long way to go. If only this shabby rig would quit breaking down on him, and if he hadn't hit that pesky shallow water sand that kept flooding his hole, he would have been much deeper by now. But he would get there, he assured me. Yes. And it would be the dolomite, he proclaimed—the Knox dolomite. There it lay trapped in fractures and between the pores of the grainy, dolomitized limestone deposited by shallow seas hundreds of millions of years ago, so far back even the dinosaurs were an unchecked item on God's things-to-do list.

Despite Oscar's claims to geological wizardry, I suspected he was neither aware of, nor concerned about, the depositional origins of the Knox formation. He only knew that the dolomite and its slimy contents waited patiently for his bit to complete its final thump.

I looked around and pointed out that there was no blowout preventer installed around the cable. The hole was wide open, in direct violation of the Alabama oil and gas code. He explained he was still too shallow to expect trouble and planned to install it on his next trip out to dress the bit. That sounded reasonable to me.

On he talked of the pay rock to come. I nodded and smiled and tried to follow his words without forgetting that Mrs. Hembree was addressing me simultaneously on an unrelated topic.

I noted his progress for my records and said goodbye. I had rounds to make. I wished them well, and with a wave and a last glance at the old rig, I drove away, hoping I might miraculously be compelled to return and congratulate him on a discovery.

A couple of weeks later the news came in a stack of papers dropped on my desk. Thumbing through them I found form OGB-11, "Report of Well Plugging." The old rig had given Oscar so much trouble that he gave up before reaching anything near his target depth. It was a dry hole. A duster. He plugged his hole and went home—wherever that was.

But the THUMP chucka chucka sang in my soul for a long time afterward as I left the employ of the government and followed my own lowdown dreams. As I poured over subsurface maps and worked around the heavy rigs, swarming with workmen and appointed with the latest technological advances, I never forgot that lonely cable-tool heartbeat.

Every time I recall it, I know I was the one who made a discovery at Oscar's dry hole. Only a buried cement plug and a half acre of scarred ground remained of his exploratory venture. Yet he left the way he came, abundantly wealthy—rich with the contentment of an honest life, rich with the call of noble dreams, rich with the love of a caring wife. And whether he knew it or not, he shared it all with me. I wondered what more an oilman could want.

Alan Cockrell
Huntsville, Alabama
2003

Glossary*

Annulus The open space between the borehole wall and the drillpipe through which drilling mud returns to the surface.

Anticline An arch-shaped fold in rock in which rock layers are upwardly convex.

Barrel 42 U.S. gallons.

Basin A depression in the crust of the earth, caused by plate tectonic activity and subsidence, in which sediments accumulate.

Bcf Billion cubic feet.

Block A group of mineral leases usually assembled for a specific drilling prospect.

Blockbuster A person who sees where oil companies are leasing and tries to get one or more leases within the company's block to gain a negotiating advantage.

Blowout An uncontrolled flow of reservoir fluids into the wellbore and sometimes catastrophically to the surface. A blowout may consist of saltwater, oil, gas, or a mixture of those. Blowouts occur in all types of exploration and production operations, not just during drilling operations.

Blowout preventer A valve at the top of a well that may be closed if the drilling crew loses control of formation fluids.

BOPD Barrels of oil per day.

Casing Pipe lowered into an open hole and cemented in place to protect freshwater formations. The operation during which the casing is put into the well bore is commonly called "running pipe."

Closure Term used when contours on a subsurface structure map close to form a dome shape, usually irregular, indicating the possible presence of an oil or gas trap.

Condensate A low-density, high API gravity liquid hydrocarbon phase that generally occurs in association with natural gas.

Contour A line that includes points of equal value such as feet below sea level, on a structure map.

Core A cylindrical sample of the formation being drilled.

CO_2 Carbon dioxide gas.

Deal A package offered for sale, including a lease block, a geological prospectus, and a drilling proposal.

Development Exploitation drilling on a field after its discovery.

Dip The angle at which a sedimentary rock layer is inclined from the horizontal.

Downthrown The lower side of a normal fault.

Driller The supervisor of the rig crew and the person who operates the pumps, drawworks, and rotary table.

Drilling mud Any of a number of liquid and gaseous fluids and mixtures of fluids and solids used in drilling operations.

Drillstem test (DST) Well tests conducted with the drillstring still in the hole, usually conducted with a downhole shut-in tool that allows the well to be opened and closed at the bottom of the hole with a surface-actuated valve.

Dry hole contribution An agreed sum of money paid by a non-participating company to a company that is drilling in order to receive technical information from the hole. The payment is made only if the hole is dry.

DST See drillstem test.

Farmout A common deal in which a leaseholder who is not interested in drilling his leases assigns them to another party who wants to drill them. In the typical farmout arrangement no money is exchanged, but if a producing well is made the original owner "backs-in" for a portion (commonly 30-40%) of his original interest, after the drilling party recovers its expenses from production.

Fault A break in rock layers in which one side of the break moves in relation to the other side. In the Gulf Coast the direction of relative movement is mostly vertical.

field An accumulation, pool, or group of pools of hydrocarbons or other mineral resources in the subsurface. A field cannot be produced until the State recognizes it officially and assigns rules to it.

fishing job The application of tools, equipment, and techniques for the removal of junk or debris from a wellbore. Such junk is commonly called "fish."

flowing well A well in which natural reservoir pressure causes oil to flow to the surface. Pumping is not required until the pressure drops.

Frac job Enhancing production by pumping fluids under enormous pressure into the reservoir to open the natural fractures in the rock formation.

Gas cap The gas that accumulates in the upper portions of a reservoir.

Graben The area between two parallel opposing normal faults in which the center section drops downward in relation to the outside blocks.

Gravity data Measurements of the earth's gravitational pull taken at intervals along intersecting lines. Minute differences can be contour-mapped to find anomalous areas that may indicate a subsurface structure.

High A high point in the subsurface that may also be called a "structure," a "feature," or a "hickey."

H$_2$S Hydrogen sulfide, a poisonous gas associated with hydrocarbons in some areas.

Isopach A contour line that links points of equal thickness.

Kick Term describing what happens when the bit encounters a porous rock zone that introduces gas, oil, or water under higher than expected pressure into the borehole. Drilling mud may be blown out of the hole, and the rig make shake or jump.

Landman Person who specializes in procuring and management of leases.

Lease A right to drill on acreage under which another party owns the minerals. The lease is obtained by paying the owner an initial "bonus" and annual "rentals" for the term of the lease, or until it is produced. The owner usually retains a royalty of one eighth.

Logs Records of technical data from a hole, usually manufactured in the form of long narrow folded paper containing graphs and depth measurements.

Look-alike An undrilled geologic prospect that looks like another one, usually nearby, that was productive.

Magnetic data Measurements of the earth's magnetic field taken at intervals along intersecting lines. Minute differences can be contour-mapped to find anomalous areas that may indicate a subsurface structure.

MCFD One thousand cubic feet of gas per day.

Mudlogger Person who "sits" at a drilling well site and makes a log of the characteristics of the hole based on his observation of the cuttings collected at the surface.

Offset A well drilled in a unit adjacent to an existing producer.

Operator Company that actively conducts drilling operations, or in the case of a producing property, the company that actively manages production and distributes revenue. There may be other partial owners who pay their share of expenses to the operator.

Overriding royalty A royalty interest over and above the mineral owner's royalty that is assigned to a third party.

Participate The act of "paying one's way" wherein a partial owner in a drilling unit pays his proportional share of expenses rather than farming his interest out.

Pay A noun describing a producing zone, usually in relation to thickness, as in "50 feet of pay."

Perforations Holes made in casing to allow hydrocarbons to enter the well.

Perm Slang for permeability.

Permeability The ability, or measurement of a rock's ability, to transmit fluids, typically measured in darcies or millidarcies.

Pinchout The termination of a porous rock in a lateral direction, which may indicate a stratigraphic trap.

Play An episode of heightened exploration tempo in a particular geologic setting. A play is usually sparked by a significant discovery that attracts other explorers. It matures over time and finally diminishes as most of the fields in the play are found.

Plug The act of setting a cement block at specific points in a hole to protect freshwater zones in dry holes or abandoned wells.

Primary recovery The first stage of hydrocarbon production, in which natural reservoir energy displaces hydrocarbons from the reservoir into the wellbore and up to surface.

Prospect A concept of where an undiscovered oil or gas field may lie. It is usually supported by a package of geologic and engineering information.

Pool A single subsurface petroleum reservoir in a porous rock.

Porosity The percentage of pore volume or void space, or the volume of a rock that can contain fluids.

Pumping well A well that is being pumped at the surface due to inadequate natural reservoir pressure to lift oil.

Reserves The amount of recoverable oil or gas in a reservoir.

Reservoir A subsurface body of rock having sufficient porosity and permeability to store commercial quantities of oil or gas.

Resistivity The ability of a material to resist electrical conduction.

Roughneck A member of the drilling crew.

Roustabout Any unskilled manual laborer on the rig site.

Royalty The landowner's share of production, free of the expenses of production.

Scout A person who tracks his company's competitors' exploration and production activity for the purpose acquiring technical data that might benefit his company. (While this might sound like spying, most of a scout's work is sharing information openly.)

Seal A relatively impermeable rock, commonly shale, that forms a barrier or cap above and around reservoir rock so that fluids cannot migrate beyond the reservoir.

Secondary recovery The second stage of hydrocarbon production during which external fluids intrinsic to the reservoir such as water or natural gas are injected into the reservoir to restore pressure artificially.

Seismic data Information showing the geometry and other properties of subsurface rock layers based on reflections of shock waves from the surface.

Show Surface observation of hydrocarbons in well cuttings or drilling fluid using various techniques and equipment.

Shut in well A well which is closed off at the surface.

Spacing A conservation measure required by a governmental regulatory agency that specifies the size of drilling/production units in acres and minimum distances from the edges of the unit. Oil wells commonly have 40 acre spacing and gas wells 320 acres, but both can be larger or smaller depending on various factors the agency takes into account.

Spud Commencement of drilling operations.

Sour Gas or oil that contains hydrogen sulfide (H_2S).

Squeeze job The act of sealing off water zones by perforating casing and squeezing cement into the annulus.

Step out A well drilled adjacent to a producing field but in an unproven area.

Stratigraphic trap A type of petroleum trap, not dependent on structure, that features a change in rock characteristics such as porosity and/or permeability in a lateral direction.

Stratigraphy The study of the composition, characteristics, and origin of sedimentary rocks.

Stripper A well that makes less than 10 BOPD.

Structure A geological feature produced by deformation of the earth's crust, such as a fold or a fault.

Trap A geometric configuration of rocks suitable for containing hydrocarbons and sealed by a relatively impermeable formation through which hydrocarbons will not migrate.

Tcf Trillion cubic feet.

TD Target depth before drilling, total depth after drilling.

Tertiary recovery The third stage of hydrocarbon production during which agents not intrinsic to the reservoir are injected to restore reservoir artificially. Such agents may be heat energy or CO_2 from an external source.

Tight (1) Term describing a relatively impermeable rock from which hydrocarbon production is difficult or impossible. (2) Term used to describe a well whose technical data is being held secret by its operator.

Tool pusher The general superintendent of drilling operations, who supervises one or more drilling crews in the field.

Tour A work shift of a drilling crew (pronounced like tower).

Trip The complete operation of removing the entire drillstring from the wellbore and running it back in the hole, usually for the purpose of changing the bit.

Unitization An act of conservation making an entire field a single production unit for the purpose maintaining reservoir pressure more efficiently. In such a case all individual owners, whether royalty owners or working-interest owners, become owners of all wells in the unit, reduced proportionally.

Upthrown The upper side of a normal fault.

Waterflooding A common secondary recovery method that takes saltwater from a field and reinjects it under pressure at strategic points to drive the remaining oil or gas toward the primary producing wells.

Wildcat An exploration well.

Working interest Type of ownership in a well characterized by paying one's proportional share of expenses related to drilling, completion, and production operations. In contrast, royalty interest owners, such as mineral owners who lease their rights, get a free ride.

Zone A specific interval or unit of rock differentiated from rock layers above or below it by various characteristics.

---

* Glossary assembled from the author's experience and from *Manual of Oil and Gas Terms* (Williams and Myers, 5th ed., 1981, Bender).

Notes

Prelude
1. Dudley Hughes, *Oil in the Deep South,* 1869-1945 (Jackson: University Press of Mississippi, 1993) 115.
2. Hughes, 154
3. Hughes, 148.
4. Hughes, 150.
5. Hughes, 15.
6. Dudley Hughes, Untitled, Unfinished manuscript, 6.
7. Hughes, 8.

Chapter 1
1. Robert Womack, Transcript of interview with Dudley Hughes and Carrol Brinson, 16 June 1987.
2. Dudley Hughes, *Oil in the Deep South,* 1869-1945 (Jackson: University Press of Mississippi, 1993) 114.
3. Hughes, 199-220.
4. Hughes, 204.
5. Hughes, 194.
6. Emmett Vaughey and William Vaughey, Transcript of interview with Carrol Brinson, 11 March 1987.
7. James Furrh, Personal interview, 10 April 2002.
8. M.E. "Bud" Norman, Transcript of interview with Dudley Hughes and Carrol Brinson, 11 November 1988.
9. Hughes, 154.
10. Mack Cox, Letter to Dudley Hughes, 5 January 1990.
11. See note 6.
12. See note 7.
13. John Callon, Personal interview, 8 January 1999.

Chapter 2
1. Merrill Harris, Transcript of interview with Dudley Hughes and Carrol Brinson, 29 March 1990.
2. Robert Hearin, Transcript of interview with Dudley Hughes and Carrol Brinson, 13 September 1988.
3. Wilbur Knight, Transcript of interview with Dudley Hughes and Carrol Brinson, 24 July 1987.
4. Dudley Hughes, *Oil in the Deep South,* 1869-1945 (Jackson: University Press of Mississippi, 1993) 204.

5. Hughes, 76.
6. Hughes, 190.
7. Emmett Vaughey and William Vaughey, Transcript of interview with Carrol Brinson, 11 March 1987
8. Dudley Hughes, Untitled, Unfinished manuscript, 29.

Chapter 3
1. Dudley Hughes, *Oil in the Deep South, 1869-1945* (Jackson: University Press of Mississippi, 1993) 39.
2. Wilbur Knight, Interview with Dudley Hughes and Carrol Brinson, 24 July 1987.
3. Fred Mellen, Transcript of interview with Carrol Brinson, 7 July 1989.
4. See note 2.
5. Hughes, 14-15.
6. Walter B. Jones, "Oil and Gas Possibilities in the Warrior Coal Basin," *The Petroleum Engineer*, September 1954.
7. Charles Williams, E-mail to author, 8 October 2004.
8. Vern Culbertson, Personal interview, 9 September 1999.

Chapter 4
1. John Callon, Personal interview with the author and Dudley Hughes, 8 January 1999.
2. Vern Culbertson, Personal interview, 9 September 1999.
3. "Promising Show of Oil," *The Brewton Standard* (Brewton, AL) 30 August 1951.
4. "Pollard Oil Boom," *Tri-cities Ledger* (Flomaton, AL), circa 1952, 2b.
5. See note 4.
6. Dudley Hughes, *Oil in the Deep South, 1869-1945* (Jackson: University Press of Mississippi, 1993) 236.
7. H. Gene White, Personal interview, 10 October 1999.

Chapter 5
1. Wilbur Knight, Transcript of interview with Dudley Hughes and Carrol Brinson, 24 July 1987.
2. Mack Cox, Letter to Dudley Hughes, 5 January 1990.
3. Ray Stevens, Transcript of interview with Dudley Hughes and Carrol Brinson, 28 March 1990.
4. Chesley Pruet, Transcript of interview with Dudley Hughes, 14 March 1998.
5. Dudley Hughes, Letter to the author, 10 June 1998.

Chapter 6
1. Robert Hearin, Transcript of interview with Dudley Hughes and Carrol Brinson, 13 September 1988.
2. "100 Years Ago," *The Mobile Register* (Mobile, AL), 12 March 2002.
3. Chesley Pruet, Transcript of interview with Dudley Hughes, 14 March 1998.
4. H. Gene White, Personal interview, 10 October 1999.

5. "Alabama Oil and Gas Industry Changed by Citronelle Field," *The Mobile Register*, Date unknown.
6. "Deep Hope Spews Black Gold," *The Mobile Register*, Circa 1955.
7. See note 3.
8. See note 4.
9. Richard Stechmann, "Significance and Development of the Citronelle Oil Field Discovery," *In Celebration, Alabama Oil and Gas Report* 18 (Tuscaloosa: Geological Survey of Alabama, 1995) 23.
10. Harold H. Martin, "The Day it Rained Money," *The Saturday Evening Post*, 16 June 1956.

Chapter 7

1. William Wooten, Personal interview with the author and Dudley Hughes, January 7, 1999.
2. Dudley Hughes, *Oil in the Deep South*, 1869-1945 (Jackson: University Press of Mississippi, 1993) 164.
3. Dudley Hughes, "Statistical Outline," 1 June 1998.
4. Richard Stechmann, "Significance and Development of the Citronelle Oil Field Discovery," *In Celebration, Alabama Oil and Gas Report* 18 (Tuscaloosa: Geological Survey of Alabama, 1995) 23.
5. "Alabama Oil Industry," *The Mobile Press Register*, December 28, 1959.
6. Tom Joiner, Personal interview, 6 June 1998.
7. Charles Hayes, Transcript of interview with Dudley Hughes, 18 November 1989.
8. Robert C. MacElvain and H. Gene White, "The Oil Industry in Alabama," *The Petroleum Engineer*, February 1989.
9. Robert Mosbacher, Telephone conversation with the author, 22 November 2004.
10. Chesley Pruet, Transcript of interview with Dudley Hughes, 14 March 1998.
11. See note 7.
12. Wilbur Knight, Transcript of interview with Dudley Hughes and Carrol Brinson, July 24, 1987.
13. Merrill Harris, Transcript of interview with Dudley Hughes and Carrol Brinson, March 29, 1990.
14. Marvin Oxley, Personal interview, June 6, 2000.
15. See note 13.

Chapter 8

1. Mack Cox, Transcript of interview with Dudley Hughes, January 5, 1990.
2. Craig Castle, Transcript of interview with Dudley Hughes, March 1, 1988.
3. Charles Hayes, Transcript of interview with Dudley Hughes, November 18, 1989.
4. Walker Watters, Personal interview, April 9, 2002.
5. Hearin, Robert, Interview with Dudley Hughes and Carrol Brinson, September 13, 1988.
6. James Furrh, Personal interview, April 10, 2002.

7. Dudley Hughes, *Oil in the Deep South*, 1869-1945 (Jackson: University Press of Mississippi, 1993) 109.
8. Chesley Pruet, Transcript of interview with Dudley Hughes, 14 March 1998.
9. Dudley Hughes, "Statistical Outline," 1 June 1998, 11.
10. William Wooten, Personal interview with the author and Dudley Hughes, 7 January 1999.
11. See note 9.
12. Alex Sartwell, Personal interview, 22 August 2001.

Chapter 9

1. Philip LaMoreaux, Personal interview, 22 August 2001.
2. Alex Sartwell, Personal interview, 22 August 2001.
3. Tom Watson, Personal interview, 21 June 2000.
4. Fred Mellen, Transcript of interview with Dudley Hughes, 3 March 1987.
5. Richard Stechmann, "Significance and Development of the Citronelle Oil Field Discovery," *In Celebration, Alabama Oil and Gas Report* 18 (Tuscaloosa: Geological Survey of Alabama, 1995) 23.
6. Jimmy Morgan, Transcript of interview with Dudley Hughes and Carroll Brinson, 18 March 1987.
7. Dudley Hughes, "Statistical Outline," 1 June 1998, 17.
8. "19th Annual Mississippi Oil Review," *Laurel Call-Times*, 18 October 1963.
9. James Stewart, Personal interview, 9 September 1999.
10. Dudley Hughes, *Oil in the Deep South*, 1869-1945 (Jackson: University Press of Mississippi, 1993) 239.
11. Chesley Pruet, Transcript of interview with Dudley Hughes, March 14, 1998.
12. Fleming Browning and Stewart Welch, Simultaneous personal interview, 12 April 2002.
13. See note 11.
14. Dudley Hughes, "Medicine and Oil Do Mix," *MD News*, July 2001.

Chapter 10

1. Dudley Hughes, "Statistical Outline," 1 June 1998, 18.
2. Norman Germany, Transcript of interview with Dudley Hughes, 27 July 1995.
3. Dudley Hughes, *Oil in the Deep South*, 1869-1945 (Jackson: University Press of Mississippi, 1993) 195.
4. Donald Moore, *History of Major Oil and Gas Developments in Alabama*, (Tuscaloosa: Geological Survey of Alabama, 1971).
5. Merill Harris, Transcript of interview with Dudley Hughes and Carrol Brinson, 29 March 1990.
6. See note 1.
7. "State's Biggest Oil Well Producing in Pelahatchie Field," *Rankin County News*, 31 August 1967.
8. Vaughan Watkins, Personal interview, 16 June 2003.
9. See note 1, p. 23.
10. Chesley Pruet, Letter to the author, 10 November 1998.
11. Harry Spooner, Personal interview with Dudley Hughes, 7 January 1999.

12. Tom Joiner, Personal interview, 6 June 1999.
13. See note 1.
14. Matt Lutz and Einar Pederson, Personal telephone interview, via conference call, 22 June 2000.
15. Robert Mosbacher, Personal interview by telephone, October 2005.

Chapter 11
1. Charles Meeks, Personal interview, 1 March 1999.
2. H. Gene White, Personal interview, 10 October 1999.
3. See note 2.
4. Fleming Browning and Stewart Welch, Personal simultaneous interview, 12 April 2002.
5. Charles Blackburn, Transcript of interview with Dudley Hughes and Carrol Brinson, 7 April 1997.

Chapter 12
1. Daniel Yergin, *The Prize* (New York: Simon & Shuster, 1990) 567.
2. Dudley Hughes, Letter to the author, 17 January 1998.
3. See note 2.
4. Charles Blackburn, Transcript of interview with Dudley Hughes and Carrol Brinson, 7 April 1997.
5. John Richart and Howard Samsel, Personal simultaneous telephone interview via conference call, 7 June 2000.
6. Ralph Hines, Personal interview, 25 March 1998.
7. Alex Sartwell, *A History of the Origins and the Early Years of the State Oil and Gas Board* (Tuscaloosa: Geological Survey of Alabama/Alabama Oil and Gas Board, 1997) 29.
8. See note 7.
9. Thomas E. McMillan Jr., Personal interview, February 1990.
10. See note 9.
11. John Appleyard, *The T.R. Miller Mill Company Story* (Brewton, Alabama: Miller Forrest Products) 160.
12. Appleyard, 161.
13. Appleyard, 161.
14. Charles Meeks, Personal interview, 1 March 1999.
15. Appleyard, 162.
16. Appleyard 11, 162.
17. Appleyard 11, 163.
18. See note 14.
19. Appleyard 11, 165.
20. Robert Hearin, Transcript of interview with Dudley Hughes and Carrol Brinson, 13 September 1988.
21. "Pollard Oil Boom," *Tri-cities Ledger*, Circa 1952, 2b.

Chapter 13
1. Lloyd Tankersley, Letter to Dudley Hughes, 23 February 1990.

2. Charles Haynes, Ph.D., Personal interview, 10 October 1999.
3. Mike Epsman, Personal interview, 10 October 1999
4. Charles Meeks, Personal interview, 1 March 1999.
5. Harry Spooner, Personal Interview with the author and Dudley Hughes, 7 January 1999.
6. Dudley Hughes, Letter to the author, May 1998.
7. Les Aultman, Personal interview, 5 June 2001.
8. Thomas Sylte, Personal telephone interview, 23 June 2003.
9. See note 7.
10. Greg Halvatzis, E-mail to Robert Schneeflock, 11 November 2000.

Chapter 14

1. Dudley Hughes, "Significance of Jurassic Oil and Gas Development in Alabama." *In Celebration, Alabama Oil and Gas Report* 18. (Tuscaloosa: Geological Survey of Alabama, 1995) 37.
2. James Files, Personal interview, 7 June 2000.
3. John Richart and Howard Samsel, Simultaneous personal interview via conference call, 7 June 2000.
4. See note 3.
5. Matthew Lutz and Einar Pederson, Simultaneous personal interview, via conference call, 22 June 2000.
6. See note 5.

Chapter 15

1. Delores Burroughs, *The Petroleum Industry in Alabama, Oil and Gas Report* 3 (Tuscaloosa: Geological Survey of Alabama, 1994), 27.
2. H. Gene White, Personal interview, 10 October 1999.
3. James Stewart, Personal interview, 7 September 1999.
4. Richard Mason, E-mail to the author.
5. Sam Cerny, Personal telephone interview, 26 April 2000.
6. See note 4.
7. Dudley Hughes, "Statistical Outline." 35.
8. Marvin Oxley, Personal interview, 6 June 2000.
9. Harry Spooner, Interview with Dudley Hughes and the author, 7 January 1999.
10. See note 3.
11. Tom Joiner, Personal interview, 15 June 1998.

Chapter 16

1. William Tucker, Personal interview, 20 October 1999.
2. H. Gene White, Personal interview, 10 October 1999.
3. William Tucker, "Significance of Oil and Gas Development in the Black Warrior Basin of Alabama." *In Celebration: Alabama Oil and Gas Report* 18: (Tuscaloosa: Geological Survey of Alabama, 1995) 12.
4. LaMoreaux, Phillip, Personal interview, 22 August 2001.

Chapter 17

1. Tom Watson, Personal interview, 21 June 2000.
2. Dudley Hughes, "Statistical Outline," 38.
3. Dudley Hughes, Letter to the author, 10 June 1998.
4. Vaughan Watkins, Personal interview, 16 June 2003.
5. See note 2.
6. Chesley Pruet, Chesley, Transcript of interview with Dudley Hughes. 14 March 1998.
7. Randy James, Personal interview by telephone, June 2003.
8. William Wooten, Personal interview with the author and Dudley Hughes, 7 January 1999.
9. Davis Cate, Personal interview, 5 June 2000.
10. Charles Morrison and Robert and Gaston, Simultaneous personal interview, 5 June 2000.
11. Jerry Zoble, Personal interview, 16 June 2003.
12. Walker Watters, Personal interview, 9 April 2002.

Chapter 18

1. William Wade, Jason Plater, and Jacqueline Kelley, *History of Coastal Alabama Natural Gas Exploration and Development Final Report, OCS Study* 99-003 (New Orleans: U.S. Department of Interior, 1999) 14. (The publication quotes Chevron geologist Gary Jacobs as using the term "sand sea.")
2. Robert Mink and Bennett Bearden, *Oil and Gas Exploration and Development in Alabama State Coastal Waters and Adjacent Federal OCS Waters, October 1951-June 1986, State Oil and Gas Board Report 7D* (Tuscaloosa: Geological Survey of Alabama, 1986) 14.
3. Santa Barbara County, California, Energy Division, "Blowout at Union Oil's Platform A," 5, 2001, November 2004<http://www.countyofsb.org/>
4. Jim Hendon, "Winning Minds by Winning Hearts," AAPG Explorer Online, June 2003, 5 November 2004<"http://www.aapg.org/explorer/>
5. Myrt Jones, *A Gadfly's Memoirs* (1st Books, 2002) 3.
6. See note 2.
7. Thomas Joiner, Personal interview, 15 June 1998.
8. Wade, Plater, and Kelley, 3.
9. Wade, Plater, and Kelley, 3.
10. Wade, Plater, and Kelley, 3.
11. Jones, 16.
12. Jones, 21.
13. Wade, Plater, and Kelley, 4.
14. Ralph Helmich, Personal interview, 4 April 2003.
15. Hefferman, Anthony, "Shaking up Mobile with Natural Gas," *Business Week*, 22 March 1976.
16. Wade, Plater, and Kelley, p. 5.
17. Jones, 27.
18. Wade, Plater, and Kelley, 7.
19. Alabama Oil and Gas Board, "Petroleum Exploration and Development

Offshore Alabama, Q&A," No date, February 2005
>http://www.ogb.state.al.us/<

20. Mink and Bearden, 19.
21. Wade, Plater, and Kelley, 54.
22. Thomas Joiner, "The Role of the State Oil and Gas Board in the Conservation and Economic Development of Alabama's Petroleum Resources," *In Celebration, Alabama Oil and Gas Report* 18 (Tuscaloosa: Geological Survey of Alabama) 20.
23. Wade, Plater, and Kelley, 11.
24. Mink and Bearden, 24.
25. Phillip Rawls, "Settlement of Coastline Dispute Could Mean Millions to Alabama," *The Birmingham News*, 23 February 1993.
26. See note 14.
27. Craig Myers, "Agency: No Rigs off Beach," *Mobile Register*, 3 August 1999.
28. Dianne McGee, E-mail to the author, 15 October 2002.

Chapter 19
1. Morton E. Wakeland Jr., Ph.D., Personal interview, 6 June 2003.
2. Ralph Helmich, Personal interview, 4 April 2003.
3. Fleming Browning and Stewart Welch, Simultaneous personal interview. 12 April 2002.
4. Dudley Hughes, "Statistical Outline," 6 June 1998, 50.
5. Les Aultman, Personal interview, 5 June 2000.
6. Jerry Sanders, "Significance of the Coalbed Methane Industry in Alabama," *In Celebration, Alabama Oil and Gas Report* 18 *(Tuscaloosa*: Geological Survey of Alabama, 1995) 41.
7. Alabama Oil and Gas Board, "Coalbed Methane Resources of Alabama," No date, February 2005 >http://www.ogb.state.al.us/<

Chapter 20
1. Charles Williams, Personal Interview, 18 July 2004.
2. See note 1.
3. Les Aultman, Personal interview, 5 June 2000
4. George Vockroth, Personal interview, 5 June 2003.
5. Douglas Gill, Douglas, "The Wily Wilcox," *The Oil and Gas Investor*, September 1969.
6. Julius Ridgway, Personal interview, 10 April 2002.
7. Vaughan Watkins, Personal interview, 16 June 2003.
8. Robert Chaney and Robert Schneeflock, Simultaneous personal interview. 5 June 2000.
9. Robert Schneeflock, Robert Chaney, and Marble, John, "Updip Smackover Hunt Heating up in U.S," *Oil and Gas Journal*, unknown date.
10. Maria Halkias, Maria, "Smacking of Success," *The Dallas Morning News*, 23 January 1990.
11. See note 3.
12. Jay Masingill, E-mail to the author, 6 December 2004.

Chapter 21

1. Robert Chaney and Robert Schneeflock, Simultaneous personal interview. 5 June 2000.
2. M.B. "Duke" Rudman, Speaker's notes.
3. See note 1.
4. Stephen Mann, Bennett Bearden, and Robert Schneeflock, "The Frisco City Sand: A New Jurassic Reservoir in South Alabama." *Geological Survey of Alabama Series 77* (Tuscaloosa: Geological Survey of Alabama).
5. See note 1.
6. Debra Davis, "Oil Well Producing Excitement for Covington County Couple," *The Montgomery Advertiser*, April 1989.
7. See note 1
8. Chris McFadyen, "Independent Oil Men Ride the Updip Range," *Business Alabama Monthly*, February 1990.
9. Louise Durham, "The Alabama Haynesville," *Oil and Gas Investor*, Vol. 13 No. 4, April 1993.
10. See note 9, p. 32.
11. See note 9, p. 32.
12. See note 9, p. 33.

Chapter 22

1. Browning, Fleming and Welch, Stewart. Simultaneous personal interview. April 12, 2002.
2. Cox, John. E-mail to the author. January 7, 2004.
3. Hughes, p. 64.
4. Denbury Resources, "East Mississippi," 2002, 5 December 2004 <http://www.denbury.com/index.htm>
5. McGowan, John. Interview with Dudley Hughes and the author. January 7, 1999.
6. Morrison, Charles. (2002) Lecture. "Mississippi Salt Dome Style and Potential." Mississippi Geological Society Spring Symposium.
7. Kauffman, Karl and Baria, Larry. Simultaneous personal interview. June 2003.
8. Magee, Kenneth. Personal interview by telephone. November 26, 2004.
9. See note 7.
10. See note 7.
11. Welch, Stewart. (2002) Lecture. "Black Warrior Deep Knox Play." Mississippi Geological Society Spring Symposium.
12. Oxley, Marvin. Personal interview. June 6, 2000.
13. Information on Jim Harris and Midroc was given to the author by Dudley Hughes in a fax dated December 7, 2004.

Chapter 23

1. Kenneth S. Deffeys, Ph.D. *Hubbert's Peak: The Impending World Oil Shortage,* (Princeton and Oxford: Princeton University Press, 2001), cover flap.
2. Richard A. Kerr, "The Next Oil Crisis Looms Large+and Perhaps Close." *Science*, 21 August 1988, 1130.

Index

Knight, Wil, 9, 10, 20, 21, 25, 30, 31, 37, 47, 50, 51, 57, 69, 70, 71, 273
Knoxo Field, 91
Kokomo Field, 91

Lackey, Bill, 69
Ladner, Hilton, 106–8, 119, 175, 176, 179–81, 200
LaFleur's Restaurant, 64
LaGrange Field, 10, 12, 21
LaMoreaux, Philip, 97–101, 102, 188–90, 212, 213, 215, 272
Landrum, Charles, 270
Landrum, Jim, 147
Langsdale Field, 45
LaRue, Ike, 24, 57, 64, 70
Laurel Field, 80
Layman, D., 207
Learned Field, 136, 239
Lebrock, Robert M., 165, 166
Lee, Dick, 248
Lee, R.A., 106, 115
Legate, Robert, 126
Lismon, Burt, 50
Little Cedar Creek Field, 264
Little Creek Field, 77, 260
Little Escambia Creek Field, 155
Little Inch Pipeline, 27
Loring Field, 81
Lower Mobile Bay–Mary Ann Field, 217
Lutz, Matt, 123–26, 171–73

Maben Field, 175, 267
MacElvain, Bobby, 75, 96
MacRay, Richard, 119
Magee, Ken, 264–66
Magnolia Field, 90
Mallard Exploration, Inc., 165
Mancini, Dr. Ernest, 182
Maple Branch Field, 200
Marble, John, 251
Marsh, Charles, 165, 166
Martinville Field, 71
Masingill, Jay, 242–43
Mason, Richard, 175–77, 180, 181
Maxie Field, 55
Mayeaux, "Cuz," 69
Maynor Creek Dome Field, 263, 264

McCamic, Charles, 30
McCaskill, Malcolm, 29, 30
McComb Field, 77, 260
McGee, Diane, 222
McGee Field, 78, 114
McGlammery, Winnie, 189
McGlothin, Tom "Sparky," 3, 4, 8
McGowan, John, 261
McGowan, N.C., 26, 27
McKinley Creek Field, 180
McMillan, Ed Leigh, 144
McMillan, Tom, Jr., 144–46
McMillan, Tom, Sr., 131, 145
McRaney Field, 203
Meeks, Charles, 131, 132, 146–49, 151, 161, 201
Mellen, Fred, 30, 101, 102, 198, 273
Meragel Field, 255
Merit Field, 80
Mid-Continent Oil & Gas Association, 256
Midroc Oil Co., 268–70
Midway Dome Field, 262
Mill Creek Field, 200, 269
Miller, Dick, 154
Miller, John R., Jr., 145
Miller Exploration, Inc., 262
Minnehan, Ed, 121, 122
Minihan, E.D., 118
Mississippi Geological Society, 69, 267
Mississippi Independent Producers & Royalty Owners Association, 240
Miss-Tex, Inc., 143
Mize Field, 103, 104
Mobil Oil Corp., 210, 219
Mobile Bay Audubon Society, 211, 222
Moncrief, W.R., 147
Monticello Field, 205
Moon, Robert, 143, 272
Moon & Hines, Inc., 143, 192
Moore, Donald, 115
Morgan, Buzz, 8, 115
Morgan, Jimmy, 104
Morrison, Charles, 205, 262
Morton, J.D., 197, 198
Mosbacher, Robert, 75, 76, 125, 164, 201, 207, 239
Moselle Dome Field, 263
Mount Olive Field, 207
Movico Field, 241

Samsel, Howard, 136, 141, 168–70, 204, 226
Sanders, Jerry, 229, 230
Sanders, T.J., 29
Sartwell, Alex, 96, 97, 144
Satartia Field, 115
Save Our Bay (SOB), 211
Schlesinger, James, 235
Schneeflock, Robert, 84, 244–58, 272
Schuett, Ed, 153
Seminary Field, 203
Silas Field, 200
Siloam Field, 32, 109, 133
Sistrunk, Walter E., Sr., 18–20, 174, 178, 181–
    84, 189, 191, 193, 273
Skelly Oil Co., 202
Skelton, D.W., 174
Smith, Claude, 30, 70
Soso Field, 56, 57, 80, 95
South Carlton Field, 42, 44, 156–60
South Center Ridge Field, 103
South Cypress Creek Field, 126
South LaGrange Field, 13
South Pisgah Field, 259
South Williamsburg Field, 203
Splunge Field, 179, 198, 199
Spooner, Harry, 121, 162, 178, 179, 226, 241,
    242, 255
Spooner Petroleum, Inc., 264
Stack, Jack, 116, 117, 148, 151
Stallworth, Carlton, 61, 62
Star Field, 192, 193
Stave Creek Field, 226
Stechmann, Richard, 60
Stephens, Richard B., 148, 149
Stephenson, Mark, 254
Stevens, Ray, 50
Stewart, James, 105–8, 175, 179–80
Stewart, Lindsey, 258
Strahan, Dick, 153
Strain, Ben, 151
Sugar Ridge Field, 165
Summerland Field, 95, 103
Sunniland Field, 110, 160
Sunnyside Field, 37
Sunoco-Felda Field, 110
Sylte, Tom, 163–65

Tallahala Creek Field, 116, 118, 128
Tankersley, Lloyd, 153, 154
Tatum, Bob, 174
Tatum's Camp Field, 207
Taurus Exploration, Inc., 230
Tchula Lake Field, 133
Teel, Clyde, 74
Tensaw Lake Field, 115
Terra Resources, Inc., 192
Theiling, Stan, 248
Thomas, Robert, 178
Thomasville Field, 135, 139, 140
Thompson-Monteith, Inc., 177
Tinsley Field, 23, 81, 117, 273
Tom Branch Field, 119
Torch Operating Co., 254
Toxey Field, 122
T.R. Miller Mill Co., 145, 149, 155
Transco, Inc., 239
Traxler Field, 93
Trebloc Field, 32
Triad Oil & Gas, Inc., 93–95, 103, 114, 119, 162
Trimble, Jim, 245, 249, 250
Tucker, Jeff, 105
Tucker, William, 96, 185–94, 198, 225
Turkey Creek Field, 136, 139, 162
Turner, Ed, 154
Twister Oil & Gas, Inc., 264
Tyler, Henry, 153

U.S. Steel Corp., 227
Ultramar, Inc., 249
Uriah Field, 155, 156
Utica Field, 239

Vasen, George, 47–52, 55
Vaughey, Emmett, 8, 9, 12, 24, 25, 32–35, 51,
    93, 114, 237
Vaughey, William, 8, 9, 12, 24, 32, 33, 64, 93,
    114, 235, 237
Verba Field, 121
Vernon, Benton, 119
Vocation Field, 155, 156
Vockroth, George, 237, 238

Wakeland, Dr. Morton, 223, 224
Wallace, Gov. George, 99, 220

Printed in the United States
by Baker & Taylor Publisher Services